Morning
BY MORNING

Morning
BY MORNING

Charles
SPURGEON

W

WHITAKER
HOUSE

All Scripture quotations are taken from the King James Version (KJV) of the Holy Bible.

Editor's note: This book has been edited for the modern reader. Words, expressions, and sentence structure have been updated for clarity and readability.

MORNING BY MORNING

ISBN: 0-88368-645-7
Printed in the United States of America
© 2001 by Whitaker House

Whitaker House
30 Hunt Valley Circle
New Kensington, PA 15068
web site: www.whitakerhouse.com

Library of Congress Cataloging-in-Publication Data

Spurgeon, C. H. (Charles Haddon), 1834–1892.
  Morning by morning / by Charles Haddon Spurgeon.
      p.   cm.
  ISBN 0-88368-645-7 (pbk.)
  1. Devotional calendars—Baptists. I. Title.
  BV4811 .S667 2001
  242'.2—dc21

                          2001002171

2 3 4 5 6 7 8 9 10 11 12 / 10 09 08 07 06 05 04 03

Preface

Poets have delighted to sing of the morning as "Mother of the Dews, sowing the earth with orient pearl." Many saints, rising from their beds at the first blush of dawn, have found the poetry of nature to be the reality of grace as they have felt the dews of heaven refreshing their spirits. Hence, morning devotions have always been dear to enlightened, heaven-loving souls, and it has been their practice never to see the face of dawn until they have first seen the face of God. The breath of morn redolent with the smell of flowers is incense offered by earth to her Creator, and people should never let the dead earth excel them in praising their God.

Those alive with the Spirit tune their hearts to sing just as birds salute the radiant mercy that reveals itself in the east. The first fresh hour of every morning should be dedicated to the Lord, whose mercy gladdens it with golden light. The eye of day opens its lids and, in so doing, opens the eyes of hosts of heaven-protected slumberers. It is fitting that those eyes should first look up to the great Father of Lights, the Fount and Source of all the good upon which the sunlight gleams. It promises for us a day of grace when we begin our day with God; the sanctifying influence of the season spent in heavenly places influences each succeeding hour.

Morning devotions anchor the soul, so that it will not very readily drift far away from God during the day. They perfume the heart so that it smells fragrant with piety until nightfall; they hold up the soul's garments so that it is less apt to stumble; they feed all their power so that the soul is not permitted to faint.

The morning is the gate of the day and should be well-guarded with prayer. It is one end of the thread on which the day's actions are strung and should be well-knit with devotion. If we felt the majesty of life more, we would be more careful of its mornings. He who rushes from his bed to his business and does not wait to worship is as foolish as if he had not put on his clothes or washed his face. He is as unwise as one who dashes into battle without being armed. Let us bathe in the softly flowing river of communion with God before the heat of the wilderness and the burden of the way begin to oppress us.

In writing these short reflections on certain passages of Scripture, I wanted to assist the believer in his private meditations. A child may sometimes console a desolate heart that might not otherwise have been cheered. Even a flower smiling upward from the ground may turn our thoughts heavenward. It is my hope that, by the Holy Spirit's grace, as the reader turns, morning by morning, to read a simple page, he will hear in it a still small voice that will speak the Word of God to his soul.

The mind wearies of one thing; therefore, I have endeavored to use variety in presenting these devotionals. I have tried to change the style constantly—sometimes exhorting, then solioquizing, then conversing. I have used the first, second, and third persons, and both the singular and the plural—all with the desire of avoiding sameness and dullness.

The subject matter, also, I hope, is wide in its range, and not altogether without a dash of freshness. Readers of my sermons may recognize thoughts and expressions that they have encountered before; but much is, to me at least, as far as anything can be when it deals with the common theme of salvation, new and original. I have written out of my own heart, and most of the portions are remembrances of words that were refreshing in my own experience; therefore, I hope that these daily meditations will be refreshing to the reader as well. In fact, I know they will be if the Spirit of God rests on them.

My ambition has led me to hope that this little volume may also enrich the worship of families where God's altar burns in the morning. We know that it has been the custom in some households to read Mason, Hawker, Bogatsky, Smith, or Jay, and without wishing to usurp the place of any of these, this devotional aspires to a position among them. My happiness will overflow if this book becomes a blessing to Christian households. Family worship is, beyond measure, important both for the present and succeeding generations, and I would consider it a great honor to be, in part, a chaplain in the houses of my friends.

I have written no prayers because I think that a prayer is good for nothing if it is not written on the heart by the Holy Spirit and made to gush forth still warm from the soul. I would as soon think of printing a model for our children to use in addressing their parents as draw up a prayer to be offered to our Father who is in heaven. It has been said in defense of forms, "Better to go on crutches than not at all," but it is my firm conviction that those who truly *go* in the sense of worshipping aright might, with a little effort and an earnest cry to the Holy Spirit for assistance, go much better on their own legs than using some wearisome aid.

If there is not time to read both the morning devotional and a portion from Scripture, I earnestly request that this book would be set aside, for it would be a sore affliction to me to know that any family read the Word of God less on my account. I have had it in my heart to inspire my friends to search their Bibles more than ever; therefore, I have culled passages out of corners and nooks of Scripture, so that curiosity might lead the reader to search for their context. I would be disappointed indeed if, after all, I frustrated my own purpose by diverting one moment of time to the perusal of my remarks that should have been given to searching the Word of God itself.

I also hope that preachers may sometimes glean a text and suggestions for a sermon from one of these daily thoughts. Certainly they are free to do so if they can. The ideas are not ours but are common property. Tossed about by cares and worried by business, men's minds are not always in a condition on Saturday evening to leave their earthly concerns behind and begin a line of meditation. But once their thoughts take wing, the very events of the week can even help their flight. Perhaps we may lift some heart upward, and, if so, God be praised. Possibly a hint given here may serve as a match to set fire to a preacher's soul, and that heart ablaze may warm and gladden hundreds. Amen, and the Lord our God says so, too.

Hoping for a favorable reception for this present work, I have already written a volume of the same size and character for evening reading.* Meanwhile, with many prayers for heaven's blessing upon this labor of love, and with earnest requests for the prayers of the faithful, this work is humbly dedicated to the honor of the triune Jehovah, and respectfully presented to the Christian church.

—*C. H. Spurgeon*

---

* *Evening by Evening* is available from Whitaker House. *Morning and Evening,* a compilation of Spurgeon's morning and evening devotionals in one volume, is also available.

They did eat of the fruit of the land of Canaan that year.
—Joshua 5:12

Israel's weary wanderings were over, and the promised rest was attained. No more moving tents, fiery serpents, fierce Amalekites, and howling wildernesses. The Israelites came to the land that flowed with milk and honey, and they ate the old corn of the land. Perhaps this year, beloved Christian reader, this may be your case or mine. The prospect is joyful, and, if faith is actively exercised, it will yield pure delight. To be with Jesus in the rest that remains for the people of God is a cheering hope indeed, and to expect this glory so soon is a double bliss. Unbelief shudders at the Jordan, which still rolls between us and the good land, but let us rest assured that we have already experienced more ills than death at its worst can cause us. Let us banish every fearful thought and rejoice with exceeding great joy in the prospect that this year we will begin to *"ever be with the Lord"* (1 Thess. 4:17). Many will this year remain on earth to do service for their Lord. If this is our lot, there is no reason that the New Year's text should not still be true. *"We which have believed do enter into rest"* (Heb. 4:3). The Holy Spirit is the guarantee of our inheritance. He gives us "glory begun below." Those who are in heaven are secure; likewise, we on earth are kept safe in Christ Jesus. There, they triumph over their enemies; here, we have victories, too. Celestial spirits enjoy communion with their Lord; this privilege is not denied to us. They rest in His love; we have perfect peace in Him. They sing His praise; it is our privilege to bless Him, too. We will this year gather celestial fruits on earthly ground, where faith and hope have made the desert like the garden of the Lord. In the past, man ate angels' food; why not now? Oh, for grace to feed on Jesus and to eat of the fruit of the land of Canaan this year!

Continue in prayer.
—Colossians 4:2

t is interesting to notice how large a portion of Scripture is occupied with the subject of prayer, either in furnishing examples, enforcing precepts, or pronouncing promises. We scarcely open the Bible before we read, *"Then began men to call upon the name of the LORD"* (Gen. 4:26), and just as we are about to close the volume, the *"Amen"* (Rev. 22:21) of an earnest supplication meets our ear. Instances are plentiful. Here we find a wrestling Jacob, there a Daniel who prayed three times a day, and a David who with all his heart called on his God. On the mountain we see Elijah, and in the dungeon Paul and Silas. We have multitudes of commands and myriads of promises. What do these examples teach us but the sacred importance and necessity of prayer? We may be certain that whatever God has made prominent in His Word, He intended to be conspicuous in our lives. If He has said much about prayer, it is because He knows we have much need of it. So deep are our needs that, until we are in heaven, we must not cease to pray. Do you have no needs? Then I fear you do not know your own poverty. Do you have no need to ask God for mercy? Then may the Lord's mercy show you your misery! A prayerless soul is a Christless soul. Prayer is the lisping of the believing infant, the shout of the fighting believer, the requiem of the dying saint falling asleep in Jesus. It is the breath, the watchword, the comfort, the strength, the honor of a Christian. If you are a child of God, you will seek your Father's face and live in your Father's love. Pray that this year you may be holy, humble, zealous, and patient. Have closer communion with Christ, and enter more often into the banqueting-house of His love. Pray that you may be an example and a blessing to others, and that you may live more to the glory of your Master. The motto for this year must be *"Continue in prayer."*

I will preserve thee, and give thee
for a covenant of the people.
—Isaiah 49:8

esus Christ is Himself the sum and substance of the covenant, and as one of its gifts, He is the property of every believer. Believer, can you estimate what you have received in Christ? *"In him dwelleth all the fulness of the Godhead bodily"* (Col. 2:9). Consider the word *God* and its infinity, and then, meditate on Christ, the perfect Man, and all His beauty; for all that Christ, as God and Man, ever had, or can have, is yours. Out of pure, free favor, it passed over to you to be your personal property forever. Our blessed Jesus, as God, is omniscient, omnipresent, and omnipotent. Will it not console you to know that all these great and glorious attributes are altogether yours? Has He power? That power is yours to support and strengthen you, to overcome your enemies, and to preserve you even to the end. Has He love? Well, there is not a drop of love in His heart that is not yours; you may dive into the immense ocean of His love, and you may say of it all, "It is mine." Has He justice? It may seem a stern attribute, but even that is yours, for He will, by His justice, see to it that all that is promised to you in the covenant of grace will be most certainly secured to you. And all that He has as perfect Man is yours. As a perfect Man, Christ received the Father's delight. He stood accepted by the Most High. Believer, God's acceptance of Christ is your acceptance; for do you not know that the love that the Father set on a perfect Christ, He sets on you now? For all that Christ did is yours. That perfect righteousness that Jesus brought about, when through His stainless life He kept the law and made it honorable, is yours and is imputed to you. Christ is in the covenant.

My God, I am yours—what a comfort divine!
   What a blessing to know that the Savior is mine!
In the heavenly Lamb thrice happy I am,
   And my heart it does dance at the sound of His name.

*Grow in grace, and in the knowledge of our Lord
and Saviour Jesus Christ.*
—2 Peter 3:18

row in grace"—not in one grace only, but in all grace. Grow in that root-grace, *faith.* Believe the promises more firmly than you have before. Let faith increase in fullness, constancy, and simplicity. Grow also in *love.* Ask that your love may become extended, more intense, more practical, influencing every thought, word, and deed. Grow likewise in *humility.* Seek to lie very low, and know more of your own nothingness. As you grow downward in humility, seek also to grow upward—having nearer approaches to God in prayer and more intimate fellowship with Jesus. May God the Holy Spirit enable you to *"grow...in the knowledge of our Lord and Saviour."* He who does not grow in the knowledge of Jesus refuses to be blessed. To know Him is *"life eternal"* (John 17:3), and to advance in the knowledge of Him is to increase in happiness. He who does not long to know more of Christ knows nothing of Him yet. Whoever has sipped this wine will thirst for more, for although Christ satisfies, yet it is such a satisfaction that the appetite is not satiated, but whetted. If you know the love of Jesus, then, *"as the hart panteth after the water brooks"* (Ps. 42:1), so will you pant after deeper depths of His love. If you do not desire to know Him better, then you do not love Him, for love always cries, "Nearer, nearer." Absence from Christ is hell, but the presence of Jesus is heaven. Do not rest content, then, without an increasing acquaintance with Jesus. Seek to know more of Him in His divine nature, in His human relationship, in His finished work, in His death, in His resurrection, in His present glorious intercession, and in His future royal advent. Abide close to the cross, and search the mystery of His wounds. An increase of love for Jesus, and a more perfect apprehension of His love for us, is one of the best tests of growth in grace.

*And God saw the light, that it was good: and God
divided the light from the darkness.*
—Genesis 1:4

ight might well be good, since it sprang from that command of goodness, *"Let there be light"* (Gen. 1:3). We who enjoy it should be more grateful for it than we are and see more of God *in* it and *by* it. *Physical* light was said by Solomon to be sweet, but *gospel* light is infinitely more precious, for it reveals eternal things and ministers to our immortal natures. When the Holy Spirit gives us spiritual light and opens our eyes to behold *"the glory of God in the face of Jesus Christ"* (2 Cor. 4:6), then we also behold sin in its true colors, and ourselves in our real position. We see the Most Holy God as He reveals Himself, the plan of mercy as He offers it, and the world to come as the Word describes it. Spiritual light has many beams and prismatic colors, but whether they are knowledge, joy, holiness, or life, they are all divinely good. If the light received is thus good, what must the essential Light be, and how glorious must the place where He reveals Himself be! O Lord, since light is so good, give us more of it, and more of Yourself, the true Light. No sooner is there a good thing in the world than a division is necessary. Light and darkness have no communion. God has divided them; let us not mistake them. Sons of light must not have fellowship with deeds, doctrines, or deceits of darkness. The children of the day must be sober, honest, and bold in their Lord's work, leaving the works of darkness to those who will dwell in it forever. Our churches should by discipline divide the light from the darkness, and we should by our distinct separation from the world do the same. In our judgments, actions, relationships, teaching, and listening, we must discern between the precious and the vile, and maintain the great distinction that the Lord made on the world's first day. O Lord Jesus, be our Light throughout the whole of this day, for Your light is the light of men.

Casting all your care upon him; for he careth for you.
—1 Peter 5:7

It is a happy way of soothing sorrow when we can feel that He cares for us. Christian, do not dishonor your faith by always wearing a brow of care. Come and cast your burden on your Lord. You are staggering beneath a weight that your Father would not feel. What seems to be a crushing burden to you would be like a little dust on the scale to Him. Nothing is so sweet as to "Lie passive in God's hands, and know no will but His." O child of suffering, be patient. God has not passed you over in His loving care. He who is the feeder of sparrows will also furnish you with what you need. Do not sit down in despair. Hope on, and hope ever. Take up the arms of faith against a sea of trouble, and your fight of faith will yet end your distresses. There is One who cares for you. His eye is fixed on you, His heart beats with pity for your sorrow, and His omnipotent hand will yet bring you the needed help. The darkest cloud will scatter itself in showers of mercy. The blackest gloom will give place to the morning. If you are one of His family, He will bind up your wounds and heal your broken heart. Do not doubt His grace because of your tribulation, but believe that He loves you as much in seasons of trouble as in times of happiness. What a serene and quiet life might you lead if you would leave providing to the God of divine care! With a little oil in the cruse and a handful of meal in the barrel, Elijah outlived the famine, and you will do the same. If God cares for you, why do you need to worry? Can you trust Him for your soul, and not for your body? He has never refused to bear your burdens; He has never fainted under their weight. Come, then, soul; be done with fretful care, and leave all your concerns in the hands of a gracious God.

For to me to live is Christ.
—Philippians 1:21

he believer did not always live for Christ. He began to do so when God the Holy Spirit convinced him of sin, and when by grace he was brought to see the dying Savior making a propitiation for his guilt. From the moment of the new and celestial birth, the believer begins to live for Christ. Jesus is to believers the *"one pearl of great price"* (Matt. 13:46), for whom we are willing to part with all that we have. He has so completely won our love that it beats alone for Him. To His glory we would live, and in defense of His Gospel we would die. He is the pattern of our life and the model after which we would sculpture our character. Paul's words mean more than most men think. Many would say that Paul's words imply that the aim and end of his life was Christ, but rather, his life itself was Jesus! In the words of an ancient saint, he did "eat and drink and sleep eternal life." Jesus was his very breath, the soul of his soul, the heart of his heart, the life of his life. Can you say, as a professing Christian, that you live up to this ideal? Can you honestly say that for you *"to live is Christ"*? Are you doing your work for Christ, or are you working toward self-aggrandizement and for family advantage? Do you ask, "Is that a base reason?" For the Christian it is. He professes to live for Christ. How can he live for another purpose without committing spiritual adultery? Many carry out this principle in some measure, but who would dare to say that he has lived wholly for Christ as the apostle did? Yet this alone is the true life of a Christian—its source, its sustenance, its fashion, its end. It is all gathered up in one word: *Jesus.* Lord, accept me. I present myself, praying to live only in You and for You. Let me be as the bullock that stands between the plough and the altar. Let my motto be: "Ready for work or for sacrifice."

The iniquity of the holy things.
—Exodus 28:38

What a veil is lifted by these words, and what a disclosure is made! It will be humbling and profitable for us to pause awhile and see this sad sight. The iniquities of our public worship—its hypocrisy, formality, lukewarmness, irreverence, wandering of heart, and forgetfulness of God—what a full measure we have there! Our work for the Lord—its rivalry, selfishness, carelessness, slackness, and unbelief—what a mass of defilement is there! Our private devotions—their laxity, coldness, neglect, sleepiness, and vanity—what a mountain of dead earth is there! If we looked more carefully, we would find this *"iniquity of the holy things"* to be far greater than appears at first sight. Dr. Payson, writing to his brother, said, "My parish, as well as my heart, very much resembles the garden of the sluggard. What is worse is that I find many of my desires for the improvement of both proceed either from pride, vanity, or laziness. I look at the weeds that overspread my garden and breathe out an earnest wish that they were eradicated. But why? What prompts the wish? It may be that I may walk out and say to myself, 'In what fine order is my garden kept!' This is pride. Or it may be that my neighbors may look over the wall and say, 'How finely your garden flourishes!' This is vanity. Or I may wish for the destruction of the weeds because I am weary of pulling them up. This is laziness." Even our desires after holiness may be polluted by wrong motives. Under the greenest sods, worms hide themselves. We do not need to look long to discover them. How cheering is the thought that when the high priest bore the *"iniquity of the holy things,"* he wore on his brow the words, "HOLINESS TO THE LORD" (Exod. 28:36). Even so, while Jesus bears our sin, He presents before His Father's face not our lack of holiness, but His own holiness. Oh, for grace to view our Great High Priest with the eyes of faith!

I…will be their God.
—Jeremiah 31:33

hristian, here in this promise is all you need. In order to be happy, you need something that will satisfy you; is this not enough? If you can pour this promise into your cup, will you not say with David, "My cup runs over. (See Psalm 23:5.) I have more than my heart could wish for"? When His promise to be your God is fulfilled, are you not a possessor of all things? Desire is as insatiable as death, but He who fills *"all in all"* (Eph. 1:23) can fill it. Who can measure the capacity of our wishes? But the immeasurable wealth of God can more than overflow it. I ask you if you are not complete when God is yours? Do you need anything but God? Is not His all-sufficiency enough to satisfy you, if all else should fail? But you need more than quiet satisfaction; you desire rapturous delight. Come, soul; here is music fit for heaven in this your portion, for God is the Maker of heaven. Not all the music played by sweet instruments or drawn from strings can yield such melody as this sweet promise, *"I…will be their God."* Here is a deep sea of bliss, a shoreless ocean of delight. Come and bathe your spirit in it. Swim for an age, and you will find no shore; dive throughout eternity, and you will find no bottom. *"I…will be their God."* If this does not make your eyes sparkle and your heart beat high with bliss, then assuredly your soul is not in a healthy state. But you need more than present delights—you crave something concerning which you may exercise hope. What more can you hope for than the fulfillment of this great promise, *"I…will be their God"?* This is the masterpiece of all the promises. Its enjoyment makes a heaven below and will make a heaven above. Dwell in the light of your Lord, and let your soul always be ravished with His love. Extract all the *"marrow and fatness"* (Ps. 63:5) that this portion yields to you. Live up to your privileges, and rejoice with unspeakable joy.

There is laid up for me a crown of righteousness.
—2 Timothy 4:8

oubting one, you have often said, "I fear I will never enter heaven." Fear not! All the people of God will enter there. I love the quaint saying of a dying man, who exclaimed, "I have no fear of going home. I have sent all before me. God's finger is on the latch of my door, and I am ready for Him to enter." "But," said one, "are you not afraid lest you should miss your inheritance?" "No," said he, "there is one crown in heaven that the angel Gabriel could not wear; it will fit no head but mine. There is one throne in heaven that Paul the apostle could not fill; it was made for me, and I will have it." O Christian, what a joyous thought! Your portion is secure; *"there remaineth...a rest"* (Heb. 4:9). "But cannot I forfeit it?" No, it is titled in your name. If I am a child of God, I will not lose it. It is mine as securely as if I were there possessing it now. Come with me, believer, and let us sit on the top of Nebo and view the bountiful land, even Canaan. Do you see that little river of death glistening in the sunlight? Do you see the pinnacles of the eternal city across it? Do you observe the pleasant country and all its joyous inhabitants? Know, then, that if you could fly across, you would see written on one of its many mansions, "This remains for such a one; it is preserved for him only. He will be caught up to dwell forever with God." Poor doubting one, see the fair inheritance; it is yours. If you believe in the Lord Jesus, if you have repented of sin, if you have been renewed in heart, you are one of the Lord's people, and there is a place reserved for you, a crown laid up for you, a harp especially provided for you. No one else will have your portion. It is reserved in heaven for you, and you will have it before long, for there will be no vacant thrones in glory when all the chosen are gathered in.

These have no root.
—Luke 8:13

My soul, examine yourself this morning in the light of today's text. You have received the Word with joy. Your feelings have been stirred, and a lively impression has been made. But remember: to receive the Word in your ears is one thing; to receive Jesus into your very soul is quite another. Superficial feeling is often joined to inward hardness of heart, and a lively impression of the Word is not always a lasting one. In the parable of the sower, the seed in one case fell on ground having a rocky bottom, covered over with a thin layer of earth. When the seed began to take root, its downward growth was hindered by the hard stone; therefore, it spent its strength in pushing its green shoot aloft as high as it could; but, having no inward moisture derived from root nourishment, it withered away. Is this my case? Have I been making a fair show in the flesh without having a corresponding inner life? Good growth takes place upward and downward at the same time. Am I rooted in sincere fidelity and love for Jesus? If my heart remains hardened and unfertilized by grace, the good seed may germinate for a season, but it must ultimately wither, for it cannot flourish on a rocky, unbroken, unsanctified heart. Let me dread a godliness as rapid in growth and as lacking in endurance as Jonah's gourd. Let me count the cost of being a follower of Jesus. Above all, let me feel the energy of His Holy Spirit, and then, I will possess an abiding and enduring seed in my soul. If my mind remains as stubborn as it was by nature, the sun of trial will scorch, and my hard heart will help to cast the heat the more terribly on the ill-covered seed. My faith will soon die, and my despair will be terrible; therefore, O heavenly Sower, plough me first, and then, cast the truth into me. Let me yield a bounteous harvest for You.

Ye are Christ's.
—1 Corinthians 3:23

ou are Christ's. You are His by donation, for the Father gave you to the Son. You are His through the purchase of His blood, for He paid the price for your redemption. You are His by dedication, for you have consecrated yourself to Him. You are His by relation, for you are named by His name, and made one of His brothers and joint heirs. Labor in practical ways to show the world that you are the servant, the friend, the bride of Jesus. When tempted to sin, reply, "I cannot do this great wickedness, for I am Christ's." Immortal principles forbid the friend of Christ to sin. When wealth is before you to be won by sin, say that you are Christ's, and do not touch it. Are you exposed to difficulties and dangers? Stand fast in the evil day, remembering that you are Christ's. Are you placed where others are sitting down idly, doing nothing? Rise to the work with all your powers; and when the sweat stands on your brow, and you are tempted to loiter, cry, "No, I cannot stop, for I am Christ's. If I were not purchased by blood, I might be like *'Issachar…couching down between two burdens'* (Gen. 49:14); but I am Christ's and cannot loiter." When the siren song of pleasure would tempt you from the path of right, reply, "Your music cannot charm me; I am Christ's." When the cause of God provides you with opportunities, give your goods and yourself away, for you are Christ's. Never contradict your profession of faith. Always be one whose manners are Christian, whose speech is like the Nazarene, whose conduct and conversation are so characteristic of heaven that all who see you may know that you are the Savior's, recognizing in you His features of love and His countenance of holiness. "I am a Roman!" was of old a reason for integrity; far more, then, let this be your argument for holiness: "I am Christ's!"

Jehoshaphat made ships of Tharshish to go to Ophir for gold: but they went not; for the ships were broken at Eziongeber.
—1 Kings 22:48

Solomon's ships had returned in safety, but Jehoshaphat's vessels never reached the land of gold. Providence prospers one and frustrates the desires of another, in the same business and at the same spot, yet the Great Ruler is as good and wise at one time as another. May we have grace today, in the remembrance of this text, to bless the Lord for ships broken at Eziongeber, as well as for vessels freighted with temporal blessings. Let us not envy the more successful or murmur at our losses as though we were singularly and specially tried. Like Jehoshaphat, we may be precious in the Lord's sight, although our schemes end in disappointment. The secret cause of Jehoshaphat's loss is well worthy of notice, for it is the root of much of the suffering of the Lord's people; it was his alliance with a sinful family, his fellowship with sinners. In 2 Chronicles 20:37, we are told that the Lord sent a prophet to declare, *"Because thou hast joined thyself with Ahaziah, the LORD hath broken thy works."* This was a fatherly chastisement, which appears to have been blessed to him, for in the verse that follows this morning's text, we find him refusing to allow his servants to sail in the same vessels with those of the wicked king. Would to God that Jehoshaphat's experience might be a warning to the rest of the Lord's people to avoid being *"unequally yoked together with unbelievers"* (2 Cor. 6:14)! A life of misery is usually the lot of those who are united in marriage, or in any other way of their own choosing, with the people of the world. Oh, for such love for Jesus that, like Him, we may be *"holy, harmless, undefiled, separate from sinners"* (Heb. 7:26); for if it is not so with us, we may expect to hear it often said, "The Lord has broken your works."

Mighty to save.
—Isaiah 63:1

We understand the words *"to save"* to mean the whole of the great work of salvation, from the first holy desire onward to complete sanctification. The words are *multum in parvo*—much in little. Indeed, here is all mercy in one word. Christ is not only *"mighty to save"* those who repent, but He is also able to make people repent. He will carry those to heaven who believe; but He is, moreover, mighty to give people new hearts and to work faith in them. He is mighty to make the one who hates holiness love it, and to constrain the despiser of His name to bend the knee before Him. This is not all the meaning, for the divine power is equally seen in the work that follows. The life of a believer is a series of miracles brought about by the mighty God. The bush burns, but it is not consumed. He is mighty enough to keep His people holy after He has made them so, and to preserve them in His fear and love until He consummates their spiritual existence in heaven. Christ's might does not lie in making a believer and then leaving him to shift for himself, but He who begins the *"good work in you will perform it until the day of Jesus Christ"* (Phil. 1:6). He who imparts the first germ of life in the dead soul prolongs the divine existence and strengthens it, until it bursts asunder every bond of sin, and the soul leaps from earth, perfected in glory. Believer, here is encouragement. Are you praying for some loved one? Oh, do not give up your prayers, for Christ is *"mighty to save."* You are powerless to reclaim the rebel, but your Lord is almighty. Lay hold of His mighty arm and rouse it to put forth its strength. Does your own case trouble you? Fear not, for His strength is sufficient for you. Whether to begin with others or to carry on the work in you, Jesus is *"mighty to save."* The best proof lies in the fact that He has saved *you*. What a thousand mercies that you have not found Him mighty to destroy!

Do as thou hast said.
—2 Samuel 7:25

God's promises were never meant to be thrown aside as wastepaper. He intended that they should be used. God's gold is not miser's money, but is minted to be traded with. Nothing pleases our Lord better than to see His promises put in circulation. He loves to see His children bring them up to Him, and say, "Lord, do as You have said." We glorify God when we plead His promises. Do you think that God will be any the poorer for giving you the riches He has promised? Do you dream that He will be any the less holy for giving holiness to you? Do you imagine that He will be any the less pure for washing you from your sins? *"Come now, and let us reason together, saith the LORD: though your sins be as scarlet, they shall be as white as snow; though they be red like crimson, they shall be as wool"* (Isa. 1:18). Faith lays hold of the promise of pardon; it does not delay, saying, "This is a precious promise, but I wonder if it is true?" Instead, it goes straight to the throne with it and pleads, "Lord, here is the promise. Do as You have said." Our Lord replies, *"Be it unto thee even as thou wilt"* (Matt. 15:28). When a Christian grasps a promise, if he does not take it to God, he dishonors Him; but when he hastens to the throne of grace and cries, "Lord, I have nothing to recommend me but this: You have said it," then his desire will be granted. Our heavenly Banker delights to cash His own notes. Never let the promise rust. Draw the word of promise out of its scabbard, and use it with holy violence. Do not think that God will be troubled by your persistence in reminding Him of His promises. He loves to hear the loud outcries of needy souls. It is His delight to bestow favors. He is more ready to hear than you are to ask. The sun is not weary of shining or the fountain of flowing. It is God's nature to keep His promises; therefore, go at once to the throne with the words, "Do as You have said."

I will help thee, saith the LORD.
—Isaiah 41:14

Let us hear the Lord Jesus speak these words to each one of us: "I will help you. It is but a small thing for Me, your God, to help you. Consider what I have done already. What! not help you? Why, I bought you with My blood. What! not help you? I have died for you; and if I have done the greater, will I not do the lesser? Help you! It is the least thing I will ever do for you. I have done more and will do more. Before the world began, I chose you. I made the covenant for you. I laid aside My glory and became a man for you. I gave up My life for you, and if I did all of this, I will surely help you now! In helping you, I am giving you what I have bought for you already. If you had need of a thousand times as much help, I would give it to you. You require little compared with what I am ready to give. It is much for you to need, but it is nothing for me to bestow. Help you? Do not fear! If there were an ant at the door of your granary asking for help, it would not ruin you to give him a handful of your wheat; you are nothing but a tiny insect at the door of My all-sufficiency. I will help you." O my soul, is this not enough? Do you need more strength than the omnipotence of the united Trinity? Do you need more wisdom than exists in the Father, more love than displays itself in the Son, or more power than is manifest in the influences of the Spirit? Bring your empty pitcher here! Surely this well will fill it. Hurry, gather up your needs, and bring them here—your emptiness, your sorrows, your deficiencies. Behold, this river of God is full for your supply. What can you desire besides? Go forth, my soul, in this your might. The eternal God is your Helper!

> Fear not, I am with thee;
>   Oh, be not dismay'd!
> For I am thy God;
>   I will still give thee aid.

And I looked, and, lo, a Lamb stood on the mount Sion.
—Revelation 14:1

he apostle John was privileged to look within the gates of heaven, and in describing what he saw, he began by saying, *"I looked, and, lo, a Lamb."* This teaches us that the chief objective of contemplation in the heavenly state is *"the Lamb of God, which taketh away the sin of the world"* (John 1:29). Nothing else attracted the apostle's attention as much as the person of that divine Being, who has redeemed us by His blood. He is the theme of the songs of all glorified spirits and holy angels. Christian, here is joy for you; you have looked, and you have seen the Lamb. Through your tears, your eyes have seen the Lamb of God taking away your sins. Rejoice, then. In a little while, when your tears will have been wiped from your eyes, you will see the same Lamb exalted on His throne. It is the joy of your heart to hold daily fellowship with Jesus. You will have the same joy to a higher degree in heaven. You will enjoy the constant vision of His presence. You will dwell with Him forever. *"I looked, and, lo, a Lamb."* Why, that Lamb is heaven itself, for as good Rutherford said, "Heaven and Christ are the same thing." To be with Christ is to be in heaven, and to be in heaven is to be with Christ. A prisoner of the Lord very sweetly wrote in one of his glowing letters, "O my Lord Jesus Christ, if I could be in heaven without You, it would be a hell; and if I could be in hell, and have You still, it would be a heaven to me, for You are all the heaven I need." It is true, is it not, Christian? Does not your soul say so?

> Not all the harps above
> Can make a heavenly place,
> If God His residence remove,
> Or but conceal His face.

All you need to be blessed, supremely blessed, is *"to be with Christ"* (Phil. 1:23).

There remaineth therefore a rest to the people of God.
—Hebrews 4:9

How different will be the state of the believer in heaven from what it is here! Here he is born to toil and suffer weariness, but in the land of the immortal, fatigue is never known. Anxious to serve his Master, he now finds his strength unequal to his zeal. His constant cry is, "Help me to serve You, O my God." If he is thoroughly active, he will have much labor; not too much for his will, but more than enough for his power, so that he will cry out, "I am not wearied *of* the labor, but I am wearied *in* it." Ah, Christian, the hot day of weariness does not last forever. The sun is nearing the horizon. It will rise again, with a brighter day than you have ever seen, on a land where they serve God day and night, and yet rest from their labors. Here, rest is but partial; there, it is perfect. Here, the Christian is always unsettled; he feels that he has not yet attained. There, all are at rest; they have attained the summit of the mountain. They have ascended to the bosom of their God. They cannot go any higher. Ah, toil-worn laborer, only envision when you will rest forever! Can you imagine it? It is a rest eternal, a rest that *"remaineth."* Here, my best joys bear *mortal* on their brow, my fair flowers fade, my delicious cups are drained to the dregs, my sweetest birds fall before Death's arrows, my most pleasant days are shadowed into nights, and the flood tides of my bliss subside into ebbs of sorrow; but there, everything is immortal. The harp remains unrusted, the crown unwithered, the eye undimmed, the voice unfaltering, and the heart unwavering. The immortal being is wholly absorbed in infinite delight. Happy day, when mortality will *"be swallowed up of life"* (2 Cor. 5:4), and the eternal Sabbath will begin!

I sought him, but I found him not.
—Song of Solomon 3:1

ell me where you lost the company of Christ, and I will tell you the most likely place to find Him. Have you lost Christ by refraining from prayer? Then it is there you must seek and find Him. Did you lose Christ by sinning? You will find Christ in no other way but by giving up sin and seeking, by the Holy Spirit, to mortify the member in which the lust dwells. Did you lose Christ by neglecting the Scriptures? You must find Christ in the Scriptures. It is a true saying, "Look for a thing where you dropped it; it is there." So look for Christ where you lost Him, for He has not gone away. But it is hard work to go back for Christ. Bunyan tells us that the pilgrim found the piece of the road back to the Arbor of Ease, where he had lost his roll, the hardest he had ever traveled. Twenty miles onward is easier to go than one mile backward for lost evidence. Take care, then, when you find your Master, to cling closely to Him. But how is it that you have lost Him? One would have thought you would never have parted with such a precious Friend, whose presence is so sweet, whose words are so comforting, and whose company is so dear to you! How is it that you did not watch Him every moment for fear of losing sight of Him? Yet, since you have let Him go, what a mercy that you are seeking Him, even though you mournfully groan, *"Oh that I knew where I might find him!"* (Job 23:3). Go on seeking, for it is dangerous to be without your Lord. Without Christ, you are like a sheep without its shepherd; like a tree without water at its roots; like a withered leaf in a tempest—not bound to the tree that gives it life. Seek Him with your whole heart, and He will be found by you. Give yourself thoroughly to the search, and truly, to your joy and gladness, you will yet discover Him.

Abel was a keeper of sheep.
—Genesis 4:2

As a shepherd, Abel sanctified his work to the glory of God and offered a sacrifice of blood on his altar. The Lord respected Abel and his offering. This early type of Christ is exceedingly clear and distinct. Like the first streak of light that tinges the East at sunrise, it does not reveal everything, but it clearly manifests the great fact that the sun is coming. As we see Abel, a shepherd and yet a priest, offering a sweet-smelling sacrifice unto God, we discern our Lord, who brings before His Father a sacrifice to which Jehovah ever has respect. Abel was hated by his brother—hated without a cause; even so was the Savior. The natural and carnal man hated the accepted man, in whom the Spirit of grace was found, and did not rest until his blood had been shed. Abel fell and sprinkled his altar and sacrifice with his own blood; therein sets forth the Lord Jesus slain by the enmity of man, while serving as a Priest before the Lord. *"The good shepherd giveth his life for the sheep"* (John 10:11). Let us weep over Him as we view Him slain by the hatred of mankind, staining the horns of His altar with His own blood. Abel's blood speaks. The Lord said to Cain, *"The voice of thy brother's blood crieth unto me from the ground"* (Gen. 4:10). The blood of Jesus has a mighty tongue, and the import of its prevailing cry is not vengeance, but mercy. It is precious beyond all preciousness to stand at the altar of our Good Shepherd—to see Him bleeding there as the slaughtered Priest, and then to hear His blood speaking peace to all His flock, peace in our consciences, peace between Jew and Gentile, peace between man and his offended Maker, peace down all the ages of eternity for blood-washed men. Abel was the first shepherd in order of time, but our hearts will ever place Jesus first in order of excellence. Great Keeper of the sheep, we the people of Your pasture bless You with our whole hearts when we see You slain for us.

And so all Israel shall be saved.
—Romans 11:26

hen Moses sang at the Red Sea, it was his joy to know that all the Israelites were safe. Not a drop of spray fell from that solid wall of water until the last of God's chosen ones had safely planted his foot on the other side of the flood. That done, immediately the waters dissolved into their proper place again, but not until then. Part of that song was, *"Thou in thy mercy hast led forth the people which thou hast redeemed"* (Exod. 15:13). In the last time, when the elect will sing *"the song of the Lamb"* and *"of Moses the servant of God"* (Rev. 15:3). This will be the boast of Jesus: *"Of them which thou gavest me have I lost none"* (John 18:9). In heaven there will not be a vacant throne.

> For all the chosen race
>   Shall meet around the throne,
> Shall bless the conduct of His grace,
>   And make His glories known.

As many as God has chosen, as many as Christ has redeemed, as many as the Spirit has called, as many as believe in Jesus—all these will safely cross the dividing sea. We are not all safely landed yet. "Part of the host have crossed the flood, and part are crossing now." The vanguard of the army has already reached the shore. We are marching through the depths. We are, on this day, following hard after our Leader into the heart of the sea. Let us be of good cheer. The rear guard will soon be where the vanguard already is; the last of the chosen ones will soon have crossed the sea, and then, when all are secure, the song of triumph will be heard. But, oh, if one were absent—if one of His chosen family were to be cast away—it would make an everlasting discord in the song of the redeemed and cut the strings of the harps of paradise, so that music could never be extorted from them again.

*Son of man, What is the vine tree more than any tree, or than
a branch which is among the trees of the forest?*
—Ezekiel 15:2

These words are for the humbling of God's people.
They are called God's vine, but what are they by nature more than others? They, by God's goodness,
have become fruitful, having been planted in a good soil.
The Lord has trained them upon the walls of the sanctuary,
and they bring forth fruit to His glory; but what are they
without their God? What are they without the continual
influence of the Spirit producing fruitfulness in them? Believer, learn to reject pride, seeing that you have no ground
for it. Whatever you are, you have nothing to make you
proud. The more you have, the more you are in debt to
God; and you should not be proud of that which makes you
a debtor. Consider your origin; look back to what you were.
Consider what you would have been had it not been for divine grace. Look on yourself as you are now. Does not your
conscience reproach you? Do not your thousand wanderings stand before you and tell you that you are unworthy to
be called His child? And if He has made you anything, are
you not taught thereby that it is grace that has changed
you? Great believer, you would have been a great sinner if
God had not transformed you. O you who are valiant for
truth, you would have been as valiant for error if grace had
not laid hold of you. Therefore, be not proud, though you
have a large estate, that is, a wide domain of grace. Once,
you did not have a single thing to call your own except
your sin and misery. Oh, strange infatuation, that you, who
have borrowed everything, would think of exalting yourself! You are a poor pensioner dependent on the bounty of
your Savior; you are one who has a life that dies without
fresh streams of life from Jesus, and yet you are still proud!
Shame on you, O lowly heart!

I have exalted one chosen out of the people.
—Psalm 89:19

hy was Christ *"chosen out of the people"*? Speak, my heart, for heart-thoughts are best. Was it not that He might be able to be our Brother in the blessed tie of kindred blood? Oh, what relationship there is between Christ and the believer! The believer can say, "I have a Brother in heaven. I may be poor, but I have a Brother who is rich and is a King. Will He permit me to be in need while He is on His throne? Oh, no! He loves me; He is my Brother." Believer, wear this blessed thought like a diamond necklace around the neck of your memory. As a golden ring, put it on the finger of remembrance and use it as the King's own seal, stamping the petitions of your faith with the confidence of success. He is a *"brother...born for adversity"* (Prov. 17:17); treat Him as such. Christ was also *"chosen out of the people"* so that He might know our needs and sympathize with us. He *"was in all points tempted like as we are, yet without sin"* (Heb. 4:15). In all our sorrows, we have His sympathy. Temptation, pain, disappointment, weakness, weariness, poverty—He knows them all, for He has felt them all. Remember this, Christian, and let it comfort you. However difficult and painful your road may be, it is marked by the footsteps of your Savior. Even when you reach the dark valley of the shadow of death and the deep waters of the swelling Jordan, you will find His footprints there. In all places, wherever we go, He has been our forerunner; each burden we have to carry has once been laid on the shoulders of Immanuel.

> His way was much rougher and darker than mine.
> Did Christ, my Lord, suffer, and shall I repine?

Take courage! Royal feet have left a bloodred track on the road and consecrated the thorny path forever.

Surely he shall deliver thee from the snare of the fowler.
—Psalm 91:3

God delivers His people *"from the snare of the fowler"* in two senses: *from* and *out of.* First, He delivers them *from* the snare; He does not let them enter it. Second, if they should be caught in it, He delivers them *out of* it. The first promise is the most precious to some; the second is the best to others. *"He shall deliver thee from the snare."* How? Trouble is often the means whereby God delivers us. God knows that our backsliding will soon end in our destruction, and, in mercy, He sends the rod. We say, "Lord, why is this happening?"—not knowing that our trouble has been the means of delivering us from far greater evil. Many have been thus saved from ruin by their sorrows and their crosses; these have frightened the birds from the net. At other times, God keeps His people from the snare of the fowler by giving them great spiritual strength, so that when they are tempted to do evil they say, *"How then can I do this great wickedness, and sin against God?"* (Gen. 39:9). But what a blessed thing it is that, if the believer does, in an evil hour, come into the net, God will bring him out of it! O backslider, you may be cast down, but do not despair. Wanderer though you have been, hear what your Redeemer says: "Return, O backsliding children; I will have mercy on you." But you say you cannot return, for you are a captive. Then listen to the promise: *"Surely he shall deliver thee from the snare of the fowler."* You will yet be brought out of all evil into which you have fallen; and though you will never cease to repent of your ways, He who has loved you will not cast you away. He will receive you and give you joy and gladness, so *"that the bones which [He has] broken may rejoice"* (Ps. 51:8). No bird of paradise will die in the fowler's net.

I will mention the lovingkindnesses of the LORD, and the praises of the LORD, according to all that the LORD hath bestowed on us.
—Isaiah 63:7

an you not do this? Are there no mercies that you have experienced? Even though you are gloomy now, can you forget that blessed hour when Jesus met you and said, "Come unto Me"? Can you not remember that rapturous moment when He snapped your fetters, dashed your chains to the earth, and said, "I came to break your bonds and set you free"? Or if you have let the love of your relationship with Christ grow cold, there must surely be some precious milestone along the road of life not quite grown over with moss, on which you can read a happy memorial of His mercy toward you. What? Did you never have a sickness like the one from which you are suffering now, and did He not restore you? Were you never poor before, and did He not supply your needs? Were you never in dire straits before, and did He not deliver you? Arise! Go to the river of your experience and pull up a few bulrushes; plait them into an ark, wherein your infant-faith may float safely on the stream. Do not forget what your God has done for you; leaf through your book of memories, and consider the days of old. Can you not remember the times of refreshing? Have you forgotten the mountaintop experiences? Have you never been helped in your times of need? I know you have. Go back, then, a little way to the choice mercies of yesterday; though all may be dark now, light up the lamps of the past. They will glitter through the darkness, and you will trust in the Lord *"until the day break, and the shadows flee away"* (Song 2:17). *"Remember, O LORD, thy tender mercies and thy lovingkindnesses; for they have been ever of old"* (Ps. 25:6)

Your heavenly Father.
—Matthew 6:26

God's people are doubly His children: they are His by creation and by adoption in Christ. Hence they are privileged to call Him, *"Our Father which art in heaven"* (Luke 11:2). *Father*—oh, what a precious word that is! Here is authority: *"If then I be a father, where is mine honour?"* (Mal. 1:6). Here is affection mingled with authority. This kind of authority does not provoke rebellion. If you are children, where is your obedience? This kind of required obedience is most cheerfully given: it would not be withheld even if it could be. The obedience that God's children yield to Him must be loving obedience. Do not approach the service of God as slaves do their taskmaster's toil, but follow His commands, because that is your Father's way. Yield your bodies *"as instruments of righteousness"* (Rom. 6:13), because righteousness is your Father's will, and His will should be the will of His child. Father!—here is a kingly attribute so sweetly veiled in love that the King's crown is forgotten in the King's face, and His scepter becomes not a rod of iron, but a silver scepter of mercy; the scepter indeed seems to be forgotten in the tender hand of Him who wields it. Father!—here is honor and love. How great is a father's love for his children! What friendship cannot do and mere benevolence will not attempt, a father's heart and hand must do for his children. They are his offspring, and he must bless them; they are his children, and he must show himself strong in their defense. If an earthly father watches over his children with unceasing love and care, how much more does our heavenly Father? "Abba, Father!" He who can say this, has uttered better music than cherubim or seraphim can reach. There is heaven in the depth of that word—*Father!* There is all I can ask, all my necessities can demand, and all my wishes can desire. I have all in all now and throughout eternity when I can say, "Father."

And of his fulness have all we received.
—John 1:16

hese words tell us that there is a fullness in Christ. There is a fullness of essential deity and a fullness of perfect manhood, for *"in him dwelleth all the fulness of the Godhead bodily"* (Col. 2:9). There is a fullness of atoning efficacy in His blood, for *"the blood of Jesus Christ his Son cleanseth us from all sin"* (1 John 1:7). There is a fullness of justifying righteousness in His life, for *"there is therefore now no condemnation to them which are in Christ Jesus"* (Rom. 8:1). There is a fullness of divine prevalence in His plea, for *"he is able also to save them to the uttermost that come unto God by him, seeing he ever liveth to make intercession for them"* (Heb. 7:25). There is a fullness of victory in His death, for through death He destroyed *"him that had the power of death, that is, the devil"* (Heb. 2:14). There is a fullness of efficacy in His resurrection from the dead, for by it we are *"begotten...again unto a lively hope"* (1 Pet. 1:3). There is a fullness of triumph in His ascension, for when He *"ascended on high, [He] led captivity captive...[and] received gifts for men"* (Ps. 68:18). (See also, Ephesians 4:8.) There is a fullness of blessings of every sort and shape: a fullness of grace to pardon, of grace to regenerate, of grace to sanctify, of grace to preserve, and of grace to perfect. There is a fullness at all times: a fullness of comfort in affliction, a fullness of guidance in prosperity. There is a fullness of every divine attribute: of wisdom, of power, of love. This fullness of blessings is impossible to survey, much less to explore. *"It pleased the Father that in him should all fulness dwell"* (Col. 1:19). Oh, what a fullness this must be of which all receive! Fullness, indeed, there must be when the stream is always flowing, and yet the well springs up as free, as rich, as full as ever. Come, believer, and find all your needs supplied. Ask largely, and you will receive largely, for this fullness is inexhaustible; it is stored up where all the needy may reach it—in Jesus, Immanuel, *"God with us"* (Matt. 1:23).

+= **January 28** +=

Perfect in Christ Jesus.
—Colossians 1:28

o you not feel in your own soul that perfection is not in you? Does not every day teach you that? Every tear that trickles from your eyes weeps "imperfection"; every harsh word that proceeds from your lips mutters "imperfection." You have too frequently had a view of your own heart to dream for a moment of any perfection in yourself. But amid this sad consciousness of imperfection, here is comfort for you—you are *"perfect in Christ Jesus."* In God's sight, you are *"complete in Him"* (Col. 2:10); even now you are *"accepted in the beloved"* (Eph. 1:6). But there is a second perfection, yet to be realized, which is sure to all the seed. Is it not delightful to look forward to the time when every stain of sin will be removed from the believer, and he will be presented faultless before the throne, *"not having spot, or wrinkle, or any such thing"* (Eph. 5:27)? The church of Christ, then, will be so pure that not even the eye of Omniscience will see a spot or blemish in her; she will be so holy and so glorious that Hart did not go beyond the truth when he said, "With my Savior's garments on, holy as the Holy One." Then we will know, taste, and feel the happiness of this vast but short sentence, "Complete in Christ." Not until then will we fully comprehend the heights and depths of the salvation of Jesus. Does not your heart leap for joy at the thought of it? Black as you are, you will be white one day; filthy as you are, you will be clean. Oh, this is a marvelous salvation! Christ takes a worm and transforms it into an angel; Christ takes a black and deformed thing and makes it clean and matchless in His glory, peerless in His beauty, and fit to be the companion of seraphim. O my soul, stand and admire this blessed truth of perfection in Christ.

The things which are not seen.
—2 Corinthians 4:18

In our Christian pilgrimage, it is a good thing, for the most part, to be looking forward. Forward lies the crown, and onward is the goal. Whether it is for hope, for joy, for consolation, or for the inspiring of our love, the future must, after all, be the grand object of the eyes of faith. Looking into the future, we see sin cast out; the body of sin and death destroyed; the soul made perfect, and fit to be a partaker *"of the inheritance of the saints in light"* (Col. 1:12). Looking further yet, the believer's enlightened eyes can see death's river passed, the gloomy stream forded, and the hills of light attained on which stands the celestial city. He sees himself enter within the pearly gates, hailed as more than conqueror, crowned by the hand of Christ, embraced in the arms of Jesus, glorified with Him, and made to sit together with Him on His throne, even as He has overcome and has sat down with the Father on His throne. The thought of this future may well relieve the darkness of the past and the gloom of the present. The joys of heaven will surely compensate for the sorrows of earth. Hush, hush, my doubts! Death is but a narrow stream, and you will soon have forded it. Time, how short—eternity, how long! Death, how brief—immortality, how endless! The road is so short! I will soon be there.

> When the world my heart is rending
>   With its heaviest storm of care,
> My glad thoughts to heaven ascending
>   Find a refuge from despair.
> Faith's bright vision shall sustain me
>   Till life's pilgrimage is past;
> Fears may vex and troubles pain me,
>   I shall reach my home at last.

When thou hearest the sound of a going in the tops of the mulberry trees,...then thou shalt bestir thyself.
—2 Samuel 5:24

The members of Christ's church should be very prayerful, always seeking the anointing of the Holy One to rest on their hearts, that the kingdom of Christ may come, and that His *"will be done in earth, as it is in heaven"* (Matt. 6:10). But there are times when God seems especially to favor Zion; such seasons ought to be to them like *"the sound of a going in the tops of the mulberry trees."* We ought, then, to be doubly prayerful, doubly earnest, wrestling more at the throne than we have been inclined to do. Action should then be prompt and vigorous. The tide is flowing; let us pull manfully for the shore. Oh, for Pentecostal outpourings and Pentecostal labors! Christian, in yourself there are times when you hear the sound of marching among the mulberry trees. You have a special power in prayer; the Spirit of God gives you joy and gladness; the Scripture is open to you; the promises are applied; you walk in the light of God's countenance; you have wonderful freedom and liberty in devotion and more closeness of communion with Christ than was your custom. Now, at such joyous periods when you hear the *"sound of a going in the tops of the mulberry trees,"* is the time to rouse yourself. Now is the time to get rid of any evil habits, while God the Spirit is helping your weaknesses. Spread your sail; but remember what you sometimes sing—"I can only spread the sail; Thou! Thou! must breathe the auspicious gale." However, be sure you have the sail up. Do not miss the gale by being unprepared for it. Seek God's help, so that you may be more earnest in duty when you are made more strong in faith; that you may be more constant in prayer when you have more liberty at the throne; that you may be more holy in your conversation while you live more closely to Christ.

THE LORD OUR RIGHTEOUSNESS.
—Jeremiah 23:6

It will always give a Christian the greatest calm, quiet, ease, and peace to think of the perfect righteousness of Christ. How often are the saints of God downcast and sad! I do not think they should be. I do not think they would be if they could always see their perfection in Christ. Some are always talking about corruption, the depravity of the heart, and the innate evil of the soul. These things are quite true, but why not go a little further and remember that we are *"perfect in Christ Jesus"* (Col. 1:28)? It is no wonder that those who are dwelling on their own corruption should wear such downcast looks; but surely, if we call to mind that *"Christ Jesus...is made unto us...righteousness"* (1 Cor. 1:30), we will be of good cheer. Even though distresses afflict me and Satan assaults me; even though there may be many things to be experienced before I get to heaven, these things are done for me in the covenant of divine grace. Nothing is lacking in my Lord! Christ has done it all! On the cross, He said, *"It is finished"* (John 19:30), and if it is finished, then I am complete in Him and can *"rejoice with joy unspeakable and full of glory"* (1 Pet. 1:8). *"Not having mine own righteousness, which is of the law, but that which is through the faith of Christ, the righteousness which is of God by faith"* (Phil. 3:9). You will not find on this side of heaven a holier people than those who receive into their hearts the doctrine of Christ's righteousness. When the believer says, "I live in Christ alone. I rest solely on Him for salvation; and I believe that, however unworthy, I am still saved in Jesus," then there rises up as a motive of gratitude these thoughts: "Will I not live for Christ? Will I not love Him and serve Him, seeing that I am saved by His merits?" *"The love of Christ constraineth us...that they which live should not henceforth live unto themselves, but unto him which died for them"* (2 Cor. 5:14–15). If we are saved by imputed righteousness, we will greatly value imparted righteousness.

They shall sing in the ways of the LORD.
—Psalm 138:5

hristians begin to *"sing in the ways of the LORD"* when they first lose their burdens at the foot of the Cross. Not even the songs of the angels seem as sweet as the first song of rapture that gushes from the inmost soul of the forgiven child of God. You know how John Bunyan described it. He said that when poor Pilgrim lost his burden at the Cross, he gave three great leaps and went on his way singing,

> Blest Cross! blest Sepulchre! blest rather be
> The Man that there was put to shame for me!

Believer, do you remember the day when your fetters fell off? Do you remember the place where Jesus met you and said, *"'I have loved [you] with an everlasting love'* (Jer. 31:3). *'I have blotted out, as a thick cloud, [your] transgressions, and, as a cloud [your] sins'* (Isa. 44:22). They will not be mentioned against you forevermore." Oh, what a sweet season it is when Jesus takes away the pain of sin! When the Lord first pardoned my sin, I was so joyous that I could scarcely refrain from dancing. I thought on my way home from the house where I had been set at liberty that I must tell the stones in the street the story of my deliverance. My soul was so full of joy that I wanted to tell every snowflake that was falling from heaven of the wondrous love of Jesus, who had blotted out the sins of one of the chief of rebels. But it is not only at the beginning of the Christian life that believers have reason for song; as long as they live, they discover reasons to sing in the ways of the Lord, and their experience of His constant lovingkindness leads them to say, *"I will bless the LORD at all times: his praise shall continually be in my mouth"* (Ps. 34:1). See to it, friend, that you magnify the Lord this day.

> Long as we tread this desert land,
> New mercies shall new songs demand.

Without shedding of blood is no remission.
—Hebrews 9:22

his is the voice of unalterable truth. In none of the Jewish ceremonies were sins, even typically, removed without the shedding of blood. In no case, by no means, can sin be pardoned without atonement. It is clear, then, that there is no hope for me apart from Christ; for there is no other shedding of blood than His that is worth a thought as an atonement for sin. Am I, then, believing in Him? Is the blood of His atonement truly applied to my soul? All men are equal as to their need of Him. Even if we are moral, generous, amiable, or patriotic, the rule will not be altered to make an exception for us. Sin will yield to nothing less potent than the blood of Him whom God has set forth as a propitiation. What a blessing that there is the one way of pardon! Why should we seek another? Persons of merely formal religion cannot understand how we can rejoice that all our sins are forgiven for Christ's sake. Their works, prayers, and ceremonies give them very little comfort. It is good that they are uneasy, for they are neglecting the one great salvation and endeavoring to get remission without blood. My soul, take the time to consider that the justice of God is obligated to punish sin. See that punishment executed on your Lord Jesus and fall down in humble joy. Kiss the dear feet of Him whose blood has made atonement for you. It is in vain when the conscience is aroused to fly to feelings and evidences for comfort: we learned this habit in the Egypt of our legal bondage. The only restorative for a guilty conscience is a sight of Jesus suffering on the cross. *"The blood is the life"* (Deut. 12:23) says the Levitical law, and let us rest assured that it is the life of faith and joy and every other holy grace.

> Oh, how sweet to view the flowing
>   Of my Savior's precious blood;
> With divine assurance knowing
>   He has made my peace with God.

Therefore, brethren, we are debtors.
—Romans 8:12

As God's creatures, we are all debtors to Him: to obey Him with all our bodies, souls, and strength. Having broken His commandments, as we all have, we are debtors to His justice, and we owe to Him a vast amount that we are not able to pay. But, of the Christian, it can be said that he does not owe God's justice anything, for Christ has paid the debt His people owed. For this reason, the believer owes even more to love. I am a debtor to God's grace and forgiving mercy; but I am no debtor to His justice, for He will never accuse me of a debt that has already been paid. Christ said, *"It is finished"* (John 19:30), and by that He meant that whatever His people owed was wiped away forever from the book of remembrance. Christ, to the uttermost, has satisfied divine justice. The account is settled. The handwriting is nailed to the cross. The receipt is given, and we are debtors to God's justice no longer. But then, because we are not debtors to our Lord in that sense, we become debtors to God ten times more than we would have been otherwise. Christian, pause and ponder for a moment. What a debtor you are to divine sovereignty! How much you owe to His unbiased love, for He gave His own Son that He might die for you. Consider how much you owe to His forgiving grace that, after ten thousand affronts, He loves you as infinitely as ever. Consider what you owe to His power: how He has raised you from your death in sin; how He has preserved your spiritual life; how He has kept you from falling; and how, though a thousand enemies have beset your path, you have been able to continue on your way. Consider what you owe to His immutability: though you have changed a thousand times, He has not changed once. You are as deep in debt as you can be to every attribute of God. To God you owe yourself, and all you have. Yield yourself as a *"living sacrifice"*; it is but your *"reasonable service"* (Rom. 12:1).

The love of the LORD.
—Hosea 3:1

Believer, look back through all your experiences and think of the ways in which the Lord your God has led you in the wilderness—how He has fed and clothed you every day; how He has tolerated your bad manners, put up with all your grumbling and all your longings after Egypt's pots of meat; how He has opened the rock to supply you, and fed you with manna from heaven. Think of how His grace has been sufficient for you in all your troubles— how His blood has been a pardon for you in all your sins, how His rod and His staff have comforted you. When you have thus looked back on the love of the Lord, then let faith survey His love in the future, for remember that Christ's covenant and blood have something more in them than the past. He who has loved you and pardoned you will never cease to love and pardon. He is Alpha, and He will be Omega also. He is first, and He will be last. Therefore, re-member, when you pass through the *"valley of the shadow of death"* (Ps. 23:4), you need fear no evil, for He is with you. When you stand in the cold floods of the Jordan, you do not need to fear, for death cannot separate you from His love. When you come into the mysteries of eternity, you do not need to tremble, *"for I am persuaded, that neither death, nor life, nor angels, nor principalities, nor powers, nor things present, nor things to come, nor height, nor depth, nor any other creature, shall be able to separate us from the love of God, which is in Christ Jesus our Lord"* (Rom. 8:38–39). Now, soul, is your love not refreshed? Does this Scripture not make you love Jesus? Does a flight through the unlimited plains of heav-enly love not inflame your heart and compel you to delight yourself in the Lord your God? Surely as we meditate on *"the love of the LORD,"* our hearts burn within us, and we long to love Him more.

The Father sent the Son to be the Saviour of the world.
—1 John 4:14

It is a sweet thought that Jesus Christ did not come forth without His Father's permission, authority, consent, and assistance. He was sent by the Father so that He might be the Savior of men. We are too apt to forget that, while there are distinctions as to the persons in the Trinity, there are no distinctions of honor. We too frequently ascribe the honor of our salvation, or at least the depths of its benevolence, more to Jesus Christ than to the Father. This is a very great mistake. What if Jesus came? Did not His Father send Him? If He spoke wondrously, did not His Father pour grace into His lips so that He might be an able minister of the new covenant? He who knows the Father, the Son, and the Holy Spirit, as he should know them, never sets one before another in his love. He sees them at Bethlehem, at Gethsemane, and on Calvary, all equally engaged in the work of salvation. O Christian, have you put your confidence in the Man Christ Jesus? Have you placed your reliance solely on Him? Are you united with Him? Then believe that you are united with the God of heaven. Since to the Man Christ Jesus you are brother, and hold closest fellowship, you are linked thereby with God the Eternal, and *"the Ancient of days"* (Dan. 7:9, 13, 22) is your Father and your Friend. Did you ever consider the depth of love that was in the heart of Jehovah, when God the Father equipped His Son for the great enterprise of mercy? If not, make this your day's meditation. The Father sent Him! Contemplate that subject. Think about how Jesus works what the Father wills. In the wounds of the dying Savior, see the love of the great I AM. Let every thought of Jesus also be connected with the Eternal, ever blessed God, for *"it pleased the LORD to bruise him; he hath put him to grief"* (Isa. 53:10).

Praying always.
—Ephesians 6:18

W hat multitudes of prayers we have said from the first moment when we learned to pray. Our first prayer was a prayer for ourselves; we asked that God would have mercy on us and blot out our sins. He heard us. But when He had blotted out our sins like a cloud, then we had more prayers for ourselves. We have had to pray for sanctifying grace, for constraining and restraining grace. We have been led to crave a fresh assurance of faith, the comfortable application of the promise, deliverance in the hour of temptation, strength in the time of duty, and help in the day of trial. We have been compelled to go to God for our souls, as constant beggars asking for everything. Bear witness, children of God: you have never been able to get anything for your souls elsewhere. All the bread your soul has eaten has come down from heaven, and all the water of which it has drunk has flowed from the living Rock—Christ Jesus the Lord. Your soul has never grown rich in itself; it has always been a pensioner on the daily bounty of God; hence, your prayers have ascended to heaven for a range of spiritual mercies all but infinite. Your needs were innumerable; therefore, the supplies have been infinitely great. Your prayers have been as varied as the mercies have been countless. Do you not have cause to say, *"I love the LORD, because he hath heard my voice and my supplications"* (Ps. 116:1)? For as your prayers have been many, so also have been God's answers to them. He has heard you in the day of trouble, has strengthened and helped you, even when you have dishonored Him by trembling and doubting at the mercy seat. Remember this, and let it fill your heart with gratitude to God, who has thus graciously heard your poor weak prayers. *"Bless the LORD, O my soul, and forget not all his benefits"* (Ps. 103:2).

Arise ye, and depart.
—Micah 2:10

he hour is approaching when the message will come to us, as it comes to all—"Arise, and leave the home in which you have dwelled. Leave the city in which you have done your business. Leave your family and friends. Arise, and take your last journey." And what do we know of the journey? What do we know of the country to which we are bound? We have read a little about it, and some has been revealed to us by the Spirit, but how little we know of the realms of the future! We know that there is a black and stormy river called Death. God bids us cross it, promising to be with us. And, after death, what comes? What wondrous world will open to our astonished sight? What scene of glory will be unfolded to our view? No traveler has ever returned to tell. But we know enough of the heavenly land to make us welcome with joy and gladness our summons there. The journey of death may be dark, but we may go forth on it fearlessly, knowing that God is with us as we walk through the gloomy valley; therefore, we need fear no evil. We will be departing from all we have known and loved here, but we will be going to our Father's house—to our Father's home, where Jesus is—to that royal *"city which hath foundations, whose builder and maker is God"* (Heb. 11:10). This will be our last removal, to dwell forever with Him whom we love, in the midst of His people, in the presence of God. Christian, meditate much on heaven. It will help you to press on and to forget the toil of the way. This vale of tears is but the pathway to the better country. This world of woe is but the stepping-stone to a world of bliss.

> Prepare us, Lord, by grace divine,
>   For Thy bright courts on high;
> Then bid our spirits rise,
>   And join the chorus of the sky.

Thou shalt call his name JESUS.
—Matthew 1:21

When a person is dear, everything connected with him becomes dear for his sake. Thus, so precious is the person of the Lord Jesus in the estimation of all true believers that everything about Him they consider to be inestimable—beyond all price. *"All thy garments smell of myrrh, and aloes, and cassia"* (Ps. 45:8), said David, as if the very clothing of the Savior were so sweetened by His person that he could not but love it. Certainly, every spot where that hallowed foot has trod, every word that those blessed lips have uttered, or any thought that His loving Word has revealed is precious to us beyond all price. And this is true of the names of Christ; they are all sweet in the believer's ear. Whether He is called the Husband of the church, her Bridegroom, her Friend; whether He is named *"the Lamb slain from the foundation of the world"* (Rev. 13:8), the King, the Prophet, or the Priest; every title of our Master—Shiloh, Immanuel, Wonderful, the Mighty Counselor—every name is like the honeycomb dripping with honey, and luscious are the drops that fall from it. But if there is one name sweeter than another in the believer's ear, it is the name of *Jesus.* Jesus! His name moves the harps of heaven to melody. If there is one name more charming, more precious than another, it is the name *Jesus,* the life of all our joys. It is woven into the very foundation of our psalmody. Many of our hymns begin with it, and scarcely any that are good for anything end without it. It is the sum total of all delights. It is the music with which the bells of heaven ring; a song in a word; an ocean for comprehension, although a drop for brevity; a matchless oratorio in two syllables; a gathering up of the hallelujahs of eternity in five letters.

Jesus, I love Thy charming name,
'Tis music to mine ear.

David inquired of the LORD.
—2 Samuel 5:23

hen David made this inquiry, he had just fought the Philistines and gained a signal victory. The Philistines had come up in great hosts, but, by the help of God, David had easily put them to flight. Note, however, that when they came a second time, David did not go up to fight them without inquiring of the Lord. Once he had been victorious, and he might have said, as many have in other cases, "I will be victorious again; I may rest quite sure that, if I have conquered once, I will triumph yet again. Why should I bother to seek the Lord's direction?" Not so, David. He had gained one battle by the strength of the Lord; he would not venture on another until he had ensured the same. He inquired, "Should I go up against them?" He waited until God's sign was given. Learn from David to take no step without God. Christian, if you would know the path of duty, take God for your compass; if you would steer your ship through the dark billows, put the tiller into the hand of the Almighty. Many rocks might be escaped, if we would let our Father take the helm; many shoals or quicksand we might well avoid, if we would leave to His sovereign will to choose and to command. The Puritan said, "As sure as ever a Christian carves for himself, he'll cut his own fingers"; this is a great truth. Said another old clergyman, "He who goes before the cloud of God's providence goes on a fool's errand"; and so he does. We must mark God's providence leading us; and if providence tarries, tarry until providence comes. He who goes before providence will be very glad to run back again. *"I will instruct thee and teach thee in the way which thou shalt go"* (Ps. 32:8) is God's promise to His people. Let us, then, take all our perplexities to Him, and say, "Lord, what would You have me to do?" Do not leave your room this morning without inquiring of the Lord.

I know how to abound.
—Philippians 4:12

Many who know *"how to be abased"* (Phil. 4:12) have not learned *"how to abound."* On top of a pinnacle, their heads grow dizzy, and they are ready to fall. The Christian more often disgraces his profession of faith in prosperity than in adversity. It is a dangerous thing to be prosperous. The crucible of adversity is a less severe trial to the Christian than the refinery of prosperity. Oh, what leanness of soul and neglect of spiritual things have been brought on through the very mercies and bounties of God! Yet this does not need to happen, for the apostle Paul said that he knew how to abound. When he had much, he knew how to use it. Abundant grace enabled him to bear abundant prosperity. When he had a full sail, he was loaded with much ballast and so floated safely. More than human skill is needed to carry an overflowing cup of mortal joy with a steady hand, yet Paul had learned that skill, for he declared, *"In all things I am instructed both to be full and to be hungry"* (Phil. 4:12). It is a divine lesson to know how to be full, for the Israelites were full once, but while the meat was yet in their mouths, the wrath of God came on them. Many have asked for mercies so that they might satisfy their own hearts' lusts. When we have much of God's providential mercies, it often happens that we have but little of God's grace and little gratitude for the bounties we have received. We are full and we forget God. Satisfied with earth, we are content to do without heaven. Rest assured that it is harder to know how to be full than it is to know how to be hungry, so desperate is the tendency of human nature to pride and forgetfulness of God. Take care that you ask in your prayers that God would teach you how to be full.

Let not the gifts Thy love bestows
Estrange our hearts from Thee.

And they took knowledge of them, that they had been with Jesus.
—Acts 4:13

A Christian should be a striking likeness of Jesus Christ. You have read accounts of the life of Christ that have been beautifully and eloquently written, but the best life of Christ is His living biography, written out in the words and actions of His people. If we were what we profess to be, and what we should be, we would be pictures of Christ. We would have such a striking likeness to Him that the world would not have to say, "Well, there seems to be somewhat of a likeness to Christ." Instead, when they saw us, they would exclaim, "He has been with Jesus! He has been taught of Him. He is like Him and has caught the very idea of the holy Man of Nazareth. He works it out in his life and everyday actions." A Christian should model Christ's boldness. Never blush to own your faith. Your profession will never disgrace you; take care that you never disgrace it. Be like Jesus, very valiant for your God. Imitate Him in your loving spirit. Think kindly, speak kindly, and do kindly, so that men may say of you, "He has been with Jesus." Imitate Jesus in His holiness. Was He zealous for His Master? So be you; always go about doing good. Do not waste time; it is too precious. Was He self-denying, never looking to His own interests? Be the same. Was He devout? Be fervent in your prayers. Did He defer to His Father's will? So submit yourselves to Him. Was He patient? So learn to endure. Best of all, as the highest portraiture of Jesus, try to forgive your enemies, as He did; let those sublime words of your Master, *"Father, forgive them; for they know not what they do"* (Luke 23:34), always ring in your ears. Forgive, as you hope to be forgiven. Heap coals of fire on the head of your enemy by your kindness to him. Good for evil, remember, is Godlike. Be Godlike, then. In all ways and by all means, live so that all may say of you, "He has been with Jesus."

*For as the sufferings of Christ abound in us, so our consolation
also aboundeth by Christ.*
—2 Corinthians 1:5

onsider this blessed proportion. The Ruler of providence bears a pair of scales: on one side, He puts His
people's trials; on the other, He puts their consolations. When the scale of trial is nearly empty, you will always find the scale of consolation in nearly the same condition; likewise, when the scale of trials is full, you will find
the scale of consolation just as heavy. When the black
clouds gather most, the light is the more brightly revealed
to us. When the night lowers and the tempest is coming on,
the heavenly Captain is always closest to His crew. It is a
blessed thing that when we are most cast down, we are
most lifted up by the consolations of the Spirit. Trials make
more room for consolation. Great hearts can be made only
by great troubles. The spade of trouble digs the reservoir of
comfort deeper and makes more room for consolation. God
comes into our hearts and finds them full. He begins to
break our comforts and to make our hearts empty, so that
there is more room for grace. The humbler a man lies, the
more true comfort he will always have, because he will be
more fit to receive it. Another reason we are often happiest
in our troubles is that then we have the closest dealings
with God. When the barn is full, man can live without God.
When the purse is bursting with gold, we try to do without
as much prayer. But take our resources away, and we need
God. Cleanse the idols out of the house, and then, we are
compelled to honor Jehovah. *"Out of the depths have I cried
unto thee, O LORD"* (Ps. 130:1). There is no cry as good as
the one that comes from the bottom of the mountains—no
prayer half as hearty as one that comes from the depths of
the soul. Hence, deep trials and afflictions bring us to God,
and we are happier; for nearness to God is happiness. Come,
troubled believer, do not fret over your heavy troubles, for
they are the heralds of weighty mercies.

Behold, what manner of love the Father hath bestowed upon us, that we should be called the sons of God: therefore the world knoweth us not, because it knew him not. Beloved, now are we the sons of God.
—1 John 3:1–2

Behold, what manner of love the Father hath bestowed upon us." Consider who we were, and what we feel ourselves to be even now when corruption is powerful in us, and you will wonder at our adoption. Yet we are called *"the sons of God."* What a significant relationship is that of a son, and what privileges it brings! What care and tenderness the son expects from his father, and what love the father feels toward the son! But all that, and more than that, we now have through Christ. As for the temporary drawback of suffering with the Elder Brother, this we accept as an honor: *"Therefore the world knoweth us not, because it knew him not."* We are content to be unknown with Him in His humiliation, for we are to be exalted with Him. *"Beloved, now are we the sons of God."* That is easy to read, but it is not so easy to feel. How is it with your heart this morning? Are you in the lowest depths of sorrow? Does corruption rise within your spirit and grace seem like a poor spark trampled underfoot? Does your faith almost fail you? Fear not! It is neither your graces nor your feelings on which you are to live: you must live simply by faith on Christ. With all these things against us, *"now"*—in the very depths of our sorrow, wherever we may be— *"now,"* as much in the valley as on the mountain, *"Beloved, now are we the sons of God."* "Ah, but," you say, "see how I am clothed! My graces are not bright; my righteousness does not shine with apparent glory." But read the next part: *"It doth not yet appear what we shall be: but we know that, when he shall appear, we shall be like him"* (1 John 3:2). The Holy Spirit will purify our minds, and divine power will refine our bodies; then we will *"see him as he is"* (v. 2).

And his allowance was a continual allowance given him of the king,
a daily rate for every day, all the days of his life.
—2 Kings 25:30

Jehoiachin was not sent away from the king's palace with a store to last him for months, but his provision was given to him as a daily pension. Herein he well depicts the happy position of all the Lord's people. A daily portion is all that a person really needs. We do not need tomorrow's supplies; that day has not yet dawned, and its needs are as yet unborn. The thirst that we may suffer in the month of June does not need to be quenched in February, for we do not feel it yet. If we have enough for each day as the days arrive, we will never know need. Sufficient for the day is all that we can enjoy. We cannot eat, drink, or wear more than the day's supply of food and clothing. The surplus gives us the care of storing it and the anxiety of watching against a thief. One walking stick helps a traveler, but a bundle of sticks is a heavy burden. Enough is not only as good as a feast, but is all that the truest glutton can enjoy. This is all that we should expect; a craving for more than this is ingratitude. When our Father does not give us more, we should be content with our daily allowance. Jehoiachin's case is ours. We have a sure portion, a portion given to us by the King. It is a gracious and a perpetual portion. Here is surely ground for thankfulness. Beloved Christian, in matters of grace, you need a daily supply. You have no store of strength. Day by day, you must seek help from above. It is a very sweet assurance that a daily portion is provided for you. In the Word, through the ministry, by meditation, in prayer, and in waiting on God, you will receive renewed strength. In Jesus, all necessary things are laid up for you. Then enjoy your ongoing allowance. Never go hungry while the daily bread of grace is on the table of mercy.

To him be glory both now and for ever.
—2 Peter 3:18

Heaven will be full of the ceaseless praises of Jesus. Eternity—your unnumbered years will speed their everlasting course, but forever and forever, *"to him be glory."* Is He not a *"priest for ever after the order of Melchisedec"* (Heb. 5:6)? *"To him be glory."* Is He not King forever?—*"King of kings, and Lord of lords"* (1 Tim. 6:15), *"the everlasting Father"* (Isa. 9:6)? *"To him be glory...for ever."* Never will His praises cease. What was bought with blood deserves to last while immortality endures. The glory of the Cross must never be eclipsed; the luster of the grave and of the Resurrection must never be dimmed. O Jesus, You will be praised forever! As long as immortal spirits live—as long as the Father's throne endures—forever, forever, unto You will be glory. Believer, you are anticipating the time when you will join the saints above in ascribing all glory to Jesus, but are you glorifying Him now? The apostle's words were, *"To him be glory both now and for ever."* Will you not this day make them your prayer? "Lord, help me to glorify You. I am poor; help me to glorify You by being content. I am sick; help me to give You honor by being patient. I have talents; help me to extol You by spending them for You. I have time, Lord; help me to redeem it, so that I may serve You. I have a heart to feel, Lord; let that heart feel no love but Yours and glow with no flame but affection for You. I have a head to think, Lord; help me to think *of* You and *for* You. You have put me in this world for something, Lord; show me what that is, and help me to work out the purpose of my life. I cannot do much, but as the widow put in her two mites, which were all her living, so, Lord, I cast my time and eternity into Your treasury. I am all Yours. Take me, and enable me to glorify You now in all that I say, in all that I do, and with all that I have."

I have learned, in whatsoever state I am, therewith to be content.
—Philippians 4:11

hese words show us that contentment is not a natural human inclination. Covetousness, discontentment, and complaining are as natural to man as weeds are to the soil. We need not sow thistles and brambles; they come up naturally enough, because they are indigenous to earth. Similarly, we do not need to teach men to complain; they complain fast enough without any education. But the precious things of the earth must be cultivated. If we would have wheat, we must plough and sow. If we want flowers, we must plant and care for a garden. Now, contentment is one of the flowers of heaven, and if we would have it, it must be cultivated. It will not grow in us by nature. It is the new nature alone that can produce it, and even then we must be especially careful and watchful that we maintain and cultivate the grace that God has sown in us. Paul said, *"I have learned...to be content."* This statement implies that he did not know how to be content at one time. It cost him some pains to arrive at the mystery of that great truth. No doubt he sometimes thought he had learned the lesson, and then broke down. And when at last he had attained it, and could say, *"I have learned, in whatsoever state I am, therewith to be content,"* he was an old gray-headed man, on the borders of the grave—a poor prisoner shut up in Nero's dungeon in Rome. We might well be willing to endure Paul's infirmities and share the cold dungeon with him, if we, too, might by any means attain his good position. Do not indulge the notion that you can be contented with learning, or learn without discipline. It is not a power that may be exercised naturally, but a science to be acquired gradually. We know this from experience. Brother, hush that grumbling, natural though it be, and continue to be a diligent pupil in the College of Contentment.

Isaac dwelt by the well Lahairoi.
—Genesis 25:11

agar had once found deliverance there at the well, and Ishmael had drunk from the water so graciously revealed by the God who lives and sees the sons of men. But Isaac's visit to the well was not a casual visit, such as worldlings pay to the Lord in times of need, when it serves their turn. They cry to Him in trouble, but forsake Him in prosperity. Isaac, however, *dwelt* there, and made the well of the living and all-seeing God his constant source of supply. The usual tenor of a man's life, the dwelling of his soul, is the true test of his state. Perhaps the providential visitation experienced by Hagar struck Isaac's mind and led him to revere the place. Its mystical name endeared it to him. His frequent musings by its brim at eventide made him familiar with the well. His meeting Rebekah there had made his spirit feel at home near the spot, but, best of all, the fact that he there enjoyed fellowship with the living God had made him select that hallowed ground for his dwelling. Let us learn to live in the presence of the living God. Let us pray to the Holy Spirit that this day, and every other day, we may feel, *"Thou God seest me"* (Gen. 16:13). May the Lord Jehovah be as a well to us, delightful, comforting, unfailing, springing up unto eternal life. The bottle of the creature cracks and dries up, but the well of the Creator never fails. Happy is he who dwells at the well and thus has abundant and constant supplies near at hand. The Lord has been a sure helper to others: His name is Shaddai, God All-sufficient. Our hearts have often had most delightful communion with Him. Through Him our soul has found her glorious Husband, the Lord Jesus. This day, *"in him we live, and move, and have our being"* (Acts 17:28). Let us, then, dwell in closest fellowship with Him. Glorious Lord, constrain us that we may never leave You, but dwell by the well of the living God.

Show me wherefore thou contendest with me.
—Job 10:2

Perhaps, O tried soul, the Lord is doing this to develop your graces. Some of your graces would never be discovered if it were not for your trials. Do you not know that your faith never looks so grand in summer weather as it does in winter? Love is too often like a glow-worm, showing but little light unless it is in the midst of surrounding darkness. Hope itself is like a star—not to be seen in the sunshine of prosperity and only to be discovered in the night of adversity. Afflictions are often the black foils in which God sets the jewels of His children's graces, to make them shine the better. It was but a little while ago that on your knees you were saying, "Lord, I fear I have no faith. Let me know that I have faith." Were you not really, though perhaps unconsciously, praying for trials—for how can you know that you have faith until your faith is exercised? Depend on it: God often sends us trials so that our graces may be discovered, and so that we may be certified of their existence. Besides, it is not merely discovery. Real growth in grace is the result of sanctified trials. God often takes away our comforts and our privileges in order to make us better Christians. He trains His soldiers not in tents of ease and luxury, but by turning them out and sending them on forced marches and into hard service. He makes them ford through streams, swim through rivers, climb mountains, and walk many long miles with heavy knapsacks of sorrow on their backs. Well, Christian, may not this account for the troubles through which you are passing? Is not the Lord bringing out your graces and making them grow? Is this not the reason that He is contending with you?

> Trials make the promise sweet;
> Trials give new life to prayer;
> Trials bring me to His feet,
> Lay me low, and keep me there.

*Thus saith the Lord GOD; I will yet for this be inquired of by the
house of Israel, to do it for them.*
—Ezekiel 36:37

rayer is the forerunner of mercy. Turn to sacred history, and you will find that scarcely ever did a great
mercy come to this world unheralded by supplication.
You have found this true in your own personal experience.
God has given you many unsolicited favors, but still great
prayer has always been the prelude of great mercy with
you. When you first found peace through the blood of the
Cross, you had been praying much, and earnestly interced-
ing with God that He would remove your doubts and deliver you from your distresses. Your assurance was the
result of prayer. When at any time you have had high and
rapturous joys, you have been obliged to look on them as
answers to your prayers. When you have had great deliverance out of painful trouble and mighty help in great danger,
you have been able to say, *"I sought the LORD, and he heard
me, and delivered me from all my fears"* (Ps. 34:4). Prayer is
always the preface to blessing. It goes before the blessing as
the blessing's shadow. When the sunlight of God's mercies
rises on our needs, it casts the shadow of prayer far down
on the plain. When God piles up a hill of mercies, He Himself shines behind them, and He casts on our spirits the
shadow of prayer, so that we may rest assured. If we are
much in prayer, our pleadings are the shadows of mercy.
Prayer is thus connected with the blessing to show us the
value of it. If we had the blessings without asking for them,
we would think them common things; but prayer makes our
mercies more precious than diamonds. The things we ask
for are precious, but we do not realize their preciousness
until we have sought for them earnestly.

Prayer makes the darken'd cloud withdraw;
 Prayer climbs the ladder Jacob saw;
Gives exercise to faith and love;
 Brings every blessing from above.

God...comforteth those that are cast down.
—2 Corinthians 7:6

Who comforts like God? Go to some poor, distressed child of God and tell him sweet promises; whisper in his ear choice words of comfort. He is like a deaf adder; he does not listen to the voice of the charmer. He is drinking from the well of bitterness, and comfort him as you may, it will be only a note or two of mournful resignation that you will get from him. You will bring forth no psalms of praise, no hallelujahs, no joyful sonnets. But let God come to His child. Let Him lift up his face, and the mourner's eyes glisten with hope. Do you not hear him sing—

> 'Tis paradise, if Thou art here;
> If Thou depart, 'tis hell?

You could not have cheered him, but the Lord has done it. He is *"the God of all comfort"* (2 Cor. 1:3). There is no balm in Gilead, but there is balm in God. There is no physician among the creatures, but the Creator is Jehovah-Rophi, *"the LORD that healeth thee"* (Exod. 15:26). It is marvelous how one sweet word of God will make whole songs for Christians. One word of God is like a piece of gold, and the Christian is the goldbeater; he can hammer that promise out for whole weeks. So, then, poor Christian, you do not need to sit down in despair. Go to the Comforter, and ask Him to give you consolation. You are a poor, dry well. You have heard it said that when a pump is dry, you must pour water down it first of all, and then you will get water. So, Christian, when you are dry, go to God. Ask Him to shed abroad His joy in your heart, and then, your joy will be full. Do not go to earthly acquaintances, for you will find them Job's comforters after all; but go first and foremost to your *"God, [who] comforteth those that are cast down,"* and you will soon say, "In the multitude of my thoughts within me, Your comforts delight my soul."

He hath said.
—Hebrews 13:5

If we can only grasp these words by faith, we have an all-conquering weapon in our hand. What doubt will not be slain by this two-edged sword? What fear is there that will not fall smitten with a deadly wound before this arrow from the bow of God's covenant? Will not the distresses of life and the pangs of death; will not the corruption within, and the snares without; will not the trials from above, and the temptations from beneath all seem but light afflictions, when we can hide ourselves beneath the bulwark of *"he hath said"*? Yes, whether for delight in our silence, or for strength in our conflict, *"he hath said"* must be our daily resort. And this may teach us the extreme value of searching the Scriptures. There may be a promise in the Word that would exactly fit your case, but you may not know of it; therefore, you miss its comfort. You are like prisoners in a dungeon, and there may be one key in the bunch that would unlock the door. You might be set free; but if you will not look for it, you may remain a prisoner still, though liberty is so near at hand. There may be a potent medicine in the great pharmacopoeia of Scripture, yet you may continue to be sick unless you examine and search the Scriptures to discover what *"he hath said."* Besides reading the Bible, should you not store your memories richly with the promises of God? You can remember the sayings of great men; you treasure up the verses of renowned poets; should you not be profound in your knowledge of the words of God, so that you may be able to quote them readily when you would solve a difficulty or overthrow a doubt? Since *"he hath said"* is the source of all wisdom and the fountain of all comfort, let it dwell in you richly, as *"a well of water springing up into everlasting life"* (John 4:14). Then you will grow healthy, strong, and happy in the divine life.

*His bow abode in strength, and the arms of his hands were made
strong by the hands of the mighty God of Jacob.*
—Genesis 49:24

he strength that God gives to His Josephs is real
strength. It is not a boasted valor; fiction; or a thing
of which men talk, but that ends in smoke; it is true,
divine strength. How did Joseph stand against temptation?
Because God gave him aid. There is nothing that we can do
without the power of God. All true strength comes from
"the mighty God of Jacob." Notice in what a blessedly familiar
way God gives this strength to Joseph: *"The arms of his
hands were made strong by the hands of the mighty God of Jacob."* Thus God is represented as putting His hands on Joseph's hands, placing His arms on Joseph's arms. As a
father teaches his children, so the Lord teaches them who
fear Him. He puts His arms on them. Marvelous condescension! God Almighty, eternal, omnipotent, stoops from His
throne and lays His hands on the child's hand, stretching
His arm on the arm of Joseph so that he may be made
strong! This strength was also covenant strength, for it is
ascribed to *"the mighty God of Jacob."* Now, wherever you
read of the God of Jacob in the Bible, you should remember
the covenant with Jacob. Christians love to think of God's
covenant. All the power, all the grace, all the blessings, all
the mercies, all the comforts, and all the things we have
flow to us from the Source, through the covenant. If there
were no covenant, then we would fail indeed; for all grace
proceeds from it, as light and heat proceed from the sun. No
angels ascend or descend, save on that ladder that Jacob
saw, at the top of which stood a covenant God. Christian, it
may be that the archers have sorely grieved you, shot at
you, and wounded you, but still your bow abides in
strength; be sure, then, to ascribe all the glory to Jacob's
God.

I will never leave thee, nor forsake thee.
—Hebrews 13:5

No promise is of private interpretation. Whatever God has said to any one saint, He has said to all. When He opens a well for one, it is that all may drink. When He opens the granary door to give out food, there may be one starving man who is the occasion of its being opened, but all hungry saints may come and feed, too. Whether He gave the word to Abraham or to Moses does not matter, believer; He has given it to you as one of the covenanted seed. There is not a high blessing too lofty for you, nor a wide mercy too extensive for you. Lift up your eyes to the north and to the south, to the east and to the west, for all this is yours. Climb to Pisgah's top, and view the utmost limit of the divine promise, for the land is all your own. There is not a brook of living water of which you may not drink. If the land flows with milk and honey, eat the honey and drink the milk, for both are yours. Be bold to believe, for He has said, *"I will never leave thee, nor forsake thee."* In this promise, God gives to His people everything. *"I will never leave thee."* Then no attribute of God can cease to be engaged for us. Is He mighty? He will show Himself strong on the behalf of those who trust Him. Is He love? Then with lovingkindness will He have mercy on us. Whatever attributes may compose the character of deity, every one of them to its fullest extent will be engaged on our side. To sum it up, there is nothing you can lack, nothing you can ask for, nothing you can need in time or in eternity, nothing living, nothing dying, nothing in this world, nothing in the next world, nothing now, nothing at the Resurrection morning, nothing in heaven that is not contained in this text: *"I will never leave thee, nor forsake thee."*

I will cause the shower to come down in his season;
there shall be showers of blessing.
—Ezekiel 34:26

Here is sovereign, divine mercy: "I will give them showers in their season." For who can say, "I will give them showers," except God? There is only one voice that can speak to the clouds and bid them to rain. Who sends down the rain upon the earth? Who scatters the showers upon the green herbs? Do not I, the Lord? So grace is the gift of God and is not created by man. It is also needed grace. What would the ground do without showers? You may break the clods; you may sow your seeds, but what can you do without the rain? As absolutely necessary is the divine blessing. In vain you labor, until God gives the plenteous shower and sends salvation down. Then it is plenteous grace. "I will send them showers." It does not say, "I will send them drops," but *"showers."* So it is with grace. If God gives a blessing, He usually gives it in such a measure that there is not room enough to receive it. Plenteous grace! Oh, we need plenteous grace to keep us humble, to make us prayerful, to make us holy; we need plenteous grace to make us zealous, to preserve us through this life, and at last to land us in heaven. We cannot do without saturating showers of grace. It is also seasonable grace. *"I will cause the shower to come down in his season."* What is your season this morning? Is it the season of drought? Then that is the season for showers. Is it a season of great heaviness and black clouds? Then that is the season for showers. *"As thy days, so shall thy strength be"* (Deut. 33:25). And here is a varied blessing. "I will give you 'showers' of blessing." The word *"showers"* is in the plural. God will send all kinds of blessings. All God's blessings go together, like links in a golden chain. If He gives converting grace, He will also give comforting grace. He will send *"showers of blessing."* Look up today, O parched plant, and open your leaves and flowers for a heavenly watering.

The wrath to come.
—Matthew 3:7

It is pleasant to pass over a country after a storm has spent itself, to smell the freshness of the herbs after the rain has passed away, and to note the drops while they glisten like purest diamonds in the sunlight. That is the position of a Christian. He is going through a land where the storm has spent itself on his Savior's head, and if there are a few drops of sorrow falling, they come from clouds of mercy, and Jesus cheers him by the assurance that they are not for his destruction. But how terrible it is to witness the approach of a tempest; to see the forewarnings of a storm; to mark the birds of heaven as they droop their wings; to see the cattle as they lay their heads low in terror; to discern the face of the sky as it grows black; to look at the sun that does not shine and the angry and frowning heavens! How terrible to await the dread advance of a hurricane—such as occurs, sometimes, in the tropics—to wait in terrible apprehension until the wind rushes forth in fury, tearing up trees from their roots, forcing rocks from their pedestals, and hurling down all the dwelling places of man! And yet, sinner, this is your present position. No hot drops have as yet fallen, but a shower of fire is coming. No terrible winds howl around you, but God's tempest is gathering its dread artillery. As yet, the floods are dammed up by mercy, but the floodgates will soon be opened. The thunderbolts of God are yet in His storehouse, but lo, the tempest hastens, and how awful will that moment be when God, robed in vengeance, will march forth in fury! Where, where, where, O sinner, will you hide your head, or where will you flee? O that the hand of mercy may now lead you to Christ! He is freely set before you in the Gospel. His riven side is the rock of shelter. You know your need of Him. Believe in Him, cast yourself on Him, and then, the fury will be gone forever.

Salvation is of the LORD.
—Jonah 2:9

alvation is the work of God. It is He alone who quickens the soul *"dead in trespasses and sins"* (Eph. 2:1), and it is He also who maintains the soul in its spiritual life. He is both *"Alpha and Omega, the beginning and the ending"* (Rev. 1:8). *"Salvation is of the LORD."* If I am prayerful, God makes me prayerful. If I have graces, they are God's gifts to me. If I hold on in a consistent life, it is because He upholds me with His hand. I do nothing whatever toward my own preservation, except what God Himself first does in me. Whatever I have, all my goodness is of the Lord alone. Wherein I sin, that is my own; but wherein I act uprightly, that is of God, wholly and completely. If I have repulsed a spiritual enemy, the Lord's strength fortified my arm. Do I live a consecrated life before men? It is not I, but Christ who lives in me. Am I sanctified? I did not cleanse myself; God's Holy Spirit sanctifies me. Am I weaned from the world? I am weaned by God's chastisements sanctified to my good. Do I grow in knowledge? The great Instructor teaches me. All my jewels were fashioned by heavenly art. I find in God all that I need, but I find in myself nothing but sin and misery. *"He only is my rock and my salvation"* (Ps. 62:2, 6). Do I feed on the Word? That Word would be no food for me unless the Lord made it food for my soul and helped me to feed on it. Do I live on the manna that comes down from heaven? What is that manna but Jesus Christ Himself incarnate, whose body and whose blood I eat and drink? Am I continually receiving fresh increase of strength? Where do I gather my might? My help comes from heaven's hills. Without Jesus, I can do nothing. As a branch cannot bring forth fruit unless it *"abide[s] in the vine"* (John 15:4), no more can I, unless I abide in Him. What Jonah learned in the great deep, let me learn this morning in my place of prayer: *"Salvation is of the LORD."*

Thou hast made the LORD, which is my refuge,
even the most High, thy habitation.
—Psalm 91:9

The Israelites in the wilderness were continually exposed to change. Whenever the pillar halted its motion, the tents were pitched. But tomorrow, before the morning sun had risen, the trumpet sounded, the ark was in motion, and the fiery, cloudy pillar was leading the way through the narrow gorges of the mountain, up the hillside, or along the arid waste of the wilderness. They had scarcely time to rest a little before they heard the sound of "Away! This is not your rest; you must still be journeying onward toward Canaan!" They never stayed in one place very long. Even wells and palm trees could not detain them, yet they had an abiding home in their God. His cloudy pillar was the supporting beam for their tents; its flame by night, their household fire. They must go onward from place to place, continually changing, never having time to settle and to say, "Now we are secure; in this place we will dwell." "Yet," said Moses, "though we are always changing, Lord, You have *'been our dwelling place in all generations'* (Ps. 90:1)." The Christian knows no change with regard to God. He may be rich today and poor tomorrow; he may be sickly today and well tomorrow; he may be in happiness today and distressed tomorrow, but there is no change with regard to his relationship to God. If He loved me yesterday, He loves me today. My unmoving mansion of rest is my blessed Lord. Let prospects be blighted; let hopes be blasted; let joy be withered; and let mildew destroy everything. I have lost nothing of what I have in God. He is *"my strong habitation, whereunto I may continually resort"* (Ps. 71:3). I am a pilgrim in the world, but at home in my God. In the earth I wander, but in God I dwell in a quiet habitation.

My expectation is from him.
—Psalm 62:5

It is the believer's privilege to use this language. If he is looking for anything from the world, it is a poor *"expectation"* indeed. But if he looks to God for the supply of his needs, whether in temporal or spiritual blessings, his expectation will not be a vain one. Constantly, he may draw from the bank of faith and have his needs supplied out of the riches of God's lovingkindness. I know this: I would rather have God for my banker than all the Rothschilds. My Lord never fails to honor His promises. When we bring them to His throne, He never sends them back unanswered. Therefore, I will wait only at His door, for He always opens it with the hand of lavish grace. At this hour I will try Him anew. But we have expectations beyond this life. We will die soon, and then, our *"expectation is from him."* Do we not expect that when we lie on the bed of sickness He will send angels to carry us to His bosom? We believe that when the pulse is faint and the heart beats heavily, some angelic messenger will stand and look with loving eyes on us and whisper, "Sister spirit, come away!" As we approach the heavenly gate, we expect to hear the welcome invitation, *"Come, ye blessed of my Father, inherit the kingdom prepared for you from the foundation of the world"* (Matt. 25:34). We are expecting harps of gold and crowns of glory; we are hoping soon to be among the multitude of shining ones before the throne. We are looking forward and longing for the time when we will be like our glorious Lord, for *"we shall see him as he is"* (1 John 3:2). Then, if these are your expectations, O my soul, live for God. Live with the desire and resolve to glorify Him from whom come all your supplies, and of whose grace in your election, redemption, and calling, it is that you have any *"expectation"* of coming glory.

With lovingkindness have I drawn thee.
—Jeremiah 31:3

he thunders of the law and the terrors of judgment are all used to bring us to Christ, but the final victory is effected by lovingkindness. The Prodigal Son set out for his father's house from a sense of need, but his father saw him a great way off and ran to meet him. The last steps he took toward his father's house were with his father's kiss still warm on his cheek and the welcome still musical in his ears.

> Law and terrors do but harden
> All the while they work alone;
> But a sense of blood-bought pardon
> Will dissolve a heart of stone.

The Master came one night to the door and knocked with the iron hand of the law. The door shook and trembled on its hinges, but the man piled every piece of furniture that he could find against the door. He said, "I will not admit the Man." The Master turned away, but by and by He came back, and with His own soft hand, using mostly that part where the nails had penetrated, He knocked again—oh, so softly and tenderly. This time the door did not shake, but, strange to say, it opened, and there on his knees the once unwilling host was found rejoicing to receive his guest. "Come in; come in. You have knocked in a way that has moved my heart for You. I could not think of Your pierced hand leaving its blood mark on my door, and of Your going away homeless. I yield, I yield; Your love has won my heart." So, in every case, lovingkindness wins the day. What Moses with the tablets of stone could never do, Christ does with His pierced hand. Such is the doctrine of effectual calling. Is this my experience? Can I say, "He drew me, and I followed on, glad to confess the voice divine?" If so, may He continue to draw me, until at last I sit down at the Marriage Supper of the Lamb.

*Awake, O north wind; and come, thou south; blow upon my garden,
that the spices thereof may flow out.*
—Song of Solomon 4:16

nything is better than the dead calm of indifference.
Our souls may wisely desire the north wind of
trouble if that alone can be sanctified to the drawing forth of the perfume of our graces. As long as it cannot
be said, *"The LORD was not in the wind"* (1 Kings 19:11), we
will not shrink from the wintriest blast that ever blew on
plants of grace. Did not the spouse in this verse humbly
submit herself to the reproofs of her Beloved? Did she not
entreat Him to send forth His grace in some form and make
no stipulation as to the particular manner in which it
should come? Did she not, like ourselves, become so utterly
weary of deadness and unholy calm that she sighed for any
visitation that would brace her to action? Yet she desired
the warm south wind of comfort, too, the smiles of divine
love, the joy of the Redeemer's presence. These are often
mightily effective in arousing our sluggish life. She desired
either one or the other, or both, so that she might be able to
delight her Beloved with the spices of her garden. She could
not endure to be unprofitable, nor can we. How cheering a
thought that Jesus can find comfort in our poor feeble
graces. Can it be? It seems far too good to be true. Well
may we court trial or even death itself if we will thereby be
aided to make Immanuel's heart glad. Oh, that our hearts
were crushed to atoms if only by such bruising our sweet
Lord Jesus could be glorified. Graces unexercised are as
sweet perfumes slumbering in the cups of flowers. The wisdom of the great Husbandman overrules diverse and opposite causes to produce the one desired result. He makes
both affliction and consolation draw forth the grateful fra-
grances of faith, love, patience, hope, resignation, joy, and
the other fair flowers of the garden. May we know, by
sweet experience, what this means.

All the Israelites went down to the Philistines, to sharpen every man his share, and his coulter, and his ax, and his mattock.
—1 Samuel 13:20

We are engaged in a great war with the Philistines of evil. Every weapon within our reach must be used. Preaching, teaching, praying, giving—all must be brought into action, and talents that have been thought too humble for service must now be employed. Coulter, ax, and mattock may all be useful in slaying Philistines. Rough tools may deal hard blows, and killing need not be elegantly done, as long as it is done effectively. Each moment of time, in season or out of season; each fragment of ability, educated or untutored; each opportunity, favorable or unfavorable, must be used, for our foes are many and our force but meager. Most of our tools need to be sharpened. We need quickness of perception, tact, energy, promptness—in a word, complete adaptation—for the Lord's work. Practical common sense is a very scarce thing among the conductors of Christian enterprises. We might learn from our enemies if we would, and so make the Philistines sharpen our weapons. This morning let us note enough to sharpen our zeal during this day by the aid of the Holy Spirit. Observe the energy of the papists, how they compass sea and land to make one proselyte. Are they to monopolize all the earnestness? Mark the heathen devotees, what tortures they endure in the service of their idols. Are they alone to exhibit patience and self-sacrifice? Observe the prince of darkness, how persevering he is in his endeavors, how unabashed in his attempts, how daring in his plans, how thoughtful in his plots, how energetic in all! The devils are united as one man in their infamous rebellion, while we believers in Jesus are divided in our service of God and scarcely ever work with unanimity. O that from Satan's infernal industry we may learn to go about like Good Samaritans, seeking whom we may bless!

I have chosen thee in the furnace of affliction.
—Isaiah 48:10

omfort yourself, tried believer, with this thought: God said, *"I have chosen thee in the furnace of affliction."* Does not the word come like a soft shower, assuaging the fury of the flame? Is it not an asbestos armor, against which the heat has no power? Let affliction come. God has chosen me! Poverty, you may stride in at my door, but God is in the house already, and He has chosen me. Sickness, you may intrude, but I have a balsam ready—God has chosen me. Whatever befalls me in this vale of tears, I know that He has *"chosen"* me. If, believer, you require still greater comfort, remember that you have the Son of Man with you in the furnace. In that silent room of yours, there sits by your side One whom you have not seen, but whom you love; and often when you do not know it, He makes your bed in your affliction and smoothes your pillow for you. You are in poverty, but in that lovely house of yours, the Lord of life and glory is a frequent visitor. He loves to come into these desolate places so that He may visit you. Your Friend sticks closely to you. You cannot see Him, but you may feel the pressure of His hands. Do you not hear His voice? Even in the valley of the shadow of death He says, *"Fear thou not; for I am with thee: be not dismayed; for I am thy God"* (Isa. 41:10). Remember that noble speech of Caesar: "Fear not, thou carriest Caesar and all his fortune." Fear not, Christian; Jesus is with you. In all your fiery trials, His presence is both your comfort and safety. He will never leave one whom He has chosen for His own. *"Fear…not, for I am with thee"* is His sure word of promise to His chosen ones in the *"furnace of affliction."* Will you not, then, take fast hold of Christ, and say,

> Through floods and flames, if Jesus lead,
> I'll follow where He goes?

My grace is sufficient for thee.
—2 Corinthians 12:9

If none of God's saints were poor and tried, we would not know half so well the consolations of divine grace. When we find the wanderer who has nowhere to lay his head, who yet can say, "Still I will trust in the Lord"; when we see the pauper starving on bread and water, who still glories in Jesus; when we see the bereaved widow overwhelmed in affliction, who yet has faith in Christ, oh, what honor it reflects on the Gospel. God's grace is illustrated and magnified in the poverty and trials of believers. Saints bear up under every discouragement, believing *"that all things work together for [their] good"* (Rom. 8:28), and that out of apparent evils a real blessing will ultimately spring—that their God will either deliver them speedily or most assuredly support them in the trouble, as long as He is pleased to keep them in it. This patience of the saints proves the power of divine grace. There is a lighthouse out at sea. It is a calm night; I cannot tell whether the edifice is firm. The tempest must rage about it, and then, I will know whether it will stand. So it is with the Spirit's work. If it were not on many occasions surrounded with tempestuous waters, we would not know that it was true and strong; if the winds did not blow on it, we would not know how firm and secure it was. The masterpieces of God are those who stand steadfast and unmovable in the midst of difficulties—"Calm mid the bewildering cry, confident of victory." He who would glorify his God must set his account on meeting with many trials. No man can be illustrious before the Lord unless his conflicts are many. If yours, then, is a much tried path, rejoice in it, because you will all the better show forth the all-sufficient grace of God. As for His failing you, never dream of it—hate the thought. The God who has been sufficient until now should be trusted to the end.

Let us not sleep, as do others.
—1 Thessalonians 5:6

here are many ways of promoting Christian wakeful-
ness. Among the rest, let me strongly advise Chris-
tians to converse together concerning the ways of the
Lord. Christian and Hopeful, as they journeyed toward the
Celestial City, said to themselves, "To prevent drowsiness in
this place, let us fall into good discourse." Christian inquired,
"Brother, where shall we begin?" Hopeful answered, "Where
God began with us." Then Christian sang this song:

> When saints do sleepy grow, let them come hither,
>> And hear how these two pilgrims talk together;
> Yea, let them learn of them, in any wise,
>> Thus to keep open their drowsy, slumb'ring eyes.
> Saints' fellowship, if it be managed well,
>> Keeps them awake, and that in spite of hell.

Christians who isolate themselves and walk alone are
very liable to grow drowsy. Keep Christian company, and
you will be kept wakeful by it and refreshed and encouraged
to make quicker progress on the road to heaven. But as you
take *"sweet counsel"* (Ps. 55:14) in the ways of God, take care
that the theme of your conversation is the Lord Jesus. Let
your eyes be constantly looking to Him; let your heart be
full of Him; let your lips speak of His worth. Friend, live
near the cross, and you will not sleep. Impress on yourself a
deep sense of the value of the place to which you are going.
If you remember that you are going to heaven, you will not
sleep on the road. If you think that hell is behind you, and
the devil is pursuing you, you will not loiter. Christian, will
you sleep while the pearly gates are open, the songs of angels are waiting for you to join them, and a crown of gold is
ready for your brow? In holy fellowship continue to *"watch
and pray, that ye enter not into temptation"* (Matt. 26:41).

Ye must be born again.
—John 3:7

Regeneration is a subject that lies at the very basis of salvation, and we should be very diligent to take heed that we really are *"born again,"* for there are many who imagine they are, who are not. Be assured that the name of a Christian is not the nature of a Christian; and that being born in a Christian land and being recognized as professing the Christian religion is of no avail whatever unless there is something more added to it—being born again is a matter so mysterious that human words cannot describe it. *"The wind bloweth where it listeth, and thou hearest the sound thereof, but canst not tell whence it cometh, and whither it goeth: so is every one that is born of the Spirit"* (John 3:8). Nevertheless, it is a change that is known and felt: known by works of holiness and felt by a gracious experience. This great work is supernatural. It is not an operation that a man performs for himself. A new principle is infused, which works in the heart, renews the soul, and affects the entire man. It is not a change of my name, but a renewal of my nature, so that I am not the person I used to be, but a *"new creature"* (2 Cor. 5:17) in Christ Jesus. To wash and dress a corpse is a far different thing from making it alive. Man can do the one, but God alone can do the other. If you have, then, been born again, your acknowledgment will be, "O Lord Jesus, the everlasting Father, You are my spiritual Parent. Unless Your Spirit had breathed into me the breath of a new, holy, spiritual life, I would have been to this day *'dead in trespasses and sins'* (Eph. 2:1). My heavenly life is wholly derived from You, and from You alone. My *'life is hid with Christ in God'* (Col. 3:3). It is no longer I who live, but Christ who lives in me (Gal. 2:20)." May the Lord enable us to be well assured on this vital point, for to be unregenerate is to be unsaved, unpardoned, without God, and without hope.

Have faith in God.
—Mark 11:22

aith is the foot of the soul by which it can march along the road of the commandments. Love can make the feet move more swiftly, but faith is the foot that carries the soul. Faith is the oil that enables the wheels of holy devotion and of earnest piety to move well. Without faith the wheels are taken from the chariot, and we drag heavily. With faith I can do all things; without faith I neither have the inclination nor the power to do anything in the service of God. If you would find the men who serve God the best, you must look for the men of the most faith. Little faith will save a man, but little faith cannot do great things for God. Bunyan's Little-faith could not have fought Apollyon; it needed Christian to do that. Poor Little-faith could not have slain Giant Despair; it required Great-heart's arm to knock that monster down. Little-faith will go to heaven most certainly, but it often has to hide itself in a nutshell, and it frequently loses all but its jewels. Little-faith says, "It is a rough road, beset with sharp thorns, and full of dangers; I am afraid to go"; but Great-faith remembers the promise, *"Thy shoes shall be iron and brass; and as thy days, so shall thy strength be"* (Deut. 33:25), and so she boldly ventures. Despondent, Little-faith mingles her tears with the flood; but Great-faith sings, *"When thou passest through the waters, I will be with thee; and through the rivers, they shall not overflow thee"* (Isa. 43:2), and she fords the stream at once. Do you want to be comfortable and happy? Do you enjoy religion? Do you want to have the religion of cheerfulness and not that of gloom? Then *"have faith in God."* If you love darkness and are satisfied to dwell in gloom and misery, then be content with little faith; but if you love the sunshine and would sing songs of rejoicing, covet earnestly this best gift: great faith.

We must through much tribulation
enter into the kingdom of God.
—Acts 14:22

od's people have their trials. It was never designed by God, when He chose His people, that they should be an untried people. They were chosen in the *"furnace of affliction"* (Isa. 48:10). They were never chosen for worldly peace and earthly joy. Freedom from sickness and the pains of mortality were never promised to them; but when their Lord drew up the charter of privileges, He included chastisements among the things to which they would inevitably be heirs. Trials are a part of our lot; they were predestinated for us in Christ's last legacy. As surely as the stars are fashioned by His hands and their orbits fixed by Him, our trials are allotted to us. He has ordained their season and their place, their intensity and the effect they will have on us. Good men must never expect to escape troubles. If they do, they will be disappointed, for none of their predecessors has been without them. Mark the patience of Job. Remember Abraham, for he had his trials, and by his faith under them, he became the "Father of the faithful." Note well the biographies of all the patriarchs, prophets, apostles, and martyrs, and you will discover none of those whom God made vessels of mercy who were not made to pass through the fire of affliction. It is ordained of old that the cross of trouble should be engraved on every vessel of mercy, as the royal mark whereby the King's vessels of honor are distinguished. But although tribulation is thus the path of God's children, they have the comfort of knowing that their Master has traversed it before them. They have His presence and sympathy to cheer them, His grace to support them, and His example to teach them how to endure. And when they reach the kingdom, it will more than make amends for the *"much tribulation"* through which they passed to enter it.

Yea, he is altogether lovely.
—Song of Solomon 5:16

The superlative beauty of Jesus is all-attracting. It is not so much to be admired as to be loved. He is more than pleasant and fair; He is lovely. Surely the people of God can fully justify the use of this golden word, for He is the object of their warmest love, a love founded on the intrinsic excellence of His person, the complete perfection of His charms. O disciples of Jesus, look to your Master's lips and say, "Are they not most sweet?" Do not His words cause your hearts to burn within you as He talks with you by the way? Worshippers of Immanuel, look up to His head of much fine gold, and tell me, are not His thoughts precious to you? Is not your adoration sweetened with affection as you humbly bow before that countenance, which *"is as Lebanon, excellent as the cedars"* (Song 5:15)? Is there not a charm in His every feature, and is not His whole person fragrant with such a savor of His good ointments, that therefore the virgins love Him? Is there one member of His glorious body that is not attractive?—one portion of His person that is not a fresh lodestone to our souls?—one office that is not a strong cord to bind your heart? Our love is not as a seal set on His heart of love alone. It is fastened on His arm of power also. Nor is there a single part of Him on which it does not fix itself. We anoint His whole person with the sweet spikenard of our fervent love. His whole life we would imitate; His whole character we would copy. In all other beings we see some lack; in Him there is all perfection. Even the best of His favored saints have had blots on their garments and wrinkles on their brows. He is nothing but loveliness. All earthly suns have their spots. The fair world itself has its wilderness. We cannot love the whole of the loveliest thing, but Christ Jesus is gold without alloy, light without darkness, glory without cloud—*"Yea, he is altogether lovely."*

In my prosperity I said, I shall never be moved.
—Psalm 30:6

oab...*settled on his lees, and hath not been emptied from vessel to vessel*" (Jer. 48:11). Give a man wealth. Let his ships bring home continually rich freights, and let the winds and waves appear to be his servants to bear his vessels across the bosom of the mighty deep. Let his lands yield abundantly, and let the weather be propitious to his crops. Let uninterrupted success attend him. Let him stand among men as a successful merchant. Let him enjoy continued health, and allow him with braced nerve and brilliant eye to march through the world and live happily. Give him a buoyant spirit. Let him have a song perpetually on his lips. Let his eyes ever sparkle with joy— and the natural consequence of such an easy state to any man, even if he is the best Christian who has ever lived, will be presumption. Even David said, *"I shall never be moved,"* and we are not better than David, nor half so good. Brother, beware of the smooth places of the way. If you are treading them, or if the way is rough, thank God for it. If God would always rock us in the cradle of prosperity; if we were always dandled on the knees of fortune; if we did not have some stain on the alabaster pillar; if there were not a few clouds in the sky; if we did not have some bitter drops in the wine of this life, we would become intoxicated with pleasure. We would dream we stand and stand we would, but it would be on a pinnacle. Like a man asleep on the mast, each moment we would be in jeopardy. We bless God, then, for our afflictions. We thank Him for our ups and downs. We extol His name for losses of property, for we feel that had He not chastened us thus, we might have become too secure. Continued worldly prosperity is a fiery trial.

Afflictions, though they seem severe,
In mercy oft are sent.

Sin...exceeding sinful.
—Romans 7:13

Beware of frivolous thoughts of sin. At the time of conversion, the conscience is so tender that we are afraid of the slightest sin. Young converts have a holy timidity, a godly fear lest they should offend God. But alas! Very soon the fine bloom on these first ripe fruits is removed by the rough handling of the surrounding world. The sensitive plant of young piety turns into a willow in later life; it grows too pliant, too easily yielding. By degrees men become familiar with sin. The ear in which the cannon has been booming will not notice slight sounds. At first a little sin startles us; but soon, we say, "Is it not a little one?" Then there comes a larger one, and then another, until by degrees we begin to regard sin as but a little transgression. Then follows an unholy presumption: "We have not fallen into open sin. True, we tripped a little, but we stood upright on the whole. We may have uttered one unholy word, but most of our conversation has been consistent." So we excuse sin. We throw a cloak over it and call it by dainty names. Christian, beware of thinking lightly of sin. Take heed lest you fall little by little. Sin, a little thing? Is it not a poison? Who knows its deadliness? Sin, a little thing? Do not the little foxes spoil the grapes (Song 2:15)? Does not the tiny coral insect build a rock that wrecks a navy? Do not little strokes fell lofty oaks? Will not droplets of water eventually wear away stones? Sin, a little thing? It circled the Redeemer's head with thorns and pierced His heart! It made Him suffer anguish, bitterness, and woe. If you could weigh the least sin on the scales of eternity, you would fly from it as from a serpent and abhor the least appearance of evil. Look on all sin as that which crucified the Savior, and you will see it to be *"exceeding sinful."*

Thou shalt love thy neighbour.
—Matthew 5:43

ove your neighbor. Perhaps he rolls in riches, and you are poor, living in your little cottage side by side with his lordly mansion. Every day you see his estates, his fine linen, and his sumptuous banquets. God has given him these gifts. Do not covet his wealth, and think no cruel thoughts concerning him. Be content with your own lot, if you cannot better it. Do not look on your neighbor and wish that he were as you. Love him, and then you will not envy him. Perhaps, on the other hand, you are rich, and the poor live near you. Do not be too proud to call them your neighbor. Accept your responsibility to love them. The world calls them your inferiors. In what are they inferior? They are far more your equals than your inferiors, for God has made *"of one blood all nations of men for to dwell on all the face of the earth"* (Acts 17:26). It is your coat that is better than theirs, but you are by no means better than they. They are men, and what are you more than that? Take heed that you love your neighbor even though he is in rags or has sunken in the depths of poverty. But, perhaps, you say, "I cannot love my neighbors, because, for all I do for them, they return ingratitude and contempt." That leaves more room for the heroism of love. Would you be a featherweight warrior, instead of bearing the rough fight of love? He who dares the most will win the most. If your path of love is rough, tread it boldly, still loving your neighbors through thick and thin. *"Heap coals of fire on* [their heads]*"* (Rom. 12:20), and if they are hard to please, do not seek to please them, but to please your Master. Remember, if they spurn your love, your Master has not spurned it, and your actions are as acceptable to Him as if they had been acceptable to them. Love your neighbor, for, in so doing, you are following the footsteps of Christ.

Why sit we here until we die?
—2 Kings 7:3

ear reader, this little book was mainly intended for the edification of believers, but if you are yet unsaved, my heart yearns over you. I would gladly say a word that may be blessed to you. Open your Bible and read the story of the lepers. Notice their position, which was much the same as yours. If you remain where you are, you will perish; if you go to Jesus, you can only die. Nothing ventured, nothing gained is the old proverb, and in your case the venture is no great one. If you sit still in despair, no one can pity you when your ruin comes; but if you die with mercy sought, if such a thing were possible, you would be the object of universal sympathy. No one will escape who refuses to look to Jesus. You know that some are saved who believe in Him, for certain of your own acquaintances have received mercy. Then why not you? The Ninevites said, *"Who can tell?"* (Jonah 3:9). Act on the same hope, and try the Lord's mercy. To perish is so awful that if there were but a straw to catch at, the instinct of self-preservation would lead you to stretch out your hand. We have thus been talking to you on your own unbelieving ground. We would now assure you, as from the Lord, that if you seek Him, you will find Him. Jesus casts out no one who comes to Him. You will not perish if you trust Him; on the contrary, you will find treasure far richer than the poor lepers gathered in Syria's deserted camp. May the Holy Spirit embolden you to go at once, and you will not believe in vain. When you are saved yourself, tell the good news to others. Do not hold your peace. Tell the church first, and unite with them in fellowship. Let the minister be informed of your discovery, and then proclaim the good news in every place. May the Lord save you before the sun goes down today.

Let him that thinketh he standeth take heed lest he fall.
—1 Corinthians 10:12

It is a curious fact that there is such a thing as being proud of grace. A man says, "I have great faith; I will not fall. Poor, Little-faith may, but I never will." "I have fervent love," says another. "I can stand; there is no danger of my going astray." He who boasts of grace has little grace of which to boast. Some who do this imagine that their graces can keep them, knowing not that the stream must flow constantly from the fountainhead, or else the brook will soon be dry. If a continuous stream of oil does not come to the lamp, though it burns brightly today, it will smoke tomorrow, and its scent will be noxious. Take heed that you do not glory in your graces, but let all your glorying and confidence be in Christ and His strength, for only then can you be kept from falling. Pray much. Spend longer times in holy adoration. Read the Scriptures more earnestly and constantly. Watch your lives more carefully. Live nearer to God. Take the best examples for your pattern. Let your conversation be holy. Let your hearts be perfumed with affection for men's souls. Live in such a way that men will know that you have been with Jesus and have learned of Him. When that happy day will come, when He whom you love will say, "Come up higher," may it be your happiness to hear Him say, "[You] *have fought a good fight,* [you] *have finished* [your] *course,* [you] *have kept the faith: henceforth there is laid up for* [you] *a crown of righteousness*" (2 Tim. 4:7–8). On, Christian, with care and caution! On, with holy fear and trembling! On, with faith and confidence in Jesus alone, and let your constant petition be, *"Uphold me according unto thy word"* (Ps. 119:116). He is able, and He alone, *"to keep you from falling, and to present you faultless before the presence of his glory with exceeding joy"* (Jude 24).

Be strong in the grace that is in Christ Jesus.
—2 Timothy 2:1

hrist has grace without measure in Himself, but He has not retained it for Himself. As the reservoir empties itself into the pipes, so has Christ emptied out His grace for His people. *"Of his fulness have all we received, and grace for grace"* (John 1:16). He seems only to have in order to dispense to us. He stands like the fountain, always flowing, but only running in order to supply the empty pitchers and the thirsty lips that draw near to it. Like a tree, He bears sweet fruit, not to hang on boughs, but to be gathered by those who have need. Grace, whether its work is to pardon, to cleanse, to preserve, to strengthen, to enlighten, to quicken, or to restore, is ever to be had from Him freely and without price. Nor is there one form of the work of grace that He has not bestowed on His people. As the blood of the body, though flowing from the heart, belongs equally to every member, so the influences of grace are the inheritance of every saint united to the Lamb. Herein there is a sweet communion between Christ and His church, inasmuch as they both receive the same grace. Christ is the Head on which the oil is first poured, but the same oil runs to the very skirts of the garments, so that the humblest saint has an unction of the same costly moisture as that which fell on the Head. This is true communion when the sap of grace flows from the stem to the branch, and when it is perceived that the stem itself is sustained by the very nourishment that feeds the branch. As we day by day receive grace from Jesus, and more constantly recognize it as coming from Him, we will behold Him in communion with us, and enjoy communion with Him. Let us make daily use of our riches and ever go to Him as to our own Lord in covenant, taking from Him the supply of all we need with as much boldness as men take money from their own pockets.

I am a stranger with thee.
—Psalm 39:12

Lord, I am a stranger *with* You, but not *to* You. All my natural alienation from You, Your grace has effectively removed. Now, in fellowship with You, I walk through this sinful world as a pilgrim in a foreign country. Lord, You are a stranger in Your own world. Man forgets You, dishonors You, sets up new laws and alien customs, and does not know You. When Your dear Son came to His own, His own did not receive Him (John 1:11). *"He was in the world, and the world was made by him, and the world knew him not"* (v. 10). Never was a foreigner considered as questionable a character as much as Your beloved Son was among His own people. It is no surprise, then, if I who live the life of Jesus am a stranger here below. Lord, I would not be a citizen where Jesus was an alien. His pierced hand has loosened the cords that once bound my soul to earth, and now I find myself a stranger in the land. Among those with whom I dwell, my speech seems to these an outlandish tongue, my manners unusual, and my actions strange. A barbarian would be more at home among genteel society than I could ever be among the company of sinners. But here is the sweetness of my lot: I am a stranger along with You. You are my fellow sufferer, my fellow pilgrim. Oh, what joy to be in such blessed society! My heart burns within me by the way when You speak to me, and though I am a sojourner, I am far more blessed than those who sit on thrones or dwell in their comfortable houses.

> To me remains nor place, nor time:
>   My country is in every clime;
> I can be calm and free from care
>   On any shore, since God is there.
> While place we seek, or place we shun,
>   The soul finds happiness in none:
> But with a God to guide our way,
>   'Tis equal joy to go or stay.

Remember the poor.
—Galatians 2:10

hy does God allow so many of His children to be poor? He could make them all rich if He pleased. He could lay bags of gold at their doors and send them a large annual income. He could scatter round their houses an abundance of provisions, as once He made the quails lie in heaps round the camp of Israel and rained bread out of heaven to feed them. There is no need for them to be poor, except that He sees it to be best. *"The cattle upon a thousand hills"* (Ps. 50:10) are His. He could supply them. He could make the richest, the greatest, and the mightiest bring all their power and riches to the feet of His children, for the hearts of all men are in His control. But He does not choose to do so; instead, He allows them to experience need. He allows them to suffer in poverty and obscurity. Why is this? There are many reasons: one is to give us, who are favored with enough, an opportunity of showing our love for Jesus. We show our love for Christ when we sing of Him and when we pray to Him, but if there were no sons of need in the world, we would lose the sweet privilege of demonstrating our love by charitably ministering to His poorer brethren. He has ordained that thus we should prove that our love stands not only in word, but also in deed and in truth. If we truly love Christ, we will care for those who are loved by Him. Those who are dear to Him will be dear to us. Let us, then, look on it not as a duty but as a privilege to relieve the poor of the Lord's flock—remembering the words of the Lord Jesus, *"Inasmuch as ye have done it unto one of the least of these my brethren, ye have done it unto me"* (Matt. 25:40). Surely this assurance is sweet enough, and this motive strong enough to lead us to help others with a willing hand and a loving heart—remembering that all we do for His people is graciously accepted by Christ as done to Himself.

Ye are all the children of God by faith in Christ Jesus.
—Galatians 3:26

The fatherhood of God is common to all His children. Ah! Little-faith, you have often said, "Oh that I had the courage of Great-heart, that I could wield his sword and be as valiant as he! But, alas, I stumble at every straw, and a shadow makes me afraid." Listen, Little-faith. Great-heart is God's child, and you are God's child, too; Great-heart is not one bit more God's child than you are. Peter and Paul, the highly favored apostles, were of the family of the Most High, and so are you also. The weak Christian is as much a child of God as the strong one.

> This cov'nant stands secure,
>   Though earth's old pillars bow;
> The strong, the feeble, and the weak,
>   Are one in Jesus now.

All the names are in the same family register. One may have more grace than another, but God our heavenly Father has the same tender heart toward all. One may do more mighty works, and may bring more glory to his Father, but he whose name is the least in the kingdom of heaven is as much the child of God as he who stands among the King's mighty men. Let this cheer and comfort us, when we draw near to God and say, "Our Father." Yet while we are comforted by knowing this, let us not rest contented with weak faith, but ask, like the apostles, to have it increased. However feeble our faith may be, if it is real faith in Christ, we will reach heaven at last; but we will not honor our Master much on our pilgrimage, neither will we abound in joy and peace. If then you desire to live for Christ's glory and be happy in His service, seek to be filled with the spirit of adoption more and more completely, until *"perfect love casteth out fear"* (1 John 4:18).

Strong in faith.
—Romans 4:20

Christian, take good care of your faith, for remember, faith is the only way whereby you can obtain blessings. If we ask blessings from God, nothing can bring them down but faith. Prayer cannot draw down answers from God's throne unless it is the earnest prayer of the man who believes. Faith is the angelic messenger between the soul and the Lord Jesus in glory. If that angel is withdrawn, we can neither send up prayer, nor receive the answers. Faith is the telegraphic wire that links earth and heaven—on which God's messages of love fly so fast that before we call He answers, and while we are yet speaking He hears us. But if that telegraphic wire of faith be snapped, how can we receive the promise? Am I in trouble? I can obtain help for trouble by faith. Am I beaten about by the enemy? My soul on her dear Refuge leans by faith. But take faith away, and in vain I call to God. There is no road between my soul and heaven. In the deepest wintertime, faith is a road on which the horses of prayer may travel—yes, and all the better for the biting frost. But blockade the road, and how can we communicate with the great King? Faith links me with divinity. Faith clothes me with the power of God. Faith engages on my side the omnipotence of Jehovah. Faith ensures every attribute of God in my defense. It helps me to defy the hosts of hell. It makes me march triumphant over the necks of my enemies. But without faith how can I receive anything of the Lord? Do not let him who wavers—who is *"like a wave of the sea"* (James 1:6)—expect that he will receive anything of God (v. 7)! O, then, Christian, watch your faith well. With it you can win all things, however poor you are, but without it you can obtain nothing. If you can believe, *"all things are possible to him that believeth"* (Mark 9:23).

My beloved.
—Song of Solomon 2:8

In her most joyous moments, the ancient church was accustomed to give this golden name, *"beloved,"* to the Anointed of the Lord. When the time of the singing of birds was come and the voice of the turtledove was heard in her land, her love note was sweeter than either, as she sang, *"My beloved is mine, and I am his: he feedeth among the lilies"* (Song 2:16). Ever in her song of songs, she calls Him by that delightful name, *"my beloved"!* Even in the long winter, when idolatry had withered the garden of the Lord, her prophets found space to lay aside the burden of the Lord for a little season, and to say, as Isaiah did, *"Now will I sing to my wellbeloved a song of my beloved touching his vineyard"* (Isa. 5:1). Though the saints had never seen His face, though as yet He was not made flesh, nor had dwelt among us, nor had man beheld His glory, yet He was *"the consolation of Israel"* (Luke 2:25), the hope and joy of all the chosen, the *"beloved"* of all those who were upright before the Most High. We, in the summer days of the church, are also inclined to speak of Christ as the best beloved of our soul and to feel that He is very precious, *"the chiefest among ten thousand"* (Song 5:10), and *"altogether lovely"* (v. 16). So true is it that the church loves Jesus, and claims Him as her beloved, that the apostle dared to defy the whole universe to separate her from the love of Christ. He declared that neither persecution, distress, affliction, peril, nor the sword has been able to do it; he joyously boasted, *"In all these things we are more than conquerors through him that loved us"* (Rom. 8:37). Oh, that we knew more of You, ever precious One!

My sole possession is Your love;
 In earth beneath or heaven above,
I have no other store;
 And though with fervent suit I pray,
And importune You day by day,
 I ask You nothing more.

*Ye shall be scattered, every man to his own,
and shall leave me alone.*
—John 16:32

Few had fellowship with the sorrows of Gethsemane. The majority of the disciples were not sufficiently advanced in grace to be admitted to behold the mysteries of His *"agony"* (Luke 22:44). Occupied with the Passover Feast at their own houses, they represent the many who live on the letter, but are mere babes as to the spirit of the Gospel. To the Twelve, no, to eleven only, was the privilege given to enter Gethsemane and see this great sight. Out of the eleven, eight were left at a distance; they had fellowship, but not of that intimate sort to which men greatly beloved are admitted. Only three highly favored ones could approach the veil of our Lord's mysterious sorrow. Within that veil, even these must not intrude; a stone's throw distance must be left between. He must tread *"the winepress alone"* (Isa. 63:3), and of the people there must be none with Him. Peter and the two sons of Zebedee represent the few eminent, experienced saints who may be written down as "Fathers." Having done business on great waters, they can, in some degree, measure the huge Atlantic waves of their Redeemer's passion. To some selected spirits it is given, for the good of others, and to strengthen them for future, special, and tremendous conflict, to enter the inner circle and hear the pleadings of the suffering High Priest. They have fellowship with Him in His sufferings and are made conformable unto His death (Phil. 3:10). Yet even these cannot penetrate the secret places of the Savior's woe. "Thine unknown sufferings" is the remarkable expression of the Greek liturgy. There was an inner room in our Master's grief, shut out from human knowledge and fellowship. There Jesus was left alone. Here Jesus was more than ever an *"unspeakable gift"* (2 Cor. 9:15). Was not Watts right when he penned, "And all the unknown joys He gives were bought with agonies unknown"?

He went a little farther, and fell on his face, and prayed.
—Matthew 26:39

here are several instructive features in our Savior's prayer in His hour of trial. It was lonely prayer. He withdrew even from His three favored disciples. Believer, be much in solitary prayer, especially in times of trial. Family prayer, social prayer, and prayer in the church will not suffice. These are very precious, but the best spice will smoke in your censer in your private devotions, where no ear hears but God's. It was humble prayer. Luke said Jesus knelt, but Matthew said He *"fell on his face."* Where, then, must be your place, humble servant of the great Master? What dust and ashes should cover your head! Humility gives us good foothold in prayer. There is no hope of prevalence with God unless we abase ourselves so that He may exalt us in due time. It was filial prayer. Jesus cried, *"Abba, Father"* (Mark 14:36). You will find it a stronghold in the day of trial to plead your adoption. You have no rights as a subject, for you have forfeited them by your treason; but nothing can forfeit a child's right to a father's protection. Do not be afraid to say, "My Father, hear my cry." Observe that it was persevering prayer. He prayed three times. Do not stop praying until you prevail. Be like the importunate widow, whose continual coming earned what her first supplication could not win. *"Continue in prayer, and watch in the same with thanksgiving"* (Col. 4:2). Last, it was the prayer of resignation. *"Nevertheless not as I will, but as thou wilt"* (Matt. 26:39). Yield, and God yields. Let it be as God wills, and God will determine for the best. Be content to leave your prayer in His hands, who knows when to give, how to give, what to give, and what to withhold. So pleading earnestly, importunately, yet with humility and resignation, you will surely prevail.

His sweat was as it were great drops of blood
falling down to the ground.
—Luke 22:44

he mental pressure arising from our Lord's struggle with temptation so forced His frame to an unnatural excitement that His pores sent forth great drops of blood that fell down to the ground. This proves how tremendous the weight of sin must have been when it was able to crush the Savior so that He sweat great drops of blood! This demonstrates the mighty power of His love. It is a very apt observation of old Isaac Ambrose that the gum that oozes from the tree without cutting is always the best. This precious camphor tree yielded the sweetest spices when it was wounded under the knotty whips, and when it was pierced by the nails on the cross; but see, it gives forth its best spice when there is no whip, no nail, no wound. This sets forth the voluntary nature of Christ's sufferings, since, without a lance, the blood flowed freely. No need to put on the leech or apply the knife; it flowed spontaneously. No need for the rulers to cry, *"Spring up, O well"* (Num. 21:17); of itself it flows in crimson torrents. If men suffer great pain of mind, apparently the blood rushes to the heart. The cheeks are pale; a fainting fit comes on; the blood has gone inward as if to nourish the inner man while passing through its trial. But see our Savior in His agony. He is so utterly oblivious of self that instead of His agony driving His blood to the heart to nourish Himself, it drives it outward to bedew the earth. The agony of Christ, inasmuch as it pours Him out upon the ground, depicts the fullness of the offering that He made for men. Do we not perceive how intense must have been the wrestling through which He passed, and will we not hear its voice to us? *"Ye have not yet resisted unto blood, striving against sin"* (Heb. 12:4). Behold the great Apostle and High Priest of our profession, and sweat even to blood rather than yield to the great tempter of your soul.

[Jesus] *was heard in that he feared.*
—Hebrews 5:7

id this fear arise from the infernal suggestion that He was utterly forsaken? There may be sterner trials than this, but surely it is one of the worst to be utterly forsaken! "See," said Satan, "You have no friends anywhere! Your Father has shut up His compassionate heart against You. Not an angel in His courts will stretch out a hand to help You. All heaven is alienated from You; You are left alone. See the companions with whom You have taken sweet counsel; what are they worth? Son of Mary, see there Your brother James. See there Your beloved disciple John and Your bold apostle Peter. How the cowards sleep when You are in Your sufferings! You have no friends left in heaven or earth. All hell is against You. I have stirred up my infernal den. I have sent my command throughout all regions, summoning every prince of darkness to set on You this night. We will spare no arrows; we will use all our infernal might to overwhelm You. What will You do, O solitary One?" It may be that this was the temptation. I think it was, because the appearance of an angel unto Him, strengthening Him, removed that fear. He *"was heard in that he feared."* He was alone no more, but heaven was with Him. It may be that this is the reason for His coming three times to His disciples. As Hart put it,

> Backward and forward thrice He ran,
> As if He sought some help from man.

He would see for Himself whether it was really true that all men had forsaken Him. He found them all asleep; but perhaps He gained some faint comfort from the thought that they were sleeping, not from treachery, but from sorrow. Their spirits indeed were willing, but their flesh was weak. (See Matthew 26:41.) At any rate, He *"was heard in that he feared."* Jesus was heard in His deepest woe; my soul, you will be heard also.

Betrayest thou the Son of man with a kiss?
—Luke 22:48

he kisses of an enemy are deceitful. Let me be on my guard when the world puts on a loving face, for it will, if possible, betray me as it did my Master—with a kiss. Whenever a man is about to attack religion, he usually professes very great reverence for it. Let me beware of the sleek-faced hypocrisy that is the armor-bearer to heresy and infidelity. Knowing the deceptiveness of unrighteousness, let me be wise as a serpent to detect and avoid the designs of the enemy. The *"young man void of understanding"* (Prov. 7:7) was led astray by the kiss of the strange woman. May my soul be so graciously instructed all this day that the *"much fair speech"* (v. 21) of the world may have no effect on me. Holy Spirit, let me not, a poor frail son of man, be betrayed with a kiss! But what if I would be guilty of the same accursed sin as Judas, that *"son of perdition"* (John 17:12)? I have been baptized into the name of the Lord Jesus; I am a member of His visible church; I sit at the Communion table—all these are like so many kisses from my lips. Am I sincere in them? If not, I am a base traitor. Do I live in the world as carelessly as others do and yet make a profession of being a follower of Jesus? If so, I expose religion to ridicule and lead men to speak evil of the holy name by which I am called. Surely if I act thus inconsistently, I am a Judas, and it would be better for me if I *"had never been born"* (Mark 14:21). Dare I hope that I am clear in this matter? Then, O Lord, keep me so. O Lord, make me sincere and true. Preserve me from every false way. Never let me betray my Savior. I love You, Jesus, and though I often grieve You, yet I desire to abide faithful even to death. O God, forbid that I would be a high-soaring professor of faith, and then fall at last into the lake of fire because I betrayed my Master with a kiss.

*Jesus answered, I have told you that I am he: if therefore
ye seek me, let these go their way.*
—John 18:8

Mark, my soul, the care that Jesus manifested toward
the sheep of His hand, even in His hour of trial!
The ruling passion is strong in death. He resigns
Himself to the enemy, but He interposes a word of power to
set His disciples free. As for Himself, *"as a sheep before her
shearers is dumb"* (Isa. 53:7), He does not open His mouth;
but for His disciples' sake, He speaks with almighty energy.
Herein is love, constant, self-forgetting, faithful love. But is
there not far more here than is to be found on the surface?
Have we not the very soul and spirit of the Atonement in
these words? The Good Shepherd lays down His *"life for the
sheep"* (John 10:11) and pleads that they must go free. The
Surety is bound, and justice demands that those for whom
He stands a substitute should go their way. In the midst of
Egypt's bondage, that voice rings as a word of power, *"Let
these go their way."* (See also Exodus 9:1.) Out of the slavery
of sin and Satan, the redeemed must come. In every cell of
the dungeons of Despair, the sound is echoed, *"Let these go
their way,"* and forth come Despondency and Much-afraid.
Satan hears the well-known voice and lifts his foot from the
neck of the fallen; Death hears it, and the grave opens her
gates to let the dead arise. Their way is one of progress,
holiness, triumph, and glory, and none will dare to keep
them from it. *"No lion shall be there, nor any ravenous beast
shall go up thereon"* (Isa. 35:9). The Hind of the morning has
drawn the cruel hunters upon Himself, and now the most
timid roes and deer of the field may graze in perfect peace
among the lilies. The thundercloud has burst over the
Cross of Calvary, and the pilgrims of Zion will never be
smitten by the bolts of vengeance. Come, my heart, rejoice
in the immunity that your Redeemer has secured for you.
Bless His name all the day, every day.

Then all the disciples forsook him, and fled.
—Matthew 26:56

He never deserted His disciples, but they, in cowardly fear of their lives, fled from Him in the very beginning of His sufferings. This is but one instructive example of the frailty of all believers, if left to themselves. They are but sheep at best, and they flee when the wolf comes. They had all been warned of the danger and had promised to die rather than to leave their Master, yet they were seized with sudden panic and took to their heels. It may be that I, at the opening of this day, have prepared my mind to bear a trial for the Lord's sake, and I imagine myself to be certain to exhibit perfect fidelity; but let me be very vigilant of myself, lest having the same evil heart of unbelief, I would depart from my Lord as the apostles did. It is one thing to make a promise and quite another to carry it out. It would have been to their eternal honor to have stood at Jesus' side; instead, they fled from honor. May I be kept from imitating them! Where else could they have been so safe as near their Master, who could presently call for twelve legions of angels? They fled from their true safety. O God, let me not play the fool also. Divine grace can make the coward brave. The smoking flax can flame forth like fire on the altar when the Lord wills it. These very apostles who were timid as rabbits grew to be bold as lions after the Spirit had descended on them. Even so, the Holy Spirit can make my fearful spirit brave to confess my Lord and witness for His truth. What anguish must have filled the Savior as He saw His friends so faithless! This was one bitter ingredient in His cup, but that cup is drained dry; do not let me put another drop in it. If I forsake my Lord, I will crucify Him afresh, and subject Him to *"open shame"* (Heb. 6:6). Keep me, O blessed Spirit, from an end so shameful.

The love of Christ, which passeth knowledge.
—Ephesians 3:19

The love of Christ, in its sweetness, its fullness, its greatness, its faithfulness, passes all human comprehension. Where will language be found that will describe His matchless, unparalleled love toward the children of men? It is so vast and boundless that, as the swallow but skims the water and does not dive into its depths, so all descriptive words but touch the surface, while depths immeasurable lie beneath. Well might the poet say, "O love, thou fathomless abyss!" for this love of Christ is indeed measureless and fathomless; none can attain unto it. Before we can have any right idea of the love of Jesus, we must understand His previous glory in its height of majesty and His incarnation on the earth in all its depths of shame. But who can tell us the majesty of Christ? When He was enthroned in the highest heavens, He was very God of very God. By Him were the heavens made, and all the hosts thereof. His own almighty arm upheld the spheres. The praises of cherubim and seraphim perpetually surrounded Him; the full chorus of the hallelujahs of the universe unceasingly flowed to the foot of His throne. He reigned supreme above all His creatures, God over all, blessed forever (Rom. 9:5). Who can tell His height of glory then? And who, on the other hand, can tell how low He descended? To be a Man was something, to be a Man of Sorrows was far more. To bleed, die, and suffer—these were much for Him who was the Son of God; but to suffer such unparalleled agony—to endure a death of shame and desertion by His Father—this is a depth of condescending love that the most inspired mind must utterly fail to fathom. Herein is love! Truly it is love that *"passeth knowledge."* Oh, let this love fill our hearts with adoring gratitude and lead us to practical manifestations of its power.

*Though he were a Son, yet learned he obedience
by the things which he suffered.*
—Hebrews 5:8

We are told that the Captain of our salvation was made perfect through suffering; therefore, we who are sinful, and who are far from being perfect, must not wonder if we are called to pass through suffering, too. Will the Head be crowned with thorns, and will the other members of the body be rocked on the dainty lap of ease? Must Christ pass through seas of His own blood to win the crown, and are we to walk to heaven in silver slippers that stay dry? No, our Master's experience teaches us that suffering is necessary, and the true-born child of God must not, would not, escape it if he could. But there is one very comforting thought in the fact of Christ's *"being made perfect"* (Heb. 5:9) *"by the things which he suffered."* It is that He can have complete sympathy with us. He is not *"an high priest which cannot be touched with the feeling of our infirmities"* (Heb. 4:15). In this sympathy of Christ we find a sustaining power. One of the early martyrs said, "I can bear it all, for Jesus suffered, and He suffers in me now. He sympathizes with me, and this makes me strong." Believer, lay hold of this thought in all times of agony. Let the thought of Jesus strengthen you as you follow in His steps. Find a sweet support in His sympathy. Remember that to suffer is an honorable thing; to suffer for Christ is glory. The apostles rejoiced that they were counted worthy to do this. Just so far as the Lord will give us grace to suffer *for* Christ, to suffer *with* Christ, just so far does He honor us. The jewels of a Christian are his afflictions. The regalia of the kings whom God has anointed are their troubles, their sorrows, and their grief. Let us not, therefore, shun being honored. Let us not turn aside from being exalted. Grief exalt us, and troubles lift us up. *"If we suffer, we shall also reign with him"* (2 Tim. 2:12).

He was numbered with the transgressors.
—Isaiah 53:12

hy did Jesus permit Himself to be included with sinners? This wonderful condescension was justified by many powerful reasons. In such a character He could better become their Advocate. In some trials there is an identification of the counselor with the client. They cannot be looked upon in the eyes of the law as separate from one another. Now, when the sinner is brought to the bar, Jesus appears there Himself. He stands to answer the accusation. He points to His side, His hands, His feet, and He challenges Justice to bring anything against the sinners whom He represents. He pleads His blood, and pleads so triumphantly, being numbered with them and having a part with them, that the Judge proclaims, "Let them go their way. *'Deliver* [them] *from going down to the pit:* [He has] *found a ransom'* (Job 33:24)." Our Lord Jesus was numbered with the transgressors in order that they might feel their hearts drawn toward Him. Who can be afraid of one who is written in the same list with us? Surely we may come boldly to Him and confess our guilt. He who is numbered with us cannot condemn us. Was He not put down in the transgressor's list that we might be written in the red roll of the saints? He was holy, and written among the holy; we were guilty, and numbered among the guilty. He transferred His name from the holy list to this black indictment, and our names were taken from the indictment and written in the roll of acceptance, for there is a complete transfer made between Jesus and His people. All our estate of misery and sin Jesus has taken, and all that Jesus has comes to us. His righteousness, His blood, and everything that He has He gives to us as our dowry. Rejoice, believer, in your union to Him who was numbered among the transgressors. Prove that you are truly saved by being manifestly numbered with those who are *"new creature*[s]*"* (2 Cor. 5:17) in Him.

With his stripes we are healed.
—Isaiah 53:5

ilate delivered our Lord to the Roman officers to be scourged. The Roman scourge was a most dreadful instrument of torture. It was made of the sinews of oxen. Sharp bones were intertwined here and there among the sinews, so that every time the lash came down, pieces of bone inflicted fearful lacerations and tore the flesh from the bone. The Savior was, no doubt, bound to the column, and thus beaten. He had been beaten before, but this beating by the Roman soldiers was probably the severest of His flagellations. My soul, stand here and weep over His poor stricken body. Believer in Jesus, can you gaze on Him without tears, as He stands before you the image of agonizing love? He is at once fair as the lily for innocence and red as the rose with the crimson of His own blood. As we feel the sure and blessed healing that His stripes have worked in us, do not our hearts melt at once with love and grief? If ever we have loved our Lord Jesus, surely we must feel that affection glowing now within our hearts.

> See how the patient Jesus stands,
>   Insulted in His lowest case!
> Sinners have bound the Almighty's hands,
>   And spit in their Creator's face.
> With thorns His temples gor'd and gash'd
>   Send streams of blood from every part;
> His back's with knotted scourges lash'd.
>   But sharper scourges tear His heart.

We would gladly go to our rooms and weep; but since our business calls us away, we will first pray for our Beloved to print the image of His bleeding self on the tablets of our hearts throughout the day. At nightfall, we will return to commune with Him, and grieve that our sin should have cost Him so much.

Let him kiss me with the kisses of his mouth.
—Song of Solomon 1:2

For several days we have been dwelling on the Savior's passion, and for some little time to come we will linger there. In beginning a new month, let us seek the same desires after our Lord as those that glowed in the heart of the elect spouse. See how she leaps at once to Him; there are no prefatory words; she does not even mention His name; she is in the heart of her theme at once, for she speaks of Him who was the only *"him"* in the world to her. How bold is her love! It was great condescension that permitted the weeping penitent to anoint His feet with spikenard. It was rich love that allowed the gentle Mary to sit at His feet and learn of Him. But here, love, strong, fervent love, aspires to higher tokens of regard and closer signs of fellowship. Esther trembled in the presence of Ahasuerus, but the spouse in joyful liberty of perfect love knows no fear. If we have received the same free spirit, we also may ask the same. By *"kisses"* we suppose to be intended those varied manifestations of affection by which the believer is made to enjoy the love of Jesus. The kiss of reconciliation we enjoyed at our conversion, and it was sweet as honey dripping from the comb. The kiss of acceptance is still warm on our brow, as we know that He has accepted our persons and our works through rich grace. The kiss of daily, present communion is what we pant after to be repeated day after day, until it is changed into the kiss of reception, which removes the soul from earth, and the kiss of consummation, which fills it with the joy of heaven. Faith is our walk, but fellowship intensely felt is our rest. Faith is the road, but communion with Jesus is the well from which the pilgrim drinks. O Lover of our souls, do not be a stranger to us; let the lips of Your blessing meet the lips of our asking. Let the lips of Your fullness touch the lips of our need, and immediately, we will feel the healing effect of Your kiss.

He answered him to never a word.
—Matthew 27:14

e was never slow of speech when He could bless the sons of men, but He would not say a single word for Himself. *"Never man spake like this man"* (John 7:46), and never was any man silent like Him. Was this singular silence the indication of His perfect self-sacrifice? Did it show that He would not utter a word to stop the slaughter of His sacred person, which He had dedicated as an offering for us? Had He so entirely surrendered Himself that He would not interfere in His own behalf, even in the minutest degree, but be bound and slain a submissive, uncomplaining victim? Was this silence a type of the defenselessness of sin? Nothing can be said to lessen or excuse human guilt; therefore, He who bore its whole weight stood speechless before His judge. Is not patient silence the best reply to a contentious world? Calm endurance answers some questions infinitely more conclusively than the loftiest eloquence. The best apologists for Christianity in the early days were its martyrs. The anvil breaks a host of hammers by quietly bearing their blows. Did not the silent Lamb of God furnish us with a grand example of wisdom? Where every word was occasion for new blasphemy, it was the line of duty to afford no fuel for the flame of sin. The ambiguous and the false, the unworthy and the contemptible, will before long overthrow and destroy themselves; therefore, the true can afford to be quiet and find silence to be their wisdom. Evidently our Lord, by His silence, furnished a remarkable fulfillment of prophecy. A long defense of Himself would have been contrary to Isaiah's prediction. *"He is brought as a lamb to the slaughter, and as a sheep before her shearers is dumb, so he openeth not his mouth"* (Isa. 53:7). By His quiet, He conclusively proved Himself to be the true Lamb of God. As such we salute Him this morning. Be with us, Jesus, and in the silence of our hearts, let us hear the voice of Your love.

They took Jesus, and led him away.
—John 19:16

He had been in agony all night. After spending the early morning at the hall of Caiaphas, He had been hurried from Caiaphas to Pilate, from Pilate to Herod, and from Herod back again to Pilate. He had, therefore, but little strength left, and yet neither refreshment nor rest were permitted Him. They were eager for His blood, so they led Him out to die, bearing the weight of the cross. O heartbreaking procession! Well may the daughters of peace weep. My soul, weep also. What do we learn here as we see our blessed Lord led forth? Do we not perceive that truth that was foreshadowed by the scapegoat? Did not the high priest bring the scapegoat and put both his hands on its head, confessing the sins of the people, so that those sins might be laid on the goat and be removed from the people? Then the man selected to lead the goat took it into the wilderness, and it carried away the sins of the people, so that if they were sought for, they could not be found. Now we see Jesus brought before the priests and rulers, who pronounce Him guilty. God Himself places the blame for our sins on Him: *"The LORD hath laid on him the iniquity of us all"* (Isa. 53:6); *"He hath made him to be sin for us"* (2 Cor. 5:21). As the substitute for our guilt, bearing our sin—represented by the cross—on His shoulders, the great Scapegoat was led away by the appointed officers of justice. Beloved, can you feel assured that He carried *your* sin? As you look at the cross on His shoulders, does it represent *your* sin? There is one way by which you can tell whether He carried your sin or not. Have you laid your hand on His head, confessed your sin, and trusted in Him? Then your sin no longer lies on you; it has all been transferred by blessed imputation to Christ, and He bears it on His shoulder as a load heavier than the cross. Do not let the picture vanish until you have rejoiced in your own deliverance and adored the loving Redeemer on whom your iniquities were laid.

For he hath made him to be sin for us, who knew no sin; that we might be made the righteousness of God in him.
—2 Corinthians 5:21

ourning Christian, why do you weep? Are you mourning over your own corruption? Look to your perfect Lord, and remember, you are complete in Him. In God's sight, you are as perfect as if you had never sinned; no, more than that, the Lord our Righteousness has put a divine garment on you, so that you have more than the righteousness of man—you have the righteousness of God! Oh, you who are mourning by reason of inbred sin and depravity, remember, none of your sins can condemn you. You have learned to hate sin, but you have also learned to know that your sin is not yours: it was laid on Christ's head. Your standing is not in yourself: it is in Christ. Your acceptance is not in yourself, but in your Lord. You are as much accepted by God today, with all your sinfulness, as you will be when you stand before His throne, free from all corruption.

Oh, I beseech you, lay hold of this precious thought of perfection in Christ! For you are *"complete in him"* (Col. 2:10). With your Savior's garment on, you are holy as the Holy One is holy. *"Who is he that condemneth? It is Christ that died, yea rather, that is risen again, who is even at the right hand of God, who also maketh intercession for us"* (Rom. 8:34). Christian, let your heart rejoice, for you are *"accepted in the beloved"* (Eph. 1:6). What do you have to fear? Let your face always wear a smile. Live close to your Master. Live in the suburbs of the Celestial City. Soon, when your time comes, you will rise up where your Jesus sits and reign at His right hand. All this will occur because the divine Lord was made *"to be sin for us, who knew no sin; that we might be made the righteousness of God in him."*

On him they laid the cross, that he might bear it after Jesus.
—Luke 23:26

We see in Simon's carrying the cross a picture of the work of the church throughout all generations; she is the cross-bearer for Jesus. Mark, then, Christian: Jesus does not suffer so as to exclude your suffering. He bears a cross, not that you may escape it, but that you may endure it. Christ exempts you from sin, but not from sorrow. Remember that, and expect to suffer. But let us comfort ourselves with this thought: that in our case, as in Simon's, it is not *our* cross, but *Christ's* cross that we carry. When you are molested for your piety or when your religion brings the trial of cruel ridicule on you, then remember that it is not *your* cross, but it is *Christ's* cross. How delightful it is to carry the cross of our Lord Jesus! You carry the cross after Him. You have blessed company; your path is marked with the footprints of your Lord. The mark of His bloodred shoulder is on that heavy burden. It is *His* cross, and He goes before you as a shepherd goes before his sheep. Take up your cross daily, and follow Him. Do not forget, also, that you bear this cross in partnership. It is the opinion of some that Simon carried only one end of the cross, and not the whole of it. That is very possible; Christ may have carried the heavier part, against the transverse beam, and Simon may have borne the lighter end. Certainly it is so with you. You carry only the light end of the cross; Christ bore the heavier end. And remember that although Simon had to bear the cross for a very little while, it gave him lasting honor. Even so the cross we carry is only for a little while at most, and then, we will receive the crown, the glory. Surely we should love the cross, and, instead of shrinking from it, count it very costly, when it works out for us *"a far more exceeding and eternal weight of glory"* (2 Cor. 4:17).

Let us go forth therefore unto him without the camp.
—Hebrews 13:13

Jesus, bearing His cross, went forth to suffer without the gate. The Christian's reason for leaving the camp of the world's sin and religion is not that he loves to be an individual, but because Jesus did so, and the disciple must follow his Master. Christ was *"not of the world"* (John 17:14). His life and His testimony were a constant protest against conformity with the world. Never did such overflowing affection for men exist as you find in Him, but still He was separate from sinners. Likewise, Christ's people must *"go forth...unto him."* They must take their position *"without the camp,"* as witness-bearers for the truth. They must be prepared to tread the straight and narrow path. They must have bold, unflinching, lionlike hearts, loving Christ first, and His truth next, and Christ and His truth above all the world. Jesus would have His people *"go forth...without the camp"* for their own sanctification. You cannot grow in grace to any great degree while you are conformed to the world. The life of separation may be a path of sorrow, but it is the highway of safety. And though the separated life may cost you many pangs and make every day a battle, yet it is a happy life after all. No joy can excel that of the soldier of Christ. Jesus reveals Himself so graciously and gives such sweet refreshment that the warrior feels more calm and peace in his daily strife than others feel in their hours of rest. The highway of holiness is the highway of communion. It is thus that we will hope to win the crown if we are enabled by divine grace faithfully to follow Christ *"without the camp."* The crown of glory will follow the cross of separation. A moment's shame will be well recompensed by eternal honor; a little while of witness-bearing will seem nothing when we are forever *"with the Lord"* (1 Thess. 4:17).

O ye sons of men, how long will ye turn my glory into shame?
—Psalm 4:2

n instructive writer has made a sad list of the honors that the blinded people of Israel awarded to their long-expected King. First, they gave Him a procession of honor, in which Roman legionaries, Jewish priests, men, and women took part, He Himself bearing His cross. This is the triumph that the world awards to Him who comes to overthrow man's direst foes. Derisive shouts are His only acclamations and cruel taunts His only tributes of praise. Next, they presented Him with the wine of honor. Instead of a golden cup of generous wine, they offered Him the criminal's stupefying death-draught, which He refused because He would preserve an uninjured taste wherewith to taste of death. Afterward, when He cried, *"I thirst"* (John 19:28), they gave Him vinegar mixed with gall, thrust to His mouth on a sponge. Oh, wretched, detestable inhospitality to the King's Son. Third, He was provided with a guard of honor, who showed their esteem of Him by gambling over His garments, which they had seized as their booty. Such was the bodyguard of the adored of heaven—a quartet of brutal gamblers. Then a throne of honor was found for Him on the bloody tree; no easier place of rest would rebellious men yield to their faithful Lord. The cross was, in fact, the full expression of the world's feeling toward Him. "There," they seemed to say, "Son of God, this is the manner in which God Himself should be treated, could we reach Him." Finally, the title of honor was nominally "King of the Jews," but that the blinded nation distinctly repudiated, and really called Him "King of thieves," by preferring Barabbas, and by placing Jesus in the place of highest shame between two thieves. His glory was thus in all things turned into shame by the sons of men, but it will yet gladden the eyes of saints and angels, world without end.

If they do these things in a green tree, what shall be done in the dry?
—Luke 23:31

mong other interpretations of this suggestive question, the following is full of teaching: "If Christ, the innocent Substitute for sinners, suffered as He did, what will be done when the sinner himself—the dry tree— falls into the hands of an angry God?" When God saw Jesus in the sinner's place, He did not spare Him; and when He finds the unregenerate without Christ, He will not spare them. O sinner, Jesus was led away by His enemies; so will you be dragged away by fiends to the place appointed for you. Jesus was deserted by God; and if He, who was only a sinner because He carried our sins, was deserted, how much more will you be? *"Eloi, Eloi, lama sabachthani"* (Mark 15:34)—what an awful shriek! But what will your cry be when you will say, "O God! O God! why have You forsaken me?" and the answer will come back, *"Ye have set at nought all my counsel, and would none of my reproof: I also will laugh at your calamity; I will mock when your fear cometh"* (Prov. 1:25– 26). If God *"spared not his own Son"* (Rom. 8:32), how much less will He spare you! What whips of burning wire will be yours when your conscience smites you with all its terrors? You richest, merriest, most self-righteous sinners—who would want to stand in your place when God will say, "Awake, O sword, against the man who rejected Me; smite him, and let him feel the pain forever"? Jesus was spit on; sinner, what shame will be yours! We cannot sum up in one word all the mass of sorrows that met on the head of Jesus who died for us; therefore, it is impossible for us to tell you what streams, what oceans of grief, must roll over your spirit if you die as you are now. You may die so; you may die now. By the agonies of Christ, by His wounds and by His blood, do not bring on yourselves the wrath to come! Trust in the Son of God, and you will never die.

There followed him a great company of people, and of women,
which also bewailed and lamented him.
—Luke 23:27

Amid the mob that hounded the Redeemer to His doom, there were some gracious souls whose bitter anguish sought expression in wailing and crying. What fit music to accompany that march of woe! When my soul can, in imagination, see the Savior bearing His cross to Calvary, it joins the godly women and weeps with them; for, indeed, there is true cause for grief, a cause that lies deeper than those mourning women thought. They bewailed innocence maltreated, goodness persecuted, love bleeding, meekness about to die; but my heart has a deeper and more bitter cause to mourn. My sins were the scourges that lacerated those blessed shoulders and crowned with thorns those bleeding brows. My sins cried, "Crucify Him! Crucify Him!" and laid the cross on His gracious shoulders. His being led forth to die is sorrow enough for one eternity, but my having been His murderer is more, infinitely more, grief than one poor fountain of tears can express. Why those women loved and wept is not hard to guess, but they could not have had greater reasons for love and grief than my heart has. Nain's widow saw her son restored, but I myself have been raised to newness of life. Peter's wife's mother was cured of the fever, but I have been cured of the greater plague of sin. Out of Mary Magdalene seven devils were cast, but a whole legion have been cast out of me. Mary and Martha were favored with visits, but He dwells with me. His mother bare His body, but He has formed in me the hope of glory. In nothing behind the holy women in debt, let me not be behind them in gratitude or sorrow.

Love and grief my heart dividing,
    With my tears His feet I'll lave—
Constant still in heart abiding,
    Weep for Him who died to save.

The place, which is called Calvary.
—Luke 23:33

he hill of comfort is the hill of Calvary; the house of consolation is built with the wood of the cross; the temple of heavenly blessing is founded on the shattered rock—split open by the spear that pierced His side. No scene in sacred history ever gladdens the soul as Calvary's tragedy does.

> Is it not strange, the darkest hour
>   That ever dawned on sinful earth
> Should touch the heart with softer power
>   For comfort than an angel's mirth?
> That to the cross the mourner's eye should turn
>   Sooner than where the stars of Bethlehem burn?

Light springs from the midday-midnight of Golgotha, and every herb of the field blooms sweetly beneath the shadow of the once accursed tree. In that place of thirst, grace has dug a fountain that ever gushes with waters pure as crystal, each drop capable of alleviating the woes of mankind. You who have had your seasons of conflict will confess that it was not at Olivet that you ever found comfort, not on the hill of Sinai, nor on Tabor; but Gethsemane, Gabbatha, and Golgotha have been a means of comfort to you. The bitter herbs of Gethsemane have often taken away the bitterness of your life, the scourge of Gabbatha has often scourged away your cares, and the groans of Calvary yield us comfort rare and rich. We never would have known Christ's love in all its heights and depths if He had not died; nor could we guess the Father's deep affection if He had not given His Son to die. The common mercies we enjoy all sing of love, just as the seashell, when we put it to our ears, whispers of the deep sea from whence it came; but if we desire to hear the ocean itself, we must not look at everyday blessings, but at the transactions of the Crucifixion. He who desires to know love, let him retire to Calvary and see the Man of Sorrows die.

I am poured out like water, and all my bones are out of joint.
—Psalm 22:14

id earth or heaven ever behold a sadder spectacle of woe? In soul and body, our Lord felt Himself to be weak as water poured on the ground. The placing of the cross in its socket had shaken Him with great violence, had strained all the ligaments, pained every nerve, and more or less dislocated all His bones. Burdened with His own weight, the majestic Sufferer felt the strain increasing every moment of those six long hours. His sense of faintness and general weakness were overpowering, while to His own consciousness He became nothing but a mass of misery and swooning sickness. When Daniel saw the great vision, he thus described his sensations, *"There remained no strength in me: for my comeliness was turned in me into corruption, and I retained no strength"* (Dan. 10:8). How much more faint must have been our greater Prophet when He saw the dread vision of the wrath of God and felt it in His own soul! To us, sensations such as our Lord endured would have been unbearable, and kind unconsciousness would have come to our rescue; but in His case, He was wounded and felt the sword; He drained the cup and tasted every drop.

> O King of Grief! (a title strange, yet true
> To Thee of all kings only due,)
> O King of Wounds! how shall I grieve for Thee,
> Who in all grief preventest me!

As we kneel before our now ascended Savior's throne, let us remember well the way by which He prepared it as a throne of grace for us. Let us in spirit drink of His cup, so that we may be strengthened for our hour of heaviness whenever it may come. In His natural body every member suffered, and so must it be in the spiritual. But as out of all His grief and woes His body came forth uninjured to glory and power, even so will His spiritual body come through the furnace with not so much as the smell of fire on it.

My heart is like wax; it is melted in the midst of my bowels.
—Psalm 22:14

ur blessed Lord experienced a terrible sinking and melting of soul. *"The spirit of a man will sustain his infirmity; but a wounded spirit who can bear?"* (Prov. 18:14). Deep depression of spirit is the most grievous of all trials; all else is as nothing. Well might the suffering Savior cry to His God, *"Be not far from me"* (Ps. 71:12), for above all other seasons a man needs his God when his heart is melted within him because of heaviness. Believer, come near the cross this morning and humbly adore the King of Glory as having once been brought far lower, in mental distress and inward anguish, than anyone among us; and mark His fitness to become a faithful High Priest, who can *"be touched with the feeling of our infirmities"* (Heb. 4:15). Especially let those of us whose sadness springs directly from the withdrawal of a present sense of our Father's love enter into near and intimate communion with Jesus. Let us not give way to despair, since through this dark room the Master has passed before us. Our souls may sometimes long and faint, and thirst even to anguish, to behold the light of the Lord's countenance. At such times let us sustain ourselves with the sweet fact of the sympathy of our great High Priest. Our drops of sorrow may well be forgotten in the ocean of His grief, but how high should our love rise! Come in, O strong and deep love of Jesus, like the sea at the flood in spring tides. Cover all my powers, drown all my sins, wash out all my cares, lift up my earthbound soul, and float it right up to my Lord's feet. There let me lie, a poor broken shell, washed up by His love, having no virtue or value, only venturing to whisper to Him that if He will put His ear to me, He will hear within my heart faint echoes of the vast waves of His own love that have brought me where it is my delight to lie, even at His feet forever.

A bundle of myrrh is my wellbeloved unto me.
—Song of Solomon 1:13

Myrrh may well be chosen to serve as a type of Jesus because of its preciousness, its perfume, and its pleasantness; its healing, preserving, and disinfecting qualities; and its connection with sacrifice. But why is He compared to *"a bundle of myrrh"?* First, for plenty. He is not a drop of it, but a barrelful. He is not a sprig or flower of it, but a whole bundle. There is enough in Christ for all my needs; let me not be slow to avail myself of Him. Our *"wellbeloved"* is compared to a bundle also for variety: for there is in Christ not only the one thing that is necessary, but *"in him dwelleth all the fulness of the Godhead bodily"* (Col. 2:9). Everything necessary is in Him. Take Jesus in His different characters, and you will see a marvelous variety: Prophet, Priest, King, Husband, Friend, Shepherd. Consider Him in His life, death, resurrection, ascension, and second advent; view Him in His virtue, gentleness, courage, self-denial, love, faithfulness, truth, righteousness. Everywhere He is a bundle of preciousness. He is *"a bundle of myrrh"* for preservation—not loose myrrh tied up, but myrrh to be stored in a container. We must value Him as our best treasure. We must prize His words and His laws. We must keep our thoughts of Him and knowledge of Him as under lock and key, lest the devil would steal anything from us. Moreover, Jesus is *"a bundle of myrrh"* for His unique qualities. The symbol suggests the idea of distinguishing, discriminating grace. From before the foundation of the world, He was set apart for His people; and He gives forth His perfume only to those who understand how to enter into communion with Him, to have close dealings with Him. Oh, blessed people whom the Lord has admitted into His secrets, and for whom He sets Himself apart. Oh, choice and happy are those who are thus made to say, *"A bundle of myrrh is my wellbeloved unto me."*

All they that see me laugh me to scorn: they shoot out the lip,
they shake the head.
—Psalm 22:7

Mockery was a great ingredient in our Lord's woe. Judas mocked Him in the garden; the chief priests and scribes laughed Him to scorn; Herod considered Him to be insignificant; the servants and the soldiers jeered at Him and brutally insulted Him; Pilate and his guards ridiculed His royalty; and on the tree all sorts of horrid jests and hideous taunts were hurled at Him. Ridicule is always hard to bear, but when we are in intense pain, it is so heartless, so cruel, that it cuts us to the quick. Imagine the Savior crucified, racked with anguish far beyond all human comprehension, and then, picture that motley multitude, all wagging their heads or thrusting out their lips in bitter contempt of one poor suffering victim! Surely there must have been something more in the Crucified One than they could see; otherwise, such a great and mixed crowd would not unanimously have honored Him with such contempt. Was it not evil confessing, in the very moment of its greatest apparent triumph, that after all it could do no more than mock at that victorious goodness that was then reigning on the cross? O Jesus, *"despised and rejected of men"* (Isa. 53:3), how could You die for men who treated you so horribly? Herein is amazing love, divine love, yes, love beyond measure. We, too, have despised You in the days of our unregeneracy, and even since our new birth, we have set the world high in our hearts. Yet You bled to heal our wounds and died to give us life. Oh, that we could set You on a glorious high throne in all men's hearts! We would ring out Your praises over land and sea until men would as universally adore You as once they unanimously rejected You.

> Thy creatures wrong You, O sovereign Good!
>   Thou are not loved, because not understood:
> This grieves me most, that vain pursuits beguile
>   Ungrateful men, regardless of Thy smile.

My God, my God, why hast thou forsaken me?
—Psalm 22:1

We here behold the Savior in the depth of His sorrows. No other place so well shows the grief of Christ as Calvary, and no other moment at Calvary is so full of agony as that in which His cry rends the air—*"My God, my God, why hast thou forsaken me?"* At this moment physical weakness was united with acute mental torture from the shame and ignominy through which He had to pass. He suffered spiritual agony surpassing all expression, resulting from the departure of His Father's presence, unbearably heightening His grief. This was the black midnight of His horror. It was then that He descended into the abyss of suffering. No man can enter into the full meaning of these words. Some of us think at times that we could cry, "My God, my God, why have You forsaken me?" There are seasons when the brightness of our Father's smile is eclipsed by clouds and darkness, but let us remember that God never really forsakes us. It is only an illusory forsaking with us, but in Christ's case, it was a real forsaking. We grieve at a little withdrawal of our Father's love; but the real turning away of God's face from His Son, who will calculate how deep the agony that it caused Him? In our case, our cry is often dictated by unbelief. In His case, it was the utterance of a dreadful fact, for God had really turned away from Him for a season. O poor, distressed soul, who once lived in the sunshine of God's face, but are now in darkness, remember that He has not really forsaken you. God in the clouds is as much our God as when He shines forth in all the luster of His grace. But since even the thought that He has forsaken us gives us agony, what must the woe of the Savior have been when He exclaimed, *"My God, my God, why hast thou forsaken me?"*

The precious blood of Christ.
—1 Peter 1:19

tanding at the foot of the cross, we see, falling from His hands, feet, and side, crimson streams of precious blood. It is precious because of its redeeming and atoning efficacy. By it, the sins of Christ's people are atoned for. They are redeemed from under the law. They are reconciled to God and made one with Him. Christ's blood is also precious in its cleansing power; it *"cleanseth us from all sin"* (1 John 1:7). *"Though your sins be as scarlet, they shall be as white as snow"* (Isa. 1:18). Through Jesus' blood there is not a spot left on any believer; no wrinkle or any such thing remains. His precious blood, which makes us clean, removes the stains of abundant iniquity and permits us to stand *"accepted in the beloved"* (Eph. 1:6), notwithstanding the many ways in which we have rebelled against our God. The blood of Christ is likewise precious in its preserving power. Under the sprinkled blood, we are safe from the destroying angel. Remember it is God's seeing the blood that is the true reason for our being spared. Here is comfort for us when the eye of faith is dim, for God's eye is still the same. The blood of Christ is precious also in its sanctifying influence. The same blood that justifies by taking away sin, in its after-action, quickens the new nature and leads it onward to subdue sin and to carry out the commands of God. There is no motive for holiness so great as that which streams from the veins of Jesus. And precious, unspeakably precious, is this blood, because it has an overcoming power. It is written, *"They overcame...by the blood of the Lamb"* (Rev. 12:11). How could they do otherwise? He who fights with the precious blood of Jesus fights with a weapon that cannot know defeat. The blood of Jesus! Sin dies at its presence, death ceases to be death, and heaven's gates are opened. The blood of Jesus! We will march on, conquering and to conquer, as long as we trust its power!

---

*Ye are come…to the blood of sprinkling, that speaketh
better things than that of Abel.*
—Hebrews 12:22, 24

R eader, have you come *"to the blood of sprinkling"?* The
question is not whether you have come to a knowledge of doctrine, an observance of ceremonies, or to a
certain form of experience, but have you come to the blood
of Jesus? The blood of Jesus is the life of all vital godliness.
If you have truly come to Jesus, we know how you came—
the Holy Spirit sweetly brought you there. You came to the
blood of sprinkling with no merits of your own. Guilty,
lost, and helpless, you came to take that blood, and that
blood alone, as your everlasting hope. You came to the
cross of Christ with a trembling and an aching heart, and
oh, what a precious sound it was to you to hear the voice of
the blood of Jesus! The dripping of His blood is as the music of heaven to the penitent sons of earth. We are full of
sin, but the Savior bids us lift our eyes to Him. As we gaze
on His streaming wounds, each drop of blood, as it falls,
cries, "It is finished! I have made an end of sin, and I have
brought in everlasting righteousness." Oh, sweet language
of the precious blood of Jesus! If you have come to that
blood once, you will come to it constantly. Your life will be
one of *"looking unto Jesus"* (Heb. 12:2). Your whole conduct
will be epitomized in this phrase: *"To whom coming"* (1 Pet.
2:4). Not to whom I *have* come, but to whom I am *always
coming.* If you have ever come to the blood of sprinkling,
you will feel your need of coming to it every day. He who
does not desire to wash in it every day has never washed in
it at all. The believer always feels it to be his joy and privilege that there is still a fountain opened. Past experiences
are doubtful food for Christians; a present coming to Christ
alone can give us joy and comfort. This morning let us
sprinkle our doorposts fresh with blood, and then, feast on
the Lamb, assured that the destroying angel must pass us
by.

She bound the scarlet line in the window.
—Joshua 2:21

ahab depended for her preservation on the promise of the spies, whom she considered to be the representatives of the God of Israel. Her faith was simple and firm, but it was very obedient. To tie the scarlet line in the window was a very trivial act in itself, but she dared not run the risk of omitting it. Come, my soul, is there not a lesson here for you? Have you been attentive to all of your Lord's will, even though some of His commands might seem nonessential? Have you observed in His own way the two ordinances of the believers' baptism and the Lord's Supper? Neglecting these sacraments points to much unloving disobedience in your heart. From now on, in all things, be blameless, even to the tying of a thread, if that is what you are commanded to do. This act of Rahab sets forth a yet more solemn lesson. Have I implicitly trusted in the precious blood of Jesus? Have I tied the scarlet cord, as with a Gordian knot in my window, so that my trust can never be removed? Or can I look out toward the Dead Sea of my sins, or the Jerusalem of my hopes, without seeing the blood, and seeing all things in connection with its blessed power? If it hangs from the window, the passerby can see a cord of so conspicuous a color; likewise, it will be well for me if my life makes the power of the Atonement conspicuous to all onlookers. What is there to be ashamed of? Let men or devils gaze if they will; the blood is my boast and my song. My soul, there is One who will see that scarlet line, even when from weakness of faith you cannot see it yourself; Jehovah, the Avenger, will see it and pass over you. Jericho's walls fell flat. Rahab's house was on the wall, and yet it stood unmoved. My nature is built into the wall of humanity, yet when destruction destroys the race, I will be secure. My soul, tie the scarlet thread in the window afresh, and rest in peace.

Behold, the veil of the temple was rent in twain
from the top to the bottom.
—Matthew 27:51

No lowly miracle was performed in the rending of so strong and thick a veil. It was not intended merely as a display of power; many lessons were taught to us in this act. The old law of ordinances was put away, and like worn-out clothes, it was torn and laid aside. When Jesus died, the sacrifices were all finished, because all were fulfilled in Him; therefore, the place of their presentation was marked with an obvious token of decay. The torn veil also revealed all the hidden things of the old dispensation: the mercy seat could now be seen, and the glory of God gleamed forth above it. By the death of our Lord Jesus, we have a clear revelation of God, for He was *"not as Moses, which put a veil over his face"* (2 Cor. 3:13). Life and immortality are now brought to light, and things that have been hidden since the foundation of the world are manifest in Him. The annual ceremony of atonement was thus abolished. The atoning blood, which was once every year sprinkled within the veil, was now offered once for all by the great High Priest, and, therefore, the place of the symbolic rite was broken up. No blood of bullocks or of lambs is needed now, for Jesus has entered within the veil with His own blood. Hence access to God is now permitted and is the privilege of every believer in Christ Jesus. There is no small space laid open through which we may peer at the mercy seat, but the tear reaches from the top to the bottom. We may come with boldness to the throne of heavenly grace (Heb. 4:16). Would we be wrong to say that the opening of the Holy of Holies in this marvelous manner by our Lord's dying cry was a foreshadowing of the opening of the gates of paradise to all the saints by virtue of the Passion? Our bleeding Lord has the key of heaven; He opens it and no man shuts it. Let us enter in with Him into the heavenly places and sit with Him there until our common enemies will be made His footstool.

That through death he might destroy him
that had the power of death.
—Hebrews 2:14

O child of God, death has lost its sting, because the devil's power over it is destroyed. Then cease to fear dying. Ask grace from God the Holy Spirit that by an intimate knowledge and a firm belief of your Redeemer's death, you may be strengthened for that dread hour. Living near the Cross of Calvary allows you to think of death with pleasure and welcome it, when it comes, with intense delight. It is sweet to die in the Lord; it is a covenant blessing to sleep in Jesus. Death is no longer banishment; it is a return from exile, a going home to the many mansions where the loved ones already dwell. The distance between glorified spirits in heaven and militant saints on earth seems great; but it is not so. We are not far from home—a moment will bring us there. The sail is spread; the soul is launched on the deep. How long will its voyage be? How many wearying winds must beat upon the sail before it will be reefed in the port of peace? How long will that soul be tossed on the waves before it comes to that sea that knows no storm? Listen to the answer, *"Absent from the body, and...present with the Lord"* (2 Cor. 5:8). The ship has just departed, but it is already at its haven. It spread its sail, and it was there. Like that ship of old, on the Lake of Galilee, a storm had tossed it, but when Jesus walked on the sea to them and said, *"It is I; be not afraid"* (John 6:20), immediately the ship came to land. Do not think that a long period intervenes between the instant of death and the eternity of glory. When the eyes close on earth, they open in heaven. The horses of fire are not on the road even for an instant. Then, O child of God, what is there for you to fear in death, seeing that, through the death of your Lord, its curse and sting are destroyed? Now it is but a Jacob's ladder whose foot is in the dark grave, but whose top reaches to everlasting glory.

I know that my redeemer liveth.
—Job 19:25

he essence of Job's comfort lies in that little word *"my"*—*"my redeemer"*—and in the fact that the Redeemer lives. Oh, to take hold of the living Christ! We must belong to Him before we can enjoy Him. What good is gold in the mine to me? It is gold in my purse that will satisfy my needs; then I can purchase the bread that I need. Of what use would be a Redeemer who does not redeem me or an Avenger who will not stand up for me? Do not rest content until by faith you can say, "Yes, I cast myself on my living Lord, and He is mine." It may be that you hold Him with a weak grip. You half think it presumption to say, "He lives as *my* Redeemer," yet remember: if you have a faith that is only the size of a grain of mustard seed, that little faith entitles you to say it. But there is also another word here, indicative of Job's strong confidence: "I *know*." To say "I hope so," or "I trust so" is easy, and there are thousands in the fold of Jesus who hardly ever get much further. But to reach the essence of consolation, you must say, "I know." *If*s, *but*s, and *perhaps*es are sure murderers of peace and comfort. Doubts are dreary things in times of sorrow. Like wasps, they sting the soul! If I have any suspicion that Christ is not mine, then there is vinegar mingled with the gall of death; but if I know that Jesus lives for me, then darkness is not dark. Even the night is light about me. Surely if Job, in those ages before the Incarnation and Advent of Christ, could say, *"I know,"* we should not speak less positively. God forbid that our confidence should be presumption. Let us see that our evidences are right, lest we build on an ungrounded hope. Then let us not be satisfied with the mere foundation, for it is from the upper rooms that we get the widest view. A living Redeemer, truly mine, is joy unspeakable.

Him hath God exalted.
—Acts 5:31

Jesus, our Lord, once crucified, dead, and buried, now sits on the throne of glory. The highest place that heaven affords is His by undisputed right. It is sweet to remember that the exaltation of Christ in heaven is a representative exaltation. He is exalted at the Father's right hand, and though as Jehovah He had eminent glories in which finite creatures cannot share, yet as the Mediator, the honors that Jesus wears in heaven are the heritage of all the saints. It is delightful to reflect how close Christ's union is with His people. We are actually one with Him. We are members of His body, and His exaltation is our exaltation. He has a crown, and He gives us crowns, too. He will give us places of honor, even as He has overcome, and is set down with His Father on His throne. He is not content with having a throne to Himself. On His right hand, there must be His queen, arrayed *"in gold of Ophir"* (Ps. 45:9). He cannot be glorified without His bride. Look up, believer, to Jesus now. Let the eye of your faith behold Him with many crowns on His head. Remember that you will one day be like Him, when you will see Him as He is. You will not be as great as He is; you will not be as divine, but still you will, in a measure, share the same honors and enjoy the same happiness and the same dignity that He possesses. Be content to live unknown for a little while and to walk your weary way through the fields of poverty or up the hills of affliction. Soon you will reign with Christ, for He has *"made us kings and priests unto God"* (Rev. 1:6), and we will reign with Him forever and ever. Oh, wonderful thought for the children of God! We have Christ for our glorious representative in heaven's courts now, and soon He will come and receive us to Himself to be with Him there, to behold His glory, and to share His joy.

*Nay, in all these things we are more than conquerors
through him that loved us.*
—Romans 8:37

We go to Christ for forgiveness, and then too often look to the law for power to fight our sins. Paul thus rebuked us, *"O foolish Galatians, who hath bewitched you, that ye should not obey the truth?...This only would I learn of you, Received ye the Spirit by the works of the law, or by the hearing of faith? Are ye so foolish? having begun in the Spirit, are ye now made perfect by the flesh?"* (Galatians 3:1–3). Take your sins to Christ's cross, for the *"old man"* (Rom. 6:6) can only be crucified there; we are crucified with Him. The only weapon with which to fight sin is the spear that pierced the side of Jesus. If you want to overcome an angry temper, how do you go about it? It is very possible you have never tried the right way of going to Jesus with it. How did I receive salvation? I came to Jesus just as I was, and I trusted Him to save me. I must kill my angry temper in the same way. It is the only way in which I can ever kill it. I must go to the Cross with it, and say to Jesus, "Lord, I trust You to deliver me from it." This is the only way to give it a death-blow. Are you covetous? Do you feel the world entangle you? You may struggle against this evil as long as you please, but if it is your recurrent sin, you will never be delivered from it in any way but by the blood of Jesus. Take it to Christ. Tell Him, "Lord, I have trusted You, and Your name is Jesus, for You save Your people from their sins. Lord, this is one of my sins; save me from it!" Laws are nothing without Christ as the means of putting these sins to death. Your prayers, your repentance, and your tears—the whole of them put together—are worth nothing apart from Him. No one but Jesus can do helpless sinners any good—or helpless saints, either. You must be conquerors through Him who has loved you, if conquerors at all. Our laurels must grow among His olives in Gethsemane.

And because of all this we make a sure covenant.
—Nehemiah 9:38

Many experiences in life may lead us, to our benefit, to renew our covenant with God. After recovery from sickness when, like Hezekiah, we have had a new term of years added to our lives, we may desire to do it. After any deliverance from trouble, when our joys bud forth anew, let us again visit the foot of the Cross and renew our consecration. Especially, let us do this after any sin that has grieved the Holy Spirit or brought dishonor to the cause of God. Let us, then, look to the blood that can make us whiter than snow and again offer ourselves to the Lord. We should not only let our troubles confirm our dedication to God, but also our prosperity should do the same. If we ever meet with occasions that deserve to be called "crowning mercies" then, surely, if He has honored us, we should honor our God. Let us bring forth anew all the jewels of the divine regalia that have been stored in the jewel boxes of our hearts, and let our God sit on the throne of our love, arrayed in royal apparel. If we would learn to profit by our prosperity, we would not need so much adversity. If we would gather from a kiss all the good it might confer upon us, we would not so often smart under the rod. Have we lately received some blessing that we little expected? Has the Lord put our feet in a large room? Can we sing of mercies multiplied? Then this is the day to put our hand on the horns of the altar, and say, "Bind me here, my God; bind me here with cords, even forever." Inasmuch as we need the fulfillment of new promises from God, let us offer renewed prayers that our old vows may not be dishonored. Let us this morning make with Him *"a sure covenant,"* because of the pains of Jesus that for the last month we have been considering with gratitude.

Rise up, my love, my fair one, and come away.
—Song of Solomon 2:10

I hear the voice of my Beloved! He speaks to me. Fair weather is smiling upon the face of the earth, and He would not have me spiritually asleep while nature is all around me awaking from her winter's rest. He bids me, *"Rise up,"* and well He may, for I have long enough been lying among the campfires of worldliness. He is risen, and I am risen in Him. Why then should I cleave to the dust? From lower loves, desires, pursuits, and aspirations, I would rise toward Him. He calls me by the sweet title of *"My love,"* and counts me fair; this is a good argument for my rising. If He has exalted me and thinks I am beautiful, how can I linger in the tents of Kedar and find congenial associates among the sons of men? He bids me, *"Come away."* Further and further from everything selfish, groveling, worldly, sinful, He calls me; yes, from the outwardly religious world that does not know Him and has no sympathy with the mystery of the higher life, He calls me. *"Come away"* has no harsh sound in it to my ear, for what is there to hold me in this wilderness of vanity and sin? O my Lord, if only I could come away, but I am taken among the thorns and cannot escape from them as I want to. I would, if it were possible, have neither eyes, nor ears, nor heart for sin. You call me to Yourself by saying, *"Come away,"* and this is a melodious call indeed. To come to You is to come home from exile, to come to land out of the raging storm, to come to rest after long labor, to come to the goal of my desires and the summit of my wishes. But Lord, how can a stone rise, or how can a lump of clay come away from the horrible pit? Oh, raise me; draw me. Your grace can do it. Send forth Your Holy Spirit to kindle sacred flames of love in my heart, and I will continue to rise until I leave life and time behind me, and indeed *"come away."*

This do in remembrance of me.
—1 Corinthians 11:24

he implication from today's text seems to be that Christians may forget Christ! There could be no need for this loving exhortation if there were not a fearful supposition that our memories might prove treacherous. Nor is this a bare supposition. It is, alas, too well confirmed in our experience, not as a possibility, but as a lamentable fact! It appears almost impossible that those who have been redeemed by the blood of the dying Lamb, who have been loved with an everlasting love by the eternal Son of God, could forget that gracious Savior. But, if startling to the ear, it is, alas, too apparent to the eye to allow us to deny the crime. Forget Him who never forgot us! Forget Him who poured His blood forth for our sins! Forget Him who loved us even to the death! Can it be possible? Yes, it is not only possible, but conscience confesses that it is too sadly a fault with all of us, that we permit Him to be as a wayfaring man tarrying but for a night. He whom we should make the abiding tenant of our memories is but a visitor therein. The Cross, where one would think that memory would linger and inattentiveness would be an unknown intruder, is desecrated by the feet of forgetfulness. Does not your conscience say that this is true? Do you not find yourselves forgetful of Jesus? Some creature steals away your heart, and you are unmindful of Him on whom your affection ought to be set. Some earthly business engrosses your attention when you should fix your eye steadily on the Cross. It is the incessant turmoil of the world and the constant attraction of earthly things that take away the soul from Christ. While memory too well preserves a poisonous weed, it permits the Rose of Sharon to wither. Let us charge ourselves to bind a heavenly forget-me-not about our hearts for Jesus our Beloved, and, whatever else we let slip, let us hold fast to Him.

God, even our own God.
—Psalm 67:6

t is strange how little use we make of the spiritual blessings that God gives us, but it is stranger still how little use we make of God Himself. Though He is *"our own God,"* we apply ourselves but little to Him and ask but little of Him. How seldom do we ask counsel at the hands of the Lord! How often do we go about our business without seeking His guidance! In our troubles how constantly do we strive to bear our burdens ourselves, instead of casting them on the Lord, so that He may sustain us! This is not because we may not, for the Lord seems to say, "I am yours, soul, come and make use of Me as you will. You may freely come to My store, and the more often, the more welcome." It is our own fault if we do not avail ourselves of the riches of our God. Then, since you have such a Friend, and He invites you, draw from Him daily. Never be in need while you have God to go to. Never fear or faint while you have God to help you. Go to your Treasure and take whatever you need. There is all that you can desire. Learn the divine skill of making God all things to you. He can supply you with all, or, better still, He can be all to you. Let me urge you, then, to make use of your God. Make use of Him in prayer. Go to Him often, because He is *your* God. Oh, will you fail to use so great a privilege? Fly to Him, and tell Him all your needs. Use Him constantly—by faith—at all times. If some dark circumstance has clouded your way, use your God as a light. If some strong enemy has attacked you, find in Jehovah a shield, for *"God is a sun and shield"* (Ps. 84:11) to His people. If you have lost your way in the mazes of life, use Him as a guide, for He will direct you. Whatever you are, and wherever you are, remember that God is just what you need and just where you need. He can do all you need.

Remember the word unto thy servant, upon which
thou hast caused me to hope.
—Psalm 119:49

hatever your special need may be, you may readily find some promise in the Bible suited to it. Are you faint and feeble because your way is rough, and you are weary? Here is the promise: *"He giveth power to the faint"* (Isa. 40:29). When you read such a promise, take it back to the great Promiser, and ask Him to fulfill His own Word. Are you seeking after Christ and thirsting for closer communion with Him? This promise shines like a star on you: *"Blessed are they which do hunger and thirst after right-eousness: for they shall be filled"* (Matt. 5:6). Take that promise to the throne continually; do not plead anything else, but go to God over and over again with this: "Lord, You have said it; do as You have said." Are you distressed because of sin and burdened with the heavy load of your iniquities? Listen to these words: *"I, even I, am he that blotteth out thy transgressions for mine own sake, and will not remember thy sins"* (Isa. 43:25). You have no merit of your own to plead for His pardon, but plead His written promises, and He will perform them. Are you afraid lest you should not be able to hold on to the end, lest, after having thought yourself a child of God, you should prove a castaway? If that is your state, take this Word of grace to the throne and plead it: *"The mountains shall depart, and the hills be removed; but my kindness shall not depart from thee, neither shall the covenant of my peace be removed"* (Isa. 54:10). If you have lost the sweet sense of the Savior's presence and are seeking Him with a sorrowful heart, remember the promises: *"Return unto me, and I will return unto you"* (Mal. 3:7). *"For a small moment have I forsaken thee; but with great mercies will I gather thee"* (Isa. 54:7). Feast your faith on God's own Word, and what-ever your fears or needs, return to the Bank of Faith with your Father's note, saying, *"Remember the word unto thy servant, upon which thou hast caused me to hope."*

Thou art my hope in the day of evil.
—Jeremiah 17:17

he path of the Christian is not always bright with sunshine. He has his seasons of darkness and of storm. True, it is written in God's Word, *"Her ways are ways of pleasantness, and all her paths are peace"* (Prov. 3:17). It is a great truth that religion is calculated to give a man happiness below as well as bliss above. But experience tells us that if the course of the just be *"as the shining light, that shineth more and more unto the perfect day"* (Prov. 4:18), yet sometimes that light is eclipsed. At certain periods clouds cover the believer's sun, and he walks in darkness and sees no light. Many have rejoiced in the presence of God for a season. They have basked in the sunshine in the earlier stages of their Christian career; they have walked along the *"green pastures"* by the side of the *"still waters"* (Ps. 23:2), but suddenly they find the glorious sky is clouded. Instead of the Land of Goshen, they have to tread the sandy desert. In the place of sweet waters, they find troubled streams, bitter to their taste. They say, "Surely, if I were a child of God, this would not happen." Oh, do not say this, you who are walking in darkness. The best of God's saints must drink from the cup of bitterness; the dearest of His children must bear the cross. No Christian has enjoyed perpetual prosperity; no believer can always keep his harp from the willows. (See Psalm 137:2.) Perhaps the Lord allotted you at first a smooth and unclouded path, because you were weak and timid. He tempered the wind to the shorn lamb, but now that you are stronger in the spiritual life, you must enter on the riper and rougher experience of God's full-grown children. We need winds and tempests to exercise our faith, to tear off the rotten bough of self-dependence, and to root us more firmly in Christ. The day of evil reveals to us the value of our glorious hope.

And all the children of Israel murmured.
—Numbers 14:2

There are complainers among Christians now, as there were in the camp of Israel of old. There are those who, when the rod falls, cry out against painful trials. They ask, "Why am I thus afflicted? What have I done to be chastened in this manner?" A word with you, O complainer! Why should you grumble against the actions of your heavenly Father? Can He treat you more harshly than you deserve? Consider what a rebel you were once, but He has pardoned you! Surely, if He in His wisdom sees fit now to chasten you, you should not complain. After all, are you smitten as harshly as your sins deserve? Consider the corruption that is in your heart, and then, will you wonder that so much of the rod is required to remove it? Weigh yourself, and discern how much dross is mingled with your gold. Do you think the fire is too hot to purge away as much dross as you have? Does not that proud, rebellious spirit of yours prove that your heart is not thoroughly sanctified? Are not those murmuring words contrary to the holy, submissive nature of God's children? Is not the correction needed? But if you will grumble against the chastening, take heed, for it will go hard with complainers. God always chastises His children twice if they do not bear the first stroke patiently. But know one thing: *"He doth not afflict willingly nor grieve the children of men"* (Lam. 3:33). All His corrections are sent in love, to purify you and to draw you nearer to Himself. Surely it must help you to bear the chastening with resignation if you are able to recognize your Father's hand. *"For whom the Lord loveth he chasteneth, and scourgeth every son whom he receiveth. If ye endure chastening, God dealeth with you as with sons"* (Heb. 12:6–7). *"Neither murmur ye, as some of them also murmured, and were destroyed of the destroyer"* (1 Cor. 10:10).

His cheeks are as a bed of spices, as sweet flowers.
—Song of Solomon 5:13

The flowery month is here! March winds and April showers have done their work, and the earth is all adorned in beauty. Come, my soul, and put on your holiday attire; go forth to gather garlands of heavenly thoughts. You know where to go, for you know well the *"bed of spices."* You have often smelled the perfume of *"sweet flowers."* You will go at once to your Well Beloved and find all loveliness and all joy in Him. That cheek—once so rudely smitten with a rod, often wet with tears of sympathy and then defiled with spittle—that cheek, as it smiles with mercy, is a fragrant aroma to my heart. You did not hide Your face from shame and spittle, O Lord Jesus; therefore, I will find my dearest delight in praising You. Those cheeks were furrowed by the plow of grief and crimsoned with red lines of blood from Your thorn-crowned temples. Such marks of limitless love cannot but charm my soul far more than great quantities of perfume. If I may not see the whole of His face, I would behold His cheeks, for the least glimpse of Him is exceedingly refreshing to my spiritual sense and yields a variety of delights. In Jesus I find not only fragrance, but *"a bed of spices"*; not one flower, but all manner of *"sweet flowers."* He is to me my Rose and my Lily, my heart's comfort and my healing balm. When He is with me, it is May all year round. My soul goes forth to wash its happy face in the morning dew of His grace and to comfort itself with the singing of the birds of His promises. Precious Lord Jesus, let me truly know the blessedness that dwells in abiding, unbroken fellowship with You. I am a poor worthless one, whose cheek You have deigned to kiss! Oh, let me kiss You in return with the kisses of my lips.

I pray not that thou shouldest take them out of the world.
—John 17:15

A sweet and blessed event that will occur to all believers in God's own time is the going home to be with Jesus. In a few more years the Lord's soldiers, who are now fighting *"the good fight of faith"* (1 Tim. 6:12), will be finished with conflict and will have entered into the joy of their Lord. But although Christ prays that His people may eventually be with Him where He is, He does not ask that they may be taken at once away from this world to heaven. He wishes them to stay here. Yet how frequently does the wearied pilgrim offer up the prayer, *"Oh that I had wings like a dove! for then would I fly away, and be at rest"* (Ps. 55:6), but Christ does not pray like that. He leaves us in His Father's hands, until, like shocks of fully ripened corn, we will each be gathered into our Master's granary. Jesus does not plead for our instant removal by death, for to abide in the flesh is necessary for others if not profitable for ourselves. He asks that we may be kept from evil, but He never asks for us to be admitted to the inheritance in glory until we are of full age. Christians often want to die when they have any trouble. Ask them why, and they tell you, "Because we would be with the Lord." We fear it is not so much that they are longing to be with the Lord, but rather that they are desiring to get rid of their troubles; otherwise, they would feel the same wish to die at other times, when not under the pressure of trial. They want to go home, not so much for the Savior's company, as to be at rest. Now it is quite right to desire to depart if we can do it in the same spirit that Paul did, because to be with Christ is far better, but the wish to escape from trouble is a selfish one. Rather let your care and wish be to glorify God by your life here as long as He pleases, even though it is in the midst of toil, conflict, and suffering, and leave it to Him to say when it is enough.

In the world ye shall have tribulation.
—John 16:33

re you asking the reason for your trials, believer? Look *upward* to your heavenly Father, and behold Him pure and holy. Do you know that you are one day to be like Him? Will you easily be conformed to His image? Will you not require much refining in the *"furnace of affliction"* (Isa. 48:10) to purify you? Will it be an easy thing to get rid of your corruption and make you perfect, *"even as your Father which is in heaven is perfect"* (Matt. 5:48)? Next, Christian, turn your eye *downward.* Do you know what foes you have beneath your feet? You were once a servant of Satan, and no king will willingly lose his subjects. Do you think that Satan will leave you alone? No, he will always be after you, for *"as a roaring lion, [he] walketh about, seeking whom he may devour"* (1 Pet. 5:8). Expect trouble, therefore, Christian, when you look beneath you. Then look *around* you. Where are you? You are in an enemy's country, a stranger and a sojourner. The world is not your friend. If it is, then you are not God's friend, for he who is the friend of the world is the enemy of God. Be assured that you will find enemies everywhere. When you sleep, think that you are resting on the battlefield; when you walk, suspect an ambush in every hedge. As mosquitoes are said to bite strangers more than natives, so will the trials of earth be sharpest to you. Last, look *within* you, into your own heart, and observe what is there. Sin and self are still within. Ah, if you had no devil to tempt you, no enemies to fight you, and no world to ensnare you, you would still find in yourself enough evil to be a painful trouble to you, for *"the heart is deceitful above all things, and desperately wicked"* (Jer. 17:9). Expect trouble, then, but do not despair because of it, for God is with you to help and to strengthen you. He has said, *"I will be with [you] in trouble; I will deliver [you], and honour [you]"* (Ps. 91:15).

Shall a man make gods unto himself, and they are no gods?
—Jeremiah 16:20

One great recurrent sin of ancient Israel was idolatry; spiritual Israel is plagued with a tendency toward the same evil. Mammon still intrudes his golden calf, and the shrines of pride are not forsaken. Self in various forms struggles to subdue the chosen ones under its dominion, and the flesh sets up its altars wherever it can find space for them. Favorite children are often the cause of much sin in believers. The Lord is grieved when He sees us doting on them above measure. They will live to be as great a curse to us as Absalom was to David, or they will be taken from us to leave our homes desolate. If Christians desire to grow thorns to stuff their sleepless pillows, let them dote on their dear ones. It is truly said that *"they are no gods,"* for the objects of our foolish love are very doubtful blessings, the solace that they yield us now is dangerous, and the help that they can give us in the hour of trouble is little indeed. Why, then, are we so bewitched with vanities? We pity the poor heathen who adore a god of stone, yet we worship a god of gold. Where is the vast superiority between a god of flesh and one of wood? The principle, the sin, the folly is the same in either case, only that in ours the crime is more aggravated because we have more light, and sin in the face of it. The heathen bows to a false deity, but he has never known the true God. We commit two evils when we forsake the living God and turn to idols. May the Lord purge us all from this grievous iniquity!

> The dearest idol I have known,
> Whate'er that idol be;
> Help me to tear it from Thy throne,
> And worship only Thee.

I will be their God, and they shall be my people.
—2 Corinthians 6:16

What a sweet title: *"my people"!* What a cheering revelation: *"their God"!* How much meaning is couched in those two words, *"my people"!* Here is a distinctive point. The whole world is God's. The heaven, even the heaven of heavens, is the Lord's, and He reigns among the children of men; but of those whom He has chosen, whom He has purchased for Himself, He says what He does not say of others—*"My people."* In this phrase there is the idea of ownership. In a special manner *"the LORD'S portion is his people; Jacob is the lot of his inheritance"* (Deut. 32:9). All the nations on earth are His. The whole world is in His power, yet His people, His chosen, are His special possession. He has done more for them than others. He has bought them with His blood and has brought them close to Himself. He has set His great heart on them and has loved them with an everlasting love, a love that many waters cannot quench, and that the revolutions of time will never suffice in the least degree to diminish. Dear friends, can you, by faith, see yourselves in that number? Can you look up to heaven and say, "My Lord and my God. You are mine by that sweet relationship that entitles me to call You 'Father.' You are mine by that hallowed fellowship that I delight to hold with You when You are pleased to manifest Yourself to me as You do not to the world"? Can you read the Book of Inspiration, and find there the indentures of your salvation? Can you read your name written in precious blood? Can you, by humble faith, lay hold of Jesus' garments, and say, "My Christ"? If you can, then God says of you, and of others like you, *"My people."* If God is your God, and Christ is your Christ, the Lord pays special attention to you. You are the object of His choice, accepted in His beloved Son.

We dwell in him.
—1 John 4:13

o you want a house for your soul? Do you ask, "What is the price?" It is something less than proud human nature would like to give. It is without money and without price. Would you like to pay a respectable rent? Would you love to do something to win Christ? Then you cannot have the house, for it is *"without price"* (Isa. 55:1). Will you take my Master's house on a lease for all eternity, with nothing to pay for it, nothing but the rent of loving and serving Him forever? Will you take Jesus and *"dwell in him"*? See, this house is furnished with all you need. It is filled with riches more than you will spend as long as you live. Here you can have intimate communion with Christ and feast on His love. Here are tables well-stored with food for you to live on forever. In it, when weary, you can find rest with Jesus. From it, you can look out and see heaven itself. Will you have the house? If you are homeless, you will say, "I would like to have the house; may I have it?" Yes, there is the key. The key is, "Come to Jesus." "But," you say, "I am too shabby for such a house." Never mind, for there are clothes inside. If you feel guilty and condemned, come; and though the house is too good for you, Christ will make you good enough for the house in time. He will wash you and cleanse you, and you will yet be able to sing, *"We dwell in him."* Believer, you are thrice blessed to have such a dwelling place! You are greatly privileged, for you have a *"strong habitation"* (Ps. 71:3) in which you are ever safe. Dwelling in Him, you have not only a perfect and secure house, but also an everlasting one. When this world will have melted like a dream, our house will live and stand more imperishable than marble, more solid than granite, self-existent as God, for it is God Himself—*"We dwell in him."*

Great multitudes followed him, and he healed them all.
—Matthew 12:15

hat an abundance of hideous sickness must have thrust itself under the eye of Jesus! Yet we do not read that He was disgusted by it; instead, He patiently waited on every case. What an unusual variety of evils must have met at His feet! What sickening ulcers and putrefying sores! Yet He was ready for every new shape of monstrous evil, and He was victor over it in every form. Let the arrow fly from what quarter it might; He quenched its fiery power. The heat of fever or the cold of dropsy; the lethargy of palsy or the rage of madness; the filth of leprosy or the darkness of blindness—all knew the power of His word and fled at His command. In every corner of the field He was triumphant over evil and received the respect of delivered captives. He came, He saw, He conquered everywhere. It is even so this morning. Whatever my own case may be, the beloved Physician can heal me. Whatever may be the state of others whom I may remember at this moment in prayer, I may have hope in Jesus that He will be able to heal them of their sins. My child, my friend, my dearest one, I can have hope for each, for all, when I remember the healing power of my Lord. On my own account, however severe my struggle with sins and infirmities, I may yet be of good cheer. He who walked on earth healing the sick still dispenses His grace and works wonders among the sons of men. Let me go to Him at once in earnest. Let me praise Him this morning, as I remember how He performed His spiritual cures, which bring Him most renown. It was by taking our sicknesses on Himself. *"With his stripes we are healed"* (Isa. 53:5). The church on earth is full of souls healed by our beloved Physician. The inhabitants of heaven itself confess that He healed them all. Come, then, my soul; tell about the virtue of His grace everywhere, and let it be *"to the LORD for a name, for an everlasting sign that shall not be cut off"* (Isa. 55:13).

He that was healed wist not who it was.
—John 5:13

Years are short to the happy and healthy, but thirty-eight years of disease must have dragged into a long time for the poor, impotent man. When Jesus, therefore, healed him by a word, while he lay at the pool of Bethesda, he was delightfully aware of a change. Likewise, the sinner who has for weeks and months been paralyzed with despair, and has wearily sighed for salvation, is very conscious of the change when the Lord Jesus speaks the word of power and gives joy and peace in believing. The evil removed is too great to be removed without our discerning it, the life imparted is too remarkable to be possessed and remain inoperative, and the change is too marvelous not to be perceived. Yet the poor man was ignorant of the Author of his cure. He did not know the sacredness of His person, the offices that He sustained, or the mission that brought Him among men. Much ignorance of Jesus may remain in hearts that yet feel the power of His blood. We must not hastily condemn men for lack of knowledge; but where we can see the faith that saves the soul, we must believe that salvation has been bestowed. The Holy Spirit makes men penitents long before He makes them holy. He who believes what he knows will soon know more clearly what he believes. Ignorance is, however, an evil, for this poor man was much tantalized by the Pharisees and was quite unable to cope with them. It is good to be able to answer the opposition, but we cannot do so if we do not know the Lord Jesus clearly and with understanding. The cure of his ignorance, however, soon followed the cure of his infirmity, for he was visited by the Lord in the temple. After that gracious manifestation, he was found testifying that *"it was Jesus, which had made him whole"* (John 5:15). Lord, if You have saved me, show me Yourself, so that I may declare You to the sons of men.

Who hath blessed us with all spiritual blessings.
—Ephesians 1:3

Christ bestows on His people all the goodness of the past, present, and the future. In the mysterious ages of the past, the Lord Jesus was His Father's first elect. In His election He gave us an interest, for we were *"chosen...in him before the foundation of the world"* (Eph. 1:4). He had from all eternity the privileges of Sonship, as His Father's Only Begotten and well-beloved Son. He has, in the riches of His grace, by adoption and regeneration, elevated us to sonship also, so that to us He has given *"power to become the sons of God"* (John 1:12). The eternal covenant, based on suretyship and confirmed by oath, is ours, for our strong consolation and security. In the everlasting settlements of predestinating wisdom and omnipotent decree, the eyes of the Lord Jesus were ever fixed on us. We may rest assured that in the whole roll of destiny there is not a line that lessens the interests of His redeemed. The great betrothal of the Prince of Glory is ours, for it is to us that He is betrothed, as the sacred nuptials will before long declare to an assembled universe. The marvelous incarnation of the God of heaven, with all the amazing condescension and humiliation that attended it, is ours. The bloody sweat, the scourge, and the cross are ours forever. Whatever blissful consequences flow from perfect obedience, finished atonement, resurrection, ascension, or intercession—all are ours by His own gift. He is now bearing our names on His breastplate; and in His authoritative pleadings at the throne, He remembers our persons and pleads our cause. He employs His dominion over principalities and powers and His absolute majesty in heaven for the benefit of those who trust in Him. His high estate is as much at our service as was His condition of abasement. He who gave Himself for us in the depths of woe and death does not withdraw the grant now that He is enthroned in the highest heavens.

But now is Christ risen from the dead.
—1 Corinthians 15:20

he whole system of Christianity rests on the fact that Christ is risen from the dead, for *"If Christ be not risen, then is our preaching vain, and your faith is also vain....Ye are yet in your sins"* (1 Cor. 15:14, 17). The divinity of Christ finds its surest proof in His resurrection, since He was *"declared to be the Son of God with power, according to the spirit of holiness, by the resurrection from the dead"* (Rom. 1:4). It would not be unreasonable to doubt His deity if He had not risen. Moreover, Christ's sovereignty depends on His resurrection, *"For to this end Christ both died, and rose, and revived, that he might be Lord both of the dead and living"* (Rom. 14:9). Again, our justification, that choice blessing of the covenant, is linked with Christ's triumphant victory over death and the grave; for He *"was delivered for our offences, and was raised again for our justification"* (Rom. 4:25). Moreover, our very regeneration is connected with His resurrection, for we are *"begotten...again unto a lively hope by the resurrection of Jesus Christ from the dead"* (1 Pet. 1:3). And most certainly our ultimate resurrection rests here, for *"if the Spirit of him that raised up Jesus from the dead dwell in you, he that raised up Christ from the dead shall also quicken your mortal bodies by his Spirit that dwelleth in you"* (Rom. 8:11). If Christ is not risen, then we will not rise; but if He is risen, then they who are asleep in Christ have not perished, but in their flesh will surely behold their God. Thus, the silver thread of resurrection runs through all the believer's blessings, from his regeneration to his eternal glory, and it binds them together. How important, then, will this glorious fact be in his estimation, and how will he rejoice that beyond a doubt it is established that *"now is Christ risen from the dead."*

The promise is fulfill'd,
　　Redemption's work is done,
Justice with mercy's reconciled,
　　For God has raised His Son.

Lo, I am with you alway.
—Matthew 28:20

It is good to know that there is One who is always the same, One who is always with us. It is good there is a stable rock in the midst of the billows of the sea of life. O my soul, do not set your affections on rusting, moth-eaten, decaying treasures, but set your heart on Him who abides forever faithful to you. Do not build your house on the moving quicksand of a deceitful world, but ground your hopes on the Rock, that, amid descending rain and roaring floods, will stand immovably secure. My soul, I charge you: lay up your treasure in the only secure cabinet; store your jewels where you can never lose them. Put your all in Christ. Set all your affections on His person, all your hope in His merit, all your trust in His efficacious blood, and all your joy in His presence, so that you may laugh at loss and defy destruction. Remember that all the flowers in the world's garden eventually fade, and the day is coming when nothing will be left but the black, cold earth. Death's black extinguisher must soon put out your candle. Oh, how sweet to have sunlight when the candle is gone! The dark flood must soon roll between you and all you have. Then wed your heart to Him who will never leave you. Trust yourself with Him who will go with you through the black and surging current of death's stream, and who will land you safely on the celestial shore and make you sit with Him in heavenly places forever. Go, sorrowing son of affliction, and tell your secrets to the Friend who sticks *"closer than a brother"* (Prov. 18:24). Trust all your concerns to Him who never can be taken from you, who will never leave you, and who will never let you leave Him, even *"Jesus Christ the same yesterday, and to day, and for ever"* (Heb. 13:8). *"Lo, I am with you alway"* is enough for my soul to live on, no matter who else might forsake me.

I will love him, and will manifest myself to him.
—John 14:21

The Lord Jesus gives special revelations of Himself to His people. Even if Scripture did not declare this, there are many children of God who could testify to the truth of it from their own experience. They have had manifestations of their Lord and Savior Jesus Christ in an unusual manner, such as no mere reading or hearing could afford. In the biographies of eminent saints, you will find many instances recorded in which Jesus has been pleased, in a very special manner, to speak to their souls and to unfold the wonders of His person. Their souls have been steeped in happiness that they have thought themselves to be in heaven, whereas they were not there, though they were very close to the threshold of it. When Jesus manifests Himself to His people, it is heaven on earth; it is paradise in embryo; it is bliss begun. Special manifestations of Christ exercise a holy influence on the believer's heart. One effect will be humility. If a man says, "I have had such-and-such spiritual communications. I am a great man," then he has never had any communion with Jesus at all, for God has *"respect unto the lowly: but the proud he knoweth afar off"* (Ps. 138:6). He does not need to come near them to know them, and He will never give them any visits of love. Another effect of a true manifestation of Christ will be happiness, for in God's presence, *"there are pleasures for evermore"* (Ps. 16:11). Holiness will be sure to follow. A man who has no holiness has never had this manifestation. Some men profess a great deal, but we must not believe anyone unless we see that his deeds match his words. *"Be not deceived; God is not mocked"* (Gal. 6:7). He will not bestow His favors on the wicked, for while He will not cast away a perfect man, neither will He respect an evildoer. Thus there will be three effects of nearness to Jesus: humility, happiness, and holiness. May God give them to you, Christian!

Weeping may endure for a night, but joy cometh in the morning.
—Psalm 30:5

Christian, if you are in a night of trial, think of tomorrow. Encourage your heart with thoughts of the coming of your Lord. Be patient, for He comes with clouds descending. Be patient! The Husbandman waits until He reaps His harvest. Be patient, for you know who has said, *"Behold, I come quickly; and my reward is with me, to give every man according as his work shall be"* (Rev. 22:12). If you are distressed now, remember,

> A few more rolling suns, at most,
> Will land you on fair Canaan's coast.

Your head may be crowned with thorny troubles now, but it will wear a starry crown before long. Your hand may be filled with cares now, but it will sweep the strings of the harp of heaven soon. Your garments may be soiled with dust now, but they will be white soon. Wait a little longer. Oh, how despicable our troubles and trials will seem when we look back on them! Looking at them here in the present, they seem immense; but when we get to heaven, we will then

> With transporting joys recount,
> The labors of our feet.

Our trials will then seem light and momentary afflictions. Let us go on boldly. Even if the night is never so dark, the morning comes, which is more than they can say who are shut up in the darkness of hell. Do you know what it is thus to live on the future—to live on expectation—to anticipate heaven? Happy believer, what joy it is to have so sure and so comforting a hope! It may be all dark now, but it will soon be light; it may be all trial now, but it will soon be all happiness. What does it matter though *"weeping may endure for a night,"* when *"joy cometh in the morning"*?

Joint-heirs with Christ.
—Romans 8:17

The boundless realms of His Father's universe are Christ's by prescriptive right. As *"heir of all things"* (Heb. 1:2), He is the sole proprietor of the vast creation of God. He has admitted us to claim the whole as ours, by virtue of that deed of joint heirship that the Lord has ratified with His chosen people. The golden streets of paradise, the pearly gates, the river of life, the transcendent bliss, and the unutterable glory are, by our blessed Lord, allotted to us for our everlasting possession. He shares all that He has with His people. The royal crown He has placed on the head of His church, appointing her a kingdom, and calling her sons *"a royal priesthood"* (1 Pet. 2:9), a generation of *"kings and priests"* (Rev. 1:6). He uncrowned Himself that we might have a coronation of glory. He would not sit on His own throne until He had procured a place on it for all who overcome by His blood. Crown the head and the whole body shares the honor. Behold here the reward of every Christian conqueror! Christ's throne, crown, scepter, palace, treasure, robes, and heritage are yours. Far superior to the jealousy, selfishness, and greed— that bring no advantages to those who practice them— Christ deems His happiness completed by His people sharing it. *"The glory which thou gavest me I have given them"* (John 17:22). *"These things have I spoken unto you, that my joy might remain in you, and that your joy might be full"* (John 15:11). The smiles of His Father are all the sweeter to Him, because His people share them. The honors of His kingdom are more pleasing, because His people appear with Him in glory. More valuable to Him are His conquests, since they have taught His people to overcome. He delights in His throne, because on it there is a place for them. He rejoices in His royal robes, since over them His skirts are spread. He delights the more in His joy, because He calls them to enter into it.

All that believe are justified.
—Acts 13:39

The believer in Christ receives a present justification. Faith does not produce this fruit in the future, but now. So far as justification is the result of faith, it is given to the soul in the moment when it surrenders to Christ and accepts Him as its all in all. Are they who stand before the throne of God justified now?—so are we, as truly and as clearly justified as they who walk in white and sing melodious praises to celestial harps. The thief on the cross was justified the moment that he turned the eye of faith to Jesus. The aged Paul, after years of service, was not more justified than was the thief with no service at all. We are today *"accepted in the beloved"* (Eph. 1:6), today absolved from sin, today acquitted at the bar of God. Oh, soul-transporting thought! There are some clusters of Eshcol's vine that we will not be able to gather until we enter heaven, but this is a bough that runs over the wall. This is not as the corn of the land, which we can never eat until we cross the Jordan. This is part of the manna in the wilderness, a portion of our daily nourishment with which God supplies us on our journey. We are pardoned even now. Even now are our sins put away. Even now we stand in the sight of God accepted, as though we had never been guilty. *"There is therefore now no condemnation to them which are in Christ Jesus"* (Rom. 8:1). There is not a sin in the Book of God, even now, against one of His people. Who dares to lay anything to their charge? There is neither speck, nor spot, nor wrinkle, nor any such thing remaining on any one believer in the matter of justification in the sight of the Judge of all the earth. Let present privilege awaken us to present duty, and now, while life lasts, let us spend and be spent for our sweet Lord Jesus.

Who giveth us richly all things to enjoy.
—1 Timothy 6:17

ur Lord Jesus is always giving. Not for a solitary instant does He withdraw His hand. As long as there is a vessel of grace not yet full to the brim, the oil will not be withheld. He is a sun that always shines. He is manna always falling round the camp. He is a rock in the desert that ever sends out streams of life from His smitten side. The rain of His grace is always falling; the river of His bounty is always flowing, and the wellspring of His love is constantly overflowing. As the King can never die, so His grace can never fail. Daily we pluck His fruit, and daily His branches bend down to our hand with a fresh store of mercy. There are seven feast days in His weeks, and as many as are the days, so many are the banquets in His years. Who has ever returned from His door unblessed? Who has ever risen from His table unsatisfied, or from His heart unloved? His mercies are *"new every morning"* (Lam. 3:23) and fresh every evening. Who can know the number of His benefits or recount the list of His bounties? Every grain of sand that drops from the glass of time is but the tardy follower of a myriad of mercies. The wings of our hours are covered with the silver of His kindness and with the gold of His affection. The river of time bears from the mountains of eternity the golden sands of His favor. The countless stars are but as the standard bearers of a more innumerable host of blessings. *"Who can count the dust of Jacob, and the number of the fourth part of Israel?"* (Num. 23:10). How will my soul extol Him *"who daily loadeth us with benefits"* (Ps. 68:19), and *"who crowneth [us] with loving-kindness"* (Ps. 103:4)? Oh, that my praise could be as ceaseless as His bounty! O miserable tongue, how can you be silent? Wake up, I pray you, lest I call you no more my glory, but my shame. *"Awake, psaltery and harp: I myself will awake early"* (Ps. 108:2).

So to walk, even as he walked.
—1 John 2:6

hy should Christians imitate Christ? They should do it for their own sakes. If they desire to be in a healthy state of soul, if they want to escape the sickness of sin and enjoy the vigor of growing grace, let Jesus be their model. For the sake of their own happiness, if they would enjoy holy and happy communion with Jesus, and if they would be lifted above the cares and troubles of this world, let them walk even as He walked. There is nothing that can assist you in walking toward heaven with good speed as much as wearing the image of Jesus on your heart to rule all its motions. It is when, by the power of the Holy Spirit, you are enabled to walk with Jesus in His very footsteps that you are happiest and most known to be the sons of God. Peter's position of being *"afar off"* (Luke 22:54) is both unsafe and uneasy. Next, for faith's sake, strive to be like Jesus. Ah, poor faith, you have been sorely shot at by cruel foes, but you have not been wounded half so dangerously by your enemies as by your friends. Who made those wounds in the fair hand of godliness? The one who professed faith but used the dagger of hypocrisy. The man with pretenses who enters the fold, being nothing but a wolf in sheep's clothing, worries the flock more than the lion outside. There is no weapon half so deadly as a Judas-kiss. Inconsistent Christians injure the Gospel more than the sneering critic or the infidel. But, especially for Christ's own sake, imitate His example. Christian, do you love your Savior? Is His name precious to you? Is His cause dear to you? Would you see the kingdoms of the world become His? Is it your desire that He would be glorified? Are you longing that souls should be won to Him? If so, imitate Jesus; be an *"epistle of Christ"* (2 Cor. 3:3), *"known and read of all men"* (v. 2).

In him dwelleth all the fulness of the Godhead bodily.
And ye are complete in him.
—Colossians 2:9–10

All the attributes of Christ, as God and man, are at our disposal. All the fullness of the Godhead, whatever that marvelous term may include, is ours to make us complete. He cannot endow us with the attributes of deity; but He has done all that can be done, for He has made even His divine power and Godhead subservient to our salvation. His omnipotence, omniscience, omnipresence, immutability, and infallibility are all combined for our defense. Arise, believer, and behold the Lord Jesus yoking the whole of His divine Godhead to the chariot of salvation! How vast His grace, how firm His faithfulness, how unswerving His immutability, how infinite His power, how limitless His knowledge! These are all made the pillars of the temple of salvation by the Lord Jesus. And all, without shortening their infinity, are covenanted to us as our perpetual inheritance. Every drop of the fathomless love of the Savior's heart is ours; every sinew in the arm of might, every jewel in the crown of majesty, the immensity of divine knowledge, and the sternness of divine justice are all ours and will be employed for us. The whole of Christ, in His adorable character as the Son of God, is by Himself made over to us most richly to enjoy. His wisdom is our direction, His knowledge our instruction, His power our protection, His justice our surety, His love our comfort, His mercy our solace, and His immutability our trust. He holds back no reserves, but opens the recesses of the mount of God and invites us to dig in its mines for the hidden treasures. "All, all, all are yours," He says. "Be satisfied with My favor and enjoy the full goodness of the Lord." Oh, how sweet it is to behold Jesus and to call on Him with the certain confidence that in seeking the intervention of His love or power, we are but asking for that which He has already faithfully promised.

*I have seen servants upon horses, and princes walking
as servants upon the earth.*
—Ecclesiastes 10:7

Upstarts frequently usurp the highest places, while the truly great pine in obscurity. This is a riddle in providence whose solution will one day gladden the hearts of the upright; but it is so common a fact, that none of us should murmur if it should fall to our own lot. When our Lord was on earth, although He is the Prince of the kings of the earth, yet He walked the footpath of weariness and service as the Servant of servants: what wonder is it if His followers, who are princes of the blood, should also be looked down on as inferior and contemptible persons? The world is upside down; therefore, the first are last and the last first. See how the servile sons of Satan lord it in the earth! What a high horse they ride! How they lift up their horn on high! Haman is in the court, while Mordecai sits in the gate; David wanders on the mountains, while Saul reigns in state; Elijah is complaining in the cave, while Jezebel is boasting in the palace; yet who would wish to take the places of the proud rebels? And who, on the other hand, might not envy the despised saints? When the wheel turns, those who are lowest rise, and the highest sink. Patience, then, believer, eternity will right the wrongs of time. Let us not fall into the error of letting our passions and carnal appetites ride in triumph, while our nobler powers walk in the dust. Grace must reign as a prince, and make the members of the body instruments of righteousness. The Holy Spirit loves order, and He therefore sets our powers and faculties in due rank and place, giving the highest room to those spiritual faculties that link us with the great King. Let us not disturb the divine arrangement, but ask for grace that we may keep under our body and bring it into subjection. We were not new created to allow our passions to rule over us, but that we, as kings, may reign in Christ Jesus over the triple kingdom of spirit, soul, and body, to the glory of God the Father.

Marvellous lovingkindness.
—Psalm 17:7

When we give our hearts along with our charitable gifts, we give well, but we must often admit to failing in this respect. Not so our Master and our Lord. His favors are always performed with the love of His heart. He does not send to us the cold meat and the broken pieces from the table of His luxury, but He dips our morsels into His own dish and seasons our provisions with the spices of His fragrant affections. When He puts the golden tokens of His grace into our palms, He accompanies the gift with such a warm pressure of our hand that the manner of His giving is as precious as the gift itself. He will come into our houses on His errands of kindness, but He will not act as some austere visitors do in a poor man's cottage; instead, He sits by our sides, not despising our poverty or blaming our weaknesses. Beloved, with what smiles does He speak! What golden sentences drop from His gracious lips! What embraces of affection He bestows on us! If He had but given us pennies, the way of His giving would have gilded them; but as it is, the costly gifts are set in a golden basket by His pleasant carriage. It is impossible to doubt the sincerity of His charity, for there is a bleeding heart stamped on the face of all His benefactions. He gives *"liberally, and up-braideth not"* (James 1:5). Not one hint that we are burdensome to Him; not one cold look for His poor pensioners; but He rejoices in His mercy and presses us to His bosom while He is pouring out His life for us. There is a fragrance in His spikenard that nothing but His heart could produce; there is a sweetness in His honeycomb that could not be in it unless the very essence of His soul's affection had been mingled with it. Oh, the rare communion that such singular sincerity produces! May we continually taste and know the blessedness of it!

If so be ye have tasted that the Lord is gracious.
—1 Peter 2:3

If"—then this is not a matter to be taken for granted concerning every one of the human race. *"If"*—then there is a possibility and a probability that some may not have tasted that the Lord is gracious. *"If"*—then this is not a general but a special mercy; and it is necessary to inquire whether we know the grace of God by inward experience. There is no spiritual favor that may not be a matter for heart-searching. But while this should be a matter of earnest and prayerful inquiry, no one ought to be content while there is any such thing as an *"if"* about his having *"tasted that the Lord is gracious."* A jealous and holy distrust of self may give rise to the question even in the believer's heart, but the continuance of such a doubt would be an evil indeed. We must not rest without a desperate struggle to clasp the Savior in the arms of faith, and say, *"I know whom I have believed, and am persuaded that he is able to keep that which I have committed unto him"* (2 Tim. 1:12). Do not rest, believer, until you have a full assurance of your interest in Jesus. Let nothing satisfy you until, by the infallible witness of the Holy Spirit bearing witness with your spirit, you are certified that you are a child of God (Rom. 8:16). Oh, do not trifle here; let no "perhaps" or "peradventure" or "if" or "maybe" satisfy your soul. Build on eternal truths, and truly build on them. Get *"the sure mercies of David"* (Isa. 55:3), and surely get them. Let your anchor be cast into that which is within the veil, and see to it that your soul is linked to the anchor by a cable that will not break. Advance beyond these dreary *if*s. Abide no more in the wilderness of doubts and fears. Cross the Jordan of distrust, and enter the Canaan of peace, where the Canaanite still lingers, but where the land does not cease to flow *"with milk and honey"* (Lev. 20:24).

He led them forth by the right way.
—Psalm 107:7

Uncertain experiences often lead the anxious believer to inquire, "Why is this happening to me?" I looked for light, but lo, darkness came; for peace, but found trouble. I said in my heart, my mountain stands firm; I will never be moved. Lord, you hide Your face, and I am troubled. It was but yesterday that I could read my title clear; today my evidences are unsure, and my hopes are clouded. Yesterday I could climb to Pisgah's top and view the distant landscape. I could rejoice with confidence in my future inheritance. Today my spirit has no hopes, but many fears; no joys, but much distress. Is this part of God's plan for me? Can this be the way in which God would bring me to heaven? Yes, it is even so. The eclipse of your faith, the darkness of your mind, the fainting of your hope—all these things are but part of God's method of making you ready for the great inheritance into which you will soon enter. These trials are for the testing and strengthening of your faith. They are waves that wash you further upon the rock; they are winds that waft your ship the more swiftly toward the desired haven. According to David's words, so it might be said of you, *"He bringeth them unto their desired haven"* (Ps. 107:30). By honor and dishonor, by evil report and by good report, by plenty and by poverty, by joy and by distress, by persecution and by peace, by all these things are the lives of your souls maintained, and by each of these are you helped on your way. Oh, believer, do not think that your sorrows are out of God's plan; they are necessary parts of it. *"We must through much tribulation enter into the kingdom of God"* (Acts 14:22). Learn, then, even to *"count it all joy when ye fall into divers temptations"* (James 1:2).

O let my trembling soul be still,
    And wait Thy wise, Thy holy will!
I cannot, Lord, Thy purpose see,
    Yet all is well since ruled by Thee.

The LORD will perfect that which concerneth me.
—Psalm 138:8

learly the confidence that the psalmist expressed here was a divine confidence. He did not say, "I have grace enough to perfect that which concerns me. My faith is so steady that it will not stagger. My love is so warm that it will never grow cold. My resolution is so firm that nothing can move it." No, his dependence was on the Lord alone. If we indulge in any confidence that is not grounded on the Rock of ages, our confidence is worse than a dream. It will fall on us and cover us with its ruins, to our sorrow and confusion. All that nature spins, time will unravel, to the eternal confusion of all who are clothed therein. The psalmist was wise. He rested on nothing short of the Lord's work. It is the Lord who has begun the good work within us. It is He who has carried it on, and if He does not finish it, it will never be completed. If there is one stitch in the celestial garment of our righteousness that we are to insert ourselves, then we are lost; but this is our confidence: the Lord who began will perfect. He has done it all, must do it all, and will do it all. Our confidence must not be in what we have done or in what we have resolved to do, but entirely in what the Lord will do. Unbelief insinuates, "You will never be able to stand. Look at the evil of your heart; you can never conquer sin. Remember the sinful pleasures and temptations of the world that besiege you; you will certainly be allured by them and led astray." Ah, yes, we would indeed perish if left to our own strength. If we had to navigate our frail vessels alone over so rough a sea, we might as well give up the voyage in despair. But thanks be to God! He *"will perfect that which concerneth [us]"* and bring us to the *"desired haven"* (Ps. 107:30). We can never be too confident when we confide in Him alone and never carry too many concerns when we have this assurance of His.

Blessed be God, which hath not turned away my prayer.
—Psalm 66:20

In looking back on the character of our prayers, if we do it honestly, we will be filled with wonder that God has ever answered them. There may be some who think their prayers are worthy of acceptance—as the Pharisee did; but the true Christian, in a more enlightened retrospect, weeps over his prayers, and if he could retrace his steps, he would desire to pray more earnestly. Remember, Christian, how cold your prayers have been. Instead of wrestling in prayer as Jacob did, your petitions have been weak and few—far removed from that humble, believing, persevering faith that cries, *"I will not let thee go, except thou bless me"* (Gen. 32:26). Yet, wonderful to say, God has heard these cold prayers of yours, and not only heard, but answered them. Reflect also on how infrequent your prayers have been, unless you have been in trouble, and then, you have gone often to the mercy seat. But when deliverance has come, where has your constant supplication been? Yet, even though you have ceased to pray as you once did, God has not ceased to bless. When you have neglected the mercy seat, God has not deserted it, but the bright light of the Shechinah has always been visible between the wings of the cherubim. Oh, it is marvelous that the Lord would regard those intermittent spasms of pleading that come and go with our needs. What a God He is to hear the prayers of those who come to Him when they have pressing needs, but neglect Him when they have received an answer; who approach Him when they are forced to come, but who almost forget to address Him when mercies are plentiful and sorrows are few! Let His gracious kindness in hearing such prayers touch our hearts, so that we may from this point on be found *"praying always with all prayer and supplication in the Spirit"* (Eph. 6:18).

Forsake me not, O LORD.
—Psalm 38:21

requently we pray that God would not forsake us in the hour of trial and temptation, but we too often forget that we need to use this prayer at all times. There is no moment of our lives, however holy, in which we can do without His constant upholding. Whether in light or in darkness, in communion or in temptation, we need the prayer, *"'Forsake me not, O LORD.'* Hold me up, and I will be safe." A little child, while learning to walk, always needs his mother's hand. The ship left by the pilot drifts at once from her course. We cannot do without continued aid from above. Let it, then, be your prayer today, "Do not forsake me, Father. Do not forsake Your child, lest he fall by the hand of the enemy. Shepherd, do not forsake Your lamb, lest he wander from the safety of the fold. Great Husbandman, do not forsake Your plant, lest it wither and die. *'Forsake me not, O LORD,'* now; and forsake me not at any moment of my life. Do not forsake me in my joys, lest they absorb my heart. Do not forsake me in my sorrows, lest I murmur against You. Do not forsake me in the day of my repentance, lest I lose the hope of pardon and fall into despair. Do not forsake me in the day of my strongest faith, lest faith degenerate into presumption. Do not forsake me, for without You I am weak, but with You I am strong. Do not forsake me, for my path is dangerous and full of snares, and I cannot do without Your guidance. The hen does not forsake her brood; will You then cover me evermore with Your feathers and permit me to find my refuge under Your wings? *'Be not far from me; for trouble is near; for there is none to help'* (Ps. 22:11). *'Leave me not, neither forsake me, O God of my salvation'* (Ps. 27:9)."

O ever in our cleansed breast,
  Bid Thine Eternal Spirit rest;
And make our secret soul to be
  A temple pure and worthy Thee.

Cast thy burden upon the LORD, and he shall sustain thee.
—Psalm 55:22

Care, even though exercised on legitimate objects, if carried to excess, has in it the nature of sin. The precept to avoid anxious care is earnestly instilled by our Savior, again and again, in His teachings. It is reiterated by the apostles, and it is one that cannot be neglected without involving transgression: for the very essence of anxious care is the imagining that we are wiser than God, and the thrusting of ourselves into His place to do for Him what He has undertaken to do for us. We attempt to think of that which we imagine He will forget. We labor to take on ourselves our weary burden, as if He were unable or unwilling to take it for us. Now this disobedience to His plain precept, this unbelief in His Word, this presumption in intruding on His province, is all sinful. Yet more than this, anxious care often leads to acts of sin. He who cannot calmly leave his affairs in God's hand, but will carry his own burden, is very likely to be tempted to use wrong means to help himself. This sin leads to a forsaking of God as our Counselor, resorting instead to human wisdom. This is going to the *"broken cisterns"* (Jer. 2:13) instead of to the *"fountain of living waters"* (v. 13)—a sin that was laid against ancient Israel. Anxiety makes us doubt God's lovingkindness, and thus our love for Him grows cold. We feel mistrust, and thus grieve the Spirit of God, so that our prayers become hindered, our consistent example marred, and our lives ones of self-seeking. Thus lack of confidence in God leads us to wander far from Him; but if through simple faith in His promise, we cast each burden as it comes upon Him, and are *"careful for nothing"* (Phil. 4:6) because He undertakes to care for us, it will keep us close to Him and strengthen us against much temptation. *"Thou wilt keep him in perfect peace, whose mind is stayed on thee: because he trusteth in thee"* (Isa. 26:3).

So Mephibosheth dwelt in Jerusalem: for he did eat continually at the king's table; and was lame on both his feet.
—2 Samuel 9:13

Mephibosheth was no great ornament to a royal table, yet he had a continual place at David's board, because the king could see in his face the features of the beloved Jonathan. Like Mephibosheth, we may cry unto the King of Glory, *"What is thy servant, that thou shouldest look upon such a dead dog as I am?"* (2 Sam. 9:8). But still, the Lord indulges us with most familiar communion with Himself, because He sees in our countenances the remembrance of His dearly beloved Jesus. The Lord's people are dear for Another's sake. Such is the love that the Father bears for His Only Begotten that for His sake He raises His lowly brethren from poverty and banishment to courtly companionship, noble rank, and royal provision. Their deformity will not rob them of their privileges. Lameness is no bar to sonship; the cripple is as much the heir as if he could run like Asahel, who *"was as light of foot as a wild roe"* (2 Sam. 2:18). Our right does not limp, though our might may. A king's table is a noble hiding place for lame legs, and at the gospel feast we learn to glory in infirmities, because the power of Christ rests on us. Yet grievous disability may mar the persons of the best-loved saints. Here is one feasted by David, and yet so lame in both his feet that he could not go up with the king when he fled from the city, and was therefore maligned and injured by his servant Ziba. Saints whose faith is weak, and whose knowledge is slender, are great losers; they are exposed to many enemies and cannot follow the king wherever he goes. This disease frequently arises from falls. Bad nursing in their spiritual infancy often causes converts to fall into a despondency from which they never recover, and sin in other cases brings broken bones. Lord, help the lame to leap like a deer and satisfy all Your people with the bread of Your table!

Whom he justified, them he also glorified.
—Romans 8:30

Here is a precious truth for you, believer. You may be poor, in pain, or unknown, but for your encouragement, review your calling and the consequences that flow from it, especially that blessed result spoken of in this morning's text. As surely as you are God's child today, so surely will all your trials soon be at an end, and you will be rich to all the intents of bliss. Wait awhile, and that weary head will wear the crown of glory, and that hand of labor will grasp the palm branch of victory. Do not lament your troubles, but rather rejoice that before long you will be where *"there shall be no more death, neither sorrow, nor crying, neither shall there be any more pain"* (Rev. 21:4). The chariots of fire are at your door, and a moment will suffice to bear you to the glorified. The everlasting song is almost on your lips. The portals of heaven stand open for you. Do not think that you can fail to enter into rest. If He has called you, nothing can separate you from His love. Distress cannot sever the bond; the fire of persecution cannot burn the link; the hammer of hell cannot break the chain. You are secure. That voice that called you at first will call you yet again from earth to heaven, from death's dark gloom to immortality's unuttered splendors. Rest assured, the heart of Him who has justified you beats with infinite love toward you. You will soon be with the glorified, where your portion is; you are waiting here only to be made ready for the inheritance; once that is done, the wings of angels will carry you far away to the mount of peace, joy, and blessedness, where,

> Far from a world of grief and sin,
> With God eternally shut in,

you will rest forever and ever.

Thou lovest righteousness, and hatest wickedness.
—Psalm 45:7

"Be ye angry, and sin not" (Eph. 4:26). There can hardly be goodness in a man if he is not angry at sin; he who loves truth must hate every false way. How our Lord Jesus hated it when the temptation came! Thrice it assailed Him in different forms, but He always met it with, *"Get thee behind me, Satan"* (Matt. 16:23; Mark 8:33; Luke 4:8). He hated sin in others—none the less fervently because He showed His hate more often in tears of pity than in words of rebuke. Yet what language could be more stern, more Elijah-like, than the words, *"Woe unto you, scribes and Pharisees, hypocrites! for ye devour widows' houses, and for a pretence make long prayer"* (Matt. 23:14). He hated wickedness, so much that He bled to wound it to the heart; He died that it might die. He was buried that He might bury it in His tomb, and He rose that He might forever trample it beneath His feet. Christ is in the Gospel, and that Gospel is opposed to wickedness in every shape. Wickedness arrays itself in fair garments and imitates the language of holiness; but the precepts of Jesus, like His famous scourge of small cords, chase it out of the temple and will not tolerate it in the church. So, too, in the heart where Jesus reigns, what war there is between Christ and Belial! And when our Redeemer will come to be our Judge, those thundering words, *"Depart from me, ye cursed"* (Matt. 25:41), which are, indeed, but a prolongation of His life's teaching concerning sin, will manifest His abhorrence of iniquity. As warm as His love is for sinners, so hot is His hatred of sin; as perfect as His righteousness is, so complete will be the destruction of every form of wickedness. O you glorious Champion of right and Destroyer of wrong, for this cause has God, even Your God, *"anointed thee with the oil of gladness above thy fellows"* (Ps. 45:7).

Take us the foxes, the little foxes, that spoil the vines.
—Song of Solomon 2:15

A little thorn may cause much suffering. A little cloud may hide the sun. *"Little foxes...spoil the vines,"* and little sins do mischief to the tender heart. These little sins burrow in the soul and make it so full of that which is hateful to Christ that He will hold no comfortable fellowship and communion with us. A great sin cannot destroy a Christian, but a little sin can make him miserable. Jesus will not walk with His people unless they drive out every known sin. He says, *"If ye keep my commandments, ye shall abide in my love; even as I have kept my Father's commandments, and abide in his love"* (John 15:10). Some Christians very seldom enjoy their Savior's presence. How is this? Surely it must be an affliction for a tender child to be separated from his father. Are you a child of God and yet satisfied to go on without seeing your Father's face? What! You are the spouse of Christ and yet content without His company! Surely you have fallen into a sad state, for the chaste spouse of Christ mourns like a dove without her mate, when he has left her. Ask, then, this question: what has driven Christ from you? He hides His face behind the wall of your sins. That wall may be built up of little pebbles, as easily as of great stones. The sea is composed of drops, and the rocks are composed of grains; the sea that separates you from Christ may be filled with the drops of your little sins, and the rock that has nearly wrecked your weak vessel may have been made by the daily working of the coral insects of your little sins. If you would live with Christ, walk with Christ, see Christ, and have fellowship with Christ, take heed of *"the little foxes, that spoil the vines: for our vines have tender grapes"* (Song 2:15). Jesus invites you to go with Him and take them. He will surely, like Samson, take the foxes at once and easily. Go with Him to the hunting.

The king also himself passed over the brook Kidron.
—2 Samuel 15:23

avid passed that gloomy brook when flying with his mourning company from his traitor son. The man after God's own heart was not exempt from trouble; no, his life was full of it. He was both the Lord's anointed and the Lord's afflicted. Why then should we expect to escape? At sorrow's gates the noblest of our race have waited with ashes on their heads; why then should we complain as though some strange thing had happened to us? The King of Kings Himself was not favored with a more cheerful or royal road. He passed over the filthy ditch of Kidron, through which the filth of Jerusalem flowed. God had one Son without sin, but not a single child without the rod. It is a great joy to believe that Jesus has been tempted in all points like as we are. What is our Kidron this morning? Is it a faithless friend, a sad bereavement, a slanderous reproach, a dark foreboding? The King has passed over all these. Is it bodily pain, poverty, persecution, or contempt? Over each of these Kidrons the King has gone before us. *"In all [our] affliction he was afflicted"* (Isa. 63:9). The idea of strangeness in our trials must be banished at once and forever, for He who is the Head of all saints knows by experience the grief that we think so peculiar. All the citizens of Zion must be free of the honorable company of mourners, of which the Prince Immanuel is Head and Captain. Notwithstanding the abasement of David, he yet returned in triumph to his city, and David's Lord arose victorious from the grave. Let us, then, be of good courage, for we also will win the day. We will yet with joy draw water out of the wells of salvation, though now for a season we have to pass by the noxious streams of sin and sorrow. Courage, soldiers of the Cross, the King Himself triumphed after going over Kidron, and so will you.

The evening and the morning were the first day.
—Genesis 1:5

as it so even in the beginning? Did light and darkness divide the realm of time in the first day? Then little wonder is it if I also have changes in my circumstances from the sunshine of prosperity to the midnight of adversity. It will not always be the blaze of noon. Even in my soul's concerns, I must expect at seasons to mourn the absence of my former joys and seek my Beloved in the night. Nor am I alone in this, for all the Lord's beloved ones have had to sing the mingled song of judgment and of mercy, of trial and deliverance, of mourning and of delight. It is one of the arrangements of Divine Providence that day and night will not cease either in the spiritual or natural creation until we reach the land of which it is written, *"There shall be no night there"* (Rev. 21:25). What our heavenly Father ordains is wise and good. What, then, my soul, is it best for you to do? Learn first to be content with this divine order, and be willing, with Job, to receive evil from the hand of the Lord as well as good. Study next to make *"the outgoings of the morning and the evening to rejoice"* (Ps. 65:8). Praise the Lord for the sun of joy when it rises, and for the gloom of evening as it falls. There is beauty both in the sunrise and sunset. Sing of their beauty, and glorify the Lord. Like the nightingale, pour forth your notes at all hours. Believe that the night is as useful as the day. The dew of grace falls heavily in the night of sorrow. The stars of promise shine forth gloriously amid the darkness of grief. Continue your service under all changes. If in the day your watchword is *labor*, at night exchange it for *watch*. Every hour has its duty. Continue in your calling as the Lord's servant until He will suddenly appear in His glory. My soul, your evening of old age and death is drawing near. Do not dread it, for it is part of the day; and the Lord has said, "I will *'cover him all the day long'* (Deut. 33:12)."

For the flesh lusteth against the Spirit,
and the Spirit against the flesh.
—Galatians 5:17

In every believer's heart there is a constant struggle between the old nature and the new. The old nature is very active, and it loses no opportunity of plying all the weapons of its deadly armory against newborn grace; while, on the other hand, the new nature is ever on the watch to resist and destroy its enemy. Grace within us will employ prayer, faith, hope, and love to cast out the evil. It takes to it the *"whole armour of God"* (Eph. 6:11) and wrestles earnestly. These two opposing natures will never cease to struggle as long as we are in this world. Bunyan's pilgrim, Christian, battled with Apollyon for three hours, but Christian's battle with himself lasted all the way from the Wicket Gate to the river Jordan. The enemy is so securely entrenched within us that he can never be driven out while we are in this body. Although we are troubled, and often in sore conflict, we have an almighty Helper, even Jesus, the Captain of our salvation. He is ever with us and assures us that we will eventually be *"more than conquerors through him"* (Rom. 8:37). With such assistance the newborn nature is more than a match for its foes. Are you fighting with the adversary today? Are Satan, the world, and the flesh all against you? Do not be discouraged or dismayed. Fight on, for God Himself is with you! Jehovah-Nissi is your banner, and Jehovah-Rophi is the healer of your wounds. Fear not, for you will overcome. Who can defeat Omnipotence? Fight on, *"looking unto Jesus"* (Heb. 12:2). Though the conflict is long and stern, sweet will be the victory and glorious the promised reward.

> From strength to strength go on;
>   Wrestle, and fight, and pray,
> Tread all the powers of darkness down,
>   And win the well-fought day.

These were the potters, and those that dwelt among plants and
hedges: there they dwelt with the king for his work.
—1 Chronicles 4:23

otters were the very highest grade of workers, but the
king needed potters; therefore, they were in royal
service, although the material on which they worked
was nothing but clay. We, too, may be engaged in the most
menial part of the Lord's work, but it is a great privilege to
do anything for our King; therefore, we will abide in our
calling, hoping that, although we *"have lien among the pots,*
yet shall [we] be as the wings of a dove covered with silver, and
her feathers with yellow gold" (Ps. 68:13). The text tells us of
those who *"dwelt among plants and hedges,"* having rough,
rustic hedging and ditching work to do. They may have
desired to live in the city, amid its life, society, and refine-
ment, but they kept their appointed places, for they were
doing the king's work. The place of our habitation is fixed,
and we are not to leave it out of whim and caprice, but seek
to serve the Lord in it, by being a blessing to those among
whom we reside. These potters and gardeners had royal
company, for *"they dwelt with the king."* Although they lived
among hedges and plants, they dwelt with the king there.
No lawful place or gracious occupation, however lowly, can
exclude us from communion with our divine Lord. In visit-
ing hovels, crowded rooming houses, workhouses, or jails,
we may go with the King. In all works of faith we may
count on Jesus' fellowship. It is when we are in His work
that we may depend on His smile. You unknown workers
who are occupied for your Lord amid the dirt and wretchedness of the lowest of the low, be of good cheer, for jewels
have been found on dunghills before now, earthen pots have
been filled with heavenly treasure, and bad weeds have been
transformed into precious flowers. Dwell with the King for
His work, and when He writes His chronicles, your name
will be recorded.

The kindness and love of God our Saviour.
—Titus 3:4

How sweet it is to behold the Savior communing with His own beloved people! There can be nothing more delightful than, by the divine Spirit, to be led into this fertile field of delight. Let the mind for an instant consider the history of the Redeemer's love, and a thousand enchanting acts of affection will suggest themselves—all of which have had for their design the weaving of the heart into Christ, and the intertwining of the thoughts and emotions of the renewed soul with the mind of Jesus. When we meditate on this amazing love and behold the all-glorious Kinsman of the church, endowing her with all His ancient wealth, our souls may well faint for joy. Who is he who can endure such a weight of love? That partial sense of it, which the Holy Spirit is sometimes pleased to afford, is more than the soul can contain; how transporting must be a complete view of it! When the soul will have understanding to discern all the Savior's gifts, wisdom wherewith to estimate them, and time in which to meditate on them, such as the world to come will afford us, we will then commune with Jesus in a nearer manner than at present. But who can imagine the sweetness of such fellowship? It must be one of the things that has not entered into the heart of man, but which God has prepared for those who love Him. Oh, to burst open the door of our Joseph's granaries and see the plenty that He has stored up for us! This will overwhelm us with love. By faith we see, as in *"a glass, darkly"* (1 Cor. 13:12), the reflected image of His unbounded treasures, but when we will actually see the heavenly things themselves, with our own eyes, how deep will be the stream of fellowship in which our soul will bathe itself! Until then, our loudest sonnets will be reserved for our loving Benefactor, Jesus Christ our Lord, whose love for us is wonderful, surpassing human love.

The LORD shut him in.
—Genesis 7:16

oah was shut in away from all the world by the hand of divine love. The door of election comes between us and the world in which the wicked one exists. We *are not of the world, even as* [Jesus was] *not of the world"* (John 17:14). Into the sin, the gaiety, the pursuits of the multitude we cannot enter; we cannot play in the streets of Vanity Fair with the children of darkness, for our heavenly Father has shut us in. Noah was shut in with his God. *"Come thou and all thy house into the ark"* (Gen. 7:1) was the Lord's invitation, by which He clearly showed that He Himself intended to dwell in the ark with His servant and his family. Thus all the chosen dwell in God and God in them. Happy people to be enclosed in the same circle that contains God in the Trinity of His persons: Father, Son, and Spirit. Let us never be inattentive to that gracious call, "Come, My people, enter into your chambers, and shut your doors about you, and hide yourself as it were for a little moment until the indignation is gone." Noah was so shut in that no evil could reach him. Floods did but lift him heavenward, and winds did but waft him on his way. Outside of the ark all was ruin, but inside all was rest and peace. Without Christ we perish, but in Christ Jesus there is perfect safety. Noah was so shut in that he could not even desire to come out, and those who are in Christ Jesus are in Him forever. They will go no more out forever, for eternal faithfulness has shut them in, and infernal malice cannot drag them out. The Prince of the house of David *"shutteth, and no man openeth"* (Rev. 3:7). When once in the last days, as Master of the house, He will rise up and shut the door, it will be in vain for mere professors of faith to knock, and cry "Lord, Lord open unto us," for that same door that shuts in the wise virgins will shut out the foolish forever. Lord, shut me in by Your grace.

Behold, I am vile.
—Job 40:4

ere is an encouraging word for you, poor lost sinner. You think you must not come to God because you are vile. Now, there is not a saint living on earth who has not been made to feel that he is vile. If Job, Isaiah, and Paul were all obliged to say they were vile, oh, poor sinner, will you be ashamed to join in the same confession? If divine grace does not eradicate all sin from the believer, how do you hope to do it yourself? And if God loves His people while they are yet vile, do you think your vileness will prevent His loving you? Believe on Jesus, you outcast of the world's society! Jesus calls you, and such as you are. "Not the righteous, not the righteous; sinners, Jesus came to call." Even now say, "You have died for sinners; I am a sinner, Lord Jesus. Sprinkle Your blood on me." If you will confess your sin, you will find pardon. If, now, with all your heart, you will say, "I am vile; wash me," you will be washed now. If the Holy Spirit will enable you from your heart to cry,

> Just as I am, without one plea
> But that Thy blood was shed for me,
> And that thou bidd'st me come to Thee,
> O Lamb of God, I come!

you will rise from reading this morning's portion with all your sins pardoned; and though you awoke this morning with every sin that man has ever committed on your head, you will rest tonight *"accepted in the beloved"* (Eph. 1:6). Though once degraded with the rags of sin, you will be adorned with a robe of righteousness and appear white as the angels are. For *"now,"* mark it, *"Now is the accepted time; behold, now is the day of salvation"* (2 Cor. 6:2). If you believe on Him who justifies the ungodly, you are saved. Oh, may the Holy Spirit give you saving faith in Him who receives the vilest.

Ye that love the LORD, hate evil.
—Psalm 97:10

Y ou have good reason to *"hate evil."* Consider what harm it has already brought you! Oh, what a world of mischief sin has brought into your heart! Sin blinded you so that you could not see the beauty of the Savior; it made you deaf so that you could not hear the Redeemer's tender invitations. Sin turned your feet into the way of death and poured poison into the very fountain of your being. It tainted your heart, and made it *"deceitful above all things, and desperately wicked"* (Jer. 17:9). Oh, what a creature you were when evil had done its utmost with you, before divine grace intervened! You were an heir of wrath even as others; you ran with the *"multitude to do evil"* (Exod. 23:2). Such were all of us; but Paul reminded us, *"Ye are washed, but ye are sanctified, but ye are justified in the name of the Lord Jesus, and by the Spirit of our God"* (1 Cor. 6:11). We have good reason, indeed, for hating evil when we look back and trace its deadly workings. Evil did such mischief to us that our souls would have been lost had not omnipotent love interfered to redeem us. Even now it is an active enemy, ever watching to do us harm and to drag us to perdition. Therefore *"hate evil,"* O Christians, unless you desire trouble. If you would strew your path with thorns and plant nettles on the pillow of your deathbed, then neglect to *"hate evil"*; but if you would live a happy life and die a peaceful death, then walk in all the ways of holiness, hating evil, even unto the end. If you truly love your Savior and would honor Him, then *"hate evil."* We know of no cure for the love of evil in a Christian like abundant communion with the Lord Jesus. Dwell with Him, and it will be impossible for you to be at peace with sin.

> Order my footsteps by Thy Word,
>   And make my heart sincere;
> Let sin have no dominion, Lord,
>   But keep my conscience clear.

There fell down many slain, because the war was of God.
—1 Chronicles 5:22

Warrior, fighting under the banner of the Lord Jesus, observe this verse with holy joy. If the war is of God, the victory is sure. The sons of Reuben, the Gadites, and the half tribe of Manasseh could barely muster forty-five thousand fighting men, yet in their war with the Hagarites, they killed a hundred thousand men, *"for they cried to God in the battle, and he was entreated of them; because they put their trust in him"* (1 Chron. 5:20). The Lord does not save by many or by few; it is ours to go forth in Jehovah's name if we are but a handful of men, for the Lord of Hosts is with us as our Captain. They did not neglect their weaponry; neither did they place their trust in it. We must use all appropriate means, but our confidence must rest in the Lord alone. He is the sword and the shield of His people. The great reason for their extraordinary success was that *"the war was of God."* In fighting sin without and within, with doctrinal or practical errors, with spiritual wickedness in high places or low places, with devils and the devil's allies, you are waging Jehovah's war. Unless He can be defeated, you do not need to fear defeat. Do not cower before superior numbers, shrink from difficulties or impossibilities, or flinch at wounds or death. Smite with the two-edged sword of the Spirit, and the slain will lie in heaps. *"The battle is the Lord's"* (1 Sam. 17:47), and He will deliver His enemies into our hands. With steadfast foot, strong hand, dauntless heart, and flaming zeal, rush to the conflict, and the hosts of evil will fly like chaff before the gale.

> Stand up! stand up for Jesus!
>   The strife will not be long;
> This day the noise of battle,
>   The next the victor's song:
> To him that overcometh,
>   A crown of life shall be;
> He with the King of Glory
>   Shall reign eternally.

The LORD hath done great things for us; whereof we are glad.
—Psalm 126:3

ome Christians are sadly prone to look on the dark side of everything and to dwell more on what they have gone through than on what God has done for them. Ask for their impression of the Christian life, and they will describe their continual conflicts, their deep afflictions, their sad adversities, and the sinfulness of their hearts, yet with scarcely any allusion to the mercy and help that God has granted to them. But a Christian whose soul is in a healthy state will come forward joyously and say, "I will speak, not about myself, but to the honor of my God. *'He brought me up also out of an horrible pit, out of the miry clay, and set my feet upon a rock, and established my goings. And he hath put a new song in my mouth, even praise unto our God'* (Ps. 40:2–3). *'The LORD hath done great things for* [me]; *whereof* [I am] *glad.'"* Such an abstract of experience as this is the very best that any child of God can present. It is true that we endure trials, but it is just as true that we are delivered out of them. It is true that we have our depravity, and mournfully do we know this, but it is quite as true that we have an all-sufficient Savior, who overcomes these corruptions and delivers us from their dominion. In looking back, it would be wrong to deny that we have been in the Slough of Despond and have crept along the Valley of Humiliation, but it would be equally wicked to forget that we have been through them safely and profitably; we have not remained in them, thanks to our almighty Helper and Leader, who has brought *"us out into a wealthy place"* (Ps. 66:12). The deeper our troubles, the louder our thanks to God, who has led us through all and preserved us until now. Our grief cannot mar the melody of our praise; we consider them to be the bass part of our lives' song, *"The LORD hath done great things for us; whereof we are glad."*

We live unto the Lord.
—Romans 14:8

If God had willed it, each of us might have entered heaven at the moment of conversion. It was not absolutely necessary for our preparation for immortality that we should tarry here. It is possible for a person to be taken to heaven and to be found ready to be a partaker of the inheritance of the saints in light, though he has but just believed in Jesus. It is true that our sanctification is a long, continual process, and we will not be perfected until we lay aside our bodies and enter within the veil; but nevertheless, had the Lord so willed it, He might have changed us from imperfection to perfection, and have taken us to heaven at once. Why, then, are we here? Would God keep His children out of paradise a single moment longer than was necessary? Why is the army of the living God still on the battlefield when one charge might give them the victory? Why are His children still wandering here and there through a maze, when a solitary word from His lips would bring them into the center of their hopes in heaven? The answer is—they are here that they may *"live unto the Lord,"* and may bring others to know His love. We remain on earth as sowers to scatter good seed; as ploughmen to break up the fallow ground; as heralds publishing salvation. We are here as the *"salt of the earth"* (Matt. 5:13), to be a blessing to the world. We are here to glorify Christ in our daily lives. We are here as workers for Him, and as *"workers together with him"* (2 Cor. 6:1). Let us see that our lives answer their end. Let us live earnest, useful, holy lives, *"to the praise of the glory of his grace"* (Eph. 1:6). Meanwhile, we long to be with Him and daily sing,

> My heart is with Him on His throne,
>   And ill can brook delay;
> Each moment listening for the voice,
>   "Rise up, and come away."

We love him, because he first loved us.
—1 John 4:19

There is no light in the planet but what proceeds from the sun; and there is no true love for Jesus in the heart but what comes from the Lord Jesus Himself. From this overflowing fountain of the infinite love of God, all our love for God must spring. This must ever be a great and certain truth: we love Him for no other reason than that He first loved us. Our love for Him is the fair offspring of His love for us. Cold admiration, when studying the works of God, anyone may have, but the warmth of love can be kindled in the heart only by God's Spirit. How great the wonder that such as we should ever have been brought to love Jesus at all! How marvelous that when we had rebelled against Him, He would, by a display of such amazing love, seek to draw us back. No, we never would have had a grain of love toward God unless it had been sown in us by the sweet seed of His love for us! Love, then, has for its parent the love of God shed abroad in the heart; but after it is thus divinely born, it must be divinely nourished. Love is an exotic plant. It is not one that will flourish naturally in human soil; it must be watered from above. Love for Jesus is a flower of a delicate nature, and if it received no nourishment but that which could be drawn from the rock of our hearts, it would soon wither. As love comes from heaven, so it must feed on heavenly bread. It cannot exist in the wilderness unless it is fed by manna from on high. Love must feed on love. The very soul and life of our love for God is His love for us.

> I love Thee, Lord, but with no love of mine,
>   For I have none to give;
> I love Thee, Lord; but all the love is Thine,
>   For by Thy love I live.
> I am as nothing, and rejoice to be
>   Emptied, and lost, and swallowed up in Thee.

Thou art weighed in the balances, and art found wanting.
—Daniel 5:27

t is well frequently to weigh ourselves in the scale of God's Word. You will find it a holy exercise to read some psalm of David, and, as you meditate on each verse, to ask yourself, "Can I say this? Have I felt as David felt? Has my heart ever been broken on account of sin, as his was when he penned his penitential psalms? Has my soul been full of true confidence in the hour of difficulty, as his was when he sang of God's mercies in the cave of Adullam or in the holds of Engedi? Do I take the cup of salvation and call on the name of the Lord?" Then turn to the life of Christ, and as you read, ask yourselves how far you are conformed to His likeness. Endeavor to discover whether you have the meekness, the humility, the lovely spirit that He constantly taught and displayed. Take, then, the epistles, and see whether you can go with the apostle in what he said of his experience. Have you ever cried out as he did—*"O wretched man that I am! who shall deliver me from the body of this death"*? (Rom. 7:24). Have you ever felt his self-abasement? Have you seemed to yourself the chief of sinners, and less than the least of all saints? Have you known anything of his devotion? Could you join with him and say, *"For to me to live is Christ, and to die is gain"* (Phil. 1:21)? If we thus read God's Word as a test of our spiritual condition, we will have good reason to stop many times and say, "Lord, I feel I have never yet been here. Oh, bring me here! Give me true penitence, such as this of which I read. Give me real faith; give me warmer zeal; inflame me with more fervent love; grant me the grace of meekness; make me more like Jesus. Let me no longer be *'found wanting'* when weighed in the balances of the sanctuary, lest I be *'found wanting'* in the scales of judgment." *"Judge not, that ye be not judged"* (Matt. 7:1).

Whosoever will, let him take the water of life freely.
—Revelation 22:17

esus says, *"Take...freely."* He wants no payment or preparation. He seeks no recommendation from our virtuous emotions. If you have no good feelings, if you are but willing, you are invited; therefore, come! If you have no belief and no repentance, come to Him, and He will give them to you. Come just as you are, and take *"freely,"* without money and without price. He gives Himself to needy ones. The drinking fountains at the corners of our streets are valuable fixtures, and we can hardly imagine anyone so foolish as to feel for his purse, when he stands before one of them, and to cry, "I cannot drink because I do not have five pounds in my pocket." However poor the man is, there is the fountain, and, just as he is, he may drink of it. Thirsty passengers, as they go by, whether they are dressed in finery or in rags, do not look for authorization to drink from the fountain; its being there is their permission for taking its water freely. The generosity of some good friends has put the refreshing crystal liquid there, and we take it and ask no questions. Perhaps the only persons who need go thirsty through the street where there is a drinking fountain are the fine ladies and gentlemen who are in their carriages. They are very thirsty, but they cannot think of being so vulgar as to get out to drink. It would demean them, they think, to drink at a common drinking fountain: so they ride by with parched lips. Oh, how many there are who are rich in their own good works and cannot therefore come to Christ! "I will not be saved," they say, "in the same way as the harlot or the swearer." What! go to heaven in the same way as a chimney sweep? Is there no pathway to glory but the path that led the thief there? I will not be saved that way. Such proud boasters must remain without the living water, but *"whosoever will, let him take the water of life freely."*

Delight thyself also in the LORD.
—Psalm 37:4

he teaching of these words must seem very surprising to those who are strangers to vital godliness, but to the sincere believer, it is only the communication of a recognized truth. The life of the believer is here described as a delight in God, and we are thus certified of the great fact that true faith overflows with happiness and joy. Ungodly persons and mere professors never look on faith as a joyful thing; to them it is service, duty, or necessity, but never pleasure or delight. If they attend to religion at all, it is either that they may gain thereby, or else because they dare not do otherwise. The thought of delight in religion is so strange to most men that no two words in their language stand further apart than *holiness* and *delight*. But believers who know Christ understand that delight and faith are so blessedly united that the gates of hell cannot prevail to separate them. They who love God with all their hearts find that His *"ways are ways of pleasantness, and all* [His] *paths are peace"* (Prov. 3:17). Such joys, such brimful delights, such overflowing blessedness do the saints discover in their Lord that so far from serving Him from custom, they would follow Him though all the world cast out His name as evil. We do not fear God because of any compulsion. Our faith is no fetter; our profession is no bondage. We are neither dragged to holiness, nor driven to duty. No, our piety is our pleasure, our hope is our happiness, and our duty is our delight. Delight and true religion are as allied as root and flower—as indivisible as truth and certainty. They are, in fact, two precious jewels glittering side by side in a setting of gold.

'Tis when we taste Thy love,
Our joys divinely grow,
Unspeakable like those above,
And heaven begins below.

And Sarah said, God hath made me to laugh,
so that all that hear will laugh with me.
—Genesis 21:6

It was far above the power of nature, and even contrary to its laws, that the aged Sarah should be honored with a son. Likewise, it is beyond all ordinary rules that I, a poor, helpless, undone sinner, should find grace to bear about in my soul the indwelling Spirit of the Lord Jesus. I, who once despaired, as well I might, for my nature was as dry, withered, barren, and accursed as a howling wilderness, even I have been made to bring forth fruit unto holiness. Well may my mouth be filled with joyous laughter, because of the singular, surprising grace that I have received from the Lord, for I have found Jesus, the promised Seed, and He is mine forever! This day will I lift up psalms of triumph unto the Lord who has remembered my low estate, for *"my heart rejoiceth in the LORD, mine horn is exalted in the LORD: my mouth is enlarged over mine enemies; because I rejoice in thy salvation"* (1 Sam. 2:1). I would have all those who hear of my great deliverance from hell, and my most blessed visitation from on high, laugh for joy with me. I would surprise my family with my abundant peace. I would delight my friends with my ever increasing happiness. I would edify the church with my grateful confessions, and even impress the world with the cheerfulness of my daily conversation. Bunyan tells us that Mercy laughed in her sleep, and no wonder when she dreamed of Jesus; my joy will not stop short of hers while my Beloved is the theme of my daily thoughts. The Lord Jesus is a deep sea of joy; my soul will dive therein, will be swallowed up in the delights of His society. Sarah looked on her Isaac and laughed with excessive rapture, and all her friends laughed with her; and you, my soul, look on your Jesus and bid heaven and earth unite in your unspeakable joy.

And I give unto them eternal life; and they shall never perish.
—John 10:28

he Christian should never think or speak lightly of unbelief. For a child of God to mistrust His love, His truth, His faithfulness, must be greatly displeasing to Him. How can we ever grieve Him by doubting His upholding grace? Christian, it is contrary to every promise of God's precious Word that you should ever be forgotten or left to perish. If it could be so, how could He be true who has said, *"Can a woman forget her sucking child, that she should not have compassion on the son of her womb? yea, they may forget, yet will I not forget thee"* (Isa. 49:15). Of what value would be the promise—*"The mountains shall depart, and the hills be removed; but my kindness shall not depart from thee, neither shall the covenant of my peace be removed, saith the* LORD *that hath mercy on thee"* (Isa. 54:10)? Where would the truth be in Christ's words—*"I give unto* [*"my sheep,"* John 10:27] *eternal life; and they shall never perish, neither shall any man pluck them out of my hand. My Father, which gave them me, is greater than all; and no man is able to pluck them out of my Father's hand"* (John 10:28–29). Where would the doctrines of grace be? They would be all disproved if one child of God would perish. Where would the veracity of God, His honor, His power, His grace, His covenant, His oath be, if any of those for whom Christ has died, and who have put their trust in Him, would nevertheless be cast away? Banish those unbelieving fears that so dishonor God. Arise, shake yourself from the dust, and put on your beautiful garments. Remember that it is sinful to doubt His Word wherein He has promised you that you will never perish. Let the eternal life within you express itself in confident rejoicing.

> The Gospel bears my spirit up:
>   A faithful and unchanging God
> Lays the foundation for my hope,
>   In oaths, and promises, and blood.

Help, LORD.
—Psalm 12:1

he prayer itself is remarkable, for it is short, but seasonable, concise, and suggestive. David mourned the scarcity of faithful men, and therefore lifted up his heart in supplication. When the creature failed, he flew to the Creator. He evidently felt his own weakness, or he would not have cried for help. At the same time, he intended honestly to exert himself for the cause of truth, for the word *"help"* is inapplicable where we ourselves do nothing. There is much directness, clearness of perception, and distinctness of utterance in this petition of two words—much more, indeed, than in the long rambling outpourings of certain professors. The psalmist runs directly to his God, with a well-considered prayer; he knows what he is seeking and where to seek it. Lord, teach us to pray in the same blessed manner. The occasions for the use of this prayer are frequent. In providential afflictions how suitable it is for tried believers who find all helpers failing them. Students, in doctrinal difficulties, may often obtain aid by lifting up this cry of *"Help, LORD,"* to the Holy Spirit, the great Teacher. Spiritual warriors in inward conflicts may send to the throne for reinforcements, and this will be a model for their request. Workers in heavenly labor may thus obtain grace in time of need. Seeking sinners, in doubts and alarms, may offer up the same weighty supplication; in fact, in all these cases, times, and places, this will serve the turn of needy souls. *"Help, LORD,"* will suit us living and dying, suffering or laboring, rejoicing or sorrowing. In Him our help is found. Let us not be slack to cry to Him. The answer to the prayer is certain, if it is sincerely offered through Jesus. The Lord's character assures us that He will not leave His people. His relationship as Father and Husband guarantees us His aid. His gift of Jesus is a pledge of every good thing, and His sure promise stands, *"Fear not; I will help thee"* (Isa. 41:13).

Thy Redeemer.
—Isaiah 54:5

Jesus, the Redeemer, is altogether ours and ours forever. All the offices of Christ are held on our behalf. He is King for us, Priest for us, and Prophet for us. Whenever we read a new title of the Redeemer, let us appropriate Him as ours under that name as much as under any other. The shepherd's staff, the father's rod, the captain's sword, the priest's miter, the prince's scepter, the prophet's mantle—all are ours. Jesus has no dignity that He will not employ for our exaltation and no prerogative that He will not exercise for our defense. His fullness of Godhead is our unfailing, inexhaustible treasure-house. His manhood also, which He took on Him for us, is ours in all its perfection. To us our gracious Lord communicates the spotless virtue of a stainless character; to us He gives the meritorious efficacy of a devoted life; on us He bestows the reward procured by obedient submission and incessant service. He makes the unsullied garment of His life our covering beauty, the glittering virtues of His character our ornaments and jewels, and the superhuman meekness of His death our boast and glory. He bequeaths us His manger, from which to learn how God came down to man, and His Cross to teach us how man may go up to God. All His thoughts, emotions, actions, utterances, miracles, and intercessions were for us. He trod the road of sorrow on our behalf and has made over to us as His heavenly legacy the full results of all the labors of His life. He is now as much ours as heretofore; and He does not blush to acknowledge Himself our Lord Jesus Christ, though He is the blessed and only Potentate, the King of Kings, and Lord of Lords. Christ everywhere and every way is our Christ, forever and ever most richly to enjoy. O my soul, by the power of the Holy Spirit, call Him this morning, *"thy Redeemer."*

And they were all filled with the Holy Ghost.
—Acts 2:4

he blessings of this day would be rich if all of us were *"filled with the Holy Ghost."* The consequences of this sacred filling of the soul would be impossible to overestimate. Life, comfort, light, purity, power, peace, and many other precious blessings are inseparable from the Spirit's benign presence. As sacred oil, He anoints the head of the believer, sets him apart to the priesthood of saints, and gives him grace to execute his office aright. As the only truly purifying water, He cleanses us from the power of sin and sanctifies us unto holiness, working in us *"to will and to do of his good pleasure"* (Phil. 2:13). As light, He manifested to us at first our lost estate, and now He reveals the Lord Jesus to us and in us and guides us in the way of righteousness. Enlightened by His pure celestial ray, we are no more darkness but light in the Lord. As fire, He both purges us from dross and sets our consecrated nature on a blaze. He is the sacrificial flame by which we are enabled to offer our whole souls as a *"living sacrifice"* (Rom. 12:1) unto God. As heavenly dew, He removes our barrenness and fertilizes our lives. Oh, that He would drop from above upon us at this early hour! Such morning dew would be a sweet beginning to the day. As the Dove, with wings of peaceful love, He broods over His church and over the souls of believers; and as the Comforter, He dispels the cares and doubts that mar the peace of His beloved. He descends on the chosen as on the Lord in Jordan, and bears witness to their sonship by working in them a filial spirit by which they cry, *"Abba, Father"* (Gal. 4:6). As the wind, He brings the breath of life to men; blowing where He pleases, He performs the quickening operations by which the spiritual creation is animated and sustained. Would to God that we might feel His presence this day and every day.

*For, lo, I will command, and I will sift the house of Israel
among all nations, like as corn is sifted in a sieve, yet shall
not the least grain fall upon the earth.*
—Amos 9:9

very sifting comes by divine command and permission. Satan must ask permission before he can lay a finger on Job. Furthermore, in some sense, our siftings are directly the work of heaven, for the text says, *"I will sift the house of Israel."* Satan, like a drudge, may hold the sieve, hoping to destroy the corn; but the overruling hand of the Master is accomplishing the purity of the grain by the very process that the enemy intended to be destructive. Precious, but much sifted, corn of the Lord's floor, be comforted by the blessed fact that the Lord directs both flail and sieve to His own glory, and to your eternal profit. The Lord Jesus will surely use the fan that is in His hand and will divide the precious from the vile. All are not Israel who are of Israel. The heap on the barn floor is not clean food; hence, the winnowing process must be performed. In the sieve true weight alone has power. Husks and chaff, being devoid of substance, must fly before the wind, and only solid corn will remain. Observe the complete safety of the Lord's wheat; even the least grain has a promise of preservation. God Himself sifts, and therefore it is stern and terrible work. He sifts them in all places, *"among all nations"*; He sifts them in the most effective manner, *"like as corn is sifted in a sieve"*; and yet for all this, not the smallest, lightest, or most shriveled grain is permitted to fall to the ground. Every individual believer is precious in the sight of the Lord. A shepherd would not lose one sheep or a jeweler one diamond or a mother one child or a man one limb of his body. Neither will the Lord lose one of His redeemed people. However little we may be, if we are the Lord's, we may rejoice that we are *"preserved in Jesus Christ"* (Jude 1).

Thou art fairer than the children of men.
—Psalm 45:2

he entire person of Jesus is but as one gem, and His life is all along but one impression of the seal. He is altogether complete; not only in His several parts, but as a gracious, all-glorious whole. His character is not a mass of fair colors mixed confusedly, nor a heap of precious stones laid carelessly one upon another. He is a picture of beauty and a breastplate of glory. In Him, all the things of good repute are in their proper places and assist in adorning each other. Not one feature in His glorious person attracts attention at the expense of others, but He is perfectly and altogether lovely. Oh, Jesus! Your power, Your grace, Your justice, Your tenderness, Your truth, Your majesty, and Your immutability make up such a man, or rather such a God-man, as neither heaven nor earth has seen elsewhere. Your infancy, Your eternity, Your sufferings, Your triumphs, Your death, and Your immortality are all woven in one gorgeous tapestry, without seam or rent. You are music without discord. You are many, and yet not divided. You are all things, and yet not diverse. As all the colors blend into one resplendent rainbow, so all the glories of heaven and earth meet in You and unite so wondrously that there is none like You in all things; if all the virtues of the most excellent were bound in one bundle, they could not rival You, mirror of all perfection. You have been anointed with the holy oil of myrrh and cassia, which Your God has reserved for You alone. As for Your fragrance, it is as the holy perfume, the like of which none other can ever mingle, even with the art of the apothecary; each spice is fragrant, but the compound is divine.

> Oh, sacred symmetry! Oh, rare connection
> Of many perfects, to make one perfection!
> Oh, heavenly music, where all parts do meet
> In one sweet strain, to make one perfect sweet!

He shall build the temple of the LORD; and he shall bear the glory.
—Zechariah 6:13

hrist Himself is the builder of His spiritual temple, and He has built it on the mountains of His unchangeable affection, His omnipotent grace, and His infallible truthfulness. But as it was in Solomon's temple, so in this; the materials need to be made ready. There are the cedars of Lebanon, but they are not framed for the building. They are not cut down, shaped, and made into those cedar planks, whose odorous beauty will *"make glad"* (Ps. 46:4) the courts of the Lord's house in paradise. There are also the rough stones still in the quarry; they must be hewn from that place and squared. All this is Christ's own work. Each individual believer is being prepared, polished, and made ready for his place in the temple; but Christ's own hand performs the preparatory work. Afflictions cannot sanctify, excepting as they are used by Him to this end. Our prayers and efforts cannot make us ready for heaven, apart from the hand of Jesus, who fashions our hearts aright. As in the building of Solomon's temple, *"there was neither hammer nor ax nor any tool of iron heard in the house"* (1 Kings 6:7), because all was brought perfectly ready for the exact spot it was to occupy. So it is with the temple that Jesus builds; the making ready is all done on earth. When we reach heaven, there will be no sanctifying us there, no squaring us with affliction, no planing us with suffering. No, we must be made ready here. Christ will do all that beforehand. And when He has done it, we will be ferried by a loving hand across the stream of death and brought to the heavenly Jerusalem, to abide as eternal pillars in the temple of our Lord.

> Beneath His eye and care,
>   The edifice shall rise,
> Majestic, strong, and fair,
>   And shine above the skies.

Ephraim is a cake not turned.
—Hosea 7:8

A cake not turned is uncooked on one side; and so Ephraim was, in many respects, untouched by divine grace. Although there was some partial obedience, there was much rebellion left. My soul, I charge you, see whether this is your case. Are you thorough in the things of God? Has grace gone through the very center of your being so as to be felt in its divine operations in all your powers, actions, words, and thoughts? To be sanctified, spirit, soul, and body, should be your aim and prayer; and although sanctification may not be perfect in you anywhere in degree, yet it must be universal in its action; there must not be the appearance of holiness in one place and reigning sin in another; otherwise, you, too, will be a cake not turned. A cake not turned is soon burned on the side nearest the fire, and although no man can have too much religion, there are some who seem burned black with bigoted zeal for that part of truth that they have received, or are charred to a cinder with a boastful Pharisaic ostentation of those religious performances that suit their character. The assumed appearance of superior sanctity frequently accompanies a total absence of all vital godliness. The saint in public is a devil in private. He deals in flour by day and in soot by night. The cake that is burned on one side is dough on the other. If it is so with me, O Lord, turn me! Turn my unsanctified nature to the fire of Your love, and let it feel the sacred glow. Let my burned side cool a little, while I learn my own weakness and lack of heat when I am removed from Your heavenly flame. Let me not be found to be a double-minded person, but one entirely under the powerful influence of reigning grace; for well I know if I am left like a cake unturned, and am not on both sides the subject of Your grace, I must be consumed forever amid *"everlasting burnings"* (Isa. 33:14).

*A certain woman of the company lifted up her voice, and said
unto him, Blessed is the womb that bare thee, and the paps which
thou hast sucked. But He said, Yea rather, blessed are they
that hear the word of God, and keep it.*
—Luke 11:27–28

It is fondly imagined by some that it must have involved very special privileges to have been the mother of our Lord, because they supposed that she had the benefit of looking into His very heart in a way in which we cannot hope to do. There may be an appearance of plausibility in the supposition, but not much. We do not know that Mary knew more than others. What she did know she did well to lay up in her heart, but she does not appear from anything we read in the Gospels to have been a better instructed believer than any other of Christ's disciples. All that she knew we also may discover. Do you wonder that we should say so? Here is a text to prove it: *"The secret of the Lord is with them that fear him; and he will show them his covenant"* (Ps. 25:14). Remember the Master's words, *"Henceforth I call you not servants; for the servant knoweth not what his lord doeth: but I have called you friends; for all things that I have heard of my Father I have made known unto you"* (John 15:15). So blessedly does this divine Revealer of secrets tell us His heart that He keeps back nothing that is profitable to us. His own assurance is, *"If it were not so, I would have told you"* (John 14:2). Does He not this day manifest Himself unto us as He does not unto the world? It is even so; therefore, we will not ignorantly cry out, *"Blessed is the womb that bare thee,"* but we will intelligently bless God that, having heard the Word and kept it, we have first of all as true a communion with the Savior as the Virgin had, and in the second place as true an acquaintance with the secrets of His heart as she can be supposed to have obtained. Happy soul to be thus privileged!

Get thee up into the high mountain.
—Isaiah 40:9

Our knowledge of Christ is somewhat like climbing one of our Welsh mountains. When you are at the base you see but little: the mountain itself appears to be but one-half as high as it really is. Confined in a little valley, you discover scarcely anything but the rippling brooks as they descend into the stream at the foot of the mountain. Climb the first rising knoll, and the valley lengthens and widens beneath your feet. Go higher, and you see the country for four or five miles round, and you are delighted with the widening prospect. Climb higher still, and the scene enlarges, until at last, when you are on the summit, and look east, west, north, and south, you see almost all of England lying before you. Yonder is a forest in some distant county, perhaps two hundred miles away, and here the sea, and there a shining river and the smoking chimneys of a manufacturing town, or the masts of the ships in a busy port. All these things please and delight you, and you say, "I could not have imagined that so much could be seen at this elevation." Now, the Christian life is of the same order. When we first believe in Christ we see but little of Him. The higher we climb, the more we discover of His beauties. But who has ever gained the summit? Who has known all the heights and depths of the *"love of Christ, which passeth knowledge"* (Eph. 3:19)? Paul, when grown old, sitting gray-haired, shivering in a dungeon in Rome, could say with greater emphasis than we can, *"I know whom I have believed"* (2 Tim. 1:12), for each experience had been like the climbing of a hill, each trial had been like ascending another summit, and his death seemed like gaining the top of the mountain, from which he could see the whole of the faithfulness and the love of Him to whom he had committed his soul. Get up, dear friend, into the high mountain.

Art thou also become like unto us?
—Isaiah 14:10

hat must be the apostate's doom when his naked soul appears before God? How will he bear that voice, "Depart, you cursed; you have rejected Me, and I reject you. You have played the harlot and departed from Me. I also have banished you forever from My presence, and I will not have mercy on you." What will be this wretch's shame at the Last Great Day when, before assembled multitudes, the apostate will be unmasked? See the profane, and sinners who never professed religion, lifting themselves up from their beds of fire to point at him. "There he is," says one. "Will he preach the Gospel in hell?" "There he is," says another. "He rebuked me for cursing and was a hypocrite himself!" "Aha!" says another. "Here comes a psalm-singing Methodist—one who was always at his meetings; he is the man who boasted of his being sure of everlasting life, and here he is!" No greater eagerness will ever be seen among satanic tormentors than in that Day when devils drag the hypocrite's soul down to perdition. Bunyan pictured this with massive but awful grandeur of poetry when he spoke of the back way to hell. Seven devils bound the wretch with nine cords and dragged him from the road to heaven, in which he had professed to walk, and thrust him through the back door into hell. Mind that back way to hell, false professors of faith! *"Examine yourselves, whether ye be in the faith"* (2 Cor. 13:5). Look well to your state; see whether you are in Christ or not. It is the easiest thing in the world to give a lenient verdict when oneself is to be tried; but oh, be just and true here. Be just to all, but be rigorous with yourself. Remember, if it is not a rock on which you build, when the house will fall, great will be *"the fall of it"* (Matt. 7:27). May the Lord give you sincerity, constancy, and firmness; and in no day, however evil, may you be led to turn aside.

Only ye shall not go very far away.
—Exodus 8:28

This is a crafty word from the lips of the arch tyrant Pharaoh. If the poor, enslaved Israelites needed to go out of Egypt, then he bargained with them that it should not be very far away—not too far for them to escape the terror of his arms and the observation of his spies. After the same fashion, the world does not love the lack of conformity of nonconformists or the dissidence of dissenters. It would have us be more charitable and not carry matters with too severe a hand. Death to the world and burial with Christ are experiences that carnal minds treat with ridicule; therefore, the law that sets them forth is almost universally neglected, and even condemned. Worldly wisdom recommends the path of compromise and talks of "moderation." According to this carnal policy, purity is admitted to be very desirable, but we are warned against being too precise; truth is, of course, to be followed, but error is not to be severely denounced. "Yes," says the world, "be spiritually minded by all means, but do not deny yourself a little frivolous society, an occasional ball, and a Christmas visit to a theater. What's the good of crying down a thing when it is so fashionable, and everybody does it?" Multitudes of professors yield to this cunning advice, to their own eternal ruin. If we would follow the Lord wholly, we must go right away into the wilderness of separation and leave the Egypt of the carnal world behind us. We must leave its maxims, its pleasures, and its religion, too, and go far away to the place where the Lord calls His sanctified ones. When the town is on fire, our house cannot be too far from the flames. When the plague is abroad, a man cannot be too far from its haunts. The further from a viper the better, and the further from worldly conformity the better. To all true believers let the trumpet call be sounded, *"Come out from among them, and be ye separate"* (2 Cor. 6:17).

Looking unto Jesus.
—Hebrews 12:2

It is always the Holy Spirit's work to turn our eyes away from self to Jesus; but Satan's work is just the opposite of this, for he is constantly trying to make us pay attention to ourselves instead of to Christ. He insinuates, "Your sins are too great for pardon; you have no faith. You do not repent enough. You will never be able to continue to the end. You do not have the joy of His children. You have such a weak hold of Jesus." All these are thoughts about self, and we will never find comfort or assurance by looking within. But the Holy Spirit turns our eyes entirely away from self. He tells us that we are nothing, but that "Christ is all in all." Remember, therefore, that it is not your hold of Christ that saves you; it is Christ. It is not your joy in Christ that saves you; it is Christ. It is not even your faith in Christ, though that is the instrument, but it is Christ's blood and His merits that save you; therefore, do not look as much to your hand, with which you are grasping Christ, as to Christ. Do not look to your hope, but to Jesus, the Source of your hope. Do not look to your faith, but to *"Jesus, the author and finisher of* [your] *faith"* (Heb. 12:2). We will never find happiness by looking at our prayers, our actions, or our feelings. It is what Jesus is, not what we are, that gives rest to the soul. If we would at once overcome Satan and have peace with God, it must be by *"looking unto Jesus."* Keep your eyes simply on Him. Let His death, His sufferings, His merits, His glories, and His intercession be fresh on your mind. When you wake in the morning, look to Him. When you lie down at night, look to Him. Oh, do not let your hopes or fears come between you and Jesus. Follow hard after Him, and He will never fail you.

> My hope is built on nothing less
>   Than Jesus' blood and righteousness:
> I dare not trust the sweetest frame,
>   But wholly lean on Jesus' name.

Them also which sleep in Jesus will God bring with him.
—1 Thessalonians 4:14

Let us not imagine that the soul sleeps anesthetized. *"To day shalt thou be with me in paradise"* (Luke 23:43) is the whisper of Christ to every dying saint. They *"sleep in Jesus,"* but their souls are before the throne of God, praising Him day and night in His temple, singing hallelujahs to Him who washed them from their sins in His blood. The body sleeps in its lonely bed of earth, beneath the coverlet of grass. But what is this sleep? The idea connected with sleep is "rest," and that is the thought that the Spirit of God would convey to us. Sleep makes each night a Sabbath for the day. Sleep shuts fast the door of the soul and bids all intruders tarry for a while, so that the life within may enter its summer garden of ease. The toilworn believer quietly sleeps, as does the weary child when he slumbers on his mother's breast. Oh, happy are those who *"die in the Lord...: they...rest from their labours; and their works do follow them"* (Rev. 14:13). Their quiet repose will never be broken until God rouses them to give them their full reward. Guarded by angel watchers, curtained by eternal mysteries, they sleep on, the inheritors of glory, until the fullness of time will bring the fullness of redemption. What an awaking will be theirs! They were laid in their last resting place, weary and worn, but as such they will not rise. They went to their rest with furrowed brows and the wasted features, but they wake up in beauty and glory. The shriveled seed, so destitute of form and comeliness, rises from the dust a beauteous flower. The winter of the grave gives way to the spring of redemption and the summer of glory. Blessed is death, since it, through the divine power, disrobes us of this workday garment, to clothe us with the wedding garment of incorruption. Blessed are those who *"sleep in Jesus."*

And the glory which thou gavest me I have given them.
—John 17:22

Behold the superlative liberality of the Lord Jesus, for He has given us His all. Although a tithe of His possessions would have made a universe of angels rich beyond all thought, yet He was not content until He had given us all that He had. It would have been surprising grace if He had allowed us to eat the crumbs of His bounty beneath the table of His mercy. But He will do nothing by halves; He makes us sit with Him and share the feast. Had He given us some small pension from His royal coffers, we would have had cause to love Him eternally; but no, He will have His bride as rich as Himself, and He will not have a glory or a grace in which she will not share. He has not been content with less than making us joint heirs with Himself, so that we might have equal possessions. He has emptied all His estate into the coffers of the church and has all things in common with His redeemed. There is not one room in His house the key of which He will withhold from His people. He gives them full liberty to take all that He has to be their own; He loves them to help themselves freely to His treasure and appropriate as much as they can possibly carry. The boundless fullness of His all-sufficiency is as free to the believer as the air he breathes. Christ has put the flagon of His love and grace to the believer's lip and has invited him to drink on forever. Could he drain it, he is welcome to do so; but since he cannot exhaust it, he is bidden to drink abundantly, for it is all his own. What truer proof of fellowship can heaven or earth afford?

When I stand before the throne
    Dressed in beauty not my own;
When I see Thee as Thou art,
    Love Thee with unsinning heart;
Then, Lord, shall I fully know—
    Not till then—how much I owe.

In summer and in winter shall it be.
—Zechariah 14:8

The streams of living water that flow from Jerusalem are not dried up by the parching heat of sultry midsummer any more than they were frozen by the cold winds of blustering winter. Rejoice, O my soul, that you are spared to testify of the faithfulness of the Lord. The seasons change and you change, but your Lord abides evermore the same, and the streams of His love are as deep, as broad, and as full as ever. The pressures of business cares and scorching trials make me need the cooling influences of the river of His grace. I may go at once and drink to the full from the inexhaustible fountain, for in summer and in winter it pours forth its flood. The upper springs are never scanty, and, blessed be the name of the Lord, the lower springs cannot fail either. Elijah found Cherith dried up, but Jehovah was still the same God of providence. Job said his brethren were like deceitful brooks, but he found his God an overflowing river of consolation. The Nile is the great confidence of Egypt, but its floods are variable; our Lord is evermore the same. By turning the course of the Euphrates, Cyrus took the city of Babylon, but no power, human or infernal, can divert the current of divine grace. The tracks of ancient rivers have been found all dry and desolate, but the streams that take their rise on the mountains of divine sovereignty and infinite love will ever be full to the brim. Generations melt away, but the course of grace is unaltered. The river of God may sing with greater truth than the brook in the poem,

> Men may come, and men may go,
> But I go on forever.

How happy are you, my soul, to be led beside such still waters! Never wander to other streams, lest you hear the Lord's rebuke, "Why go to Egypt to drink from the muddy river?" (See Jeremiah 2:18.)

Our heart shall rejoice in him.
—Psalm 33:21

Blessed is the fact that Christians can rejoice even in the deepest distress. Although trouble may surround them, they still sing; and, like many birds, they sing best in their cages. The waves may roll over them, but their souls soon rise to the surface and see the light of God's countenance. They have a buoyancy about them that keeps their heads always above the water and helps them to sing amid the tempest, "God is with me still." To whom will the glory be given? Oh, to Jesus—it is all by Jesus. Trouble does not necessarily bring consolation with it to the believer, but the presence of the Son of God in the fiery furnace with him fills his heart with joy. He is sick and suffering, but Jesus visits him and makes his bed for him. He is dying, and the cold chilly waters of Jordan are gathering about him up to the neck, but Jesus puts His arms around him and cries, "Fear not, beloved; to die is to be blessed; the waters of death have their source in heaven. They are not bitter; they are sweet as nectar, for they flow from the throne of God." As the departing saint wades through the stream, and the billows gather around him, and heart and flesh fail him, the same voice sounds in his ears, *"Fear thou not; for I am with thee: be not dismayed; for I am thy God"* (Isa. 41:10). As he nears the borders of the infinite unknown and is almost too afraid to enter the realm of shadows, Jesus says, *"Fear not, little flock; for it is your Father's good pleasure to give you the kingdom"* (Luke 12:32). Thus strengthened and consoled, the believer is not afraid to die. He is even willing to depart, for since he has seen Jesus as the Morning Star, he longs to gaze on Him as the sun in its strength. Truly, the presence of Jesus is all the heaven we desire. He is at once "the glory of our brightest days; the comfort of our nights."

*The ill favoured and leanfleshed kine did eat up
the seven well favoured and fat kine.*
—Genesis 41:4

haraoh's dream has too often been my waking experience. My days of sloth have ruinously destroyed all that I had achieved in times of zealous industry. My seasons of coldness have frozen all the genial glow of my periods of fervency and enthusiasm, and my fits of worldliness have thrown me back from my advances in the divine life. I need to beware of lean prayers, lean praises, lean duties, and lean experiences, for these will eat up the fat of my comfort and peace. If I neglect prayer for ever so short a time, I lose all the spirituality to which I had attained. If I draw no fresh supplies from heaven, the old corn in my granary is soon consumed by the famine that rages in my soul. When the caterpillars of indifference, the cankerworms of worldliness, and the palmerworms of self-indulgence lay my heart completely desolate and make my soul to languish, all my former fruitfulness and growth in grace avails me nothing at all. How anxious should I be to have no lean-fleshed days, no ill-favored hours! If every day I journeyed toward the goal of my desires, I would soon reach it, but backsliding leaves me still far off from the prize of my high calling and robs me of the advances that I had so laboriously made. The only way in which all my days can be like the *"fat kine"* is to feed them in the right meadow, to spend them with the Lord, in His service, in His company, in His fear, and in His way. Why should not every year be richer than the past, in love, usefulness, and joy? I am nearer the celestial hills; I have had more experience of my Lord and should be more like Him. O Lord, keep the curse of leanness of soul far from me. Do not let me have to cry, *"My leanness, my leanness, woe unto me!"* (Isa. 24:16), but may I be well-fed and nourished in Your house, so that I may praise Your name.

Sanctify them through thy truth.
—John 17:17

anctification begins in regeneration. The Spirit of God infuses into man that new living principle by which he becomes *"a new creature"* (2 Cor. 5:17) in Christ Jesus. This work, which begins in the new birth, is carried on in two ways: through mortification, whereby the lusts of the flesh are subdued and kept under; and through vivification, by which the life that God has put within us is made to be a *"well of water springing up into everlasting life"* (John 4:14). This is carried on every day in what is called *perseverance,* by which the Christian is preserved and continued in a gracious state and is made to *"abound to every good work"* (2 Cor. 9:8) unto the praise and glory of God; and it culminates or comes to perfection in glory, when the soul, being thoroughly purged, is caught up to dwell with holy beings at the right hand of the Majesty on high. But while the Spirit of God is thus the Author of sanctification, yet there is a visible agency employed that must not be forgotten. Jesus said, *"Sanctify them through thy truth: thy word is truth"* (John 17:17). The passages of Scripture that prove that the instrument of our sanctification is the Word of God are many. The Spirit of God brings to our minds the precepts and doctrines of truth and applies them with power. These are heard in the ear, and being received in the heart, they work in us *"both to will and to do of* [God's] *good pleasure"* (Phil. 2:13). The truth is the sanctifier, and if we do not hear or read the truth, we will not grow in sanctification. We only progress in sound living as we progress in sound understanding. *"Thy word is a lamp unto my feet, and a light unto my path"* (Ps. 119:105). Do not say of any error, "It is a mere matter of opinion." No man indulges an error of judgment without sooner or later tolerating an error in practice. Hold fast the truth, for by so holding the truth, you will be sanctified by the Spirit of God.

Called to be saints.
—Romans 1:7

We are very apt to regard the apostolic saints as if they were saints in a more special manner than the other children of God. All are saints whom God has called by His grace and sanctified by His Spirit; but we are apt to look on the apostles as extraordinary beings, scarcely subject to the same weaknesses and temptations as ourselves. Yet in so doing we are forgetful of this truth, that the nearer a man lives to God the more intensely has he to mourn over his own evil heart; and the more his Master honors him in His service, the more also does the evil of the flesh vex and tease him day by day. The fact is, if we had seen the apostle Paul, we would have thought him remarkably like the rest of the chosen family. And if we had talked with him, we would have said, "We find that his experience and ours are much the same. He is more faithful, more holy, and more deeply taught than we are, but he has the selfsame trials to endure. In some respects, he is more sorely tried than we." Do not, then, look on the ancient saints as being exempt either from infirmities or sins, and do not regard them with that mystic reverence that will almost make us idolaters. Their holiness is attainable even by us. We are *"called to be saints"* by that same voice that constrained them to their high vocation. It is a Christian's duty to force his way into the inner circle of sainthood. And if these saints were superior to us in their attainments, as they certainly were, let us follow them; let us emulate their ardor and holiness. We have the same light that they had; the same grace is accessible to us. Why should we, then, rest satisfied until we have equaled them in heavenly character? They lived with Jesus, and they lived for Jesus; therefore, they grew to be like Jesus. Let us live by the same Spirit as they did, *"looking unto Jesus"* (Heb. 12:2), and our sainthood will soon be apparent.

*Whoso hearkeneth unto me shall dwell safely,
and shall be quiet from fear of evil.*
—Proverbs 1:33

Divine love is rendered conspicuous when it shines in the midst of judgments. Fair is that lone star that smiles through the rifts of the thunderclouds. Bright is the oasis that blooms in the wilderness of sand. So fair and so bright is love in the midst of wrath. When the Israelites provoked the Most High by their continued idolatry, He punished them by withholding both dew and rain, so that their land was visited by a sore famine. But while He did this, He took care that His own chosen ones would be secure. If all other brooks are dry, yet will there be one reserved for Elijah; and when that fails, God will still preserve for him a place of sustenance. No, not only for one, because the Lord did not have simply one "Elijah," but He had a remnant according to the election of grace, who were hidden by fifties in a cave; and though the whole land was subject to famine, yet these fifties in the cave were fed, and fed from Ahab's table, too, by His faithful, God-fearing steward, Obadiah. Let us from this draw the inference: come what may, God's people are safe. Let convulsions shake the solid earth, let the skies themselves be rent in twain, yet amid the wreck of worlds, the believer will be as secure as in the calmest hour of rest. If God cannot save His people under heaven, He will save them in heaven. If the world becomes too hot to hold them, then, heaven will be the place of their reception and their safety. Be confident, then, when you *"hear of wars and rumours of wars"* (Matt. 24:6). Let no agitation distress you, but be quiet from fear of evil. Whatever comes on the earth, you, beneath the broad wings of Jehovah, will be secure. Abide on His promises, and rest in His faithfulness. Bid defiance to the blackest future, for there is nothing in it direful for you. Your sole concern should be to show forth to the world the blessedness of listening to the voice of wisdom.

Brethren, pray for us.
—1 Thessalonians 5:25

We reserved this one morning in the year to refresh the reader's memory on the subject of prayer for ministers, and we most earnestly implore every Christian household to grant the fervent request of the text first uttered by an apostle and now repeated by us. Brethren, our work is solemnly momentous, involving well-being or woe to thousands. We deal with souls for God on eternal business, and our word is either the aroma of life to life, or of death to death. A very heavy responsibility rests on us, and it will be no small mercy if at the last we are found clear of the blood of all men. As officers in Christ's army, we are the special target of the hatred of men and devils; they watch for our halting and labor to take us by the heels. Our sacred calling involves us in temptations from which you are exempt. Above all it too often draws us away from our personal enjoyment of truth into a ministerial and official consideration of it. We meet with many knotty cases, and our wits are confounded. We observe very sad backslidings, and our hearts are wounded; we see millions perishing, and our spirits sink. We wish to benefit you by our preaching. We desire to be a blessing to your children. We long to be useful both to saints and sinners; therefore, dear friends, intercede for us with our God. Miserable men are we if we miss the aid of your prayers, but happy are we if we live in your supplications. You do not look to us but to our Master for spiritual blessings, and yet how many times has He given those blessings through His ministers. Ask, then, again and again, that we may be the earthen vessels into which the Lord may put the treasure of the Gospel. We, the whole company of missionaries, ministers, city missionaries, and students, do in the name of Jesus beseech you, *"Brethren, pray for us."*

Tell me, I pray thee, wherein thy great strength lieth.
—Judges 16:6

Where lies the secret strength of faith? It lies in the food it feeds on; for faith studies what the promise is—an emanation of divine grace, an overflowing of the great heart of God. And faith says, "My God could not have given this promise, except from love and grace; therefore, it is quite certain His Word will be fulfilled." Then faith thinks, "Who gave this promise?" It considers not so much its greatness, as, "Who is the author of it?" Faith remembers that it is God who cannot lie—God omnipotent, God immutable; and therefore concludes that the promise must be fulfilled. Faith advances forward in this firm conviction. She remembers why the promise was given—namely, for God's glory. She feels perfectly sure that God's glory is safe, that He will never stain His own armor or mar the luster of His own crown; therefore, the promise must and will stand. Then faith also considers the amazing work of Christ as being a clear proof of the Father's intention to fulfill His word. *"He that spared not his own Son, but delivered him up for us all, how shall he not with him also freely give us all things?"* (Rom. 8:32). Moreover, faith looks back on the past, for her battles have strengthened her, and her victories have given her courage. She remembers that God has never failed her; no, that He never once has failed any of His children. She recollects times of great peril, when deliverance came; hours of awful need, when strength was found to meet the demands of the day, and she cries, "No, I never will be led to think that He can change and leave His servant now. *'Hitherto hath the LORD helped us'* (1 Sam. 7:12), and He will help me still." Thus faith views each promise in its connection with the Promise-giver, and, because she does so, can with assurance say, *"Surely goodness and mercy shall follow me all the days of my life"* (Ps. 23:6).

Forget not all his benefits.
—Psalm 103:2

It is a delightful and profitable occupation to mark the hand of God in the lives of ancient saints and to observe His goodness in delivering them, His mercy in pardoning them, and His faithfulness in keeping His covenant with them. But would it not be even more interesting and profitable for us to notice the hand of God in our own lives? Should we not look on our own history as being at least as full of God, as full of His goodness and of His truth, as much a proof of His faithfulness and veracity, as the lives of any of the saints who have gone before? We do our Lord an injustice when we suppose that He wrought all His mighty acts and showed Himself strong for those in the early times, but does not perform wonders or *"bare his holy arm"* (Isa. 52:10) for the saints who are now on the earth. Let us review our own lives. Surely in these we may discover some happy incidents, refreshing to ourselves and glorifying to our God. Have you had no deliverances? Have you passed through no rivers, supported by the divine presence? Have you walked through no fires unharmed? Have you had no manifestations? Have you had no choice favors? The God who gave Solomon the desire of his heart, has He never listened to you and answered your requests? That God of lavish bounty of whom David sang, *"Who satisfieth thy mouth with good things"* (Ps. 103:5), has He never satiated you with fatness? Have you never been made to lie down in green pastures? Have you never been led by the still waters? Surely the goodness of God has been the same to us as to the saints of old. Let us, then, weave His mercies into a song. Let us take the pure gold of thankfulness and the jewels of praise and make them into another crown for the head of Jesus. Let our souls give forth music as sweet and as exhilarating as came from David's harp, while we praise the Lord whose mercy endures forever.

Fellowcitizens with the saints.
—Ephesians 2:19

hat does it mean to be a citizen of heaven? It means that we are under heaven's government. Christ the King of heaven reigns in our hearts; our daily prayer is, *"Thy will be done in earth, as it is in heaven"* (Matt. 6:10). The proclamations issued from the throne of glory are freely received by us; the decrees of the Great King we cheerfully obey. Then, as citizens of the New Jerusalem, we share heaven's honors. The glory that belongs to beatified saints belongs to us, for we are already sons of God, already princes of the blood imperial; already we wear the spotless robe of Jesus' righteousness; already we have angels for our servants, saints for our companions, Christ for our Brother, God for our Father, and a crown of immortality for our reward. We share the honors of citizenship, for we have come to the general assembly and church of the firstborn whose names are written in heaven. As citizens, we have common rights to all the property of heaven. Ours are its gates of pearl and walls of chrysolite; ours the azure light of the city that needs no candle nor light of the sun; ours the river of the water of life, and the twelve manner of fruits that grow on the trees planted on the banks thereof; there is nothing in heaven that does not belong to us. *"Things present, or things to come"* (1 Cor. 3:22) are all ours. Also as citizens of heaven we enjoy its delights. Do they there rejoice over sinners who repent—prodigals who have returned? So do we. Do they chant the glories of triumphant grace? We do the same. Do they cast their crowns at Jesus' feet? Such honors as we have we cast there, too. Are they charmed by His smile? It is not less sweet to us who dwell below. Do they look forward, waiting for His second advent? We also look and long for His appearing. If, then, we are thus citizens of heaven, let our walk and actions be consistent with our high dignity.

After that ye have suffered a while, make you perfect,
stablish, strengthen, settle you.
—1 Peter 5:10

Y ou have seen the arch of heaven as it spans the plain:
glorious are its colors and rare its hues. It is beautiful, but, alas, it passes away. The fair colors give way
to fleecy clouds, and the sky is no longer brilliant with the
tints of heaven. It is not established. How can it be? A glorious show made up of transitory sunbeams and passing
raindrops, how can it last? The graces of the Christian
character must not resemble the rainbow in its transitory
beauty, but, on the contrary, must be established, settled,
abiding. Seek, believer, that every good thing you have may
be an abiding thing. May your character not be a writing
on the sand, but an inscription on the rock! May your faith
be no "baseless fabric of a vision," but may it be built of material able to endure that awful fire that will consume the
"wood, hay, [and] stubble" (1 Cor. 3:12) of the hypocrite.
May you be *"rooted and grounded in love"* (Eph. 3:17). May
your convictions be deep, your love real, and your desires
earnest. May your whole life be so settled and established
that all the blasts of hell and all the storms of earth will
never be able to remove you. But notice how this blessing
of being *"stablished in the faith"* (Col. 2:7) is gained. The
apostle's words point us to suffering as the means employed: *"After that ye have suffered a while."* It is of no use to
hope that we will be well rooted if no rough winds pass
over us. All those old gnarlings on the root of the oak tree
and those strange twistings of the branches tell of the many
storms that have swept over it, and they are also indicators
of the depth into which the roots have forced their way. So
the Christian is made strong and firmly rooted by all the
trials and storms of life. Do not shrink, then, from the tempestuous winds of trial, but take comfort, believing that by
their rough discipline God is fulfilling this benediction to
you.

Sanctified by God the Father.
—Jude 1

anctified in Christ Jesus" (1 Cor. 1:2). *"Through sancti-fication of the Spirit"* (1 Pet. 1:2). Mark the union of the three divine persons in all their gracious acts. How unwisely do those believers talk who make prefer-ences in the persons of the Trinity; who think of Jesus as if He were the embodiment of everything lovely and gracious, while the Father they regard as severely just, but destitute of kindness. Equally wrong are those who magnify the de-cree of the Father, and the Atonement of the Son, so as to depreciate the work of the Spirit. In deeds of grace none of the persons of the Trinity act apart from the rest. They are as united in their deeds as in their essence. In their love to-ward the chosen, they are one, and in the actions that flow from that great central source, they are still undivided. Take special notice of this in the matter of sanctification. While we may without mistake speak of sanctification as the work of the Spirit, yet we must take heed that we do not view it as if the Father and the Son had no part therein. It is correct to speak of sanctification as the work of the Father, of the Son, and of the Spirit. Still does Jehovah say, *"Let us make man in our image, after our likeness"* (Gen. 1:26), and thus we are *"his workmanship, created in Christ Jesus unto good works, which God hath before ordained that we should walk in them"* (Eph. 2:10). See the value that God sets on real holi-ness, since the three persons in the Trinity are represented as working together to produce a church without *"spot, or wrinkle, or any such thing"* (Eph. 5:27). And you, believer, as the follower of Christ, must also set a high value on holi-ness—on purity of life and godliness of conversation. Value the blood of Christ as the foundation of your hope, but never speak disparagingly of the work of the Spirit that qualifies you for the *"inheritance of the saints in light"* (Col. 1:12). This day let us so live as to manifest the work of the triune God in us.

God said to Jonah, Doest thou well to be angry?
—Jonah 4:9

nger is not always or necessarily sinful, but it has such a tendency to run wild that whenever it displays itself, we should be quick to question its character with this inquiry, *"Doest thou well to be angry?"* It may be that we can answer, "Yes." Very frequently anger is the madman's firebrand, but sometimes it is Elijah's fire from heaven. We do well when we are angry with sin, because of the wrong that it commits against our good and gracious God; or with ourselves because we remain so foolish after so much divine instruction; or with others when the sole cause of anger is the evil that they do. He who is not angry at transgression becomes a partaker in it. Sin is a loathsome and hateful thing, and no renewed heart can patiently endure it. God Himself is angry with the wicked every day, and it is written in His Word, *"Ye that love the LORD, hate evil"* (Ps. 97:10). Far more frequently it is to be feared that our anger is not commendable or even justifiable, and then, we must answer, "No." Why should we be fretful with children, angry with servants, and irate with companions? Is such anger honorable to our Christian profession or glorifying to God? Is it not the old evil heart seeking to gain dominion, and should we not resist it with all the might of our newborn nature? Many false believers give way to temper as though it were useless to attempt resistance; but let the true believer remember that he must be a conqueror in every point, or else he cannot be crowned. If we cannot control our tempers, what has grace done for us? Someone told Mr. Jay that grace was often grafted on the stump of a crab apple tree. "Yes," said he, "but the fruit will not be crabs." We must not make natural infirmity an excuse for sin, but we must fly to the cross and pray to the Lord to crucify our tempers and renew us in gentleness and meekness after His own image.

If thou lift up thy tool upon it, thou hast polluted it.
—Exodus 20:25

God's altar was to be built of unhewn stones, so that no trace of human skill or labor might be seen on it. Human wisdom delights to trim and arrange the doctrines of the cross into a system more artificial and more congenial with the depraved tastes of fallen nature; however, instead of improving the Gospel, carnal wisdom pollutes it, until it becomes another gospel, and not the truth of God at all. All alterations and amendments of the Lord's own Word are defilements and pollutions. The proud heart of man is very anxious to have a hand in the justification of the soul before God; preparations for Christ are dreamed of, humblings and repentings are trusted in, good works are cried up, natural ability is much vaunted, and by all means the attempt is made to lift up human tools on the divine altar. It were well if sinners would remember that so far from perfecting the Savior's work, their carnal confidences only pollute and dishonor it. The Lord alone must be exalted in the work of atonement, and not a single mark of man's chisel or hammer will be endured. There is an inherent blasphemy in seeking to add to what Christ Jesus in His dying moments declared to be finished, or to improve that in which the Lord Jehovah finds perfect satisfaction. Trembling sinner, away with your tools. Fall on your knees in humble supplication. Accept the Lord Jesus to be the altar of your atonement, and rest in Him alone. Many professors of faith may take warning from this morning's text as to the doctrines in which they believe. There is among Christians far too much inclination to square and reconcile the truths of revelation; this is a form of irreverence and unbelief. Let us strive against it and receive truth as we find it, rejoicing that the doctrines of the Word are unhewn stones, and so are all the more suitable to build an altar for the Lord.

The fire shall ever be burning upon the altar; it shall never go out.
—Leviticus 6:13

Keep the altar of private prayer burning. This is the very life of all piety. The sanctuary and family altars borrow their fires here; therefore, let this burn well. Secret devotion is the very essence, evidence, and barometer of vital and experimental religion. Burn here the fat of your sacrifices. Let your private seasons of prayer be, if possible, regular, frequent, and undisturbed. Effectual prayer avails much. Have you nothing to pray for? Let us suggest the church, the ministry, your own soul, your children, your relations, your neighbors, your country, and the cause of God and truth throughout the world. Let us examine ourselves on this important matter. Do we engage with lukewarmness in private devotion? Is the fire of devotion burning dimly in our hearts? Do the chariot wheels drag heavily? If so, let us be alarmed at this sign of decay. Let us go with weeping and ask for the Spirit of grace and of supplications. Let us set apart special seasons for extraordinary prayer. For if this fire would be smothered beneath the ashes of a worldly conformity, it will dim the fire on the family altar and lessen our influence both in the church and in the world. The text also applies to the altar of the heart. This is a golden altar indeed. God loves to see the hearts of His people glowing toward Himself. Let us give to God our hearts, all blazing with love, and seek His grace, so that the fire may never be quenched; for it will not burn if the Lord does not keep it burning. Many foes will attempt to extinguish it, but if the unseen hand behind the wall pour the sacred oil on it, it will blaze higher and higher. Let us use texts of Scripture as fuel for our heart's fire. They are live coals. Let us pay attention to sermons, but above all, let us be much alone with Jesus.

They gathered [manna] every morning.
—Exodus 16:21

Labor to maintain a sense of your entire dependence on the Lord's goodwill and pleasure for the continuance of your richest enjoyments. Never try to live on the old manna or seek to find help in Egypt. All must come from Jesus, or you are ruined forever. Old anointings will not suffice to impart unction to your spirit; your head must have fresh oil poured upon it from the golden horn of the sanctuary, or it will cease from its glory. Today you may be on the summit of the mount of God, but He who has put you there must keep you there; otherwise, you will sink far more speedily than you ever dreamed. Your mountain only stands firm when He settles it in its place; if He hides His face, you will soon be troubled. If the Savior should see fit, there is not a window through which you see the light of heaven that He could not darken in an instant. Joshua ordered the sun to stand still, but Jesus can shroud it in total darkness. He can withdraw the joy of your heart, the light of your eyes, and the strength of your life. In His hand your comforts lie, and at His will they can depart from you. Our Lord is determined that we will feel and recognize this hourly dependence, for He permits us to pray only for *"daily bread"* (Matt. 6:11), and only promises that *"as [our] days, so shall [our] strength shall be"* (Deut. 33:25). Is it not best for us that it should be this way, so that we may often repair to His throne and constantly be reminded of His love? Oh, how rich is the grace that supplies us so continually and does not refrain itself because of our ingratitude! The golden shower never ceases; the cloud of blessing tarries evermore above our habitation. O Lord Jesus, we would bow at Your feet, conscious of our utter inability to do anything without You, and in every favor that we are privileged to receive, we would adore Your blessed name and acknowledge Your inexhaustible love.

Knowing, brethren beloved, your election of God.
—1 Thessalonians 1:4

Many persons want to know their election before they look to Christ, but they cannot learn it thus; it is only to be discovered by *"looking unto Jesus"* (Heb. 12:2). If you desire to be sure of your own election, assure your heart before God by asking the following questions: Do you feel yourself to be a lost, guilty sinner? Then go immediately to the cross of Christ and tell Jesus so. Tell Him that you have read in the Bible, *"Him that cometh to me I will in no wise cast out"* (John 6:37). Tell Him that He has said, *"This is a faithful saying, and worthy of all acceptation, that Christ Jesus came into the world to save sinners"* (1 Tim. 1:15). Look to Jesus and believe on Him, and you be confident of your election directly, for as surely as you believe, you are elect. If you will give yourself wholly up to Christ and trust Him, then, you are one of God's chosen ones; but if you stop and say, "I want to know first whether I am elect," you do not know what you are asking. Go to Jesus; although you are ever so guilty, go just as you are. Leave all curious inquiry about election alone. Go straight to Christ and hide in His wounds, and you will know your election. The assurance of the Holy Spirit will be given to you, so that you will be able to say, *"I know whom I have believed, and am persuaded that he is able to keep that which I have committed unto him"* (2 Tim. 1:12). Christ was at the everlasting council. He can tell you whether you were chosen or not, but you cannot find it out in any other way. Go and put your trust in Him, and His answer will be, *"I have loved thee with an everlasting love: therefore with lovingkindness have I drawn thee"* (Jer. 31:3). There will be no doubt about His having chosen *you*, when you have chosen *Him*.

Sons we are through God's election,
Who in Jesus Christ believe.

They shall go hindmost with their standards.
—Numbers 2:31

he camp of Dan brought up the rear when the armies of Israel were on the march. The Danites occupied the hindmost place, but what did their position matter, since they were as truly a part of the host as were the foremost tribes? They followed the same fiery, cloudy pillar; they ate of the same manna; drank of the same spiritual rock; and journeyed to the same inheritance. Come, my heart, cheer up. Although you are the last and the least, it is your privilege to be in the army and to fare as they fare who lead the way. Someone must be hindmost in honor and esteem; someone must do menial work for Jesus, and why should it not be I? In a poor village among an ignorant peasantry or in a back street among degraded sinners, I will work on, and *"go hindmost with* [my standard]*."* The Danites occupied a very useful place. Stragglers have to be picked up along the march, and lost property has to be gathered from the field. Fiery spirits may dash forward over untrodden paths to learn fresh truth and win more souls to Jesus, but some with more conservative spirits may be well engaged in reminding the church of her ancient faith and restoring her fainting sons. Every position has its duties, and the slowly moving children of God will find their particular state one in which they may be eminently a blessing to the whole host. The rear guard is a place of danger. There are foes behind us as well as before us. Attacks may come from any side. We read that Amalek fell on Israel and slew some of the rear guard. The experienced Christian will find much work for his weapons in aiding those poor, doubting, despondent, wavering souls who are hindmost in faith, knowledge, and joy. These must not be left unaided; therefore, it should be the business of well-taught saints to bear their standards among the rear guard. My soul, tenderly watch to help the hindmost this day.

The LORD our God hath showed us his glory.
—Deuteronomy 5:24

God's great design in all His works is the manifestation of His own glory. Any aim less than this would be unworthy of Him. But how will the glory of God be manifested to such fallen creatures as we are? Man's eye is not single; he always has a side-glance toward his own honor. He has too high an estimate of his own powers, and so he is not qualified to behold the glory of the Lord. It is clear, then, that self must stand out of the way, so that there may be room for God to be exalted. This is the reason that He often brings His people into problems and difficulties, so that, being made conscious of their own folly and weakness, they may be fitted to behold the majesty of God when He comes forth to work their deliverance. He whose life is one even, smooth path will see only a little of the glory of the Lord, for he has few occasions of self-emptying; hence, he has only a little fitness for being filled with the revelation of God. Those who navigate little streams and shallow creeks know little of the God of tempests, but those who *"do business in great waters"* (Ps. 107:23) see *"his wonders in the deep"* (v. 24). Among the huge Atlantic waves of bereavement, poverty, temptation, and reproach, we learn the power of Jehovah, because we feel the inadequacy of man. Thank God, then, if you have been led by a rough road. It is this that has given you your experience of God's greatness and lovingkindness. Your troubles have enriched you with a wealth of knowledge to be gained by no other means. Your trials have been the cleft of the rock in which Jehovah has set you, as He did His servant Moses, so that you might behold His glory as it passes by. Praise God that you have not been left to the darkness and ignorance that continued prosperity might have involved, but that in the great fight of affliction, you have been equipped for the outshinings of His glory in His wonderful dealings with you.

The earnest of our inheritance.
—Ephesians 1:14

h, what enlightenment, what joys, what consolation, what delight of heart is experienced by that man who has learned to feed on Jesus, and on Jesus alone! Yet the realization that we have of Christ's preciousness is, in this life, imperfect at best. As an old writer says, "'Tis but a taste!" We *"have tasted that the Lord is gracious"* (1 Pet. 2:3), but we do not yet know *how* good and gracious He is, although what we know of His sweetness makes us long for more. We have enjoyed the firstfruits of the Spirit, and they have set us hungering and thirsting for the fullness of the heavenly vintage. We groan within ourselves, waiting for the adoption. Here we are like Israel in the wilderness, who had but one cluster from Eshcol; there we will be in the vineyard. Here we see the manna falling small, like coriander seed, but there we will eat the bread of heaven and the old corn of the kingdom. We are but beginners now in spiritual education. Although we have learned the first letters of the alphabet, we cannot read words yet, much less put sentences together. But as one says, "He who has been in heaven but five minutes knows more than the general assembly of divines on earth." We have many ungratified desires at present, but soon every wish will be satisfied. All our powers will find the sweetest employment in that eternal world of joy. O Christian, anticipate heaven for a few years. Within a very little time you will be rid of all your trials and your troubles. Your eyes now suffused with tears will weep no longer. You will gaze in indescribable rapture on the splendor of Him who sits on the throne. Even more, you will sit on His throne. The triumph of His glory will be shared by you. His crown, His joy, and His paradise will be yours, and you will be co-heir with Him who is the *"heir of all things"* (Heb. 1:2).

The daughter of Jerusalem hath shaken her head at thee.
—Isaiah 37:22

eassured by the Word of the Lord, the poor trembling citizens of Zion grew bold and shook their heads at Sennacherib's boastful threats. Strong faith enables the servants of God to look with calm contempt on their haughtiest foes. We know that our enemies are attempting impossibilities. They seek to destroy the eternal life, which cannot die while Jesus lives; to overthrow the citadel, against which the gates of hell will not prevail. They *"kick against the pricks"* (Acts 9:5) to their own wounding and rush upon the raised ornamentation of Jehovah's shield to their own hurt. We know their weaknesses. What are they but men? And what is man but a worm? They roar and swell like waves of the sea, foaming out their own shame. When the Lord arises, they will fly as chaff before the wind and be consumed as crackling thorns. Their utter powerlessness to do damage to the cause of God and His truth may make the weakest soldiers in Zion's ranks laugh them to scorn. Above all, we know that the Most High is with us, and when He dresses Himself in arms, where are His enemies? If He comes forth from His place, the *"potsherds of the earth"* (Isa. 45:9) will not long contend with their Maker. His *"rod of iron"* will *"dash them in pieces like a potter's vessel"* (Ps. 2:9), and their very *"remembrance shall perish from the earth"* (Job 18:17). Away, then, all fears! The kingdom is safe in the King's hands. Let us shout for joy, for the Lord reigns, and His foes will be like straw for the dunghill.

> As true as God's own Word is true;
>   Nor earth, nor hell, with all their crew,
> Against us shall prevail.
>   A jest, and byword, are they grown.
> God is with us; we are his own.
>   Our victory cannot fail.

I am married unto you.
—Jeremiah 3:14

hrist Jesus is joined with His people in the union of marriage. In love He espoused His church as a chaste virgin, long before she fell under the yoke of bondage. Full of burning affection, Christ toiled, like Jacob for Rachel, until the whole of her purchase-money had been paid. And now, having sought her by His Spirit, and brought her to know and love Him, Christ awaits the glorious hour when their mutual bliss will be consummated at the Marriage Supper of the Lamb. Not yet has the glorious Bridegroom presented His betrothed, perfected and complete, before the Majesty of heaven; not yet has she actually entered into the enjoyment of her privileges as His wife and queen. She is as yet a wanderer in a world of woe, a dweller *"in the tents of Kedar"* (Ps. 120:5); but she is even now the bride, the spouse of Jesus, dear to His heart, precious in His sight, written on His hands, and united with His person. On earth He exercises toward her all the affectionate offices of Husband. He makes rich provision for her needs, pays all her debts, and allows her to assume His name and to share in all His wealth. Nor will He ever act otherwise to her. The word *divorce* He will never mention, for He *"hateth putting away"* (Mal. 2:16). Death must sever the conjugal tie between the most loving mortals, but it cannot divide the links of this immortal marriage. In heaven they do not marry, but are as the angels of God; yet there is this one marvelous exception to the rule, for in heaven Christ and His church will celebrate their joyous nuptials. Because this affinity is more lasting, it is more intimate than earthly wedlock. Although the love of a husband may be so pure and fervent, it is but a faint picture of the flame that burns in the heart of Jesus. Surpassing all human union is that mystical cleaving unto the church, for which Christ left His Father and became one flesh with her.

Even thou wast as one of them.
—Obadiah 1:11

Brotherly kindness was due from Edom to Israel in their time of need, but instead, the men of Esau joined forces with Israel's foes. Special stress in the sentence before us is laid on the word *"thou,"* as when Caesar cried to Brutus, "and *thou* Brutus." A bad action may be all the worse because of the person who has committed it. When we, who are the chosen favorites of heaven, sin, ours is a crying offense, because we are so highly favored. If an angel would lay his hand on us when we are doing evil, he would not need to use any other rebuke than the question, "What, you? What are you doing here?" Much forgiven, much delivered, much instructed, much enriched, much blessed—will we dare to put forth our hand unto evil? God forbid! A few minutes of confession may be beneficial to you, gentle reader, this morning. Have you never been as the wicked? At an evening party certain men laughed at uncleanness, and the joke was not altogether offensive to your ear; *"even thou wast as one of them."* When hard things were spoken concerning the ways of God, you were bashfully silent; and so, to onlookers, you were as one of them. When worldlings were bartering in the market and driving hard bargains, were you not as one of them? When they were pursuing vanity, were you not as greedy for gain as they were? Could any difference be discerned among you and them? Is there any difference? Here the truth hits close to home. Be honest with your own soul, and make sure that you are a *"new creature"* (2 Cor. 5:17) in Christ Jesus. Even when your faith is true, be vigilant in your Christian walk, lest any should again be able to say, *"Even thou wast as one of them."* You would not desire to share their eternal doom, so why be like them here? Do not join their practices, lest you be united with them in their ruin. Side with the afflicted people of God, and not with the world.

Stand still, and see the salvation of the LORD.
—Exodus 14:13

hese words contain God's command to the believer when he is reduced to great straits and brought into extraordinary difficulties. He cannot retreat; he cannot go forward. He is shut up on the right hand and on the left. What is he to do now? The Master's word to him is, *"Stand still."* It will be well for him if at such times he listens only to his Master's word, for evil advisers come with their suggestions. Despair whispers, "Lie down and die; give it all up." But God would have us put on a cheerful courage, and even in our worst times, rejoice in His love and faithfulness. Cowardice says, "Retreat; go back to the world's way of doing things. You cannot play the Christian's part; it is too difficult. Relinquish your principles." However much Satan may urge this course upon you, you cannot follow it if you are a child of God. His divine command has bid you to *"go from strength to strength"* (Ps. 84:7), and so you will, and neither death nor hell will turn you away from your course. If for a while you are called to stand still, this is but to renew your strength for some greater advance in due time. Hastiness cries, "Do something! Stir yourself! To stand still and wait is sheer idleness." We must be doing something at once. We must do it, so we think, instead of looking to the Lord, who will not only do something but will do everything. Presumption boasts, "If the sea is before you, march into it and expect a miracle." But Faith listens neither to Presumption, nor to Despair, nor to Cowardice, nor to Hastiness, but it hears God say, *"Stand still"*; and immovable as a rock, it stands. *"Stand still."* Keep the posture of an upright man: ready for action, expecting further orders, cheerfully and patiently awaiting the directing voice. It will not be long before God will say to you, as distinctly as He told Moses to say it to the people of Israel, *"Go forward"* (Exod. 14:15).

He left his garment in her hand, and fled, and got him out.
—Genesis 39:12

In contending with certain sins there remains no mode of victory but flight. The ancient naturalists wrote much of basilisks, whose eyes fascinated their victims and rendered them easy victims; likewise, the mere gaze of wickedness puts us in solemn danger. He who would be safe from acts of evil must run away from occasions of it. A covenant must be made with our eyes not even to look on the cause of temptation, for such sins need only a spark to begin, and a blaze follows in an instant. Who would wantonly enter the leper's prison and sleep amid its horrible corruption? Only he who desires to be leprous himself would thus court contagion. If the mariner knew how to avoid a storm, he would do anything rather than run the risk of weathering it. Cautious pilots have no desire to see how near to quicksand they can sail, or how often they may touch a rock without springing a leak. Their aim is to keep as far away as possible from danger and navigate in the middle of a safe channel. This day I may be exposed to great peril; let me have the serpent's wisdom to keep out of it and avoid it. The wings of a dove may be of more use to me today than the jaws of a lion. It is true that I may be an apparent loser by declining evil company, but I would rather lose my coat than my character. It is not necessary that I should be rich, but it is imperative upon me to be pure. No ties of friendship, no accumulation of beauty, no displays of talent, no shafts of ridicule must turn me from the wise resolve to flee from sin. I am *to "resist the devil, and he will flee from* [me]*"* (James 4:7); but the lusts of the flesh, I must flee, or they will surely overcome me. O God of holiness, preserve your Josephs, so that they will not be bewitched by vile suggestions. May the horrible trinity of the world, the flesh, and the devil never overcome us!

Add to your faith virtue; and to virtue knowledge....Give diligence.
—2 Peter 1:5, 10

If you would enjoy the eminent grace of the full assurance of faith, under the blessed Spirit's influence and assistance, do what the Scripture tells you: *"Give diligence."* Take care that your faith is of the right kind—that it is not a mere belief of doctrine, but a simple faith, depending on Christ, and on Christ alone. Give diligent heed to your courage. Plead with God that He would give you the face of a lion, that you may, with a consciousness of right, go on boldly. Study the Scriptures well, and get knowledge; for a knowledge of doctrine will lead to the confirmation of your faith. Try to understand God's Word; let it *"dwell in you richly"* (Col. 3:16). When you have done this, *"Add to your...knowledge temperance"* (2 Pet. 1:5–6). Pay attention to your body: practice moderation without. Pay attention to your soul: practice moderation within. Restrain your lips, your life, your heart, and your thoughts. Add to this, by God's Holy Spirit, patience. Ask Him to give you the patience that endures affliction, which, when it is tried, will *"come forth as gold"* (Job 23:10). Adorn yourself with patience, so that you may not complain or be depressed in your afflictions. When that grace is won, look to godliness. Godliness is something more than religion. Make God's glory your purpose in life. Live in His sight, and dwell closely to Him. Seek fellowship with Him, and you will be godly. To godliness, add brotherly love. Have a love for all the saints; and add to that love a charity that opens its arms to all people and loves their souls. When you are adorned with these jewels, and just in proportion as you practice these heavenly virtues, will you come to know by clearest evidence *"your calling and election"* (2 Pet. 1:10). *"Give diligence,"* if you would find assurance, for lukewarmness and doubting very naturally go hand in hand.

Exceeding great and precious promises.
—2 Peter 1:4

If you would know the preciousness of the promises and enjoy them in your own heart, meditate much on them. There are promises that are like grapes in the wine-press; if you will tread on them, the juice will flow. Thinking over the hallowed words will often be the prelude to their fulfillment. While you are meditating on them, the blessings that you are seeking will gradually come to you. Many Christians who have thirsted for the promise have found the favor that it ensured gently distilling into their souls even while they have been considering the divine record. They have rejoiced that they were led to lay the promises near their hearts. But besides meditating on the promises, seek in your soul to receive them as being the very words of God. Speak to your soul, saying, "If I were dealing with a man's promise, I would carefully consider the ability and the character of the man who had covenanted with me. So with the promise of God; my eye must not be focused as much on the greatness of the mercy—that may stagger me—as on the greatness of the Promiser— that will cheer me. My soul, it is God, even your God, God who cannot lie, who speaks to you. This word of His that you are now considering is as true as His own existence. He is an unchangeable God. He has not altered the words that have gone out of His mouth, nor has He called back one single comforting sentence. Nor does He lack any power. It is the God who made the heavens and the earth who has spoken thus. Nor can He fail in wisdom as to the time when He will bestow the favors, for He knows when it is best to give and when it is better to withhold. Therefore, seeing that it is the word of a God so true, so immutable, so powerful, so wise, I will and must believe the promise." If we meditate on the promises, and consider the Promiser, we will experience their sweetness and obtain their fulfillment.

So foolish was I, and ignorant: I was as a beast before thee.
—Psalm 73:22

Remember this is the confession of the man after God's own heart; and in telling us his inner life, David wrote, *"So foolish was I, and ignorant."* The word *"foolish"* here means more than it signifies in everyday language. David, in the third verse of this psalm, wrote, *"I was envious at the foolish, when I saw the prosperity of the wicked,"* which shows that the folly he intended had sin in it. He put himself down as being *"foolish,"* and added a word that gave intensity to it, *"so foolish was I"* (emphasis added). How foolish, he could not tell. It was a sinful folly, a folly that was not to be excused by frailty, but to be condemned because of its perverseness and willful ignorance; for he had been envious of the present prosperity of the ungodly and forgetful of the dreadful end awaiting them. And are we better than David that we should call ourselves wise? Do we profess that we have attained perfection or that we have been so chastened that the rod has taken all our willfulness out of us? Ah, this is pride indeed! If David was foolish, how foolish would we be in our own esteem if we could but see ourselves! Look back, believer. Think of your doubting God when He has been so faithful to you. Think of your foolish outcry of "Not so, my Father," when He crossed His hands in affliction to give you the larger blessing. Think of the many times when you have read His providences in the dark, misinterpreted His dispensations, and groaned out, "All these things are against me," when they are all working together for your good! Think how often you have chosen sin because of its pleasure, when indeed, that pleasure was a root of bitterness to you! Surely, if we know our own hearts, we must plead guilty to the indictment of a sinful folly. Conscious of this "foolishness," we must make David's consequent resolve our own: *"Thou shalt guide me with thy counsel"* (Ps. 73:24).

Nevertheless I am continually with thee.
—Psalm 73:23

"Nevertheless"—notwithstanding all the foolishness and ignorance that David had just been confessing to God, not one atom the less was it true and certain that David was saved, accepted, and blessed by the constant presence of God. Fully conscious of his own lost state, and of the deceitfulness and vileness of his nature, yet, by a glorious outburst of faith, he sang, *"Nevertheless I am continually with thee."* Believer, you are forced to enter into the psalmist's confession and acknowledgment; endeavor in the same spirit to say, "Nevertheless, since I belong to Christ, I am continually with God!" This means that I am continually on His mind; He is always thinking of me for my good. I am continually before His eye; the eye of the Lord never sleeps, but is perpetually watching over my welfare. I am continually in His hand, so that none will be able to pluck me from it. I am continually on His heart, worn there as a memorial, even as the high priest bore the names of the twelve tribes on his heart forever. You always think of me, O God. Your love continually reaches out to me. You are always making providence work for my good. You have set me as a signet on Your arm. Your love is as *"strong as death"* (Song 8:6). *"Many waters cannot quench [it], neither can the floods drown it"* (v. 7). Surprising grace! You see me in Christ, and, though in myself abhorred, You behold me as wearing Christ's garments, washed in His blood; thus, I stand accepted in Your presence. I am continually in Your favor—*"continually with thee."* Here is comfort for the tried and afflicted soul: vexed with the tempest within, look at the calm without. *"Nevertheless"*—Oh, say it in your heart, and take the peace it gives. *"Nevertheless I am continually with thee."*

And when he thought thereon, he wept.
—Mark 14:72

It has been thought by some that as long as Peter lived, the fountain of his tears began to flow whenever he remembered his denying his Lord. It is not unlikely that it was so, for his sin was very great, and grace in him had afterward a perfect work. This same experience is common to all the redeemed family according to the degree in which the Spirit of God has removed the natural heart of stone. We, like Peter, remember our boastful promise: *"Though all men shall be offended because of thee, yet will I never be offended"* (Matt. 26:33). We eat our own words with the bitter herbs of repentance. When we think of what we vowed we would be, and of what we have been, we may weep whole showers of grief. He thought about his denying his Lord: the place in which he did it, the insignificant reason that led him into such heinous sin, the oaths and blasphemies with which he sought to confirm his falsehood, and the dreadful hardness of heart that drove him to do so again and yet again. Can we, when we are reminded of our sins, and their exceeding sinfulness, remain impassive and stubborn? Will we not make our house a place of weeping and cry to the Lord for renewed assurances of pardoning love? May we never take a dry-eyed look at sin, unless before long we have a tongue parched in the flames of hell. Peter also thought about his Master's look of love. The Lord followed up the cock's warning voice with an admonishing look of sorrow, pity, and love. That glance was never out of Peter's mind as long as he lived. It was far more effective than ten thousand sermons would have been without the Spirit. The penitent apostle would be sure to weep when he remembered the Savior's full forgiveness, which restored him to his former place. To think that we have offended so kind and good a Lord is more than sufficient reason for being constant weepers. Lord, smite our rocky hearts and make the waters flow.

I in them.
—John 17:23

If such is the union that exists between our souls and the person of our Lord, how deep and broad is the channel of our communion! This is no narrow pipe through which a thread-like stream may wind its way. It is a channel of amazing depth and breadth, along whose glorious length a ponderous volume of living water may roll its floods. Behold, He has set before us an open door; let us not be slow to enter. This city of communion has many pearly gates. Each gate is of one pearl and is thrown wide open so that we may enter, assured of being welcome. If there were but one small hole through which to talk with Jesus, it would be a high privilege to thrust a word of fellowship through the narrow door. How much we are blessed in having so large an entrance! Had the Lord Jesus been far away from us, with many stormy seas between, we would have longed to send a messenger to Him to carry Him our love and bring us tidings from His Father's house. But note His kindness: He has built His house next door to ours; no, even more, He lodges with us and tabernacles in our poor, humble hearts, so that He may have perpetual contact with us. Oh, how foolish we must be, if we do not live in habitual communion with Him! When the road is long, dangerous, and difficult, we do not need to wonder that friends seldom meet each other, but when they live together, will Jonathan forget his David? A wife may, when her husband is on a journey, endure many days without being able to talk with him, but she could never tolerate being separated from him if she knew he was in one of the rooms of their very own house. Why, believer, do you not sit at His banquet of wine? Seek your Lord, for He is near. Embrace Him, for He is your Brother. Hold Him fast, for He is your Husband. Press Him to your heart, for He is of your own flesh.

Let me now go to the field, and glean ears of corn.
—Ruth 2:2

owncast and troubled Christian, come and glean to-day in the broad field of promises. Here is an abundance of precious promises that exactly meet your needs. Take this one: *"A bruised reed shall he not break, and the smoking flax shall he not quench"* (Isa. 42:3). Does that fit your case? A helpless and weak reed; a bruised reed, out of which no music can come; a reed weaker than weakness itself; an insignificant reed, and yet, He will not break you. On the contrary, He will restore and strengthen you. You are like the smoking flax. No light or warmth can come from you, but He will not quench you. He will blow with His sweet breath of mercy until He fans you into a flame. Would you glean another ear? *"Come unto me, all ye that labour and are heavy laden, and I will give you rest"* (Matt. 11:28). What inviting words! Your heart is tender, and the Master knows it; therefore, He speaks so gently to you. Will you not obey Him and come to Him even now? Take another ear of corn: *"Fear not...; I will help thee, saith the LORD, and thy redeemer, the Holy One of Israel"* (Isa. 41:14). How can you fear with such a wonderful assurance as this? You may gather ten thousand golden ears such as these! *"I have blotted out, as a thick cloud, thy transgressions, and, as a cloud, thy sins"* (Isa. 44:22). Or this, *"Though your sins be as scarlet, they shall be as white as snow; though they be red like crimson, they shall be as wool"* (Isa. 1:18). Or this, *"The Spirit and the bride say, Come. And let him that...is athirst come. And whosoever will, let him take the water of life freely"* (Rev. 22:17). Our Master's field is very rich; behold the handfuls of available promises. See them there before you, poor timid believer! Gather them up, and make them your own; for Jesus invites you to take them. Do not be afraid; only believe! Grasp these sweet promises, thresh them out by meditation, and feed on them with joy.

Who worketh all things after the counsel of his own will.
—Ephesians 1:11

Our belief in God's wisdom supposes and necessitates that He has a settled purpose and plan in the work of salvation. What would Creation have been without His design? Is there a fish in the sea or a fowl in the air that was left to chance for its formation? No, in every bone, joint, muscle, sinew, gland, and blood vessel, you observe the presence of a God working everything according to the design of infinite wisdom. And will God be present in creation, ruling over all, and not in grace? Will the new creation have the fickle genius of free will to preside over it when divine counsel rules the old creation? Look at Providence! Who does not know that not even a sparrow falls to the ground without your Father's knowledge? Even the hairs of your head are all numbered. God weighs the mountains of our grief on scales, and the hills of our tribulation on balances. And will there be a God in providence and not in grace? Will the shell be ordained by wisdom and the kernel be left to blind chance? No, He knows the end from the beginning. He sees in its appointed place, not merely the Cornerstone, which He has laid in fair colors in the blood of His dear Son, but He beholds in their ordained position each of the chosen stones taken out of the quarry of nature and polished by His grace. He sees the whole from corner to cornice, from base to roof, from foundation to pinnacle. He has in His mind a clear knowledge of every stone that will be laid in its prepared space, how vast the edifice will be, and when the top-stone will be brought forth with shoutings of "Grace! Grace! unto it." At the last it will be clearly seen that in every chosen vessel of mercy, Jehovah did as He willed with His own; and that in every part of the work of grace, He accomplished His purposes and glorified His own name.

The Lamb is the light thereof.
—Revelation 21:23

Quietly contemplate the Lamb as the light of heaven. Light in Scripture is the symbol of joy. The joy of the saints in heaven is comprised of this: Jesus chose us, loved us, bought us, cleansed us, robed us, kept us, and glorified us. We are here entirely through the Lord Jesus. Each one of these thoughts is like a cluster of the grapes of Eshcol. Light is also the cause of beauty. Nothing of beauty is left when light is gone. Without light no radiance flashes from the sapphire, no peaceful ray proceeds from the pearl; thus, all the beauty of the saints above comes from Jesus. As planets, they reflect the light of the Sun of Righteousness; they live as beams proceeding from the central orb. If He withdrew, they would die; if His glory were veiled, their glory would expire. Light is also the symbol of knowledge. In heaven our knowledge will be perfect, but the Lord Jesus Himself will be the fountain of it. Dark providences, never understood before, will then be clearly seen, and all that puzzles us now will become plain to us in the light of the Lamb. Oh, what revelations there will be and what glorifying of the God of love! Light also means manifestation. Light manifests. In this world it does *"not yet appear what we shall be"* (1 John 3:2). God's people are a hidden people, but when Christ receives His people into heaven, He will touch them with the wand of His own love and change them into the image of His manifested glory. They were poor and wretched, but what a transformation! They were stained with sin, but one touch of His finger, and they are as bright as the sun and as clear as crystal. Oh, what a manifestation! All this proceeds from the exalted Lamb. Whatever there may be of radiant splendor, Jesus will be the center and soul of it all. Oh, to be present and to see Him in His own light, the King of Kings and Lord of Lords!

The people that do know their God shall be strong.
—Daniel 11:32

very believer understands that to know God is the highest and best form of knowledge. This spiritual knowledge is a source of strength to the Christian. It strengthens his faith. Believers are constantly spoken of in the Scriptures as being persons who are enlightened and taught of the Lord; they are said to *"have an unction from the Holy One"* (1 John 2:20), and it is the Spirit's special office to lead them into all truth, and all this for the increase and the fostering of their faith. Knowledge strengthens love, as well as faith. Knowledge opens the door, and then, through that door, we see our Savior. To use another metaphor, knowledge paints the portrait of Jesus, and when we see that portrait, then, we love Him. We cannot love a Christ whom we do not know, at least, in some degree. If we know only a little of the virtues of Jesus, what He has done for us, and what He is doing now, we cannot love Him much; but the more we know Him, the more we will love Him. Knowledge also strengthens hope. How can we hope for a thing if we do not know of its existence? Hope may be the telescope, but until we receive instruction, our ignorance stands in front of the glass, and we can see nothing whatsoever. Knowledge removes the interposing object, and when we look through the bright glass, we discern the glory to be revealed and anticipate it with joyous confidence. Knowledge supplies us reasons for patience. How will we have patience unless we know something of the sympathy of Christ and understand the good that is to come out of the correction that our heavenly Father sends us? Nor is there one single grace of the Christian that, under God, will not be fostered and brought to perfection by holy knowledge. How important, then, is it that we should grow not only *"in grace,"* but also *"in the knowledge of our Lord and Savior Jesus Christ"* (2 Pet. 3:18).

*We know that all things work together for good
to them that love God.*
—Romans 8:28

n some points a believer is absolutely sure. He knows, for instance, that God sits with the passengers of the vessel when it rocks the most. He believes that an invisible hand is always on the world's tiller, and that wherever providence may lead the vessel, Jehovah steers it. That reassuring knowledge prepares him for everything. He looks over the raging waters and sees the spirit of Jesus treading the billows. He hears a voice saying, *"It is I; be not afraid"* (Matt. 14:27). He knows, too, that God is always wise; knowing this, he is confident that there can be no accidents, no mistakes. Nothing can occur that should not happen. He can say, "If I would lose all that I have, it is better that I should lose it than keep it, if God so wills. The worst calamity is the wisest and the kindest thing that could happen to me if God ordains it." *"We know that all things work together for good to them that love God."* The Christian does not merely hold this as a theory, but he knows it as a matter of fact. Everything has worked for good so far. The poisonous drugs mixed in proper proportions have worked the cure; the sharp cuts of the scalpel have cleansed out the ulcerous flesh and facilitated the healing. Every event thus far has worked out the most divinely blessed results. And so, believing that God rules all, that He governs wisely, that He brings good out of evil, the believer's heart is assured, and he is enabled calmly to meet each trial as it comes. The believer can in the spirit of true resignation pray, "Send me what You will, my God, as long as it comes from You. A bad portion has never come from Your table to any of Your children." Do not say, my soul,

> From whence can God relieve my care?
>> Remember that Omnipotence has servants everywhere.
> His method is sublime; His heart profoundly kind.
> God never is before His time and never is behind.

Watchman, what of the night?
—Isaiah 21:11

W hat enemies are abroad? Numerous errors abound, and new ones appear every hour. What heresy must I guard against? Sins creep from their lurking places when darkness reigns. I must climb the watchtower and be attentive in prayer. Our heavenly Protector foresees all the attacks that are about to be made on us, and when as yet the evil designed for us is but Satan's desire, Jesus prays for us that our faith will not fail, when Satan tries to *"sift [us] as wheat"* (Luke 22:31). Continue, O gracious Watchman, to forewarn us of our foes, and for Zion's sake do not hold Your peace. *"Watchman, what of the night?"* What weather is coming for the church? Are the clouds lowering, or is it all clear and fair overhead? We must care for the church of God with anxious love; and now that infidelity is threatening, let us observe the signs of the times and prepare for conflict. *"Watchman, what of the night?"* What stars are visible? What precious promises suit our present case? You sound the alarm; give us the consolation also. Christ, the North Star, is ever fixed in His place, and all the stars are secure in the right hand of their Lord. But watchman, when will the morning come? The Bridegroom tarries. Are there no signs of His coming forth as the Sun of Righteousness? Has not the morning star arisen as the pledge of day? When will the day dawn, and the shadows flee away? O Jesus, if You do not come in person to Your waiting church this day, then come in Spirit to my sighing heart, and make it sing for joy.

> Now all the earth is bright and glad
>   With the fresh morn;
> But all my heart is cold, and dark and sad:
> Sun of the soul, let me behold Thy dawn!
>   Come, Jesus, Lord,
> O quickly come, according to Thy word.

The upright love thee.
—Song of Solomon 1:4

Believers love Jesus with a deeper affection than they dare to give to any other being. They would sooner lose father and mother than part with Christ. They hold all earthly comforts with a loose hand, but they carry Him locked securely in their hearts. They voluntarily deny themselves for His sake, but they are not to be driven to deny Him. It is a meager love that the fire of persecution can dry up; the true believer's love is a deeper stream than this. Men have labored to divide the faithful from their Master, but their attempts have been fruitless in every age. Neither crowns of honor nor frowns of anger have untied this Gordian knot. This is no everyday attachment that the world's power may at length dissolve. Neither man nor devils have found a key that opens this lock. Never has the craft of Satan been more at fault than when he has exercised it in seeking to tear apart this union of two divinely welded hearts. It is written, and nothing can blot out the sentence, *"The upright love thee."* The intensity of the love of the upright, however, is not so much to be judged by what it appears as by what the upright long for. It is our daily lament that we cannot love enough. Would that our hearts were capable of holding more and reaching further. Like Samuel Rutherford, we sigh and cry, "Oh, for as much love as would go round about the earth, and over heaven—yea, the heaven of heavens, and ten thousand worlds—that I might let all out upon fair, fair, only fair Christ." Alas, our longest reach is but a span of love, and our affection is but a drop in a bucket compared with what He is due. Measure our love by our intentions, and it is high indeed; we trust that this is how our Lord judges it. Oh, that we could give all the love in all hearts in one great mass, a gathering together of all loves to Him who *"is altogether lovely"* (Song 5:16)!

They...weave the spider's web.
—Isaiah 59:5

ook at a spider's web, and see in it a most suggestive picture of the hypocrite's religion. It is meant to catch its prey: the spider fattens himself on flies, and the Pharisee has his reward. Foolish persons are easily entrapped by the loud professions of pretenders, and even the more judicious cannot always escape. Philip baptized Simon Magus, whose guileful declaration of faith was soon exploded by the stern rebuke of Peter. Custom, reputation, praise, advancement, and other flies are the small game that hypocrites capture in their nets. A spider's web is a marvel of skill: look at it and admire the cunning hunter's wiles. Is not a deceiver's religion equally wonderful? How does he make so barefaced a lie appear to be the truth? How can he make his tinsel answer so well the purpose of gold? A spider's web comes all from the creature's own insides. The bee gathers its wax from flowers; the spider sucks no flowers, yet it spins out its material to any length. In the same way, a hypocrite finds his trust and hope within himself; his anchor is forged on his own anvil, and his cable is twisted by his own hands. He lays his own foundation and hews out the pillars of his own house, disdaining to be a debtor to the sovereign grace of God. But a spider's web is very frail. It is curiously wrought, but not enduringly manufactured. It is no match for the servant's broom or the traveler's staff. The hypocrite needs no battery of high-pressure hydraulics to blow his hope to pieces; a mere puff of wind will do it. Hypocritical cobwebs will soon come down when the broom of destruction begins its purifying work. This reminds us of one more thought: such cobwebs are not to be endured in the Lord's house. He will see to it that they and those who spin them will be destroyed forever. Oh, my soul, rest on something better than a spider's web. May the Lord Jesus be your eternal hiding place.

The city had no need of the sun, neither of the moon, to shine in it.
—Revelation 21:23

Yonder in the better world, the inhabitants are independent of all creature comforts. They have no need of clothing. Their white robes never wear out; neither will they ever be defiled. They require no medicine to heal diseases, for the inhabitants will never need to say, "I am sick." They do not need any sleep to refresh their bodies. They do not rest day or night, but without ever growing weary, they praise Him in His temple. They have no need of social relationships to bring them comfort. Whatever happiness they may derive from association with their fellow saints is not essential to their bliss, for their Lord's presence is enough for their largest desires. They have no need for teachers there. Undoubtedly, they talk with one another concerning the things of God, but they do not require this by way of instruction; they will all *"be taught of the LORD"* (Isa. 54:13). Ours are the alms at the king's gate, but they feast at the table itself. Here we lean on a friendly arm, but there they lean on their Beloved and on Him alone. Here we must have the help of our companions, but there they find all they need in Christ Jesus. Here we look to meat that perishes and to clothing that can be destroyed by moths, but there they find everything in God. We use a bucket to fetch water from the well, but there they drink from the Fountainhead and put their lips to the living water. Here the angels bring us blessings, but we will need no messengers from heaven then. They need no Gabriels there to bring them love notes from God, for there they will see Him face to face. Oh, what a blessed time that will be when we rest in the arms of God! What a glorious hour when God, and not His creatures; the Lord, and not His works, will be our daily joy! Our souls will then have attained the perfection of bliss.

Christ, who is our life.
—Colossians 3:4

aul's marvelously rich expression indicates that Christ is the source of our lives. *"You hath he quick-ened, who were dead in trespasses and sins"* (Eph. 2:1). The same voice that brought Lazarus out of the tomb raised us to *"newness of life"* (Rom. 6:4). He is now the sub-stance of our spiritual life. It is by His life that we live. He is in us, the hope of glory, the spring of our actions, the central thought that directs every other thought. Christ is the sustenance of our lives. What can the Christian feed on but Jesus' flesh and blood? *"This is the bread which cometh down from heaven, that a man may eat thereof, and not die"* (John 6:50). Oh, weary pilgrims in this wilderness of sin, you never get a morsel to satisfy the hunger of your spirits, unless you find it in Him! Christ is the solace of our lives. All our true joys come from Him; and in times of trouble, His presence is our consolation. There is nothing worth living for but Him; and His *"lovingkindness is better than life"* (Ps. 63:3)! Christ is the object of our lives. As the ship speeds toward the port, so the believer hurries toward the haven of his Savior's heart. As the arrow flies to its target, so the Christian flies toward the perfecting of his fellowship with Christ Jesus. As the soldier fights for his captain and is honored by his captain's victory, so the believer contends for Christ and receives his triumph out of the triumphs of his Master. For him *"to live is Christ"* (Phil. 1:21). Christ is the example of our lives. Where there is the same life within, there will, there must be to a great extent, the same developments without. If we live in close fellowship with the Lord Jesus, we will grow like Him. We will set Him before us as our divine Example, and we will seek to walk in His footsteps, until He becomes the crown of our lives in glory. Oh, how safe, how honored, how happy is the Chris-tian, since Christ is his life!

Oh that I were as in months past.
—Job 29:2

Numbers of Christians can view the past with pleasure, but regard the present with dissatisfaction. They look back on the days that they have passed in communing with the Lord as being the sweetest and the best they have ever known, but the present is clad in a sable garb of gloom and dreariness. Once they lived near to Jesus, but now they feel that they have wandered from Him, and they say, *"Oh that I were as in months past."* They complain that they have lost their assurance, that they are not experiencing present peace of mind, that they have no enjoyment in the means of grace, that their consciences are not so tender, or that they no longer have as much zeal for God's glory. The causes of this mournful state of things are manifold. It may arise through a comparative neglect of prayer, for a neglected prayer life is the beginning of all spiritual decline. Or it may be the result of idolatry. The heart has been occupied with something else, more than with God; the affections have been set on the things of earth, instead of on the things of heaven. A jealous God will not be content with a divided heart. He must be loved first and best. He will withdraw the sunshine of His presence from a cold, wandering heart. Or the cause may be found in self-confidence and self-righteousness. Pride is busy in the heart, and self is exalted instead of lying low at the foot of the cross. Christian, if you are not now as you *"were…in months past,"* do not rest satisfied with wishing for a return of former happiness, but go at once to seek your Master and tell Him about your sad state. Ask for His grace and strength to help you to walk more closely with Him. Humble yourself before Him, and He will lift you up and cause you yet again to enjoy the light of His countenance. Do not sit down to sigh and lament. While the beloved Physician lives, there is hope; no, there is a certainty of recovery for the worst cases.

The LORD reigneth; let the earth rejoice.
—Psalm 97:1

here are no reasons for anxiety as long as today's blessed text is true. On earth, the Lord's power as readily controls the rage of the wicked as the rage of the sea. His love as easily refreshes the poor with mercy as the earth with showers. Majesty gleams in flashes of fire amid the tempest's horrors, and the glory of the Lord is seen in its grandeur in the fall of empires and the crash of thrones. In all our conflicts and tribulations, we may behold the hand of the divine King.

> God is God; He sees and hears
> All our troubles, all our tears.
> Soul, forget not, 'mid thy pains,
> God o'er all forever reigns.

In hell, evil spirits acknowledge, with misery, His undoubted supremacy. When they are permitted to roam abroad, it is with a chain at their heels. The bit is in the mouth of the behemoth, and the hook in the jaws of the leviathan. Death's darts are under the Lord's lock, and the grave's prisons have divine power as their warden. The terrible vengeance of the Judge of all the earth makes fiends cower and tremble, even as dogs fear the hunter's whip.

> Fear not death, nor Satan's thrusts,
> God defends who in Him trusts;
> Soul, remember, in thy pains,
> God o'er all forever reigns.

In heaven, none doubt the sovereignty of the King Eternal, but all fall on their faces to pay Him homage. Angels are His courtiers, the redeemed His favorites, and all delight to serve Him day and night. May we soon reach the city of the great King!

> For this life's long night of sadness
> He will give us peace and gladness.
> Soul, remember, in thy pains,
> God o'er all forever reigns.

The cedars of Lebanon, which he hath planted.
—Psalm 104:16

Lebanon's cedars are symbolic of the Christian, in that they owe their planting entirely to the Lord. This is quite true of every child of God. He is not man-planted or self-planted, but God-planted. The mysterious hand of the divine Spirit dropped the living seed into a heart that He had Himself prepared for its reception. Every true heir of heaven acknowledges the great Husbandman as his planter. Moreover, the cedars of Lebanon are not dependent on man for their watering. They stand on the lofty rock, not moistened by human irrigation, yet our heavenly Father provides for them. Thus it is with the Christian who has learned to live by faith. He is independent of man, even in temporal things. For his continued maintenance, he looks to the Lord his God, and to Him alone. The dew of heaven is his portion, and the God of heaven is his fountain. Again, the cedars of Lebanon are not protected by any mortal power. They owe nothing to man for their preservation from stormy wind and tempest. They are God's trees, kept and preserved by Him, and by Him alone. It is precisely the same with the Christian. He is not a hothouse plant, sheltered from temptation; he stands in the most exposed position. He has no shelter, no protection, except this: the broad wings of the eternal God always cover the cedars that He Himself has planted. Like cedars, believers are full of sap having vitality enough to always be green, even amid winter's snows. Last, the flourishing and majestic condition of the cedar is to the praise of God only. The Lord, even the Lord alone, has been everything to the cedars; therefore, David very sweetly put it in one of the psalms, *"Praise the LORD...fruitful trees, and all cedars"* (Ps. 148:7, 9). In the believer there is nothing that can magnify man. He is planted, nourished, and protected by the Lord's own hand, and to Him let all the glory be ascribed!

Thou, LORD, hast made me glad through thy work.
—Psalm 92:4

Do you believe that your sins are forgiven and that Christ has made a full atonement for them? Then what a joyful Christian you ought to be! How you should live above the common trials and troubles of the world! Since sin is forgiven, can it matter what happens to you now? Luther said, "Smite, Lord, smite, for my sin is forgiven; if Thou hast but forgiven me, smite as hard as Thou wilt." In a similar spirit you may say, "Send sickness, poverty, losses, crosses, persecution; send what You will, for You have forgiven me, and my soul is glad." Christian, if you are thus saved, while you are glad, be grateful and loving. Cling to the cross that took your sin away; serve Him who served you. *"I beseech you therefore, brethren, by the mercies of God, that ye present your bodies a living sacrifice, holy, acceptable unto God, which is your reasonable service"* (Rom. 12:1). Do not let your zeal evaporate in some little exuberant outburst of song. Show your love in expressive ways. Love the brethren of Him who loved you. If there is a Mephibosheth anywhere who is lame or halt, help him for Jonathan's sake. If there is a poor tried believer, weep with him and bear his cross for the sake of Him who wept for you and carried your sins. Since you are thus forgiven freely for Christ's sake, go and tell to others the joyful news of pardoning mercy. Do not be content with this unspeakable blessing for yourself alone, but publish abroad the story of the Cross. Holy gladness and holy boldness will make you a good preacher, and all the world will be a pulpit for you to preach in. Cheerful holiness is the most forcible of sermons, but the Lord must give it to you. Seek it this morning before you go into the world. When it is the Lord's work in which we rejoice, we do not need to be afraid of being too glad.

Isaac went out to meditate in the field at the eventide.
—Genesis 24:63

Isaac spent his time in an admirable pursuit. If those who spend so many hours in idle company, light reading, and useless pastimes could learn wisdom, they would find more profitable society and more interesting engagements in meditation than in the vanities that now have such charms for them. We would all know more, live nearer to God, and grow in grace, if we were alone more. Meditation chews the cud and extracts the real nutriment from the mental food gathered elsewhere. When Jesus is the theme, meditation is sweet indeed. Isaac found Rebekah while engaged in private musings; many others have found their best beloved there. Isaac's choice of place was admirable as well. In the field we have a study hung round with texts for thought. From the cedar to the hyssop, from the soaring eagle down to the chirping grasshopper, from the blue expanse of heaven to a drop of dew, all things are full of teaching; and when the eye is divinely opened, that teaching flashes upon the mind far more vividly than from written books. Our little rooms are neither as healthy, as suggestive, as agreeable, or as inspiring as the fields. Let us count nothing common or unclean, but feel that all created things point to their Maker, and the field will at once be hallowed. Isaac's choice of time for meditation was also wise. The season of sunset as it draws a veil over the day befits that repose of the soul when earthly cares yield to the joys of heavenly communion. The glory of the setting sun excites our wonder, and the solemnity of approaching night awakens our awe. If the business of this day will permit it, it will be well, dear reader, if you can spare an hour to walk in the field at eventide; if not, the Lord is in the town, too, and will meet with you in your house or on the crowded street. Let your heart go forth to meet Him.

Give unto the LORD the glory due unto his name.
—Psalm 29:2

God's glory is the result of His nature and acts. He is glorious in His character, for there is such a store of everything that is holy, good, and lovely in God that He must be glorious. The actions that flow from His character are also glorious; while He intends that they should manifest to His creatures His goodness, mercy, and justice, He is equally concerned that the glory associated with them should be given only to Himself. Nor is there anything in ourselves in which we may glory, for who makes us different from another? And what do we have that we did not receive from the God of all grace? Then how careful we should be to walk humbly before the Lord! The moment we glorify ourselves, since there is room for one glory only in the universe, we set ourselves up as rivals of the Most High. Will the insect of an hour glorify itself against the sun that warmed it into life? Will pottery exalt itself above the one who fashioned it on the wheel? Will the dust of the desert strive with the whirlwind? Or the drops of the ocean struggle with the tempest? Give to the Lord, all righteous people. *"Give unto the LORD the glory due unto his name."* Yet it is, perhaps, one of the hardest struggles of the Christian life to learn this sentence— *"Not unto us, O LORD, not unto us, but unto thy name give glory"* (Ps. 115:1). It is a lesson that God is ever teaching us, and teaching us sometimes through the most painful discipline. Let a Christian begin to boast, *"I can do all things,"* without adding *"through Christ which strengtheneth me"* (Phil. 4:13), and before long he will have to groan, "I can do nothing," and moan himself into the dust. When we do anything for the Lord, and He is pleased to accept our actions, let us lay our crown at His feet and exclaim, *"Not I, but the grace of God which was with me"* (1 Cor. 15:10)!

The mercy of God.
—Psalm 52:8

editate a little on this mercy of the Lord. It is *tender* mercy. With gentle, loving touch, He heals the broken in heart and binds up their wounds. He is as gracious in the manner of His mercy as in the matter of it. It is *great* mercy. There is nothing little in God. His mercy is like Himself: it is infinite. You cannot measure it. His mercy is so great that it forgives great sins to great sinners, after great lengths of time, and then, it gives great favors and great privileges, and raises us up to great enjoyments in the great heaven of the great God. It is *undeserved* mercy, as indeed all true mercy must be, for deserved mercy is only a misnomer for justice. There was no right on the sinner's part to the kind consideration of the Most High. Had the rebel been doomed at once to eternal fire, he would have truly deserved the sentence. But if he was delivered from wrath, sovereign love alone was the reason, for there was no goodness in the sinner himself. It is *rich* mercy. Some things are great, but have little efficacy in them, but this mercy is an encouragement to drooping spirits; a golden ointment to bleeding wounds; a heavenly bandage to broken bones; a royal chariot for weary feet; and an embrace of love for trembling hearts. It is *manifold* mercy. As Bunyan said, "All the flowers in God's garden are double." There is no single mercy. You may think you have but one mercy, but you will find it to be a whole cluster of mercies. It is *abounding* mercy. Millions have received it, yet far from its being exhausted, it is as fresh, as full, and as free as ever. It is *unfailing* mercy. It will never leave you. If mercy is your friend, mercy will be with you in temptation to keep you from yielding; with you in trouble to prevent you from sinking; with you in living to be the light and life of your countenance; and with you in dying to be the joy of your soul when earthly comfort is ebbing fast.

Strangers are come into the sanctuaries of the LORD'S house.
—Jeremiah 51:51

In this account the faces of the Lord's people were covered with shame, for it was a terrible thing that men would intrude into the Holy Place that was reserved for the priests alone. Everywhere about us we see similar reasons for sorrow. How many ungodly men are now being educated with the view of entering the ministry! What a crying sin is that solemn lie by which our whole population is nominally included in a national church! How fearful it is that ordinances should be pressed upon the unconverted, and that among the more enlightened churches of our land, there should be such laxity of discipline. If the thousands who will read this portion will all take this matter before the Lord Jesus this day, He will intercede and avert the evil that otherwise will come on His church. To adulterate the church is to pollute a well, to pour water on fire, to sow a fertile field with stones. May we all have grace to maintain in our own proper way the purity of the church, as being an assembly of believers, and not an unsaved community of unconverted men. Our zeal must, however, begin at home. Let us examine ourselves as to our right to eat at the Lord's Table. Let us see to it that we have on our wedding garment, lest we ourselves be intruders in the Lord's sanctuaries. *"Many are called, but few are chosen"* (Matt. 22:14); *"strait is the gate, and narrow is the way, which leadeth unto life"* (Matt. 7:14). Oh, for grace to come to Jesus aright, with the faith of God's elect. He who smote Uzzah (see 2 Samuel 6:3–7) for touching the ark is very jealous of His two ordinances. As a true believer, I may approach them freely; as a stranger, I must not touch them lest I die. To search one's heart is the duty of all who are baptized or come to the Lord's Table. *"Search me, O God, and know my heart: try me, and know my thoughts"* (Ps. 139:23).

He shall stand and feed in the strength of the LORD.
—Micah 5:4

hrist's reign in His church is that of a Shepherd-King. He has supremacy, but it is the superiority of a wise and tender Shepherd over His needy and loving flock. He commands and receives obedience, but it is the willing obedience of the well-cared-for sheep, rendered joyfully to their beloved Shepherd, whose voice they know so well. He rules by the force of love and the energy of goodness. His reign is practical in its character. It is said, *"He shall stand and feed."* The great Head of the church is actively engaged in providing for His people. He does not sit down on the throne in an empty state or hold a scepter without wielding it in government. No! He stands and feeds. The word *"feed,"* in the original, is analogous to one in the Greek that means to "shepherdize," to do everything expected of a shepherd: to guide, to watch, to preserve, to restore, to tend, as well as to feed. His reign is continual in its duration. It is said, *"He shall stand and feed"*; not "He will feed now and then, and leave His position"; not "He will one day grant a revival, and then the next day leave His church to barrenness." His eyes never slumber, and His hands never rest. His heart never ceases to beat with love, and His shoulders are never weary of carrying His people's burdens. His reign is completely powerful in its action. He feeds in the strength of Jehovah. Wherever Christ is, there is God; and whatever Christ does is the act of the Most High. Oh, it is a joyful truth to consider that He who stands today representing the interests of His people is very God of very God, to whom every knee will bow! We are happy to belong to such a Shepherd, whose humanity communes with us, and whose divinity protects us. Let us worship and bow down before Him as *"the people of his pasture"* (Ps. 95:7).

The sweet psalmist of Israel.
—2 Samuel 23:1

Among all the saints whose lives are recorded in Holy Writ, David possessed an experience of the most striking, varied, and instructive character. In his history, we meet with trials and temptations not to be discovered, as a whole, in other saints of ancient times; hence, he is all the more suggestive a type of our Lord. David knew the trials of all ranks and conditions of men. Kings have their troubles, and David wore a crown. The peasant has his cares, and David handled a shepherd's crook. The wanderer has many hardships, and David abode in the caves of Engedi. The captain has his difficulties, and David found the sons of Zeruiah too hard for him. The psalmist was also tried by his friends. His counselor Ahithophel forsook him: *"Mine own familiar friend, in whom I trusted, which did eat of my bread, hath lifted up his heel against me"* (Ps. 41:9). His worst foes were those of his own household, and his children were his greatest affliction. The temptations of poverty and wealth, of honor and reproach, of health and weakness, all tried their power on him. He had temptations from without to disturb his peace, and from within to mar his joy. David no sooner escaped from one trial than he fell into another; he no sooner emerged from one season of despondency and alarm than he was again brought into the lowest depths, and all God's waves and billows rolled over him. It is probably this reason that David's psalms are so universally the delight of experienced Christians. Whatever our frame of mind, whether ecstasy or depression, David has exactly described our emotions. He was an able master of the human heart because he had been tutored in the best of all schools—the school of heartfelt, personal experience. As we are instructed in the same school, as we grow mature in grace and in years, we increasingly appreciate David's psalms and find them to be *"green pastures"* (Ps. 23:2). My soul, let David's experience cheer and counsel you this day.

He that watereth shall be watered also himself.
—Proverbs 11:25

ere we are taught the great lesson that to receive, we must give; that to accumulate, we must scatter; that to make ourselves happy, we must make others happy; and that in order to become spiritually vigorous, we must seek the spiritual good of others. In watering others, we are ourselves watered. How? Our efforts to be useful bring out our powers for usefulness. We have latent talents and dormant faculties that are brought to light by exercise. Our strength for labor is hidden even from ourselves, until we venture forth to fight the Lord's battles or to climb the mountains of difficulty. We do not know what tender sympathies we possess until we try to dry the widow's tears or soothe the orphan's grief. We often find in attempting to teach others that we gain instruction for ourselves. Oh, what gracious lessons some of us have learned at sickbeds! We went to teach the Scriptures, and we came away blushing that we knew so little of them. In our conversations with poor saints, we are taught the way of God more perfectly for ourselves and receive a deeper insight into divine truth. So that watering others makes us humble. We discover how much grace there is where we had not looked for it, and how much the poor saint may outstrip us in knowledge. Our own comfort is also increased by our working for others. We endeavor to cheer them, and the consolation gladdens our own heart. Like the two men in the snow, one rubbed the other's limbs to keep him from dying, and in so doing kept his own blood in circulation and saved his own life. The poor widow of Sarepta gave from her scanty store a supply for the prophet's needs, and from that day she never again knew what it was to be in need. *"Give, and it shall be given unto you; good measure, pressed down, and shaken together, and running over"* (Luke 6:38).

I charge you, O daughters of Jerusalem, if ye find my beloved,
that ye tell him, that I am sick of love.
—Song of Solomon 5:8

uch is the language of the believer panting after present fellowship with Jesus: he is sick for his Lord. Gracious souls are never perfectly at ease unless they are
in a state of nearness to Christ, for when they are away
from Him, they lose their peace. The nearer to Him, the
nearer they are to the perfect calm of heaven; the nearer to
Him, the fuller their heart is, not only of peace, but also of
life, vigor, and joy, for these all depend on constant communion with Jesus. What the sun is to the day, what the
moon is to the night, what the dew is to the flower, such is
Jesus Christ to us. What bread is to the hungry, clothing to
the naked, the shadow of a great rock to the traveler in a
weary land, such is Jesus Christ to us; therefore, if we are
not consciously one with Him, it is little wonder if our
spirits cry in the words of the Song, *"I charge you, O daugh-*
ters of Jerusalem, if ye find my beloved, that ye tell him, that I am
sick of love." This earnest longing after Jesus has a blessing
attending it: *"Blessed are they which do hunger and thirst after*
righteousness" (Matt. 5:6). Supremely blessed, therefore, are
those who thirst after the Righteous One. Blessed is that
hunger, since it comes from God. If I may not have the full-
blown blessedness of being filled, I would seek the same
blessedness in its sweet budding stages of emptiness and
eagerness, until I am filled with Christ. If I may not feed on
Jesus, it will be next door to heaven to hunger and thirst
after Him. There is a blessedness about that hunger, since it
sparkles among the beatitudes of our Lord. But the blessing
involves a promise. Such hungry ones *"shall be filled"* (v. 6)
with what they are desiring. If Christ thus causes us to long
after Himself, He will certainly satisfy those longings; and
when He does come to us, as come He will, oh, how sweet it
will be!

The voice of weeping shall be no more heard.
—Isaiah 65:19

he glorified weep no more, for all outward causes of grief are gone. There are no broken friendships or blighted prospects in heaven. Poverty, famine, peril, persecution, and slander are unknown there. No pain distresses; no thought of death or bereavement saddens. They weep no more, for they are perfectly sanctified. No *"evil heart of unbelief"* (Heb. 3:12) prompts them to depart from the living God. They are without fault before His throne and are fully conformed to His image. Well may they cease to mourn who have ceased to sin. They weep no more, because all fear of change is past. They know that they are eternally secure. Sin is shut out, and they are shut in. They live in a city that will never be stormed. They bask in a sun that will never set. They drink from a river that will never run dry, and they pick fruit from a tree that will never wither. Countless cycles may revolve, but eternity will not be exhausted; while eternity endures, their immortality and blessedness will coexist with it. They are forever with the Lord. They weep no more, because every desire is fulfilled. They cannot wish for anything that they do not already have in their possession. Eye and ear, heart and hand, judgment, imagination, hope, desire, will, and all the faculties are completely satisfied. As imperfect as our present ideas are of the things that God has prepared for those who love Him, we know enough by the revelation of the Spirit to know that the saints above are supremely blessed. The joy of Christ, which is an infinite fullness of delight, is in them. They bathe themselves in the bottomless, shoreless sea of infinite beatitude. That same joyful rest remains for us. It may not be far distant. Before long the weeping willow will be exchanged for the palm branch of victory, and sorrow's dewdrops will be transformed into the pearls of everlasting bliss. *"Wherefore comfort one another with these words"* (1 Thess. 4:18).

The breaker is come up before them.
—Micah 2:13

ecause Jesus has gone before us, things are not the same as they would have been had He never passed that way. He has conquered every foe that obstructed the way. Cheer up now, you fainthearted warrior. Not only has Christ traveled the road, but He has slain your enemies. Do you dread sin? He has nailed it to His cross. Do you fear death? He has been the death of death. Are you afraid of hell? He has barred it against the advent of any of His children; they will never see the gulf of perdition. Whatever foes may be before the Christian, they are all overcome. There are lions, but their teeth are broken; there are serpents, but their fangs are extracted; there are rivers, but they are bridged or fordable; there are flames, but we wear that matchless garment that makes us invulnerable to fire. The sword that has been forged against us is already blunted. The instruments of war that the enemy is preparing have already lost their point. God has taken away in the person of Christ all the power that anything can have to hurt us. The army may safely march on, then, and you may go joyously along your journey, for all your enemies are conquered beforehand. What will you do but march on to take the prey? They are beaten; they are vanquished. All you have to do is to divide the spoil. You will, it is true, often engage in combat; but your fight will be with a vanquished foe. His head is broken. He may attempt to injure you, but his strength will not be sufficient for his malicious design. Your victory will be easy, and your treasure will be beyond counting.

Proclaim aloud the Savior's fame,
    Who bears the Breaker's wond'rous name;
Sweet name; and it becomes Him well,
    Who breaks down earth, sin, death, and hell.

His fruit was sweet to my taste.
—Song of Solomon 2:3

aith, in the Scripture, is spoken of as pertaining to all the senses. It is sight: *"Look unto me, and be ye saved"* (Isa. 45:22). It is hearing: *"Hear, and your soul shall live"* (Isa. 55:3). Faith is smelling: *"All thy garments smell of myrrh, and aloes, and cassia"* (Ps. 45:8); *"thy name is as ointment poured forth"* (Song 1:3). Faith is spiritual touch. By this faith the woman came behind and touched the hem of Christ's garment, and by this we handle the things of the good word of life. Faith is equally the spirit's taste. *"How sweet are thy words unto my taste! yea, sweeter than honey to my mouth"* (Ps. 119:103). Jesus said, *"Except ye eat the flesh of the Son of man, and drink his blood, ye have no life in you"* (John 6:53). This taste is faith in one of its highest operations. One of the first performances of faith is hearing. We hear the voice of God, not with the outward ear alone, but with the inward ear. We hear it as God's Word, and we believe it to be so. That is the hearing of faith. Then our mind looks on the truth as it is presented to us; that is to say, we understand it; we perceive its meaning. That is the seeing of faith. Next we discover its preciousness. We begin to admire it, and find how fragrant it is. That is faith in its smell. Then we appropriate the mercies that are prepared for us in Christ; that is faith in its touch. Hence follow the enjoyments—peace, delight, and communion—which are faith in its taste. Any one of these acts of faith is saving. To hear Christ's voice as the sure voice of God in the soul will save us, but what gives true enjoyment is the aspect of faith wherein Christ, by holy taste, is received into us, and made, by inward and spiritual understanding of His sweetness and preciousness, to be the food of our souls. It is then we sit *"under his shadow with great delight"* (Song 2:3) and find *"his fruit sweet to [our] taste."*

He hath commanded his covenant for ever.
—Psalm 111:9

The Lord's people delight in the covenant. It is an unfailing source of consolation to them as often as the Holy Spirit leads them into its banqueting house and waves its banner of love. They delight to contemplate the antiquity of that covenant, remembering that before the sun knew its place or planets followed their orbits, the interests of the saints were made secure in Christ Jesus. It is particularly pleasing to them to remember the sureness of the covenant, while meditating on *"the sure mercies of David"* (Isa. 55:3). They delight to celebrate it as signed, sealed, and ratified, in all things ordered well. It often makes their hearts swell with joy to think of its immutability, as a covenant that neither time nor eternity, life nor death, will ever be able to violate—a covenant as old as eternity and as everlasting as the Rock of ages. They rejoice also to feast on the fullness of this covenant, for they see in it all things provided for them. God is their portion, Christ their Companion, the Spirit their Comforter, earth their house, and heaven their home. They see in it an inheritance reserved and assigned to every soul possessing an interest in its ancient and eternal gift. Their eyes sparkled when they saw it as a gold mine in the Bible; but oh, how their souls were gladdened when they saw in the last will and testament of their divine Kinsman that it was bequeathed to them! More especially it is the pleasure of God's people to contemplate the graciousness of this covenant. They see that the law was made void because it was a covenant of works and depended on merit; but this they perceive to be enduring because grace is the basis, grace the condition, grace the strain, grace the bulwark, grace the foundation, grace the top-stone. The covenant is a treasury of wealth, a granary of food, a fountain of life, a storehouse of salvation, a charter of peace, and a haven of joy.

How long will it be ere they believe me?
—Numbers 14:11

Strive with all diligence to keep out that monster of unbelief. It so dishonors Christ, that He will withdraw His visible presence if we insult Him by indulging it. It is true it is a weed, the seeds of which we can never entirely extract from the soil, but we must aim at its root with zeal and perseverance. Among hateful things it is the most to be abhorred. Its injurious nature is so venomous that he who exercises it and he on whom it is exercised are both hurt by it. In your case, believer, it is most wicked, for the mercies of your Lord in the past increase your guilt in doubting Him now. When you distrust the Lord Jesus, He may well cry out, *"Behold, I am pressed under you, as a cart is pressed that is full of sheaves"* (Amos 2:13). This is crowning His head with thorns of the sharpest kind. It is very cruel for a well-beloved wife to mistrust a kind and faithful husband. The sin is needless, foolish, and unwarranted. Jesus has never given the slightest ground for suspicion, and it is hard to be doubted by those to whom our conduct is uniformly affectionate and true. Jesus is the Son of the Highest and has unbounded wealth; it is shameful to doubt Omnipotence and distrust His all-sufficiency. The cattle on a thousand hills will suffice for our hungriest feeding, and the granaries of heaven are not likely to be emptied by our eating. If Christ were only a cistern, we might soon exhaust His fullness, but who can drain a fountain? Myriads of spirits have drawn their supplies from Him, and not one of them has murmured at the scantiness of His resources. Banish this lying traitor, unbelief, for his only errand is to cut the bonds of communion and make us mourn an absent Savior. Bunyan said that unbelief has "as many lives as a cat." If that is so, let us kill one life now, and continue the work until the whole nine are gone. Down with you, traitor. My heart abhors you!

Oil for the light.
—Exodus 25:6

My soul, how much you need this oil, for your lamp will not continue to burn long without it. Your snuff will smoke and become an offense if light is gone, and gone it will be if oil is absent. You have no oil well springing up in your human nature; therefore, you must go to them who sell and buy for yourself, or like the foolish virgins, you will have to cry, *"Our lamps are gone out"* (Matt. 25:8). Even the consecrated lamps could not give light without oil. Although they shone in the tabernacle, they needed to be fed. Even though no rough winds blew on them, they needed to be trimmed, and your need is equally as great. Under the happiest of circumstances, you cannot give light for another hour unless the fresh oil of grace is given to you. Not every oil could be used in the Lord's service. Neither the petroleum that exudes so plentifully from the earth nor that which is produced by fish nor that extracted from nuts would be accepted. Only the best olive oil was selected. Pretended grace from natural goodness or imaginary grace from priestly hands or from outward ceremonies will never serve the true saint of God. He knows that the Lord would not be pleased with rivers of such oil. He goes to the olive press of Gethsemane and draws his supplies from Him who was crushed therein. The oil of gospel grace is free from impurities; hence, the light that is fed on it is clear and bright. Our churches are the Savior's golden candelabra, and if they are to be lights in this dark world, they must have much holy oil. Let us pray for ourselves, our ministers, and our churches that they may never lack oil for the light. Truth, holiness, joy, knowledge, and love are all beams of the sacred light, but we cannot exemplify them in our lives unless we receive oil from God the Holy Spirit in private.

Have mercy upon me, O God.
—Psalm 51:1

When Dr. Carey was suffering from a serious illness, he was asked, "If this sickness should prove fatal, what passage would you select as the text for your funeral sermon?" He replied, "Oh, I feel that such a poor sinful creature is unworthy to have anything said about him, but if a funeral sermon must be preached, let it be from the words, *'Have mercy upon me, O God, according to thy lovingkindness: according unto the multitude of thy tender mercies blot out my transgressions'* (Ps. 51:1)." In the same spirit of humility he directed in his will that the following inscription, and nothing more, should be cut on his gravestone:

WILLIAM CAREY, BORN AUGUST 17, 1761; DIED
A wretched, poor, and helpless worm,
On Thy kind arms I fall.

Only on the footing of free grace can the most experienced and most honored of the saints approach their God. The best of men are conscious above all others that they are men at best. Empty boats float high, but heavily laden vessels are low in the water; mere professors of faith can boast, but true children of God cry for mercy, recognizing their unworthiness. We need the Lord's mercy on our good works, our prayers, our preaching, our almsgiving, and our holiest things. The blood was sprinkled not only on the doorposts of Israel's dwelling houses, but also on the sanctuary, the mercy seat, and the altar, because as sin intrudes into our holiest things, the blood of Jesus is needed to purify them from defilement. If mercy is needed to be exercised toward our duties, what will be said of our sins? How sweet to remember that inexhaustible mercy is waiting to be gracious to us, to restore our backslidings, and to make our broken bones rejoice!

Wait on the LORD.
—Psalm 27:14

t may seem to be an easy thing to wait, but it is one of the postures that a Christian soldier does not learn without years of teaching. Marching is much easier for God's warriors than standing still. There are hours of perplexity when the most willing spirit, anxiously desirous to serve the Lord, does not know what action to take. Then what will it do? Vex itself by despair? Fly back in cowardice, turn to the right hand in fear, or rush forward in presumption? No, it must simply wait. Wait in prayer, however. Call on God, and spread the case before Him. Tell Him your difficulty and plead His promise of aid. In dilemmas between one duty and another, it is sweet to be humble as a child and to wait with simplicity of soul on the Lord. It is sure to be well with us when we feel and know our own folly and are heartily willing to be guided by the will of God. But wait in faith. Express your unstaggering confidence in Him. Unfaithful, untrusting waiting is an insult to the Lord. Believe that if He keep you tarrying even until midnight, He will come at the right time. The vision will come and will not tarry. Wait in quiet patience, not rebelling because you are under affliction, but blessing your God for it. Never murmur as the children of Israel did against Moses. Never wish you could go back to the world again, but accept the situation as it is and put it as it stands, simply and with your whole heart, without any self-will, into the hand of your covenant God. Say, "Now, Lord, not my will, but Yours be done. I do not know what to do. I am brought to extremities, but I will wait until You divide the floods or drive back my foes. I will wait, even if You keep me waiting for many days, because my heart is fixed on You alone, O God. My spirit waits for You in the full conviction that You will yet be my joy and my salvation, my refuge and my strong tower."

On mine arm shall they trust.
—Isaiah 51:5

In seasons of severe trial, the Christian has nothing on earth that he can trust in; therefore, he is compelled to cast himself on God alone. When his vessel is on its beam's end, and no human deliverance can avail, he must simply and entirely trust himself to the providence and care of God. Happy storm that wrecks a man on such a rock as this! O blessed hurricane that drives the soul to God and God alone! There is no communing with our God sometimes because of the multitude of our friends. But when a man is so poor, so friendless, so helpless that he has nowhere else to turn, he flies into his Father's arms and is blessedly embraced! When he is burdened with troubles so pressing and so unique that he cannot tell them to anyone but to God, he may be thankful for them. He will learn more of his Lord, then, than at any other time. Oh, tempest-tossed believer, it is a happy trouble that drives you to your Father! Now that you have only your God to trust, see that you put your full confidence in Him. Do not dishonor your Lord and Master by unworthy doubts and fears; but be strong in faith, giving glory to God. Show the world that your God is worth ten thousand worlds to you. Show rich men how rich you are in your poverty when the Lord God is your Helper. Show the strong man how strong you are in your weakness when underneath you are the *"everlasting arms"* (Deut. 33:27). Now is the time for feats of faith and valiant exploits. Be strong and courageous, and the Lord your God will certainly, as surely as He built the heavens and the earth, glorify Himself in your weakness and magnify His might in the midst of your distress. The grandeur of the arch of heaven would be spoiled if the sky were supported by a single visible column, and your faith would lose its glory if it rested on anything discernible by the carnal eye. May the Holy Spirit help you to rest in Jesus this closing day of the month.

Thou shalt guide me with thy counsel,
and afterward receive me to glory.
—Psalm 73:24

he psalmist felt his need of divine guidance. He had just been discovering the foolishness of his own heart, and lest he would be constantly led astray by it, he resolved that God's counsel would henceforth guide him. A sense of our own folly is a great step toward being wise, when it leads us to rely on the wisdom of the Lord. The blind man leans on his friend's arm and reaches home in safety. Likewise, we should give ourselves up implicitly to divine guidance, nothing doubting, assured that though we cannot see, it is always safe to trust the all-seeing God. *"Thou shalt"* is a blessed expression of confidence. He was sure that the Lord would not decline the condescending task. There is a word for you, believer; rest in it. Be assured that your God will be your counselor and friend. He will guide you and will direct all your ways. In His written Word you have this assurance in part fulfilled, for Holy Scripture is His counsel to you. We are happy to have God's Word always to guide us! What would the mariner be without his compass? And what would the Christian be without the Bible? This is the unerring chart, the map in which every shoal is described, and all the channels from the quicksands of destruction to the haven of salvation are mapped and marked by One who knows all the way. Bless You, O God, that we may trust You to guide us now, and guide us even to the end! After this guidance through life, the psalmist anticipated a divine reception at last—*"and afterward receive me to glory."* What a thought for you, believer! God Himself will receive you to glory—you! Though you are wandering, erring, straying, yet He will bring you safe at last to glory! This is your portion. Live on it this day, and if perplexities should surround you, go, in the strength of this text, straight to the throne.

But Simon's wife's mother lay sick of a fever,
and anon they tell him of her.
—Mark 1:30

his little peep into the house of the apostolic fisherman is very interesting. We see at once that household joys and cares are no hindrance to the full
exercise of ministry. In fact, since they furnish an opportunity for personally witnessing the Lord's gracious work on
one's own flesh and blood, they may even instruct the
teacher better than any other earthly discipline. Papists and
other Nonconformists may decry marriage, but true Christianity and household life go well together. Peter's house
was probably a poor fisherman's hut, but the Lord of Glory
entered it, lodged in it, and worked a miracle in it. If our
little book is read this morning in some very humble cottage, let this fact encourage those who reside there to seek
the company of King Jesus. God is in small homes more
often than in rich palaces. Jesus is looking around your
room now and is waiting to be gracious to you. Sickness
had entered Simon's house; fever in a deadly form had pros-
trated his mother-in-law. As soon as Jesus came, they told
Him of the sad affliction, and He hurried to the patient's
bed. Do you have any sickness in your house this morning?
You will find Jesus to be the best physician by far. Go to
Him at once and tell Him all about the matter. Immediately
lay the case before Him. It concerns one of His people;
therefore, it will not be trivial to Him. Observe that the
Savior restored the sick woman immediately. No one can
heal as He does. We may not be certain that the Lord will
remove all disease right away from those we love, but we
do know that believing prayer for the sick is far more likely
to be followed by restoration than anything else in the
world. Where prayer does not avail, we must meekly bow
to His will by whom life and death are determined. The
tender heart of Jesus waits to hear our grief. Let us pour
them into His patient ear.

Thou whom my soul loveth.
—Song of Solomon 1:7

It is wonderful to be able, without any *if* or *but*, to say of the Lord Jesus—*"Thou whom my soul loveth."* Many can say of Jesus only that they *hope* they love Him; they *trust* they love Him; but only a poor and shallow experience will be content to stay here. No one should give any rest to his spirit until he feels quite sure about this vitally important matter. We should not be satisfied with a superficial hope that Jesus loves us or with a bare trust that we love Him. The old saints did not generally speak with *but*s, *if*s, *hope*s, and *trust*s, but they spoke positively and plainly. *"I know whom I have believed"* (2 Tim. 1:12), Paul said. *"I know that my redeemer liveth"* (Job 19:25), said Job. Get positive knowledge of your love for Jesus, and do not be satisfied until you can speak of your interest in Him as a reality, which you have made certain by having received the witness of the Holy Spirit and His seal on your soul by faith. True love for Christ is in every case the Holy Spirit's work, and it must be wrought in the heart by Him. He is the Agent of it, but the logical reason for our love for Jesus lies in Himself. Why do we love Jesus? *"Because he first loved us"* (1 John 4:19). Why do we love Jesus? Because He *"gave himself for us"* (Titus 2:14). We have life through His death; we have peace through His blood. *"Though he was rich, yet for* [our] *sakes he became poor"* (2 Cor. 8:9). Why do we love Jesus? Because of the excellency of His person. We are filled with a sense of His beauty, an admiration of His charms, and a consciousness of His infinite perfection! His greatness, goodness, and loveliness, in one resplendent ray, combine to enchant the soul until it is so ravished that it exclaims, *"Yea, he is altogether lovely"* (Song 5:16). This is a blessed love, a love that binds the heart with chains that are softer than silk, yet firmer than stone!

I will; be thou clean.
—Mark 1:41

Primeval darkness heard the Almighty command, *"Let there be light"* (Gen. 1:3), and immediately *"there was light"* (v. 3). The word of the Lord Jesus is equal in majesty to that ancient word of power. Redemption, like Creation, has its word of might. Jesus speaks, and it is done. Leprosy yielded to no human remedies, but it fled at once at the Lord's *"I will."* The disease exhibited no hopeful signs or tokens of recovery. Nature contributed nothing to its own healing, but the unaided word effected the entire work on the spot and forever. The sinner is in a plight more miserable than the leper. Let him imitate the leper's example and go to Jesus, *"beseeching him, and kneeling down to him"* (Mark 1:40). Let him exercise what little faith he has, even though it should go no further than, "Lord, *'if thou wilt, thou canst make me clean'* (v. 40)." There need be no doubt as to the result of the application. Jesus heals all who come and casts out none. In reading the narrative in which our morning's text occurs, it is worthy of devout notice that Jesus touched the leper. This unclean person had broken through the regulations of the ceremonial law and pressed into the house, but Jesus, far from chiding him, broke through the law Himself in order to meet him. Jesus made an interchange with the leper, for while He cleansed him, He contracted by that touch a Levitical defilement. Likewise, Jesus Christ was made sin for us, although in Himself He knew no sin, so that we might be made the righteousness of God in Him. Oh, that poor sinners would go to Jesus, believing in the power of His blessed substitutionary work, and they would soon learn the power of His gracious touch. That hand that multiplied the loaves, that saved sinking Peter, that upholds afflicted saints, that crowns believers, that same hand will touch every seeking sinner and in a moment make him clean. The love of Jesus is the source of salvation. He loves, He looks, He touches us, and we live!

Woe is me, that I sojourn in Mesech, that I dwell in the tents of Kedar!
—Psalm 120:5

s a Christian you have to live in the midst of an ungodly world, and it is of little use for you to cry
"Woe is me." Jesus did not pray that you would be
taken out of the world, and what He did not pray for, you
do not need to desire. It is far better to meet the difficulty
in the Lord's strength and to glorify Him in it. The enemy
is always on watch to detect inconsistency in your conduct;
therefore, be very holy. Remember that the eyes of all are
on you, and that more is expected from you than from other
men. Strive to give no occasion for blame. Let your goodness be the only fault they can discover in you. Like Daniel,
compel them to say of you, *"We shall not find any occasion
against this Daniel, except we find it against him concerning the
law of his God"* (Dan. 6:5). Seek to be useful as well as consistent. Perhaps you think, "If I were in a more favorable
position, I might serve the Lord's cause; but I cannot do
any good where I am." But the worse the people are around
you, the more they need your good example. If they are
crooked, the more they need you to set them straight. If
they are perverse, the more they need for you to turn their
proud hearts to the truth. Where should the physician be
but where there are many sick? Where is honor to be won
by the soldier but in the hottest fire of the battle? And
when weary of the strife and sin that meets you on every
hand, consider that all the saints have endured the same
trial. They were not carried on beds of down to heaven, and
you must not expect to travel more easily than they. They
had to hazard their lives to the death in the high places of
the field, and you will not be crowned until you also have
endured *"hardness, as a good soldier of Jesus Christ"* (2 Tim.
2:3). Therefore, *"stand fast in the faith, quit you* [conduct
yourselves] *like men, be strong"* (1 Cor. 16:13).

In the midst of a crooked and perverse nation,
among whom ye shine as lights in the world.
—Philippians 2:15

We use lights in order to see things more clearly. A Christian should so shine in his life that a person could not live with him a week without knowing the Gospel. His conversation should be such that all who are around him would clearly perceive whose he is and whom he serves. People should see the image of Jesus reflected in his daily actions. Lights are intended for guidance. We are to help those around us who are in the dark. We are to hold forth the Word of life to them. We are to point sinners to the Savior and the weary to a divine resting place. Men sometimes read their Bibles and fail to understand them. We should be ready, like Philip, to instruct the inquirer in the meaning of God's Word, the way of salvation, and the life of godliness. Lights are also used for warning. On our rocks and shoals a lighthouse is sure to be erected. Christians should know that there are many false lights shining everywhere in the world; therefore, the right light is needed. The wreckers of Satan are always abroad, tempting the ungodly to sin under the name of pleasure. They hoist the wrong light. It is our responsibility to put up the true light on every dangerous rock, to point out every sin, and tell what it leads to, so that we may be clear of the blood of all men, shining as lights in the world. Lights also have a very cheering influence, and so do Christians. A Christian should be a comforter, with kind words on his lips and sympathy in his heart; he should carry sunshine wherever he goes and diffuse happiness around him.

> Gracious Spirit, dwell with me;
>   I myself would gracious be,
> And with words that help and heal
>   Would your life in mine reveal,
> And with actions bold and meek
>   Would for Christ my Savior speak.

*And when they could not come nigh unto him for the press,
they uncovered the roof where he was: and when they had broken
it up, they let down the bed wherein the sick of the palsy lay.*
—Mark 2:4

aith is full of inventions. The house was full, a crowd blocked the door, but faith found a way of getting at the Lord and placing the palsied man before Him. If we cannot get sinners where Jesus is by ordinary methods, we must use extraordinary ones. It seems, according to Luke 5:19, that tiles from the roof had to be removed, which would make dust and cause a measure of danger to those below. But where the case is very urgent, we must not mind running some risks and shocking some proprieties. Jesus was there to heal, and come what may, faith ventured all so that her poor paralyzed charge might have his sins forgiven. Oh, that we had more daring faith among us! Cannot we, dear reader, seek it this morning for ourselves and for our fellow workers, and will we not try today to perform some gallant act for the love of souls and the glory of the Lord? The world is constantly inventing; genius serves all the purposes of human desire. Cannot faith invent, too, and reach, by some new means, the outcasts who lie perishing around us? It was the presence of Jesus that excited victorious courage in the four bearers of the palsied man. Is the Lord not among us now? Have we seen His face for ourselves this morning? Have we felt His healing power in our own souls? If so, then through door, through window, or through roof, let us, breaking through all impediments, labor to bring poor souls to Jesus. All means are good and decorous when faith and love are truly set on winning souls. If hunger for bread can break through stone walls, surely hunger for souls is not to be hindered in its efforts. O Lord, make us quick to suggest methods of reaching Your poor sin-sick ones, and make us bold to carry them out, regardless of the hazards.

From me is thy fruit found.
—Hosea 14:8

ur fruit is found from our union with God. The fruit of the branch is directly traceable to the root. Sever the connection, and the branch dies; thus, no fruit is produced. By virtue of our union with Christ, we bring forth fruit. Every bunch of grapes has first been in the root. It has passed through the stem, flowed through the sap vessels, and fashioned itself externally into fruit. But it was first in the stem. Likewise, every good work was first in Christ, and then is brought forth in us. Christian, prize this precious union with Christ, for it must be the source of all the fruitfulness that you can hope to know. If you were not joined to Jesus Christ, you would be a barren bough indeed. Our fruit comes from God's spiritual providence. When the dewdrops fall from heaven, when the cloud looks down from on high and is about to distill its liquid treasure, when the bright sun swells the berries of the cluster, each heavenly blessing may whisper to the tree and say, *"From me is thy fruit found."* The fruit owes much to the root—that is essential to fruitfulness—but it also owes much to external influences. How much we owe to God's gracious providence! He provides us constantly with quickening, teaching, consolation, strength, or whatever else we need. To this we owe all of our usefulness or virtue. Our fruit comes from God as a result of His wise husbandry. The gardener's sharp-edged knife promotes the fruitfulness of the tree by thinning the clusters and by cutting off superfluous shoots. So is it, Christian, with the pruning that the Lord gives to you. *"My Father is the husbandman. Every branch in me that beareth not fruit he taketh away: and every branch that beareth fruit, he purgeth it, that it may bring forth more fruit"* (John 15:1–2). Since our God is the Author of our spiritual graces, let us give to Him all the glory of our salvation.

I will answer thee, and show thee great and mighty things,
which thou knowest not.
—Jeremiah 33:3

here are different translations of these words. One version renders it, *"I will show thee great and fortified things"*; another, *"great and reserved things."* Now, there are reserved and special things in Christian experience: all the developments of spiritual life are not equally easy to attain. There are the common frames and feelings of repentance, faith, joy, and hope, which are enjoyed by the entire family; but there is an upper realm of rapture, of communion, and of conscious union with Christ that is far from being the common dwelling place of believers. Not all of us have John's high privilege of leaning on Jesus' bosom or of Paul's being caught up into the third heaven. There are heights in the knowledge of the things of God that the eagle's eye of acumen and philosophic thought has never seen. God alone can bear us there. But the chariot in which He takes us up, and the fiery steeds with which that chariot is dragged, are prevailing prayers. Prevailing prayer is victorious over the God of mercy: *"By his strength he had power with God: yea, he had power over the angel, and prevailed: he wept, and made supplication unto him: he found him in Bethel, and there he spake with us"* (Hosea 12:3–4). Prevailing prayer takes the Christian to Carmel and enables him to cover heaven with clouds of blessing and earth with floods of mercy. Prevailing prayer bears the Christian aloft and shows him the inheritance reserved. It elevates and transfigures us, until in the likeness of our Lord, as He is, so are we also in this world. If you would reach to something higher than the ordinary experience, look to the *"rock that is higher than* [you]*"* (Ps. 61:2), and gaze with the eyes of faith through the window of persistent prayer. When you open the window on your side, it will not be bolted on the other!

And he goeth up into a mountain, and calleth unto him whom he would: and they came unto him.
—Mark 3:13

Here was sovereignty. Impatient spirits may fret and fume because they are not called to the highest places in the ministry. But, reader, rejoice that Jesus calls whom He will. If He permits me to be a doorkeeper in His house, I will cheerfully bless Him for His grace in allowing me to do anything in His service. The call of Christ's servants comes from above. Jesus stands on the mountain, evermore above the world in holiness, earnestness, love, and power. Those whom He calls must go up the mountain to Him. They must seek to rise to His level by living in constant communion with Him. They may not be able to mount to classic honors or attain scholastic eminence, but they must, like Moses, go up into the mount of God and have close communion with the unseen God; otherwise, they will never be fitted to proclaim the gospel of peace. Jesus went apart to hold high fellowship with the Father, and we must enter into the same divine companionship if we would bless our fellowmen. No wonder the apostles were clothed with power when they came down fresh from the mountain where Jesus was. This morning we must endeavor to ascend the mount of communion, so that there we may be ordained to the lifework for which we are set apart. Let us not see the face of man today until we have seen Jesus. Time spent with Him is laid out at blessed interest. We, too, will cast out devils and work wonders if we go down into the world girded with that divine energy that Christ alone can give. It is of no use going to the Lord's battle until we are armed with heavenly weapons. We must see Jesus; this is essential. At the mercy seat we will linger until He manifests Himself to us as He does not unto the world, and until we can truthfully say, "We were with Him on the Holy Mount."

Be ye separate.
—2 Corinthians 6:17

The Christian, while *in* the world, is not to be *of* the world. He should be distinguished from it in the great objectives of his life. For him, *"to live* [should be] *Christ"* (Phil. 1:21). Whether he eats, drinks, or whatever he does, he should *"do all to the glory of God"* (1 Cor. 10:31). You may store up treasures, but store them in heaven, *"where neither moth nor rust doth corrupt, and where thieves do not break through nor steal"* (Matt. 6:20). You may strive to be rich, but let it be your ambition to be *"rich in faith"* (James 2:5) and *"rich in good works"* (1 Tim. 6:18). You may have pleasure, but when you are merry, *"sing psalms"* (James 5:13) and make *"melody in your heart to the Lord"* (Eph. 5:19). In your spirit, as well as in your aim, you should differ from the world. Waiting humbly before God, always conscious of His presence, delighting in communion with Him, and seeking to know His will, you will prove that you are of heavenly race. You should be separate from the world in your actions. If a thing is right, though you lose by it, it must be done. If it is wrong, though you would gain by it, you must scorn the sin for your Master's sake. You must have no fellowship with the unfruitful works of darkness, but rather reprove them. *"Walk worthy"* (Eph. 4:1) of your high calling and dignity. Remember, Christian, you are a child of the King of Kings. Therefore, keep yourself unspotted from the world. Do not soil the fingers that are soon to sweep celestial strings; do not let your eyes, which are soon to see the King in His beauty, become the windows of lust. Do not let your feet, which are soon to walk the golden streets, be defiled in miry places. Do not let your heart, which before long will be filled with heaven, be filled with pride and bitterness.

Then rise my soul and soar away above the thoughtless crowd;
Above the pleasures of the gay and splendors of the proud;
Up where eternal beauties bloom and pleasures all divine;
Where wealth, that never can consume,
And endless glories shine.

God is jealous.
—Nahum 1:2

Your Lord is very jealous of your love, believer. Did He choose you? He cannot bear that you should choose another. Did He buy you with His own blood? He cannot endure that you should think that you are your own or that you belong to this world. He loved you with such a love that He would not stop in heaven without you; He would sooner die than see you perish. He cannot endure anything standing between your heart's love and Himself. He is very jealous of your trust. He will not permit you to trust in an arm of flesh. He cannot bear that you should hew out broken cisterns, when the overflowing fountain is always free to you. When we lean on Him, He is glad; but when we transfer our dependence to another, when we rely on our own wisdom or the wisdom of a friend—worst of all, when we trust in any works of our own—He is displeased and will chasten us so that He may bring us to Himself. He is also very jealous of our company. There should be no one with whom we converse as much as with Jesus. To abide in Him only is true love; but to commune with the world, to find sufficient solace in our carnal comforts, or to prefer even the society of our fellow Christians to intimate time with Him, this is grievous to our jealous Lord. He is happy to have us abide in Him and enjoy constant fellowship with Him. Many of the trials that He sends us are for the purpose of weaning our hearts from the creature and fixing them more closely on Him. Let this jealousy, which would keep us near to Christ, also be a comfort to us; for if He loves us so much as to care thus about our love, we may be sure that He will not allow anything to harm us, and He will protect us from all our enemies. Oh, that we may have grace this day to keep our hearts in sacred chastity for our Beloved alone, with sacred jealousy shutting our eyes to all the fascinations of the world!

Who passing through the valley of Baca make it a well;
the rain also filleth the pools.
—Psalm 84:6

his teaches us that the comfort obtained by one may often prove serviceable to another, just as wells would be used by the company who came after. We read a book full of consolation, which is like Jonathan's rod, dripping with honey. We think our brother has been here before us and dug this well for us as well as for himself. Many wells have been dug by one pilgrim for himself but have proved quite as useful to others. We notice this especially in the Psalms, such as the ones that say, *"Why art thou cast down, O my soul?"* (Ps. 42:5, 11; 43:5). Travelers have been delighted to see the footprint of a man on a barren shore, and we love to see the signposts of pilgrims while passing through the vale of tears. The pilgrims dig the well, but, strangely enough, it fills from the top instead of the bottom. We use the means, but the blessing does not spring from the means. We dig a well, but heaven fills it with rain. *"The horse is prepared against the day of battle: but safety is of the LORD"* (Prov. 21:31). The means are connected with the end, but they do not of themselves produce it. See here the rain fills the pools so that the wells become useful as reservoirs for the water. Labor is not lost, yet it does not supersede divine help. Grace may well be compared to rain for its purity, for its refreshing and vivifying influence, for its coming alone from above, and for the sovereignty with which it is given or withheld. May our readers have showers of blessing, and may the wells they have dug be filled with water! Oh, what are means and laws without the smile of heaven! They are as clouds without rain and pools without water. O God of love, open the windows of heaven and pour out a blessing on us!

There were also with him other little ships.
—Mark 4:36

Jesus was the Lord High Admiral of the sea that night, and His presence preserved the whole convoy. It is well to sail with Jesus, even though it is in a little ship. When we sail in Christ's company, we may not have a guarantee of fair weather; for great storms may toss the vessel that carries the Lord Himself, and we must not expect to find the sea less boisterous around our little boat. If we go with Jesus, we must be content to fare as He fares; and when the waves are rough to Him, they will be rough to us. It is by tempest and tossing that we will come to land, as He did before us. When the storm swept over Galilee's dark lake, all faces gathered blackness, and all hearts dreaded shipwreck. When all creature-help was useless, the slumbering Savior arose and, with a word, transformed the riot of the tempest into the deep quiet of a calm. Then were the other little vessels at rest as well as the one that carried the Lord. Jesus is the star of the sea; although there may be sorrow on the sea, when Jesus is on it, there is joy, too. May our hearts make Jesus their anchor, their rudder, their lighthouse, their lifeboat, and their harbor. His church is the Admiral's flagship. Let us attend her movements and cheer her officers with our presence. He Himself is the great attraction. Let us follow ever in His wake, mark His signals, steer by His chart, and never fear while He is within reach of our call. Not one ship in the convoy will suffer wreck; the great Commodore will steer every boat in safety to the desired haven. By faith we will slip our cable for another day's cruise and sail forth with Jesus into a sea of tribulation. Winds and waves will not spare us, but they all obey Him; therefore, whatever squalls may occur without, faith will feel a blessed calm within. He is ever in the center of the weather-beaten company. Let us rejoice in Him. His vessel has reached the haven, and so will ours.

He shall not be afraid of evil tidings.
—Psalm 112:7

hristian, you should not dread the arrival of evil tidings. If you are distressed by them, how are you different from other men? Other men do not have your God to go to. They have never proved His faithfulness as you have done. It is no wonder if they are bowed down with alarm and cowed with fear, but you profess to be of another spirit. You have been *"begotten...again unto a lively hope"* (1 Pet. 1:3), and your heart lives in heaven and not on earthly things. Now, if you are seen to be distracted as other men, what is the value of that grace that you profess to have received? Where is the dignity of that new nature that you claim to possess? If you would be filled with alarm, as others are, you would, doubtless, be led into the sins so common to others under trying circumstances. The ungodly, when they are overtaken by evil tidings, rebel against God. They murmur and think that God deals harshly with them. Will you fall into that same sin? Will you provoke the Lord as they do? Moreover, unconverted men often run to wrong means in order to escape from difficulties, and you will be sure to do the same if your mind yields to the present pressure. Trust in the Lord, and *"wait patiently for him"* (Ps. 37:7). Your wisest course is to do as Moses did at the Red Sea, *"Stand still, and see the salvation of the LORD"* (Exod. 14:13). If you give way to fear when you hear of evil tidings, you will be unable to meet the trouble with that calm composure that strengthens for duty and sustains under adversity. How can you glorify God if you play the coward? Saints have often sung God's high praises in the fires, but will your doubt and despair, as if you had none to help you, magnify the Most High? Then take courage, and relying in sure confidence on the faithfulness of your covenant God, do not let *"your heart be troubled, neither let it be afraid"* (John 14:27).

Partakers of the divine nature.
—2 Peter 1:4

o be a partaker of the divine nature is not, of course, to become God. That cannot be. The essence of deity is not to be participated in by the creature. Between the creature and the Creator there must ever be a gulf fixed in respect of essence. But as the first man Adam was made in the image of God, so we, by the renewal of the Holy Spirit, are in a diviner sense made in the image of the Most High and are partakers of the divine nature. We are, by grace, made like God. *"God is love"* (1 John 4:16). We become love: *"Every one that loveth is born of God"* (v. 7). God is truth; we become true, and we love that which is true. God is good, and He makes us good by His grace, so that we become the *"pure in heart"* who *"shall see God"* (Matt. 5:8). Moreover, we become *"partakers of the divine nature"* in even a higher sense than this—in fact, in as lofty a sense as can be conceived, short of our being absolutely divine. Do we not become members of the body of the divine person of Christ? Yes, the same blood that flows in the head flows in the hand, and the same life that quickens Christ quickens His people, for *"Ye are dead, and your life is hid with Christ in God"* (Col. 3:3). As if this were not enough, we are married to Christ. He has betrothed us unto Himself in righteousness and in faithfulness, and he who is joined to the Lord is one spirit. Oh, marvelous mystery! We look into it, but who can understand it? One with Jesus—so one with Him that the branch is not more one with the vine than we are a part of the Lord, our Savior and our Redeemer! While we rejoice in this, let us remember that those who are made *"partakers of the divine nature"* will manifest their high and holy relationship in their fellowship with others. It will be evident by their daily walk and conversation that they have *"escaped the corruption that is in the world through lust"* (2 Pet. 1:4). Oh, for more divine holiness of life!

Bring him unto me.
—Mark 9:19

espairingly, the poor, disappointed father turned away from the disciples to their Master. His son was in the worst possible condition, and all means had failed. But the pitiful child was soon delivered from the evil one when the parent, in faith, obeyed the Lord Jesus' word, *"Bring him unto me."* Children are a precious gift from God, but much anxiety comes with them. They may be a great joy or a great bitterness to their parents. They may be filled with the Spirit of God or possessed with the spirit of evil. In all cases, the Word of God gives us one prescription for the curing of all their ills, *"Bring* [them] *unto me."* Oh, for more agonizing prayer on their behalf while they are yet babies! Sin is there, so let our prayers begin to attack it. Our cries for our offspring should precede those cries that announce their actual advent into a world of sin. In the days of their youth, we will see sad indicators of that dumb and deaf spirit that will neither pray aright, nor hear the voice of God in the soul. Still, Jesus commands, *"Bring* [them] *unto me."* When they are grown up, they may wallow in sin and display enmity against God. Then, when our hearts are breaking, we should remember the Great Physician's words, *"Bring* [them] *unto me."* We must never cease to pray until they cease to breathe. No case is hopeless while Jesus lives. The Lord sometimes allows His people to be driven into a corner so that they may know how necessary He is to them. Ungodly children, when they show us our own powerlessness against the depravity of their hearts, drive us to flee to the Strong One for strength, and this is a great blessing to us. Whatever our morning's need may be, let it, like a strong current, bear us to the ocean of divine love. Jesus can soon remove our sorrow. He delights to comfort us. Let us hasten to Him while He waits to meet us.

If we live in the Spirit, let us also walk in the Spirit.
—Galatians 5:25

The two most important things in our holy religion are the *life of faith* and the *walk of faith*. He who rightly understand these is not far from being a master in practicing theology, for they are vital points to a Christian. You will never find true faith unattended by true godliness; on the other hand, you will never discover a truly holy life that is not rooted in a living faith based on the righteousness of Christ. Woe unto those who seek after the one without the other! There are some who cultivate faith and forget holiness; these may be very high in orthodoxy, but they will be very deep in condemnation, for they *"hold the truth in unrighteousness"* (Rom. 1:18). There are others who have strained after holiness of life, but have denied the faith, like the Pharisees of old, whom the Master said were like whitewashed tombs. We must have faith, for this is the foundation; we must have holiness of life, for this is the superstructure. Of what service is the mere foundation of a building to a man in the day of tempest? Can he hide himself there? He needs a house to cover him, as well as a foundation for that house. Even so we need the superstructure of spiritual life if we would have comfort in the day of doubt. But do not seek a holy life without faith, for that would be to erect a house that can afford no permanent shelter, because it has no foundation on a rock. Let faith and a holy life be put together, and, like the two abutments of an arch, they will make our piety enduring. Like light and heat streaming from the same sun, they are both full of blessing. Like the two pillars of the temple, they are for glory and for beauty. They are two streams from the fountain of grace, two lamps lit with holy fire, two olive trees watered by heavenly care. O Lord, give us this day life within, and it will reveal itself without to Your glory.

*Stand fast therefore in the liberty wherewith Christ
hath made us free.*
—Galatians 5:1

his *"liberty"* makes us free to heaven's charter—the
Bible. Here is a choice passage, believer: *"When thou
passest through the waters, I will be with thee"* (Isa. 43:2).
You are free to that. Here is another: *"The mountains shall
depart, and the hills be removed; but my kindness shall not depart
from thee"* (Isa. 54:10). You are free to that. You are a welcome guest at the table of the promises. Scripture is a
never-failing treasury filled with boundless stores of grace.
It is the bank of heaven; you may draw from it as much as
you please, without permission or hindrance. Come in faith,
and you are welcome to all covenant blessings. There is not
a promise in the Word that will be withheld. In the depths
of tribulations, let this freedom comfort you. Amid waves of
distress, let it cheer you. When sorrow surrounds you, let it
be your solace. This is your Father's love-token. You are
free to it at all times. You are also free to the throne of
grace. It is the believer's privilege to have access at all
times to his heavenly Father. Whatever our desires, our
difficulties, our needs, we are at liberty to spread all before
Him. It does not matter how much we may have sinned; we
may ask for and expect pardon. No matter how wealthy or
how poor we are, we may plead His promise that He will
provide all things that we need. We have permission to approach His throne at all times—in midnight's darkest hour
or in noontide's most burning heat. Exercise your right,
believer, and live up to your privilege. You are free to all
that is treasured up in Christ: wisdom, righteousness, sanctification, and redemption. It does not matter what your
need is, for there is fullness of supply in Christ, and it is
there for you! Oh, what a freedom is yours—freedom from
condemnation, freedom to the promises, freedom to the
throne of grace, and, at last, freedom to enter heaven!

The sword of the LORD, and of Gideon.
—Judges 7:20

Gideon ordered his men to do two things. Covering up a torch in an earthen pitcher, he told them, at an appointed signal, to break the pitcher and let the light shine. Then they were to sound the trumpet, crying, *"The sword of the LORD, and of Gideon!"* This is precisely what all Christians must do. First, you must shine; break the pitcher that conceals your light. Throw aside the bushel that has been hiding your candle and shine. Let your light shine before men; let your good works be such that, when men look on you, they will know that you have been with Jesus. Then there must be the sound, the blowing of the trumpet. There must be active exertions for the ingathering of sinners by proclaiming Christ crucified. Take the Gospel to them. Carry it to their door. Put it in their way. Do not allow them to escape it; blow the trumpet right against their ears. Remember that the true war cry of the church is Gideon's watchword, *"The sword of the LORD, and of Gideon!"* God must do it; it is His own work. But we are not to be idle. Instrumentality is to be used—*"The sword of the LORD, and of Gideon!"* If we only cry, *"The sword of the LORD!"* we will be guilty of an idle presumption; and if we shout, *"The sword of Gideon!"* alone, we will manifest idolatrous reliance on an arm of flesh: we must blend the two in practical harmony, *"The sword of the LORD, and of Gideon!"* We can do nothing of ourselves, but we can do everything by the help of our God. Let us, therefore, in His name determine to go out personally and serve with our flaming torch of holy example and with our trumpet tones of earnest declaration and testimony. God will be with us, our enemy will be put to confusion, and the Lord of Hosts will reign forever and ever.

I will rejoice over them to do them good.
—Jeremiah 32:41

ow encouraging to the believer is the delight that God has in His saints! We cannot see any reason in ourselves why the Lord should take pleasure in us. We cannot take delight in ourselves, for we often have to groan, being burdened. We are conscious of our sinfulness and deplore our unfaithfulness. We fear that God's people cannot take much delight in us, for they must perceive so many of our imperfections and our follies that they may rather lament our infirmities than admire our graces. But we love to dwell on this transcendent truth, this glorious mystery: as the bridegroom rejoices over the bride, so the Lord rejoices over us. We do not read anywhere that God delights in the cloud-capped mountains or the sparkling stars, but we do read that He delights *"in the habitable part of his earth,"* and that His delights are *"with the sons of men"* (Prov. 8:31). We do not find it written that even angels give His soul delight. Nor does He say, concerning cherubim and seraphim, *"Thou shalt be called Hephzibah,...for the* LORD *delighteth in thee"* (Isa. 62:4), but He does say all that to poor fallen creatures like ourselves, debased and depraved by sin, but saved, exalted, and glorified by His grace. In what strong language He expresses His delight in His people! Who could have conceived of the Eternal One as bursting forth into a song? Yet it is written, *"He will rejoice over thee with joy; he will rest in his love, he will joy over thee with singing"* (Zeph. 3:17). As He looked on the world He had made, He said, "It is very good"; but when He beheld those who are the purchase of Jesus' blood, His own chosen ones, it seemed as if the great heart of the Infinite could restrain itself no longer, but overflowed in divine exclamations of joy. Should we not utter our grateful response to such a marvelous declaration of His love and sing, *"I will rejoice in the* LORD, *I will joy in the God of my salvation"* (Hab. 3:18)?

Let Israel rejoice in him.
—Psalm 149:2

Be glad of heart, believer, but take care that your gladness springs from the Lord. You have much cause for gladness in your God, for you can sing with David, *"God my exceeding joy"* (Ps. 43:4). Be glad that the Lord reigns, that Jehovah is King! Rejoice that He sits on the throne and rules all things! Every attribute of God should become a fresh ray in the sunlight of our gladness. Knowing that He is wise should make us glad, as we look at our own foolishness. Knowing that He is mighty should cause us to rejoice, as we tremble at our weakness. Knowing that He is everlasting should always be a theme of joy, as we consider that we wither as the grass. Knowing that He is unchanging should perpetually yield us a song, since we change every hour. Knowing that He is full of grace, that He is overflowing with it, and that this grace in covenant He has given to us; that it is ours to cleanse us, ours to keep us, ours to sanctify us, ours to perfect us, ours to bring us to glory—all this should tend to make us glad in Him. This gladness in God is like a deep river. We have only as yet touched its brink. We know a little of its clear, sweet, heavenly streams, but onward the depth is greater, and the current more impetuous in its joy. The Christian feels that he may delight himself not only in what God is, but also in all that God has done in the past. The Psalms show us that God's people in olden times were inclined to think much of God's actions, and to have a song concerning each of them. So let God's people now rehearse the deeds of the Lord! Let them tell of His mighty acts and *"sing unto the LORD, for he hath triumphed gloriously"* (Exod. 15:1). Nor let them ever cease to sing, for as new mercies flow to them day by day, so should their gladness in the Lord's loving acts in providence and in grace show itself in continued thanksgiving. Be glad, children of Zion, and rejoice in the Lord your God.

Accepted in the beloved.
—Ephesians 1:6

hat a privilege! It includes our justification before God, but the term *acceptance* in the Greek means more than that. It signifies that we are the objects of divine pleasure, or even more, of divine delight. How marvelous that we—worms, mortals, sinners—should be the objects of divine love! But it is only *"in the beloved."* Some Christians seem to be accepted in their own experience; at least, that is their understanding. When their spirit is lively and their hopes bright, they think God accepts them, for they feel so high, so heavenly-minded, so drawn above the earth! But when their souls cleave to the dust, they are the victims of the fear that they are no longer accepted. If they could but see that all their high joys do not exalt them, and all their low times of despair do not really depress them in their Father's sight; instead, they stand accepted in One who never alters, in One who is always the beloved of God, always perfect, always without spot or wrinkle. How much happier they would be, and how much more they would honor the Savior, if they realized this truth! Rejoice, then, believer! You are *"accepted in the beloved."* You look within and say, "There is nothing acceptable here!" But look at Christ and see if there is not everything acceptable there. Your sins trouble you, but God has cast your sins behind His back, and you are accepted in the Righteous One. You have to fight with corruption and to wrestle with temptation, but you are already accepted in Him who has overcome the powers of evil. The devil tempts you, but be of good cheer. He cannot destroy you, for you are accepted in Him who has broken Satan's head. Know by full assurance your glorious standing. Even glorified souls are not more accepted than you are. They are only accepted in heaven *"in the beloved,"* and you are even now accepted in Christ after the same manner.

For I was ashamed to require of the king a band of soldiers and horsemen to help us against the enemy in the way: because we had spoken unto the king, saying, The hand of our God is upon all them for good that seek him; but his power and his wrath is against all them that forsake him.
—Ezra 8:22

For many reasons, a convoy would have been desirable for the pilgrim band, but a holy shamefacedness would not allow Ezra to seek one. He feared lest the heathen king would think his professions of faith in God to be mere hypocrisy or imagine that the God of Israel was not able to preserve His own worshippers. He could not bring his mind to lean on an arm of flesh in a matter so evidently of the Lord; therefore, the caravan set out with no visible protection, guarded by Him who is the sword and shield of His people. It is to be feared that few believers feel this holy jealousy for God. Even those who, in a measure, walk by faith occasionally mar the luster of their lives by craving aid from man. It is a most blessed thing to have no props and no buttresses, but to stand upright on the Rock of Ages, upheld by the Lord alone. Would any believers seek state endowments for their church if they remembered that the Lord is dishonored by their asking for Caesar's aid? As if the Lord could not supply the needs of His own cause! Would we run so hastily to friends and relatives for assistance if we remembered that the Lord is magnified by our implicit reliance on His solitary arm? My soul, wait only on God. "But," says one, "are not means to be used?" Assuredly they are; but our fault seldom lies in their neglect. Far more frequently it springs out of foolishly believing in them instead of believing in God. Few run too far in neglecting the creature's arm, but many sin greatly in making too much of it. Learn, dear reader, to glorify the Lord by leaving means untried, if by using them you would dishonor the name of the Lord.

Just, and the justifier of him which believeth in Jesus.
—Romans 3:26

Being justified by faith, we have peace with God" (Rom. 5:1). Conscience no longer accuses. Judgment now decides *for* the sinner instead of *against* him. Memory looks back on past sins with deep sorrow for the sin, yet with no dread of any penalty to come. Christ paid the debt of His people to the last jot and tittle and received the divine receipt. Unless God can be so unjust as to demand double payment for one debt, no soul for whom Jesus died as a substitute can ever be cast into hell. It seems to be one of the very principles of our enlightened nature to believe that God is just. We feel that it must be so, and this causes us terror at first; but is it not marvelous that this very same belief that God is just afterward becomes the pillar of our confidence and peace! If God is just, I, a sinner, alone and without a substitute, must be punished. But Jesus stands in my stead and is punished for me. Now, if God is just, I, a sinner, standing in Christ, can never be punished. God must change His nature before one soul for whom Jesus was a substitute can ever by any possibility suffer the penalty of the law. Therefore, Jesus having taken the place of the believer, having rendered a full equivalent to divine wrath for all that His people ought to have suffered as the result of sin, the believer can shout with glorious triumph, *"Who shall lay any thing to the charge of God's elect?"* (Rom. 8:33). Not God, for He has justified. Not Christ, for He has died, *"yea rather,…[has] risen again"* (v. 34). My hope lives, not because I am not a sinner, but because I am a sinner for whom Christ died. My trust is not that I am holy, but that being unholy, He is my righteousness. My faith does not rest on what I am or will be or feel or know, but in what Christ is, in what He has done, and in what He is now doing for me. On the lion of justice the fair maid of hope rides like a queen.

I saw by night, and behold a man riding upon a red horse, and he stood among the myrtle trees that were in the bottom.
—Zechariah 1:8

he vision in this chapter describes the condition of Israel in Zechariah's day. Being interpreted in its aspect toward us, it describes the church of God as we find it now in the world. The church is compared to a myrtle grove flourishing in a valley. It is hidden, unobserved, secret. It courts no honor and attracts no observation from the careless gazer. The church, like her Head, has a glory, but it is concealed from carnal eyes, for the time of her breaking forth in all her splendor is not yet come. The idea of tranquil security is also suggested to us, for the myrtle grove in the valley is still and calm, while the storm sweeps over the mountain summits. Tempests spend their force on the craggy peaks of the Alps, but down where the stream flows that makes glad the city of our God, the myrtles flourish by the still waters, all unshaken by the impetuous wind. How great is the inward tranquility of God's church! Even when opposed and persecuted, she has a peace that the world does not give, and which, therefore, it cannot take away. The peace of God that passes all understanding keeps the hearts and minds of God's people. Does not the metaphor forcibly picture the peaceful, perpetual growth of the saints? The myrtle sheds not its leaves; it is always green. And the church, in her worst time, still has a blessed verdure of grace about her; in fact, she has sometimes exhibited the healthiest growth when her winter has been sharpest. She has prospered most when her adversities have been the most severe. Hence the text hints at victory. The myrtle is the symbol of peace and a significant token of triumph. The brows of conquerors were bound with myrtle and with laurel. Is not the church always victorious? Are not Christians *"more than conquerors"* (Rom. 8:37) through Christ who loves them? Living in peace, do not the saints fall asleep in the arms of victory?

Happy art thou, O Israel: who is like unto thee,
O people saved by the LORD!
—Deuteronomy 33:29

He who affirms that Christianity makes men miserable is himself an utter stranger to it. It would be strange, indeed, if it made us wretched, for see to what a position it exalts us! It makes us children of God. Do you suppose that God will give all the happiness to His enemies and reserve all the mourning for His own family? Will His foes have mirth and joy, and will His own children inherit sorrow and wretchedness? Will the sinner, who has no part in Christ, call himself rich in happiness, and will we go mourning as if we were penniless beggars? No, we will *"rejoice in the Lord alway[s]"* (Phil. 4:4), and glory in our inheritance, for we *"have not received the spirit of bondage again to fear; but [we] have received the Spirit of adoption, whereby we cry, Abba, Father"* (Rom. 8:15). The rod of chastisement must rest on us in our measure, but it works for us the comfortable fruits of righteousness; therefore, by the aid of the divine Comforter, we, the people saved by the Lord, will joy in the God of our salvation. We are married to Christ. Will our great Bridegroom permit His spouse to linger in constant grief? Our hearts are knit to Him. We are His members, and though for a while we may suffer as our Head once suffered, yet we are even now blessed with heavenly blessings in Him. We have the guarantee of our inheritance in the comforts of the Spirit, which are neither few nor small. Inheritors of joy forever, we have foretastes of our portion. There are streaks of the light of joy to herald our eternal rising sun. Our riches are beyond the sea. Our city with firm foundations lies on the other side the river. Gleams of glory from the spirit world cheer our hearts and urge us onward. Truly is it said of us, *"Happy art thou, O Israel: who is like unto thee, O people saved by the LORD!"*

The LORD looketh from heaven; he beholdeth all the sons of men.
—Psalm 33:13

erhaps no figure of speech represents God in a more gracious light than when He is spoken of as stooping from His throne and coming down from heaven to attend to the needs and to behold the sorrows of mankind. We love Him, who, when Sodom and Gomorrah were full of iniquity, would not destroy those cities until He had made a personal visitation to them. We cannot help pouring out our hearts in affection for our Lord, who inclines His ear from the highest glory and puts it to the lips of the dying sinner, whose failing heart longs for reconciliation. How can we but love Him when we know that He numbers the very hairs of our heads, marks our path, and orders our ways? This great truth is especially brought near to our hearts when we remember how attentive He is, not merely to the temporal interests of His creatures, but to their spiritual concerns. Though a long distance lies between the finite creature and the infinite Creator, yet there are links uniting both. When you weep, do not think that God does not see your tears, for *"like as a father pitieth his children, so the LORD pitieth them that fear him"* (Ps. 103:13). Your sigh is able to move the heart of Jehovah; your whisper can incline His ear unto you; your prayer can stay His hand; your faith can move His arm. Do not think that God sits on high paying no attention to you. Remember that however poor and needy you are, the Lord thinks about you. *"For the eyes of the LORD run to and fro throughout the whole earth, to show himself strong in the behalf of them whose heart is perfect toward him"* (2 Chron. 16:9). Oh, then, repeat the truth that never tires: No God is like the God my soul desires. He, at whose voice heaven trembles, even He, great as He is, knows how to stoop to me.

Behold, if the leprosy have covered all his flesh,
he shall pronounce him clean that hath the plague.
—Leviticus 13:13

This regulation appears to be strange, yet there was wisdom in it, for the throwing out of the disease proved that the constitution was sound. This morning it may be well for us to see the typical teaching of so unusual a rule. We, too, are lepers and may read the law of lepers as applicable to ourselves. When a man sees himself to be altogether lost and ruined, covered all over with the defilement of sin, with no part free from pollution; when he disclaims all righteousness of his own and pleads guilty before the Lord, then is he made clean through the blood of Jesus and the grace of God. Hidden, unfelt, unconfessed iniquity is the true leprosy; but when sin is seen and felt, it has received its deathblow, and the Lord looks with eyes of mercy on the soul afflicted with it. Nothing is more deadly than self-righteousness or more hopeful than contrition. We must confess that we are nothing else but sin, for no confession short of this will be the whole truth. If the Holy Spirit is at work within us, convincing us of sin, there will be no difficulty about making such an acknowledgment. It will spring spontaneously from our lips. What comfort this Scripture affords to those under a deep sense of sin! Sin that is mourned and confessed, however black and foul, will never shut a man out from the Lord Jesus. Whoever comes to Him, He *"will in no wise cast out"* (John 6:37). Though dishonest as the thief, though unchaste as the woman who was a sinner, though fierce as Saul of Tarsus, though cruel as Manasseh, though rebellious as the Prodigal, the great heart of love will look on the man who feels himself to have no soundness in himself and will pronounce him clean when he trusts in Jesus crucified. Come to Him, then, poor heavy-laden sinner.

Come needy, come guilty, come loathsome and bare.
You can't come too filthy; come just as you are.

Sing forth the honour of his name: make his praise glorious.
—Psalm 66:2

It is not left to our own choice whether we will praise God or not. Praise is God's most righteous due; every Christian, as the recipient of His grace, is bound to praise God from day to day. It is true we have no authoritative rule for daily praise; we have no commandment prescribing certain hours of song and thanksgiving. But the law written on the heart teaches us that it is right to praise God, and the unwritten mandate comes to us with as much force as if it had been recorded on the tablets of stone or handed to us from the top of thundering Sinai. Yes, it is the Christian's duty to praise God. It is not only a pleasurable exercise, but also the absolute obligation of his life. Do not think that you who are always mourning are guiltless in this respect or imagine that you can discharge your duty to your God without songs of praise. You are bound by the bonds of His love to bless His name as long as you live, and His praise should *"continually be in* [your] *mouth"* (Ps. 34:1), for you are blessed, in order that you may bless Him. *"This people have I formed for myself; they shall show forth my praise"* (Isa. 43:21). If you do not praise God, you are not bringing forth the fruit that He, as the Divine Husbandman, has a right to expect at your hands. Do not let your harp hang on the willows, but take it down, and strive, with a grateful heart, to bring forth its loudest music. Arise and sing His praise. With every morning's dawn, lift up your notes of thanksgiving, and let every setting sun be followed with your songs. Cover the earth with your praises. Surround it with an atmosphere of melody, and God Himself will hearken from heaven and accept your music.

> E'en so I love Thee, and will love,
>   And in Thy praise will sing,
> Because Thou art my loving God,
>   And my redeeming King.

*Pleasant fruits, new and old, which I have
laid up for thee, O my beloved.*
—Song of Solomon 7:13

he spouse desires to give all that she produces to Jesus. Our hearts have *"all manner of pleasant fruits"*
(Song 7:13) both *"new and old,"* and they are laid up
for our Beloved. At this rich autumn season of fruit, let us
survey our harvest. We have *"new"* fruits. We desire to feel
new life, new joy, new gratitude. We wish to make new re-
solves and carry them out by new labors. Our hearts blos-
som with new prayers, and our souls pledge themselves to
new efforts. But we have some *"old"* fruits, too. There is our
first love. What a choice fruit! Jesus delights in it. There is
our first faith. It is the simple faith by which, having nothing, we became possessors of all things. There is our joy
when first we knew the Lord; let us revive it. We have our
old remembrances of the promises. How faithful God has
been! In sickness, how softly He made our beds! In deep
waters, how placidly He lifted us up! In the flaming furnace,
how graciously He delivered us. Old fruits, indeed! We have
many of them, for His mercies have been more than the
hairs of our heads. Old sins we must regret, but then we
have had times of repentance that He has given us, by
which we have wept our way to the cross and learned the
merit of His blood. We have fruits, this morning, both new
and old; but here is the point—they are all laid up for Jesus.
Truly, those are the best and most acceptable services in
which Jesus is the solitary aim of the soul, and His glory,
without any addition whatever, is the end of all our efforts.
Let our many fruits be laid up only for our Beloved. Let us
display them when He is with us and not hold them up before the gaze of men. Jesus, we will turn the key in our garden door, and none will enter to rob You of one good fruit
from the soil that You have watered with Your bloody
sweat. Our all will be Yours, Yours only, O Jesus, our Beloved!

The hope which is laid up for you in heaven.
—Colossians 1:5

ur hope in Christ for the future is the mainspring and the mainstay of our joy here. It will animate our hearts to think often of heaven, for all that we can desire is promised there. Here we are weary and toilworn, but yonder is the land of rest where the sweat of labor will no more moisten the worker's brow, and fatigue will be forever banished. To those who are weary and spent, the word *rest* is full of heaven. We are always in the field of battle. We are so tempted within, and so molested by foes without, that we have little or no peace. But in heaven we will enjoy the victory, when the banner will be waved aloft in triumph, the sword will be sheathed, and we will hear our Captain say, *"Well done, thou good and faithful servant"* (Matt. 25:21). We have suffered bereavement after bereavement, but we are going to the land of the immortal, where graves are unknown things. Here sin is a constant grief to us, but there we will be perfectly holy. By no means will anything that defiles enter into that kingdom. Hemlock cannot spring up in the furrows of celestial fields. Oh, is it not joy, that you are not to be in banishment forever, that you are not to dwell eternally in this wilderness, but will soon inherit Canaan? Nevertheless, let it never be said of us that we are dreaming about the future and forgetting the present. Let the future sanctify the present to its highest uses. Through the Spirit of God, the hope of heaven is the most potent force for the product of virtue. It is a fountain of joyous effort; it is the cornerstone of cheerful holiness. The man who has this hope in him goes about his work with vigor, for the joy of the Lord is his strength. He fights against temptation with ardor, for the hope of the next world repels the fiery darts of the adversary. He can labor without present reward, for he looks for a reward in the world to come.

*Are they not all ministering spirits, sent forth to minister for them
who shall be heirs of salvation?*
—Hebrews 1:14

ngels are the unseen attendants of the saints of
God. They bear us up in their hands, lest we dash
our foot against a stone. Loyalty to their Lord leads
them to take a deep interest in the children of His love.
They rejoice over the return of the Prodigal to his father's
house below, and they welcome the advent of the believer
to the King's palace above. In olden times, the sons of God
were favored with their visible appearance, and at this day,
although unseen by us, heaven is still opened, and the angels of God ascend and descend on the Son of Man so that
they may visit the heirs of salvation. Seraphim still fly with
live coals from off the altar to touch the lips of men who are
greatly beloved. If our eyes could be opened, we would see
horses and chariots of fire around the servants of the Lord;
for we have come to an innumerable company of angels,
who are all watchers and protectors of the royal seed. Ed-
mund Spenser's line is no poetic fiction, where he sings,

> How oft do they with golden pinions cleave
> The flitting skies, like flying pursuivant
> Against foul fiends to aid us militant!

To what dignity are the chosen elevated when the brilliant courtiers of heaven become their willing servants! Into
what communion are we raised since we have fellowship
with spotless celestials! How well are we defended since all
the twenty thousand chariots of God are armed for our deliverance! To whom do we owe all this? Let the Lord Jesus
Christ be forever endeared to us, for through Him we are
made to sit *"in heavenly places"* (Eph. 2:6) far above principalities and powers. He it is whose camp is *"round about them that
fear him"* (Ps. 34:7). He is the true Michael whose foot is on
the dragon. All hail, Jesus! To You, the Angel of Jehovah's
presence, this family offers its morning vows.

At evening time it shall be light.
—Zechariah 14:7

Often we look with foreboding to the time of old age, forgetful that at eventide it will be light. To many saints, old age is the choicest season in their lives. A balmier air fans the mariner's cheek as he nears the shore of immortality. Fewer waves ruffle his sea, and quiet reigns, deep, still, and solemn. From the altar of age the flashes of the fire of youth are gone, but the more real flame of earnest feeling remains. The pilgrims have reached Beulah land, that happy country, whose days are as the days of heaven on earth. Angels visit it, celestial gales blow over it, flowers of paradise grow in it, and the air is filled with seraphic music. Some dwell here for years, and others come to it but a few hours before their departure, but it is an Eden on earth. We may well long for the time when we will recline in its shady groves and be satisfied with hope until the time of fruition comes. The setting sun seems larger than when aloft in the sky, and a splendor of glory tinges all the clouds that surround its going down. Pain does not break the calm of the sweet twilight of age, for *"strength…made perfect in weakness"* (2 Cor. 12:9) bears up with patience under it all. Ripe fruits of choice experience are gathered as the rare repast of life's evening, and the soul prepares itself for rest. The Lord's people will also enjoy light in the hour of death. Unbelief laments as it sees the shadows fall, the night coming, and existence ending. "Ah, no," cries faith. "The night is far spent; the true day is at hand." Light is come, the light of immortality, the light of a Father's countenance. Gather up your feet in the bed; see the waiting bands of spirits! Angels carry you away. Farewell, beloved one. You wave your hand; you are gone. Ah, now it is light. The pearly gates are open. The golden streets shine in the jasper light. We cover our eyes, but you behold the unseen. Farewell, brother; you have light at eventide, such as we have not yet seen.

He arose, and did eat and drink, and went in the strength of that
meat forty days and forty nights.
—1 Kings 19:8

All the strength supplied to us by our gracious God is meant for service, not for wantonness or boasting. When the prophet Elijah found the cake baked on the coals and the cruse of water placed at his head as he lay under the juniper tree, he was no gentleman to be gratified with dainty fare so that he might stretch himself at his ease; far from it. He was commissioned to go forty days and forty nights in the strength of it, journeying toward Horeb, the mount of God. When the Master invited the disciples to *"come and dine"* (John 21:12) with Him, after the feast was concluded, He said to Peter, *"Feed my sheep"* (vv. 16–17). He further said, *"Follow me"* (v. 19). This is true with us also. We eat the bread of heaven so that we may expend our strength in the Master's service. We come to the Passover and eat of the Paschal Lamb with loins girded and staff in hand, so as to start off at once when we have satisfied our hunger. Some Christians are for living *on* Christ, but are not so anxious to live *for* Christ. Earth should be a preparation for heaven, and heaven is the place where saints feast most and work most. They sit down at the table of our Lord, and they serve Him day and night in His temple. They eat of heavenly food and give perfect service. Believer, in the strength you daily gain from Christ, labor for Him. Some of us have yet to learn much concerning the design of our Lord in giving us His grace. We are not to retain the precious grains of truth as the Egyptian mummy held the wheat for ages, without giving it an opportunity to grow. We must sow it and water it. Why does the Lord send down the rain on the thirsty earth and give the genial sunshine? Is it not that these may all help the fruits of the earth to yield food for man? Even so, the Lord feeds and refreshes our souls so that afterward we may use our renewed strength in the promotion of His glory.

*Whosoever drinketh of the water that I shall give him
shall never thirst.*
—John 4:14

He who is a believer in Jesus finds enough in his Lord to satisfy him now and to keep him content forevermore. The believer is not the man whose days are weary for lack of comfort or whose nights are long from absence of heart-cheering thoughts. He finds in Christ such a spring of joy, such a fountain of consolation, that he is content and happy. Put him in a dungeon, and he will find good company. Place him in a barren wilderness, and he will eat the bread of heaven. Drive him away from friendship, and he will meet the *"friend that sticketh closer than a brother"* (Prov. 18:24). Blast all his gourds, and he will find shadow beneath the Rock of Ages. Sap the foundation of his earthly hopes, and his heart will still be fixed, trusting in the Lord. The heart is as insatiable as the grave until Jesus enters it, and then, it is a cup full to overflowing. There is such a fullness in Christ that He alone is the believer's all. The true saint is so completely satisfied with the all-sufficiency of Jesus that he thirsts no more—unless it is for deeper draughts of the living Fountain. In that sweet manner, believer, you will thirst. It will not be a thirst of pain, but of loving desire; you will find it a sweet thing to be panting after a fuller enjoyment of Jesus' love. One, in days of yore, said, "I have often been sinking my bucket down into the well, but now my thirst after Jesus has become so insatiable that I long to put the well itself to my lips and drink right from it." Is this the feeling of your heart now, believer? Do you feel that all your desires are satisfied in Jesus and that you have no lack now, but to know more of Him and to have closer fellowship with Him? Then come continually to the Fountain, and *"take the water of life freely"* (Rev. 22:17). Jesus will never think you take too much, but will ever welcome you, saying, "Drink, yes, drink abundantly, beloved."

Wherefore hast thou afflicted thy servant?
—Numbers 11:11

Our heavenly Father sends us frequent troubles to try our faith. If our faith is worth anything, it will stand the test. Gilt is afraid of fire, but gold is not. The artificial gem dreads to be touched by the diamond, but the true jewel fears no test. It is a weak faith that can trust God only when friends are true, the body is full of health, and business is profitable. True faith holds by the Lord's faithfulness when friends are gone, when the body is sick, when spirits are depressed, and when the light of our Father's countenance is hidden. A faith that can say, in the direst trouble, *"Though he slay me, yet will I trust in him"* (Job 13:15) is heaven-born faith. The Lord afflicts His servants to glorify Himself, for He is greatly glorified in the graces of His people, which are His own handiwork. When *"tribulation worketh patience; and patience, experience; and experience, hope"* (Rom. 5:3), the Lord is honored by these growing virtues. We would never know the music of the harp if the strings were left untouched or enjoy the juice of the grape if it were not trodden in the winepress or discover the sweet perfume of cinnamon if it were not pressed and beaten or feel the warmth of fire if the coals were not utterly consumed. The wisdom and power of the great Workman are discovered by the trials through which His vessels of mercy are permitted to pass. Present afflictions tend also to heighten future joy. There must be shadows in the picture to bring out the beauty of the light. Could we be so supremely blessed in heaven if we had not known the curse of sin and the sorrow of earth? Will not peace be sweeter after conflict, and rest more welcome after toil? Will not the remembrance of past sufferings enhance the bliss of the glorified? There are many other comforting answers to the question with which we opened our brief meditation. Let us ponder these thoughts all day long.

Launch out into the deep, and let down your nets for a draught.
—Luke 5:4

e learn from this narrative the necessity of human involvement. The draught of fish was miraculous, yet neither the fisherman nor his boat nor his fishing tackle were ignored. All were used to catch the fish. Likewise, in the saving of souls, God uses many different means. While the present economy of grace will stand, God is pleased by the foolishness of preaching to save those who believe. When God works without instruments, undoubtedly, He is glorified; but He Himself has selected this plan by which He is most magnified in the earth. Means, by themselves, are utterly unavailing. *"Master, we have toiled all the night, and have taken nothing"* (Luke 5:5). What was the reason for this? Were they not fishermen plying their special calling? Verily, they were no raw hands; they understood the work. Had they gone about the toil unskillfully? No. Had they lacked industry? No, they had toiled. Had they lacked perseverance? No, they had toiled all night. Was there a deficiency of fish in the sea? Certainly not, for as soon as the Master came, they swam to the net in shoals. What, then, is the reason? It is because there is no power in the means, by themselves, apart from the presence of Jesus. We can do nothing without Him. But with Christ we can do all things. Christ's presence confers success. Jesus sat in Peter's boat, and His will, by a mysterious influence, drew the fish to the net. When Jesus is lifted up in His church, His presence is the church's power—the shout of a king is in the midst of her. *"I, if I be lifted up, will draw all men unto me"* (John 12:32).

Let us go out this morning on our work of soul-fishing, looking up in faith and around us in solemn concern. Let us toil until night comes, and we will not labor in vain. He who bids us let down the net will fill it with fish.

Able to keep you from falling.
—Jude 24

In one sense the path to heaven is very safe, but in other respects, there is no road as dangerous. It is surrounded with difficulties. One false step—and how easy it is to take that if grace is absent—and down we go. What a slippery path some of us have to tread! How many times have we exclaimed with the psalmist, *"My feet were almost gone; my steps had well nigh slipped"* (Ps. 73:2). If we were strong, surefooted mountaineers, this would not matter so much; but in ourselves, how weak we are! On the best roads we soon falter; on the smoothest paths we quickly stumble. These feeble knees of ours can scarcely support our tottering weight. A straw may throw us, and a pebble can wound us. We are mere children tremblingly taking our first steps in the walk of faith. Our heavenly Father holds us by the arms, or we would soon be down. Oh, if we are kept from falling, how must we bless the patient power that watches over us day by day! Think how prone we are to sin, how apt to choose danger, how strong our tendency to cast ourselves down, and these reflections will make us sing more sweetly than we have ever done: "Glory be to Him, who is *'able to keep* [us] *from falling.'"* We have many foes who try to push us down. The road is rough, and we are weak. In addition, enemies lurk in ambush who rush out when we least expect them. They labor to trip us up or hurl us down the nearest precipice. Only an almighty arm can preserve us from these unseen foes who are seeking to destroy us. Such an arm is engaged for our defense. He is faithful who has promised. He is able to keep us from falling, so that with a deep sense of our utter weakness, we may cherish a firm belief in our perfect safety. We may say, with joyful confidence,

> Against me earth and hell combine,
>   But on my side is power divine;
> Jesus is all, and He is mine!

Faultless before the presence of his glory.
—Jude 24

onder this wondrous word *"faultless"*! We are far from it now, but since our Lord never stops short of perfection in His work of love, we will reach it one day. The Savior who will keep His people to the end will also present them at last to Himself as *"a glorious church, not having spot, or wrinkle, or any such thing; but that is should be holy and without blemish"* (Eph. 5:27). All the jewels in the Savior's crown are of first quality and without a single flaw. All the maids of honor who attend the Lamb's wife are pure virgins without spot or stain. But how will Jesus make us faultless? He will wash us from our sins in His own blood until we are white and fair as God's purest angel. We will be clothed in His righteousness—that righteousness that makes the saint who wears it positively faultless, yes, perfect in the sight of God. We will be without blame and without reproof even in His eyes. His law will not only have no charge against us, but also will be magnified in us. Moreover, the work of the Holy Spirit within us will be altogether complete. He will make us so perfectly holy that we will have no lingering tendency to sin. Judgment, memory, will, every power and passion will be emancipated from the slavery of evil. We will be holy even as God is holy, and in His presence we will dwell forever. Saints will not be out of place in heaven. Their beauty will be as great as that of the place prepared for them. Oh, the rapture of that hour when the everlasting doors will be lifted up, and we, being made ready for the inheritance, will dwell with the saints in light. Sin gone, Satan shut out, temptation past forever, and ourselves *"faultless"* before God—this will be heaven indeed! Let us be joyful now as we rehearse the song of eternal praise so soon to roll forth in full chorus from all the blood-washed host. Let us copy David's praise before the ark as a prelude to our ecstasies before the throne.

Let us lift up our heart with our hands unto God in the heavens.
—Lamentations 3:41

he act of prayer teaches us our unworthiness, which is a very beneficial lesson for such proud beings as we are. If God gave us favors without constraining us to pray for them, we would never know how poor we are. A true prayer is an inventory of needs, a catalogue of necessities, a revelation of hidden poverty. While it is an application to divine wealth, it is a confession of human emptiness. The healthiest state of a Christian is to be always empty and poor in self, constantly depending on the Lord for supplies, rich in Jesus, weak as water personally, but mighty through God to do great exploits. Hence, the use of prayer, because, while it adores God, it lays the creature where it should be, in the very dust. Prayer is in itself, apart from the answer that it brings, a great benefit to the Christian. As the runner gains strength for the race by daily exercise, so for the great race of life we acquire energy by the hallowed labor of prayer. Prayer plumes the wings of God's young eaglets so that they may learn to mount above the clouds. Prayer girds the loins of God's warriors and sends them forth to combat with their sinews braced and muscles firm. An earnest pleader comes out of his prayer time, even as the sun rises from the chambers of the east, rejoicing like a strong man to run his race. Prayer is that uplifted hand of Moses that routs the Amalekites more than the sword of Joshua. It is the arrow shot from the chamber of the prophet foreboding defeat to the Syrians. Prayer girds human weakness with divine strength, turns human folly into heavenly wisdom, and gives to troubled mortals the peace of God. We cannot think of anything that prayer cannot do! We thank You, great God, for the mercy seat, a choice proof of Your marvelous lovingkindness. Help us to use it aright throughout this day!

I will meditate in thy precepts.
—Psalm 119:15

here are times when solitude is better than society, and silence is wiser than speech. We would be better Christians if we spent more time alone, waiting on God and gathering, through meditation on His Word, spiritual strength for labor in His service. We ought to meditate on the things of God, because we thus get the real nutrition out of them. Truth is something like the cluster of the vine. If we would have wine from it, we must bruise it; we must press and squeeze it many times. The bruiser's feet must come down joyfully on the bunches; otherwise, the juice will not flow. They must tread the grapes well, or else much of the precious liquid will be wasted. So we must, by meditation, tread the clusters of truth, if we would get the wine of consolation from it. Our bodies are not supported by merely taking food into the mouth. The process that really supplies the muscle, nerve, sinew, and the bone is the process of digestion. It is by digestion that the outward food becomes assimilated with the inner life. Our souls are not nourished merely by listening for a while to this, and then to that, and then to the other part of divine truth. Hearing, reading, marking, and learning all require inward digesting to complete their usefulness, and the inward digesting of the truth lies for the most part in meditating on it. Why is it that some Christians, although they hear many sermons, make slow advances in the divine life? Because they neglect their prayer time and do not thoughtfully meditate on God's Word. They love the wheat, but they do not grind it. They want the corn, but they will not go forth into the fields to gather it. The fruit hangs on the tree, but they will not pluck it; the water flows at their feet, but they will not stoop to drink it. Lord, deliver us from such folly, and be this our resolve this morning, *"I will meditate in thy precepts."*

Godly sorrow worketh repentance.
—2 Corinthians 7:10

Genuine, spiritual mourning for sin is the work of the Spirit of God. Repentance is too choice a flower to grow in nature's garden. Pearls grow naturally in oysters, but penitence never shows itself in sinners unless divine grace works it in them. If you have one particle of real hatred for sin, God must have given it to you, for human nature's thorns never produced a single fig. *"That which is born of the flesh is flesh"* (John 3:6). True repentance has a distinct reference to the Savior. When we repent of sin, we must have one eye on sin and another on the cross. It will be better still if we fix both our eyes on Christ and see our transgressions only in the light of His love. True sorrow for sin is eminently practical. No man may say he hates sin if he lives in it. Repentance makes us see the evil of sin, not merely as a theory, but experientially—as a burned child dreads fire. We will be as much afraid of it as a man who has recently been stopped and robbed is afraid of the thief on the highway. We will shun it—shun it in everything—not only in great things, but also in little things, as men shun little vipers as well as great snakes. True mourning for sin will make us very jealous over our tongues, lest we should say a wrong word. We will be very watchful over our daily actions, lest in anything we offend. Each night we will close the day with painful confessions of our shortcomings, and each morning we will awaken with anxious prayers that this day God would hold us up so that we may not sin against Him. Sincere repentance is continual. Believers repent until their dying day. Their sadness over sin is not intermittent. Every other sorrow yields to time, but this dear sorrow grows with our growth, and it is so sweet as well as bitter that we thank God we are permitted to enjoy and to suffer it until we enter our eternal rest.

I count all things but loss for the excellency of the knowledge
of Christ Jesus my Lord.
—Philippians 3:8

piritual knowledge of Christ will be a personal knowledge. I cannot know Jesus through another person's
acquaintance with Him. No, I must know Him myself.
I must know Him on my own account. It will be an intelli-
gent knowledge. I must know Him, not as the visionary
dreams of Him, but as the Word reveals Him. I must know
His natures, both divine and human. I must know His offices, His attributes, His works, His shame, and His glory. I
must meditate on Him until I *"comprehend with all saints
what is the breadth, and length, and depth, and height;
and…know the love of Christ, which passeth knowledge"* (Eph.
3:18–19). It will be an affectionate knowledge of Him. Indeed, if I know Him at all, I must love Him. An ounce of
heart knowledge is worth a ton of head learning. Our
knowledge of Him will be a satisfying knowledge. When I
know my Savior, my mind will be full to the brim. I will feel
that I have that which my spirit longed for. Jesus said, *"I
am the bread of life: he that cometh to me shall never hunger"*
(John 6:35). At the same time, it will be an exciting knowledge. The more I know of my Beloved, the more I will want
to know. The higher I climb, the loftier will be the summits
that invite my eager footsteps. I will want all the more as I
get more. Like the miser's treasure, my gold will make me
covet more. In conclusion, this knowledge of Christ Jesus
will be a most happy one. In fact, it will be so elevating that
sometimes it will completely bear me up above all trials,
doubts, and sorrows. It will, while I enjoy it, make me
something more than a *"man that is born of a woman* [who]
is of few days, and full of trouble" (Job 14:1). It will fling about
me the immortality of the ever-living Savior and gird me
with the golden girdle of His eternal joy. Come, my soul, sit
at Jesus' feet and learn of Him all this day.

> *But who may abide the day of his coming?*
> —Malachi 3:2

is first coming was without external pomp or show of power. Yet, in truth, there were few who could abide its testing might. Herod and all Jerusalem were stirred at the news of the wondrous birth. Those who supposed themselves to be waiting for Him showed the fallacy of their professions by rejecting Him when He came. His life on earth was a winnowing fan, which tried the great heap of religious profession, and few could abide the process. But what will His second advent be? What sinner can endure to think of it? *"He shall smite the earth with the rod of his mouth, and with the breath of his lips shall he slay the wicked"* (Isa. 11:4). When in His humiliation He said to the soldiers, *"I am he"* (John 18:5), they fell backward. What will be the terror of His enemies when He will more fully reveal Himself as the "I am"? His death shook earth and darkened heaven. What will be the dreadful splendor of that day in which, as the living Savior, He summons the living and the dead before Him? Oh, that the terrors of the Lord would persuade men to forsake their sins and *"kiss the Son, lest he be angry"* (Ps. 2:12)! Though a lamb, He is yet the *"Lion of the tribe of Juda"* (Rev. 5:5), rending the prey in pieces; though *"a bruised reed shall he not break"* (Isa. 42:3), He will break His enemies *"with a rod of iron"* and *"dash them in pieces like a potter's vessel"* (Ps. 2:9). None of His foes will bear up before the tempest of His wrath or hide themselves from the sweeping hail of His indignation. His beloved blood-washed people, though, look for His appearing with joy and hope to abide it without fear. To them He sits as a refiner even now, and when He has tried them, they will *"come forth as gold"* (Job 23:10). Let us search ourselves this morning and make our calling and election sure, so that the coming of the Lord may cause no dark foreboding in our minds. Oh, for grace to cast away all hypocrisy and to be found sincere and without rebuke in the day of His appearing!

Jesus saith unto them, Come and dine.
—John 21:12

In these words, the believer is invited to a holy near-ness to Jesus. *"Come and dine"* implies the same table and the same meat; yes, and sometimes it means to sit side by side and lean our head on the Savior's bosom. It is being brought into the banquet room where the banner of redeeming love waves. *"Come and dine"* gives us a vision of union with Jesus, because the only food that we can feast on when we dine with Jesus is Himself. Oh, what union this is! It is a depth that reason cannot fathom, that we thus feed on Jesus. *"He that eateth my flesh, and drinketh my blood, dwelleth in me, and I in him"* (John 6:56). It is also an invitation to enjoy fellowship with the saints. Christians may differ on a variety of points, but they all have one spiritual appetite. If we cannot all feel alike, we can all feed alike on the Bread of Life sent down from heaven. At the table of fellowship with Jesus, we are one bread and one cup. As the loving cup goes around, we pledge our love and unity to one another heart-ily. Get nearer to Jesus, and you will find yourself linked more and more in spirit to all who are like yourself, sup-ported by the same heavenly manna. If we were closer to Jesus, we would be closer to one another. We likewise see in these words the source of strength for every Christian. To look at Christ is to live, but for strength to serve Him you must *"come and dine."* We labor under much unneces-sary weakness on account of neglecting this percept of the Master. None of us needs to put himself on a low-calorie diet; on the contrary, we should fatten ourselves on the marrow and fatness of the Gospel, so that we may accumu-late strength from it and urge every power to its full ten-sion in the Master's service. Thus, if you would realize nearness to Jesus, union with Jesus, love for His people, and strength from Jesus, *"come and dine"* with Him by faith.

And David said in his heart, I shall now perish one day
by the hand of Saul.
—1 Samuel 27:1

he thought of David's heart at this time was a false thought. He certainly had no ground for thinking that God's anointing him by Samuel was intended to be left as an empty, meaningless act. Never on any occasion had the Lord deserted His servant. He had been placed in perilous positions often, but not one instance had occurred in which divine intervention had not delivered him. The trials to which he had been exposed had been varied; they had not assumed one form only, but many. Yet, in every case, He who sent the trial had also graciously ordained a way of escape. David could not put his finger on any entry in his diary and say of it, "Here is evidence that the Lord will forsake me," for the entire tenor of his life had proved the very reverse. He should have realized from what God had done for him that God would be his defender still. But do we not doubt God's help in this same way? Is it not mistrust without a cause? Have we ever had the shadow of a reason to doubt our Father's goodness? Have not His lovingkindnesses been marvelous? Has He once failed to justify our trust? Ah, no! Our God has not left us at any time. We have had dark nights, but the star of love has shone forth amid the blackness. We have been in stern conflicts, but He has held aloft the shield of our defense over our heads. We have gone through many trials, but never to our detriment, always to our advantage. The conclusion from our past experiences is that He who has been with us in six troubles will not forsake us in the seventh. What we have known of our faithful God proves that He will keep us to the end. Let us not, then, reason contrary to evidence. How can we ever be so ungenerous as to doubt our God? Lord, throw down the Jezebel of our unbelief, and let the dogs devour it.

Thy paths drop fatness.
—Psalm 65:11

any are *"the paths of the LORD"* (Ps. 25:10) that *"drop fatness,"* but a special one is the path of prayer. No believer who spends much time in prayer will have any need to cry, *"My leanness, my leanness, woe unto me!"* (Isa. 24:16). Starving souls live at a distance from the mercy seat and become like parched fields in times of drought. Prevalence with God in wrestling prayer is sure to make the believer strong—if not happy. The nearest place to the gate of heaven is the throne of heavenly grace. Spend much time alone with Jesus, and you will have much assurance; spend little time alone with Him, and your religion will be shallow, polluted with many doubts and fears, not sparkling with the joy of the Lord. Since the soul-enriching path of prayer is open to the very weakest saint; since no high attainments are required; since you are not bidden to come because you are an advanced saint, but freely invited if you are a saint at all; see to it, dear reader, that you are often in the place of private devotion. Spend much time on your knees, for so Elijah drew the rain down on famished Israel's fields. There is another special path dripping with fatness to those who walk therein: it is the secret walk of communion. Oh, the delights of fellowship with Jesus! Earth has no words that can set forth the holy calm of a soul leaning on Jesus' breast. Few Christians understand it. They live in the lowlands and seldom climb to the mountaintop. They live in the outer court. They do not enter the holy place. They do not take up the privilege of priesthood. At a distance they see the sacrifice, but they do not sit down with the priest to eat of it and to enjoy the fat of the burnt offering. But, reader, always sit under the shadow of Jesus. Come up to that palm tree and take hold of the branches of it. Let your Beloved be to you as the apple tree in the woods, and you will be satisfied as with marrow and fatness. Jesus, visit us with Your salvation!

Babes in Christ.
—1 Corinthians 3:1

Are you mourning, believer, because you are so weak in the divine life, because your faith is so little, your love so feeble? Cheer up, for you have reason for gratitude. Remember that in some things you are equal to the greatest and most mature Christian. You are as much bought with blood as he is. You are as much an adopted child of God as any other believer. An infant is as truly a child of its parents as is the full-grown man. You are as completely justified, for your justification is not a thing of degrees. Your little faith has made you completely clean. You have as much right to the precious things of the covenant as the most advanced believers, for your right to covenant mercies does not lie in your growth, but in the covenant itself. Your faith in Jesus is not the measure but the token of your inheritance in Him. You are as rich as the richest, if not in enjoyment, in real possession. The smallest star that gleams is set in heaven. The faintest ray of light has affinity with the great orb of day. In the family register of glory the small and the great are written with the same pen. You are as dear to your Father's heart as the greatest in the family. Jesus is very tender over you. You are like the smoking flax. A rougher spirit would say, "Put out that smoking flax. It fills the room with an offensive odor!" But *"the smoking flax shall he not quench"* (Isa. 42:3). You are like a bruised reed; and any less tender hand than that of the Chief Musician would tread on you or throw you away, but He will never break the bruised reed (v. 3). Instead of being downcast because of what you are, you should triumph in Christ. Am I but little in Israel? Yet in Christ I am made to sit in heavenly places. Am I poor in faith? Still in Jesus I am heir of all things. Though I have nothing about which to boast, if the root of the matter is in me, I can and will rejoice in the Lord and glory in the God of my salvation.

Grow up into him in all things.
—Ephesians 4:15

Many Christians remain stunted and dwarfed in spiritual things, so as to present the same appearance year after year. No advanced and refined feelings are manifest in them. They exist but do not *"grow up into him in all things."* Should we rest content with being in the green blade when we might advance to the ear and eventually ripen into the full corn in the ear? Should we be satisfied to believe in Christ, and to say, "I am safe," without wishing to know in our own experience more of the fullness that is to be found in Him? It should not be so. We should, as good traders in heaven's market, covet to be enriched in the knowledge of Jesus. It is all very well to keep other men's vineyards, but we must not neglect our own spiritual growth and ripening. Why should it always be wintertime in our hearts? We must have our seed time, it is true, but, oh, for a springtime—yes, a summer season that gives promise of an early harvest! If we would ripen in grace, we must live near to Jesus—in His presence—ripened by the sunshine of His smiles. We must hold sweet communion with Him. We must leave the distant view of His face and come near, as John did, and pillow our head on His breast. Then will we find ourselves advancing in holiness, in love, in faith, in hope—yes, in every precious gift. As the sun rises first on the mountaintops and gilds them with its light, it presents one of the most charming sights to the eye of the traveler. So is it one of the most delightful contemplations in the world to notice the glow of the Spirit's light on the head of some saint, who has risen in spiritual stature, like Saul, above his fellows. Like the mighty snowcapped Alps, he reflects first among the chosen the beams of the Sun of Righteousness. Then he bears the sheen of His brilliant glory high aloft for all to see, and seeing it, he brings glory to His Father who is in heaven.

The love of Christ constraineth us.
—2 Corinthians 5:14

ow much do you owe to my Lord? Has He ever done anything for you? Has He forgiven your sins? Has He covered you with a robe of righteousness? Has He set your feet on a rock? Has He established your goings? Has He prepared heaven for you? Has He prepared you for heaven? Has He written your name in His book of life? Has He given you countless blessings? Has He laid up for you a store of mercies, which *"eye hath not seen, nor ear heard"* (1 Cor. 2:9)? Then do something for Jesus worthy of His love. Do not give a mere wordy offering to a dying Redeemer. How will you feel when your Master comes, if you have to confess that you did nothing for Him, but kept your love shut up like a stagnant pool, neither flowing forth to His poor or to His work? Let such love as that be gone! What do men think of a love that never shows itself in action? Why, they say, *"Open rebuke is better than secret love"* (Prov. 27:5). Who will accept a love so weak that it does not motivate you to a single deed of self-denial, of generosity, of heroism, or zeal? Think how He has loved you and given Himself for you! Do you know the power of that love? Then let it be like a rushing, mighty wind to your soul to sweep out the clouds of your worldliness and clear away the mists of sin. May the words "For Christ's sake" be the tongue of fire that will sit upon you. May they be the divine rapture, the heavenly inspiration to bear you aloft from earth, the divine spirit that will make you bold as lions and swift as eagles in your Lord's service. Love should give wings to the feet of service and strength to the arms of labor. Fixed on God with a constancy that is not to be shaken, resolute to honor Him with a determination that is not to be turned aside, and pressing on with an ardor never to be wearied, let us manifest the constraints of love for Jesus. May the divine lodestone draw us heavenward toward itself.

I will heal their backsliding, I will love them freely.
—Hosea 14:4

his sentence is a body of divinity in miniature. He who understands its meaning is a theologian, and he who can dive into its fullness is a true master in Israel. It is a condensation of the glorious message of salvation that was delivered to us in Christ Jesus our Redeemer. The meaning hinges on the word *"freely."* This is the glorious, suitable, divine way by which love streams from heaven to earth, a spontaneous love flowing forth to those who neither deserved it, purchased it, or sought after it. It is, indeed, the only way in which God can love us as we are. The text is a deathblow to all sorts of fitness: *"I will love them freely."* Now, if there were any suitability necessary in us, then He would not love us freely; at the least, this would be a mitigation and a drawback to the freeness of it. But it stands, *"I will love [you] freely."* We complain, "Lord, my heart is so hard." He responds, *"I will love [you] freely."* We say, "But I do not feel my need of You as I wish I could. I do not feel that softening of spirit that I should desire." And He answers, "I will not love you because you feel your need. *'I will love [you] freely.'"* Remember, the softening of spirit is not a condition, for there are no conditions. The covenant of grace has no stipulations whatsoever. We, without any worthiness, may venture on the promise of God that was made to us in Christ Jesus, when He said, *"He that believeth on him is not condemned"* (John 3:18). It is a blessing to know that the grace of God is free to us at all times, without preparation, without suitability, without money, and without price! *"I will love them freely."* These words invite backsliders to return: indeed, the text was especially written for such—*"I will heal their backsliding, I will love them freely."* Backslider, surely the generosity of the promise will at once break your heart, and you will return and seek your injured Father's face.

Will ye also go away?
—John 6:67

Many have forsaken Christ and have walked no more with Him. But what reason do you have to make a change? Has there been any reason for it in the past? Has not Jesus proved Himself all-sufficient? He appeals to you this morning: *"Have I been a wilderness unto [you]?"* (Jer. 2:31). When your soul has simply trusted Jesus, have you ever been confounded? Have you not up until now found your Lord to be a compassionate and generous friend to you, and has not simple faith in Him given you all the peace your spirit could desire? Can you so much as dream of a better friend than He has been to you? Then do not change the old and tried for the new and false. As for the present, can that compel you to leave Christ? When we are troubled by this world or with severe trials within the church, we find it a most blessed thing to pillow our head on the bosom of our Savior. This is the joy we have today— that we are saved in Him. If this joy is satisfying, why would we think of changing? Who barters gold for dross? We will not reject the sun until we find a better light or leave our Lord until a brighter lover will appear. Since this can never be, we will hold Him with an immortal grasp and bind His name as a seal on our arm. As for the future, can you suggest anything that can arise that will render it necessary for you to mutiny or to desert the old flag to serve under another captain? We think not. If life is long, He does not change. If we are poor, what could be better than to have Christ who can make us rich? When we are sick, what more do we need than Jesus to make our bed in our sickness? When we die, is it not written that *"neither death, nor life, nor angels, nor principalities, nor powers, nor things present, nor things to come, nor height, nor depth, nor any other creature, shall be able to separate us from the love of God, which is in Christ Jesus our Lord"* (Rom. 8:38–39)? We say with Peter, *"Lord, to whom shall we go?"* (John 6:68).

The trees of the LORD are full of sap.
—Psalm 104:16

Without sap the tree cannot flourish or even exist. Vitality is essential to a Christian. There must be life—a vital principle infused into us by God the Holy Spirit, or we cannot be trees of the Lord. The mere name of being a Christian is but a dead thing. We must be filled with the spirit of divine life. This life is mysterious. We do not understand the circulation of the sap, by what force it rises, and by what power it descends again. So the life within us is a sacred mystery. Regeneration is wrought by the Holy Spirit entering into a believer and becoming his life. This divine life afterward feeds on the flesh and blood of Christ and is thus sustained by divine food, but where it comes and where it goes—who will explain it to us? What a secret thing the sap is! The roots go searching through the soil, but we cannot see them suck out the various gases or transmute the mineral into the vegetable. This work is done down in the dark. Our root is Christ Jesus, and our life is hidden in Him. This is the secret of the Lord. The primary source of the Christian life is as secret as the life itself. How permanently active is the sap in the cedar! In the Christian, the divine life is always full of energy—not always in fruit-bearing, but in inward operations. The believer's graces are not all in constant motion, but his life never ceases to palpitate within. He is not always working for God, but his heart is always living on Him. As the sap manifests itself in producing the foliage and fruit of the tree, so it must be with a truly healthy Christian. His grace is externally manifested in his walk and conversation. If you talk with him, he cannot help speaking about Jesus. If you notice his actions, you will see that he has been with Jesus. He has so much sap within that it must fill his conduct and conversation with life.

For the truth's sake, which dwelleth in us,
and shall be with us for ever.
—2 John 2

Once the truth of God obtains an entrance into the human heart and subdues the whole person to itself, no power—human or infernal—can dislodge it. We entertain it not as a guest, but as the master of the house. This is a Christian necessity; he is no Christian who does not thus believe. Those who feel the vital power of the Gospel and know the might of the Holy Spirit, as He opens, applies, and seals the Lord's Word, would sooner be torn to pieces than be torn away from the Gospel of their salvation. What a thousand mercies are wrapped up in the assurance that the truth will be with us forever; will be our living support, our dying comfort, our rising song, our eternal glory. This is the Christian's privilege; without it our faith would be of little worth. Some truths we outgrow and leave behind, for they are but rudiments and lessons for beginners. But we cannot deal this way with divine truth, for though it is sweet food for babies, it is in the highest sense strong meat for men. The truth that we are sinners is painfully with us to humble us and make us watchful. The more blessed truth, that whoever believes on the Lord Jesus will be saved, abides with us as our hope and joy. Experience, far from loosening our hold of the doctrines of grace, has knit us to them more and more firmly. Our grounds and motives for believing are now stronger and more numerous than ever. We have reason to expect that it will be so until in death we clasp the Savior in our arms. Wherever this abiding love of truth can be discovered, we are bound to exercise our love. No narrow circle can contain our gracious sympathies; wide as the election of grace must be our communion of heart. Much error may be mingled with truth received. Let us war against the error, but still love the brother for the measure of truth that we see in him. Above all, let us love and spread the truth ourselves!

Ye looked for much, and, lo, it came to little; and when ye brought it home, I did blow upon it. Why? saith the LORD of hosts. Because of mine house that is waste, and ye run every man unto his own house.
—Haggai 1:9

Churlish souls limit their contributions to the ministry and missionary endeavors and call such savings good economy. Little do they dream that they are impoverishing themselves. Their excuse is that they must care for their own families, and they forget that to neglect the house of God is the sure way to bring ruin on their own houses. Our God has a method in providence by which He can bless our endeavors beyond our expectations or can defeat our plans to our confusion and dismay. By a turn of His hand, He can steer our vessel in a profitable channel or run it aground in poverty and bankruptcy. It is the teaching of Scripture that the Lord enriches the liberal and leaves the miserly to find out that withholding leads to poverty. In a very wide sphere of observation, I have noticed that the most generous Christians of my acquaintance have always been the happiest, and almost invariably the most prosperous. I have seen the liberal giver rise to wealth of which he never dreamed, and I have as often seen the stingy, ungenerous person descend to poverty by the very penny-pinching by which he thought to succeed. Men trust good stewards with larger and larger sums, and so it frequently is with the Lord. He gives by cartloads to those who give by bushels. Where wealth is not bestowed, the Lord turns the little into much through the contentment that the sanctified heart feels in proportion to the dedication with which the tithe has been given to the Lord. Selfishness looks first at home, but godliness seeks *"first the kingdom of God, and his righteousness"* (Matt. 6:33). In the long run, selfishness is loss, and godliness is great gain. It takes faith to act toward our God with an open hand, but surely He deserves it of us. All that we can do is a very poor acknowledgment of our amazing indebtedness to His goodness!

It is a faithful saying.
—2 Timothy 2:11

aul had four of these *"faithful"* sayings. The first occurs in 1 Timothy 1:15, *"This is a faithful saying, and worthy of all acceptation, that Christ Jesus came into the world to save sinners."* The next is in 1 Timothy 4:8–9, *"Godliness is profitable unto all things, having promise of the life that now is, and of that which is to come. This is a faithful saying and worthy of all acceptation."* The third is in 2 Timothy 2:11–12, *"It is a faithful saying:…If we suffer, we shall also reign with him."* The fourth is in Titus 3:8, *"This is a faithful saying,…that they which have believed in God might be careful to maintain good works."* We may trace a connection among these faithful sayings. The first one lays the foundation of our eternal salvation in the free grace of God, as shown to us in the mission of the great Redeemer. The next affirms the double blessedness that we obtain through this salvation—the blessings of the upper and lower springs—of time and of eternity. The third shows one of the duties to which the chosen people are called. We are ordained to suffer for Christ with the promise that *"if we suffer, we shall also reign with him"* (2 Tim. 2:12). The last sets forth the active form of Christian service, bidding us to diligently maintain good works. Thus we have the root of salvation in free grace; next, the privileges of that salvation in the life which now is, and in that which is to come; and we also have the two great branches of suffering with Christ and serving with Christ, loaded with the fruits of the Spirit. Treasure up these faithful sayings. Let them be the guides of your life, your comfort, and your instruction. The apostle of the Gentiles proved them to be faithful; they are faithful still. Not one word will fall to the ground. They are worthy of acceptance. Let us accept them now and prove their faithfulness. Let these four faithful sayings be written on the four corners of your house.

I have chosen you out of the world.
—John 15:19

ere is distinguishing grace and discriminating regard, for some are made the special objects of divine affection. Do not be afraid to dwell on this high doctrine of election. When your mind is heaviest and most depressed, you will find this assuring tenet to be a bottle of soothing medicine. Those who doubt the doctrines of grace or who cast them into the shade miss the richest clusters of Eshcol; they lose the well-refined wines or the richest delicacies full of marrow. There is no balm in Gilead comparable to it. If the honey in Jonathan's wood, when but touched, enlightened the eyes, this is honey that will enlighten your heart to love and learn the mysteries of the kingdom of God. Eat, and do not worry about being too full. Live on this choice dainty, and do not fear that it will be too delicate a diet. Meat from the King's table will hurt none of His courtiers. Desire to have your mind enlarged so that you may comprehend more and more the eternal, everlasting, discriminating love of God. When you have mounted as high as election, tarry on its sister mount, the covenant of grace. Covenant engagements are the defense of stupendous rocks behind which we lie entrenched; covenant engagements with the Surety, Christ Jesus, are the quiet resting places of trembling spirits.

> His oath, His covenant, His blood,
>   Support me in the raging flood;
> When every earthly prop gives way,
>   This still is all my strength and stay.

If Jesus undertook to bring me to glory, and if the Father promised that He would give me to the Son to be a part of the infinite reward of the travail of His soul, then, my soul, until God Himself is unfaithful, until Jesus ceases to be the Truth, you are safe. When David danced before the ark, he told Michal that election made him do so. Come, my soul, and rejoice before the God of grace; leap for joy of heart.

After this manner therefore pray ye: Our Father which art in heaven.
—Matthew 6:9

his prayer begins where all true prayer must begin, with the spirit of adoption, *"Our Father."* There is no acceptable prayer until we can say, *"I will arise and go to my father"* (Luke 15:18). This childlike spirit soon perceives the grandeur of the Father *"in heaven"* and ascends to devout adoration, *"Hallowed be thy name"* (Matt. 6:9). The child lisping, "Abba, Father," grows into the cherub crying, "Holy, Holy, Holy." There is but a single step from rapturous worship to the glowing missionary spirit, which is a sure outgrowth of filial love and reverent adoration, *"Thy kingdom come. Thy will be done in earth, as it is in heaven"* (v. 10). Next follows the heartfelt expression of dependence on God, *"Give us this day our daily bread"* (v. 11). Being further illuminated by the Spirit, the one who prays discovers that he is not only dependent, but also sinful, hence he entreats for mercy, *"Forgive us our debts, as we forgive our debtors"* (v. 12). The man who is really forgiven is anxious not to offend again; the possession of justification leads to an anxious desire for sanctification. *"Forgive us our debts"* (v. 12)—that is justification. *"Lead us not into temptation, but deliver us from evil"* (v. 13)—that is sanctification in its negative and positive forms. Being pardoned, having the righteousness of Christ imputed, and knowing his acceptance with God, the one who prays humbly supplicates for holy perseverance, *"Lead us not into temptation"* (v. 13). As the result of all this, there follows a triumphant ascription of praise, *"Thine is the kingdom, and the power, and the glory, for ever. Amen"* (v. 13). We rejoice that our King reigns in providence and will reign in grace, from the river even to the ends of the earth, and of His dominion there will be no end. Thus, this short model prayer conducts the soul from a sense of adoption to fellowship with our reigning Lord. Lord, teach us thus to pray.

I will praise thee, O LORD.
—Psalm 9:1

raise should always follow answered prayer, just as the mist of earth's gratitude rises when the sun of heaven's love warms the ground. Has the Lord been gracious to you and inclined His ear to the voice of your supplication? Then praise Him as long as you live. Let the ripe fruit drop on the fertile soil from which it drew its life. Do not deny a song to Him who has answered your prayer and given you the desire of your heart. To be silent over God's mercies is to incur the guilt of ingratitude. It is to act as basely as the nine lepers, who, after they had been cured of their leprosy, did not return to give thanks to the healing Lord. To forget to praise God is to refuse to benefit ourselves. Praise, like prayer, is one great means of promoting the growth of the spiritual life. It helps to remove our burdens, to excite our hopes, to increase our faith. It is a healthful and invigorating exercise that quickens the pulse of the believer and strengthens him for fresh enterprises in his Master's service. To bless God for mercies received is also the way to benefit our fellowmen: *"The humble shall hear thereof, and be glad"* (Ps. 34:2). Others who have been in similar circumstances will take comfort if we can say, *"O magnify the LORD with me, and let us exalt his name together....This poor man cried, and the LORD heard him"* (vv. 3, 6). Weak hearts will be strengthened, and drooping saints will be revived as they listen to our *"songs of deliverance"* (Ps. 32:7). Their doubts and fears will be rebuked, as we teach and admonish *"one another in psalms and hymns and spiritual songs"* (Col. 3:16). They too will *"sing in the ways of the LORD"* (Ps. 138:5) when they hear us magnify His holy name. Praise is the most heavenly of Christian duties. The angels do not pray, but they do not cease to praise both day and night; and the redeemed, clothed in white robes, with palm branches in their hands, are never weary of singing the new song, *"Worthy is the Lamb"* (Rev. 5:12).

Renew a right spirit within me.
—Psalm 51:10

backslider, if there is a spark of life left in him, will groan after restoration. In this renewal, the same exercise of grace is required as at our conversion. We needed repentance then, and we certainly need it now. At first, we needed faith so that we might come to Christ. Now, only the same grace can bring us to Jesus. Then, we needed a word from the Most High, a word from the lips of the loving One, to end our fears; we will soon discover, when under a sense of present sin, that we need it now. No one can be renewed without as real and true a manifestation of the Holy Spirit's energy as he felt at first, because the work is as great, and flesh and blood are as much in the way now as they ever were. Let your personal weakness, Christian, be an argument to make you pray earnestly to your God for help. Remember that David, when he felt himself to be powerless, did not fold his arms or close his lips; instead, he hastened to the mercy seat with this prayer: *"Renew a right spirit within me."* Do not let the doctrine that you, unaided, can do nothing make you sleep; but let it be a goad in your side to drive you with an extreme earnestness to Israel's strong Helper. Oh, that you may have grace to plead with God, as though you pleaded for your very life. "Lord, *'renew a right spirit within me.'*" He who sincerely prays to God to do this will prove his honesty by using the means through which God works. Be much in prayer; live much on the Word of God. Kill the lusts that have driven your Lord from you; be careful to watch over the future uprisings of sin. The Lord has His own appointed ways. Sit by the wayside, and you will be ready when He passes by. Continue in all those blessed ordinances that will foster and nourish your dying graces. Knowing that all the power must proceed from Him, do not cease to cry, *"Renew a right spirit within me."*

The church in thy house.
—Philemon 2

Is there a church in your house? Are parents, children, and friends all members of it, or are some still unconverted? Let us pause here and let the question be asked of each one: Am I a member of the church in this house? How a father's heart would leap for joy and a mother's eyes fill with holy tears if all were saved from the eldest to the youngest! Let us pray for this great mercy until the Lord grants it to us. Probably it had been the dearest object of Philemon's desires to have all his household saved, but it was not at first granted him in its fullness. He had a wicked servant, Onesimus, who, having wronged him, ran away from his service. His master's prayers followed him, though, and, at last, as God would have it, Onesimus was led to hear Paul preach. His heart was touched, and he returned to Philemon, not only to be a faithful servant, but a beloved brother, adding another member to the church in Philemon's house. Is there an unconverted member of the household absent this morning? Make special supplication that such may, on his return home, gladden all hearts with good news of what grace has done! Is there an unconverted person present? Let him partake in the same earnest entreaty. If there is such a church in your house, order it well, and let all act as in the sight of God. Move in the common affairs of life with studied holiness, diligence, kindness, and integrity. More is expected of a church than of an ordinary household. Family worship must, in such a case, be heartier and more devout. Internal love must be warmer and unbroken, and external conduct must be more sanctified and Christlike. We do not need to fear that the smallness of our number will remove us from the list of churches, for the Holy Spirit has here enrolled a family-church in the inspired book of remembrance. As a church, let us now draw near to the great Head of the one universal church, and let us ask Him to give us grace to shine before men to the glory of His name.

I am the LORD, I change not.
—Malachi 3:6

It is well for us that, amid all the variableness of life, there is One whom change cannot affect, One whose heart can never alter, and One on whose brow mutability can make no furrows. Everything else has changed or is changing. The sun itself grows dim with age. The world is growing old. The folding up of worn-out garments has begun. The heavens and earth must soon pass away; they will perish and will become old as does a garment. But there is only One who has immortality, of whose years there is no end, and in whose person there is no change. The delight that the mariner feels when, after having been tossed about for many days, he steps again on the solid shore is the satisfaction of a Christian when, amid all the changes of this stormy life, he rests the foot of his faith on this truth: *"I am the LORD, I change not."* The stability that the anchor gives the ship when it has at last obtained a holdfast is like that which the Christian's hope affords him when it fixes itself on this glorious truth. With God *"is no variableness, neither shadow of turning"* (James 1:17). Whatever His attributes were of old, they are now. His power, His wisdom, His justice, and His truth are all unchanged. He has always been the refuge of His people, their *"strong hold in the day of trouble"* (Nah. 1:7), and He is their sure Helper still. He is unchanged in His love. He has loved His people with *"an everlasting love"* (Jer. 31:3). He loves them now as much as He ever did, and when all earthly things will have melted in the last conflict, His love will still wear the *"dew of [its] youth"* (Ps. 110:3). Precious is the assurance that He does not change! The wheel of providence revolves, but its axle is eternal love.

> Death and change are busy ever,
>   Man decays, and ages move;
> But His mercy waneth never;
>   God is wisdom, God is love.

Behold, he prayeth.
—Acts 9:11

Prayers are instantly noticed in heaven. The moment Saul began to pray, the Lord heard him. Here is comfort for the distressed but praying soul. Often a poor, brokenhearted one bends his knees, but can only utter his wailing in the language of sighs and tears. Yet that groan has made all the harps of heaven thrill with music; that tear has been caught by God and is treasured in heaven. *"Put thou my tears into thy bottle"* (Ps. 56:8) implies that they are caught as they flow. The suppliant, whose fears prevent his words, will be well understood by the Most High. He may only look up with misty eyes, but "prayer is the falling of a tear." Tears are the diamonds of heaven; sighs are a part of the music of Jehovah's court and are numbered with "the sublimest strains that reach the Majesty on high." Do not think that your prayer, however weak or trembling, will be unregarded. Jacob's ladder is lofty, but our prayers will lean on the Angel of the covenant and so climb its starry rounds. Our God not only hears prayer but also loves to hear it. *"He forgetteth not the cry of the humble"* (Ps. 9:12) True, He does not regard high looks and lofty words and does not care for the pomp and pageantry of kings. He does not listen to the swell of martial music. He does not regard the triumph and pride of man. But wherever there is a heart that is full of sorrow, lips that are quivering with agony, a deep groan, or a penitential sigh, the heart of Jehovah is open. He marks it down in the registry of His memory. He puts our prayers, like rose leaves, between the pages of His book of remembrance, and when the volume is opened at last, there will be a precious fragrance springing up from it.

Faith asks no signal from the skies,
   To show that prayers accepted rise,
Our Priest is in His holy place,
   And answers from the throne of grace.

For my strength is made perfect in weakness.
—2 Corinthians 12:9

A primary qualification for serving God with any amount of success, and for doing God's work well and triumphantly, is a sense of our own weakness. When God's warrior marches forth to battle, strong in his own might, and boasts, "I know that I will conquer. My own right arm and my conquering sword will bring me victory," defeat is not far away. God will not go forth with that man who marches in his own strength. He who counts on victory has calculated wrongly, for it is *"not by might, nor by power, but by my spirit, saith the LORD of hosts"* (Zech. 4:6). Those who go forth to fight, boasting of their prowess, will return with their colorful banners trailed in the dust and their armor stained with disgrace. Those who serve God must serve Him in His own way, and in His strength, or He will never accept their service. What man does unaided by divine strength, God can never own. The mere fruits of the earth He casts away. He will reap only that corn whose seed was sown from heaven, watered by grace, and ripened by the sun of divine love. God will empty out all that you have before He will put His own into you. He will first clean out your granaries before He will fill them with the finest of the wheat. The river of God is full of water, but not one drop of it flows from earthly springs. God will have no strength used in His battles but the strength that He Himself imparts. Are you mourning over your own weakness? Take courage, for there must be a consciousness of weakness before the Lord will give you victory. Your emptiness is but the preparation for your being filled, and your casting down is but the making ready for your lifting up.

> When I am weak then am I strong,
> Grace is my shield and Christ my song.

No weapon that is formed against thee shall prosper.
—Isaiah 54:17

his day is notable in English history for two great deliverances wrought by God for us. On this day in 1605, the Gun Powder Plot, the conspiracy to destroy our Houses of Parliament, was discovered.

> While for our princes they prepare
> In caverns deep a burning snare,
> He shot from heaven a piercing ray,
> And the dark treachery brought to day.

Second, today is the anniversary of the landing of King William III at Torbay in 1688, by which a Protestant monarchy and religious liberty were secured. This day ought to be celebrated, not by the unrestrained celebrations of youth, but by the songs of saints. Our Puritan forefathers most devoutly made it a special time of thanksgiving. There is still in existence a record of the annual sermons preached by Matthew Henry on this day. Our Protestant feeling, and our love of liberty, should make us regard its anniversary with holy gratitude. Let our hearts and lips exclaim, *"We have heard with our ears, O God, our fathers have told us, what work thou didst in their days, in the times of old"* (Ps. 44:1). You have made this nation the home of the Gospel; and when the foe has risen against her, You have shielded her. Help us to offer repeated songs for repeated deliverances. Grant us more and more a hatred of the spirit of the Antichrist, and hasten on the day of its entire extinction. Until then, we believe the promise, *"No weapon that is formed against thee shall prosper."* On this day, should it not be laid on the heart of every lover of the Gospel of Jesus to plead for the overturning of false doctrines and the extension of divine truth? Would it not be good to search our own hearts and eradicate any of the lumber of self-righteousness that may lie concealed therein?

I will pour water upon him that is thirsty.
—Isaiah 44:3

Hen a believer has fallen into a low, sad state of feeling, he often tries to lift himself out of it by chastening himself with dark and doleful fears. This is not the way to rise from the dust, but to continue in it. You might as well chain the eagle's wing to make it mount as to doubt in order to increase your grace. It is not the law, but the Gospel that saves the seeking soul at first; and it is not a legal bondage, but gospel liberty that can restore the fainting believer afterward. Slavish fear does not bring the backslider back to God, but the sweet wooings of love allure him to Jesus' bosom. Are you thirsting for the living God this morning and unhappy because you cannot find Him to the delight of your heart? Have you lost the joy of religion, and is this your prayer, *"Restore unto me the joy of thy salvation"* (Ps. 51:12)? Are you conscious also that you are barren like the dry ground and that you are not bringing forth the *"fruit unto God"* (Rom. 7:4) that He has a right to expect of you? Are you aware that you are not as useful in the church or in the world as your heart desires to be? Then here is exactly the promise that you need, *"I will pour water upon him that is thirsty."* You will receive the grace you so much require, and you will have it to the utmost extent of your needs. Water refreshes the thirsty: you will be refreshed, and your desires will be gratified. Water quickens sleeping vegetable life; your life will be quickened by fresh grace. Water swells the buds and makes the fruits ripen; you will have grace that will make you fruitful in the ways of God. Whatever good quality there is in divine grace, you will enjoy it to the full. All the riches of divine grace you will receive in abundance. You will be, as it were, drenched with it. As sometimes the meadows become flooded by the bursting rivers and the fields are turned into pools, so will you be; the thirsty land will be transformed into springs of water.

Behold, I have graven thee upon the palms of my hands.
—Isaiah 49:16

No doubt a part of the wonder that is concentrated in the word *"behold"* is increased by the unbelieving lamentation of this earlier sentence, *"Zion said, The LORD hath forsaken me, and my Lord hath forgotten me"* (Isa. 49:14). How amazed the divine mind seems to be at this wicked unbelief! What can be more astounding than the unfounded doubts and fears of God's favored people? The Lord's loving word of rebuke should make us blush. He cries, "How can I have forgotten you, when *'I have graven you on the palms of my hands'*? How dare you doubt My constant remembrance, when the memorial is set on My very flesh?" O unbelief, how strange a marvel you are! We do not know which to wonder at most: the faithfulness of God or the unbelief of His people. He keeps His promise a thousand times, and yet the next trial makes us doubt Him. He never fails. He is never a dry well. He is never as a setting sun, a passing meteor, or a melting vapor; yet we are as continually vexed with anxieties, molested with suspicions, and disturbed with fears, as if our God were the mirage of the desert. *"Behold"* is a word intended to incite admiration. Here, indeed, we have a theme for marveling. Heaven and earth may well be astonished that rebels should obtain so great a nearness to the heart of infinite love as to be written on the palms of His hands. *"I have graven thee."* It does not say, "Thy name." The name is there, but that is not all: *"I have graven thee."* See the fullness of this! I have graven your person, your image, your case, your circumstances, your sins, your temptations, your weaknesses, your needs, your works. I have graven you, everything about you, all that concerns you. I have put you altogether there. Will you ever say again that your God has forsaken you when He has *"graven [you] upon the palms of [His] hands"*?

As ye have therefore received Christ Jesus the Lord.
—Colossians 2:6

he life of faith is represented as receiving—an act that implies the very opposite of anything involving merit. It is simply the acceptance of a gift. As the earth drinks in the rain, as the sea receives the streams, as night accepts light from the stars, so we, giving nothing, partake freely of the grace of God. By nature, the saints are not wells or streams; they are only cisterns into which the living water flows. They are empty vessels into which God pours His salvation. The idea of receiving implies a sense of realization, making the matter a reality. One cannot very well receive a shadow; we receive that which is substantial. So is it in the life of faith. Christ becomes real to us. While we are without faith, Jesus is a mere name to us—a person who lived a long time ago, so long ago that His life is only history to us now! By an act of faith, Jesus becomes a real person in the consciousness of our hearts. But receiving also means grasping or gaining possession. The thing that I receive becomes my own. I take hold for myself what is given. When I receive Jesus, He becomes my Savior, so much mine that neither life nor death will be able to rob me of Him. All this is to receive Christ—to take Him as God's free gift, to realize Him in my heart, and to appropriate Him as mine. Salvation may be described as the blind receiving sight, the deaf receiving hearing, the dead receiving life; but we have received not only these blessings, but also Christ Jesus Himself! It is true that He gave us life from the dead. He gave us pardon of sin and imputed righteousness. These are all precious things, but we are not content with them; we have received Christ Himself! The Son of God has been poured into us, and we have received Him and taken hold of Him. What a heartful Jesus must be, for heaven itself cannot contain Him!

As ye have therefore received Christ Jesus the Lord,
so walk ye in him.
—Colossians 2:6

If we have received Christ Himself in our inmost hearts, our new lives will manifest their intimate acquaintance with Him by a walk of faith in Him. Walking implies action. Our religion is not to be confined to our private prayer times. We must carry out into practical actions that which we believe. If a person walks in Christ, then he acts as Christ would act. Since Christ is in him as his hope, his love, his joy, his life, he is the reflection of the image of Jesus. People say of that person, "He is like his Master; he lives like Jesus Christ." Walking signifies progress. *"So walk ye in him."* Proceed from grace to grace. Run forward until you reach the uttermost degree of knowledge that a person can attain concerning our Beloved. Walking implies continuance. There must be a perpetual abiding in Christ. How many Christians think that in the morning and evening they ought to come into the company of Jesus, but then they give their hearts to the world all day? But this is poor living. We should always be with Him, treading in His steps and doing His will. Walking also implies habit. When we speak of a man's walk and conversation, we mean his habits and the constant character of his life. Now, if we sometimes enjoy Christ, and then forget Him; sometimes call Him ours, and immediately lose our hold, that is not a habit. We do not walk in Him. We must keep close to Him, cling to Him, never let Him go; we should live and have our being in Him. *"As ye have therefore received Christ Jesus the Lord, so walk ye in him."* Persevere in the same way in which you began. As at the first Christ Jesus was the trust of your faith, the source of your life, the principle of your action, and the joy of your spirit, so let Him be the same until life's end—the same when you walk through the valley of the shadow of death and enter into the joy and the rest that remains for the people of God. Holy Spirit, enable us to obey this heavenly precept.

The eternal God is thy refuge.
—Deuteronomy 33:27

The word *"refuge"* may be translated "mansion" or "abiding place," which gives the thought that God is our abode, our home. There is a fullness and sweetness in the metaphor, for dear to our hearts are our homes, although they may be the humblest cottages. Far dearer is our blessed God, *"for in him we live, and move, and have our being"* (Acts 17:28). It is at home that we feel safe. We shut the world out and dwell in quiet security. So when we are with our God, we *"fear no evil"* (Ps. 23:4). He is our shelter and retreat, our abiding refuge. At home, we rest, and it is there we find repose after the fatigue and toil of the day. And so our hearts find rest in God when, wearied with life's conflicts, we turn to Him, and our souls dwell at ease. At home, also, we let our hearts loose; we are not afraid of being misunderstood, nor of our words being misconstrued. So when we are with God, we can commune freely with Him, laying open all our hidden desires; for if the *"secret of the LORD is with them that fear him"* (Ps. 25:14), the secrets of them that fear Him ought to be, and must be, with their Lord. Home, too, is the place of our truest and purest happiness. It is in God that our hearts find their deepest delight. We have joy in Him that far surpasses all other joy. It is also for home that we work and labor. The thought of it gives strength to bear the daily burdens and quickens the fingers to perform the task; in this sense, we may also say that God is our home. Love for Him strengthens us. We think of Him in the person of His dear Son, and a glimpse of the suffering face of the Redeemer constrains us to labor in His cause. We feel that we must work, for we have friends and loved ones yet to be saved, and we have our Father's heart to make glad by bringing home His wandering ones. We would fill the sacred family among whom we dwell with holy mirth. Happy are those who have the God of Jacob for their refuge!

Underneath are the everlasting arms.
—Deuteronomy 33:27

od, the eternal God, is Himself our support at all times, especially when we are sinking in deep trouble. There are seasons when the Christian sinks very low in humiliation. Under a deep sense of his great sinfulness, he is humbled before God until he scarcely knows how to pray, because he appears, in his own sight, so worthless. Well, child of God, remember that when you are at your worst and lowest point, *"underneath [you] are the everlasting arms."* Sin may drag you low, but Christ's great atonement is still under all. You may have descended into deep distress, but you cannot have fallen so low as *"the uttermost"* (Heb. 7:25), and to the uttermost He saves. Again, the Christian sometimes sinks very deeply in sore trials from without. Every earthly prop is cut away. What then? Still underneath him are *"the everlasting arms."* He cannot fall so deep in distress and affliction without the covenant grace of an ever-faithful God still encircling him. The Christian may be sinking under trouble from within through fierce conflict, but even then he cannot be brought so low as to be beyond the reach of the *"everlasting arms."* They are underneath him, and, while thus sustained, all Satan's efforts to harm him avail nothing. This assurance of support is a comfort to any weary but earnest worker in the service of God. It implies a promise of strength for each day, grace for each need, and power for each duty. Further, when death comes, the promise will still hold good. When we stand in the midst of Jordan, we will be able to say with David, *"I will fear no evil: for thou art with me"* (Ps. 23:4). We will descend into the grave, but we will go no lower, for the eternal arms prevent our further fall. All through life, and at its close, we will be upheld by the *"everlasting arms"*—arms that neither flag nor lose their strength, for *"the everlasting God, the LORD, the Creator of the ends of the earth, fainteth not, neither is weary"* (Isa. 40:28).

The trial of your faith.
—1 Peter 1:7

Untried faith may be true faith, but it is sure to be little faith, and it is likely to remain stunted as long as it is without trials. Faith never prospers as well as when all things are against her. Tempests are her trainers, and lightning is her illuminator. When calm reigns on the sea, spread the sails as you will, but the ship will not move to its harbor; for on a slumbering ocean, the keel sleeps, too. But let the howling winds rush forth, and let the waters lift up themselves. Though the vessel may rock, her deck may be washed with waves, and her mast may creak under the pressure of the full and swelling sail, it is then that she makes headway toward her desired haven. No flowers wear as lovely a blue as those that grow at the foot of the frozen glacier. No stars gleam as brightly as those that glisten in the polar sky. No water tastes as sweet as that which springs amid the desert sand; and no faith is as precious as that which lives and triumphs in adversity. Tried faith brings experience. You could not have believed your own weakness had you not been compelled to pass through the rivers; and you would never have known God's strength had you not been supported amid the flooding waters. Faith increases in solidity, assurance, and intensity the more it is exercised with tribulation. Faith is precious, and its trial is precious, too. Let not this, however, discourage those who are young in faith. You will have trials enough without seeking them; the full portion will be measured out to you in due season. Meanwhile, if you cannot yet claim the results of long experience, thank God for what grace you have. Praise Him for that degree of holy confidence that you have already attained. Walk according to that rule, and you will yet have more and more of the blessings of God, until your faith will remove mountains and conquer impossibilities.

The branch cannot bear fruit of itself.
—John 15:4

ow did you begin to bear fruit? It was when you came to Jesus and cast yourselves on His great atonement and rested on His finished righteousness. Ah, what fruit you had then! Do you remember those early days? Then indeed the vine flourished, the tender grape appeared, the pomegranates budded forth, and the beds of spices gave forth their smell. Have you declined since then? If you have, we charge you to remember that time of love and repent; do your first works. Be most engaged in those experiences that have proven to draw you nearest to Christ, because it is from Him that all your fruit proceeds. Any holy exercise that will bring you to Him will help you to bear fruit. The sun is, no doubt, a great aid in creating fruit among the trees of the orchard. Jesus is even more so among the trees of His garden of grace. When have you been the most fruitless? Has it not been when you have lived farthest from the Lord Jesus Christ, when you have slackened in prayer, and when you have departed from the simplicity of your faith? Has it not been when your graces have engrossed your attention instead of your Lord, when you have said, "My mountain stands firm. I will never be moved," and have forgotten where your strength dwells? Has it not been then that your fruit has ceased? Some of us have been taught by terrible humility of the heart before the Lord that we are nothing apart from Christ. When we have seen the utter barrenness and death of all creature-power, we have cried in anguish, "From Him all my fruit must be found, for no fruit can ever come from me." We are taught, by past experience, that the more simply we depend on the grace of God in Christ and wait on the Holy Spirit, the more we will bring forth fruit unto God. Oh, to trust Jesus for fruit as well as for life!

I will cut off the remnant of Baal from this place, and…them that
worship the host of heaven upon the housetops; and them that swear
by the LORD, and that swear by Malcham.
—Zephaniah 1:4–5

Such persons thought themselves safe because they were with both parties. They went with the followers of Jehovah and bowed at the same time to Malcham. But duplicity is abominable with God, and His soul hates hypocrisy. The idolater who distinctly gives himself to his false god has one sin less than he who brings his polluted and detestable sacrifice to the temple of the Lord while his heart is with the world and the sins thereof. To hold with the hare and run with the hounds is a coward's policy. In the common matters of daily life, a double-minded man is despised, but in religion he is loathsome to the last degree. The penalty pronounced in the verse before us is terrible, but it is well deserved. How should divine justice spare the sinner, who knows the right, approves it, and professes to follow it, and all the while loves evil and gives it dominion in his heart? My soul, search yourself this morning, and see whether you are guilty of double-dealing. You profess to be a follower of Jesus, but do you truly love Him? Is your heart right with God? Are you of the family of old Father Honest, or are you a relative of Mr. Stretch-the-Truth? A good name is of little value if I am indeed dead in trespasses and sins. To have one foot on the land of truth and another on the sea of falsehood will involve a terrible fall and total ruin. Christ will be all or nothing. God fills the whole universe; therefore, there is no room for another god. If He reigns in my heart, there will be no space for another reigning power. Do I rest alone on Jesus crucified and live alone for Him? Is it my desire to do so? Is my heart set on doing so? Then, blessed be the mighty grace that has led me to salvation. If this is not the case, O Lord, pardon my sad offense and unite my heart to fear Your name.

The LORD'S portion is his people.
—Deuteronomy 32:9

ow are they His? By His own sovereign choice. He chose them and set His love on them. He did this altogether apart from any goodness in them at the time, or any goodness that He foresaw in them. He had mercy on whom He would have mercy and ordained a chosen company unto eternal life; therefore, they are His by His unconstrained election. They are His not only by choice, but also by purchase. He has bought and paid for them to the last cent; hence, there can be no dispute about His title. The Lord's portion has been fully redeemed, *"not...with corruptible things, as silver and gold,...but with the precious blood of Christ"* (1 Pet. 1:18–19). There is no mortgage on His estate; no suits can be raised by opposing claimants. The price was paid in open court, and the church is the Lord's property forever. See the bloodmark on all the chosen, invisible to human eye, but known to Christ, for *"the Lord knoweth them that are his"* (2 Tim. 2:19). He does not forget any of those whom He has redeemed from among men. He counts the sheep for whom He laid down His life and remembers well the church for which He gave Himself. They are also His by conquest. What a battle He had in us before we would be won! How long He laid siege to our hearts! How often He sent us terms of capitulation, but we barred our gates and fenced our walls against Him. Do we not remember that glorious hour when He carried our hearts by storm? When He placed His cross against the wall and scaled our ramparts, planting on our strongholds the bloodred flag of His omnipotent mercy? Yes, we are, indeed, the conquered captives of His omnipotent love. Thus chosen, purchased, and subdued, the rights of our divine Possessor are inalienable. We rejoice that we can never be our own, and we desire, day by day, to do His will and to show forth His glory.

The LORD is my portion, saith my soul.
—Lamentations 3:24

his verse does not say, "The Lord is partly my por-tion" or "The Lord is in my portion," but He Himself makes up the sum total of my soul's inheritance. Within the circumference of that circle lies all that we possess or desire. *"The LORD is my portion"*—not His grace merely or His love or His covenant, but Jehovah Himself! He has chosen us for His portion, and we have chosen Him for ours. It is true that the Lord must first choose our inheritance for us, or else we will never choose it for ourselves; but if we are really called according to the purpose of electing love, we can sing

> Lov'd of my God for Him again
> With love intense I burn;
> Chosen of Him ere time began,
> I choose Him in return.

The Lord is our all-sufficient portion. God fills Himself; and if God is all-sufficient in Himself, He must be all-sufficient for us. It is not easy to satisfy man's desires. When he dreams that he is satisfied, immediately he awakens to the perception that there is something yet beyond, and the greed in his heart cries, "Give! Give!" But all that we can wish for is to be found in our divine portion, so that we ask, *"Whom have I in heaven but thee? and there is none upon earth that I desire beside thee"* (Ps. 73:25). Well may we delight in the Lord who makes us to drink of the river of His pleasures. Our faith stretches her wings and mounts like an eagle into the heaven of divine love as to her proper dwelling place. *"The lines are fallen unto me in pleasant places; yea, I have a goodly heritage"* (Ps. 16:6). Let us rejoice in the Lord always. Let us show the world that we are a happy and blessed people, and thus cause them to exclaim, "We will go with you, for we have heard that God is with you."

To whom be glory for ever. Amen.
—Romans 11:36

o whom be glory for ever." This should be the single desire of the Christian. All other wishes must be subservient to this one. The Christian may wish for prosperity in his business, but only so far as it may help him to promote this cause—"To Him be glory forever." He may desire to attain more gifts and more graces, but it should only be for God's glory. You are not acting as you should when you are moved by any other motive than a single eye to your Lord's glory. As a Christian, you are *of* God, and *through* God; then live *to* God. Let nothing ever set your heart beating so mightily as love for Him. Let this ambition fire your soul. May this be the foundation of every enterprise on which you enter and your sustaining motive whenever your zeal would grow cold. Make God your only object. Depend on it. Where self begins, sorrow begins. But if God is my supreme delight and only purpose,

> To me 'tis equal whether love ordain
> My life or death—appoint me ease or pain.

Let your desire for God's glory be a growing desire. You blessed Him in your youth; do not be content with such praises as you gave Him then. Has God prospered you in business? Give Him more as He has given you more. Has God given you experience? Praise Him by stronger faith than you exercised at first. Does your knowledge grow? Then sing more sweetly. Do you enjoy happier times than you once had? Have you been restored from sickness, and has your sorrow been turned into peace and joy? Then give Him more music. Put more coals and more sweet frankincense into the censer of your praise. Practically in your life give Him honor, putting the "Amen" to this doxology to your great and gracious Lord by your own individual service and increasing holiness.

A spring shut up, a fountain sealed.
—Song of Solomon 4:12

In this metaphor, which has reference to the inner life of a believer, we have very plainly the idea of secrecy. It is *"a spring shut up."* Just as there were springs in the East, over which an edifice was built, so that none could reach them except those who knew the secret entrance, so is the heart of a believer when it is renewed by grace. There is a mysterious life within that no human skill can touch. It is a secret that no other man knows; no, the very man who is the possessor of it cannot tell it to his neighbor. The text includes not only secrecy, but separation. It is not the common spring, of which every passerby may drink; it is one kept and preserved from all others. It is a fountain bearing a particular mark—a king's royal seal, so that all can perceive that it is not a common fountain, but a fountain owned by a proprietor and placed especially by itself. So is it with the spiritual life. The chosen of God were separated in the eternal decree. They were separated by God in the day of redemption, and they are separated by the possession of a life that others do not have. It is impossible for them to feel at home with the world or to delight in its pleasures. There is also the idea of sacredness. The *"spring shut up"* is preserved for the use of some special person, and such is the Christian's heart. It is a spring kept for Jesus. Every Christian should feel that he has God's seal on him. He should be able to say with Paul, *"From henceforth let no man trouble me: for I bear in my body the marks of the Lord Jesus"* (Gal. 6:17). Another prominent idea is that of security. Oh, how sure and safe is the inner life of the believer! If all the powers of earth and hell could combine against it, that immortal principle must still exist, for He who gave it pledged His life for its preservation. And who is He that will harm you, when God is your protector?

Avoid foolish questions.
—Titus 3:9

ur days are few and are far better spent in doing good than in disputing over matters which are, at best, of minor importance. In the past, men have done a world of mischief by their incessant discussion of subjects of no practical importance. Our churches suffer as well from petty wars over obscure points and unimportant questions. After everything has been said that can be said, neither party is any wiser; therefore, the discussion no more promotes knowledge than love, and it is foolish to sow in so barren a field. Questions on points wherein Scripture is silent, on mysteries that belong to God alone, on prophecies of doubtful interpretation, and on mere modes of observing human ceremonials are all foolish, and wise men avoid them. Our business is neither to ask nor answer foolish questions, but to avoid them altogether. If we observe the apostle's precept to *"be careful to maintain good works"* (Titus 3:8), we will find ourselves far too occupied with profitable business to take much interest in unworthy, contentious, needless strivings. There are, however, some questions that are the reverse of foolish ones, questions that we must not avoid, but fairly and honestly meet, such as these: Do I believe in the Lord Jesus Christ? Am I renewed in the spirit of my mind? Am I walking not after the flesh, but after the Spirit? Am I growing in grace? Does my conversation adorn the doctrine of God my Savior? Am I looking for the coming of the Lord and watching as a servant who expects his master should? What more can I do for Jesus? Such inquiries as these urgently demand our attention. If we have been at all given to quibbling, let us now turn our critical abilities to a service so much more profitable. Let us be peacemakers and endeavor to lead others, both by our precept and example, to *"avoid foolish questions."*

O Lord, thou hast pleaded the causes of my soul;
thou hast redeemed my life.
—Lamentations 3:58

otice how positively the prophet spoke. He did not say, "I hope, I trust, I sometimes think that God has pleaded the causes of my soul." Instead, he spoke of it as a matter of fact not to be disputed. *"Thou hast pleaded the causes of my soul."* Let us, by the aid of the gracious Comforter, shake off those doubts and fears that so often mar our peace and comfort. May this be our prayer: that we may be done with the harsh, croaking voice of surmise and suspicion and be able to speak with the clear, melodious voice of full assurance. Notice how gratefully the prophet spoke, ascribing all the glory to God alone! There was not a word concerning himself or his own pleadings. He did not ascribe his deliverance in any measure to any man, much less to his own merit; but he said, *"Thou"*—*"O Lord, thou hast pleaded the causes of my soul; thou hast redeemed my life."* A grateful spirit should be cultivated by the Christian; especially after deliverances we should prepare a song for our God. Earth should be a temple filled with the songs of grateful saints, and every day should be a smoking censor, filled with the sweet incense of thanksgiving. How joyful Jeremiah seemed to be while he recorded the Lord's mercy! How triumphantly he lifted up the strain! He had been in the low dungeon, and even now, he is considered to be the weeping prophet; yet in the very book that is called Lamentations, clear as the song of Miriam when she dashed her fingers against the tabor, shrill as the note of Deborah when she met Barak with shouts of victory, we hear the voice of Jeremiah going up to heaven— *"Thou hast pleaded the causes of my soul; thou hast redeemed my life."* Children of God, seek after a vital experience of the Lord's lovingkindness. When you have it, speak positively of it, sing gratefully, and shout triumphantly.

Grieve not the holy Spirit of God.
—Ephesians 4:30

All that the believer has must come from Christ, but it comes solely through the channel of the Spirit of grace. Moreover, as all blessings thus flow to you through the Holy Spirit, so also no good thing can come out of you in holy thought, devout worship, or gracious actions, apart from the sanctifying operation of the same Spirit. Even if the good seed is sown in you, it lies dormant unless He works *"in you both to will and to do of his good pleasure"* (Phil. 2:13). Do you desire to speak for Jesus—how can you unless the Holy Spirit touches your tongue? Do you desire to pray? Alas, what dull work it is unless the *"Spirit itself maketh intercession for [you]"* (Rom. 8:26)! Do you desire to subdue sin? Would you be holy? Would you imitate your Master? Do you desire to rise to superlative heights of spirituality? Are you wanting to be made like the angels of God, full of zeal and ardor for the Master's cause? You cannot without the Spirit—*"Without me ye can do nothing"* (John 15:5). Branch of the vine, you can have no fruit without the sap! Child of God, you have no life within you apart from the life that God gives you through His Spirit! Then let us not grieve Him or provoke Him to anger by our sins. Let us not quench Him in one of His faintest motions in our souls. Let us foster every suggestion and be ready to obey every prompting. If the Holy Spirit is indeed so mighty, let us attempt nothing without Him. Let us begin no project and carry on no enterprise and conclude no transaction without imploring His blessing. Let us give Him the due homage of feeling our entire weakness apart from Him, and then, depending alone on Him, have this as our prayer, "Open my heart and my whole self to Your incoming. Uphold me with Your free Spirit when I will have received that Spirit in my inmost being."

Israel served for a wife, and for a wife he kept sheep.
—Hosea 12:12

Jacob, while reasoning with Laban, described his own toil in this way, *"This twenty years have I been with thee....That which was torn of beasts I brought not unto thee; I bare the loss of it; of my hand didst thou require it, whether stolen by day, or stolen by night. Thus I was; in the day the drought consumed me, and the frost by night; and my sleep departed from mine eyes"* (Gen. 31:38–39). Even more toilsome than this was the life of our Savior here below. He watched over all His sheep until He gave as His last account, *"Of them which thou gavest me have I lost none"* (John 18:9). His hair was wet with dew, and His locks with the drops of the night. Sleep departed from His eyes, for all night He was in prayer, wrestling for His people. One night Peter must be pleaded for; then another claims His tearful intercession. No shepherd sitting beneath the cold skies, looking up at the stars, could ever utter such complaints because of the hardness of his toil as Jesus Christ might have done, if He had chosen to do so, because of the difficulty of His service in order to procure His spouse.

> Cold mountains and the midnight air,
>   Witnessed the fervor of His prayer;
> The desert His temptations knew,
>   His conflict and His victory, too.

It is sweet to dwell on the spiritual parallel of Laban having required all the sheep at Jacob's hand. If they were attacked and destroyed by beasts, Jacob must make it good; if any of them died, he must stand as surety for the whole. Was not the toil of Jesus for His church the toil of one who was under suretyship obligations to bring every believing one safe to the hand of Him who had committed them to His charge? Look on toiling Jacob, and you see a representation of Him of whom we read, *"He shall feed his flock like a shepherd"* (Isa. 40:11).

Fellowship with him.
—1 John 1:6

When we were united by faith to Christ, we were brought into such complete fellowship with Him that we were made one with Him. His interests and ours became mutual and identical. We have fellowship with Christ in His love. What He loves, we love. He loves the saints; so do we. He loves sinners; so do we. He loves the poor perishing race of man and longs to see earth's deserts transformed into the garden of the Lord; so do we. We have fellowship with Him in His desires. He desires the glory of God; we also labor for the same. He desires that the saints may be with Him where He is; we desire to be with Him there, too. He desires to drive out sin; behold, we fight under His banner. He desires that His Father's name may be loved and adored by all His creatures; we pray daily, *"Thy kingdom come. Thy will be done in earth, as it is in heaven"* (Matt. 6:10). We have fellowship with Christ in His sufferings. We are not nailed to the cross, nor do we die a cruel death; but when He is reproached, we are reproached. It is a very sweet thing to be blamed for His sake, to be despised for following the Master, to have the world against us. *"The disciple is not above his master, nor the servant above his lord"* (Matt. 10:24). In our measure we commune with Him in His labors, ministering to people by the word of truth and by deeds of love. Our meat and our drink, like His, *"is to do the will of him that sent [us], and to finish his work"* (John 4:34). We also have fellowship with Christ in His joys. We are happy in His happiness, and we rejoice in His exaltation. Have you ever tasted that joy, believer? There is no purer or more thrilling delight to be known this side of heaven than that of having Christ's joy fulfilled in us so that our joy may be full. His glory awaits us to complete our fellowship, for His church will sit with Him on His throne, as His well-beloved bride and queen.

The glorious LORD will be unto us a place
of broad rivers and streams.
—Isaiah 33:21

road rivers and streams" produce fertility and abundance in the land. Places near broad rivers are remarkable for the variety of their plants and their
plentiful harvests. God is all this to His church. Having
God, she has abundance. What can she ask for that He will
not give her? What need can she mention that He will not
supply? *"In this mountain shall the LORD of hosts make unto all
people a feast of fat things"* (Isa. 25:6). Do you want the bread
of life? It drops like manna from the sky. Do you want refreshing streams? The rock follows you, and that Rock is
Christ. If you suffer any lack, it is your own fault. If you are
suffering any deficiency, you are not deficient in Him, but in
your own hearts. Broad rivers and streams also point to
commerce. Our glorious Lord is to us a place of heavenly
merchandise. Through our Redeemer, we have commerce
with the past; the wealth of Calvary, the treasures of the
covenant, the riches of the ancient days of election, and the
stores of eternity all come to us down the broad stream of
our gracious Lord. We have commerce, too, with the future.
What boats, laden to the water's edge, come to us from the
Millennium! What visions we have of the days of heaven on
earth! Through our glorious Lord, we have commerce with
angels and communion with the bright spirits washed in
His blood, who sing before the throne. Better still, we have
fellowship with the Infinite One. Broad rivers and streams
are especially intended to set forth the idea of security. Rivers were a defense in the past. Beloved, what a defense God
is to His church! The devil cannot cross this broad river of
God. How he wishes he could turn the current, but do not
fear, for God abides immutably the same. Satan may worry,
but he cannot destroy us. No boat with oars will invade our
river; neither will stately ships pass thereby.

To preach deliverance to the captives.
—Luke 4:18

No one but Jesus can give deliverance to the captives. Real liberty comes only from Him. It is a liberty righteously bestowed; for the Son, who is Heir of all things, has a right to make men free. The saints honor the justice of God, which now secures their salvation. It is a liberty that has been dearly purchased. Christ speaks it by His power, but He bought it by His blood. He makes you free, but it is by His own bonds. You go clear, because He bore your burden for you. You are set at liberty, because He has suffered in your place. But, though dearly purchased, He freely gives it. Jesus asks nothing of us as a preparation for this liberty. He finds us sitting in sackcloth and ashes and invites us to put on the beautiful array of freedom. He saves us just as we are, and all without our help or merit. When Jesus sets free, the liberty is perpetually given; no chains can bind again. Let the Master say to me, "Captive, I have delivered you," and it is done forever. Satan may plot to enslave us, but if the Lord is on our side, whom will we fear? The world, with its temptations, may seek to ensnare us, but mightier is He who is for us than all they who are against us. *"If God be for us, who can be against us?"* (Rom. 8:31). The schemes of our own deceitful hearts may harass and annoy us, but *"he which hath begun a good work"* (Phil. 1:6) in us will carry it on and perfect it to the end. The foes of God and the enemies of man may gather their hosts together and come with concentrated fury against us, but if God acquits, *"who is he that condemneth?"* (Rom. 8:34). The eagle that mounts to his rocky nest, and afterward outsoars the clouds, is not any freer than the soul that Christ has delivered. If we are no more under the law, but free from its curse, let our liberty be practically exhibited in our serving God with gratitude and delight. *"I am thy servant, and the son of thine handmaid: thou hast loosed my bonds"* (Ps. 116:16). *"Lord, what wilt thou have me to do?"* (Acts 9:6).

Whatsoever thy hand findeth to do, do it with thy might.
—Ecclesiastes 9:10

"Whatsoever thy hand findeth to do" refers to works that are possible. There are many things that our hearts find to do that we will never do. It is well it is in our hearts, but if we would be eminently useful, we must not be content with forming schemes in our hearts and talking about them. We must practically carry out whatever our hands find to do. One good deed is worth more than a thousand brilliant theories. Let us not wait for large opportunities or for different kinds of work, but do the things that we find to do day by day. We have no other time in which to live. The past is gone; the future has not arrived. We will never have any time but the present. Then do not wait until your experience has ripened into maturity before you attempt to serve God. Endeavor now to bring forth fruit. Serve God now, but be careful as to the way in which you perform what you find to do—*"do it with thy might."* Do it promptly. Do not fritter away your life in thinking of what you intend to do tomorrow, as if that could make up for the idleness of today. No man ever served God by doing things tomorrow. If we honor Christ and are blessed, it is by the things that we do today. Whatever you do for Christ, throw your whole soul into it. Do not give Christ a little shoddy labor, done as a matter of course now and then. When you serve Him, do it with your heart, soul, and strength. But where is the might of a Christian? It is not in himself, for he is perfect weakness. His strength lies in the Lord of Hosts. Then let us seek His help; let us proceed with prayer and faith, and when we have done what our *"hand findeth to do,"* let us wait on the Lord for His blessing. What we do thus will be well done and will not fail in its purpose.

Joshua the high priest standing before the angel of the LORD.
—Zechariah 3:1

In Joshua, the high priest, we see a picture of each and every child of God who has been *"made nigh by the blood of Christ"* (Eph. 2:13) and has been taught to minister in holy things and enter into that which is within the veil. Jesus has made us *"kings and priests unto God"* (Rev. 1:6), and even here on earth, we exercise the priesthood of consecrated living and hallowed service. But this high priest is said to be *"standing before the angel of the LORD,"* that is, standing to minister. This should be the perpetual position of every true believer. Every place is now God's temple, and His people can as truly serve Him in their daily employment as in His house. They are always to be ministering, offering the spiritual sacrifice of prayer and praise and presenting themselves a *"living sacrifice"* (Rom. 12:1). But notice where it is that Joshua stands to minister; it is before the angel of Jehovah. It is only through a mediator that we poor, defiled ones can ever become priests unto God. I present what I have before the messenger, the Angel of the covenant, the Lord Jesus. Through Him, my prayers find acceptance wrapped up in His prayers; my praises become sweet as they are bound up with bundles of myrrh, aloe, and cassia from Christ's own garden. If I can bring Him nothing but my tears, He will put them with His own tears in His own bottle, for He once wept. If I can bring Him nothing but my groans and sighs, He will accept these as an acceptable sacrifice, for He once was broken in heart, and sighed heavily in spirit. I myself, standing in Him, am *"accepted in the beloved"* (Eph. 1:6); and all my polluted works, though in themselves only objects of divine abhorrence, are received so that God smells a sweet savor. He is content, and I am blessed. See, then, the position of the Christian—a *"priest standing before the angel of the LORD."*

For I rejoiced greatly, when the brethren came and testified of the
truth that is in thee, even as thou walkest in the truth.
—3 John 3

he truth was in Gaius, and Gaius walked in the truth. If the first had not been the case, the second could never have occurred; and if the second could not have been said of him, the first would have been a mere pretense. Truth must enter into the soul, penetrate and saturate it, or else it is of no value. Doctrines held as a matter of creed are like bread in the hand, which ministers no nourishment to the frame. But doctrine accepted by the heart is as digested food, which, by assimilation, sustains and builds up the body. In us truth must be a living force, an active energy, an indwelling reality, a part of the essence of our being. If it is in us, we cannot part with it. A man may lose his clothes or his limbs, but his inward parts are vital and cannot be torn away without absolute loss of life. A Christian can die, but he cannot deny the truth. Now it is a rule of nature that the inward affects the outward, as light shines from the center of the lantern through the glass. When, therefore, the truth is kindled within, its brightness soon shines forth in the outward life and conversation. It is said that the food of certain worms colors the cocoons of silk that they spin. In the same way, the nutriment on which a man's inward nature lives gives a tinge to every word and deed proceeding from him. To walk in the truth signifies a life of integrity, holiness, faithfulness, and simplicity—the natural product of those principles of truth that the Gospel teaches and that the Spirit of God enables us to receive. We may judge of the secrets of the soul by their manifestation in the man's conversation. Be it ours today, O gracious Spirit, to be ruled and governed by Your divine authority, so that nothing false or sinful may reign in our hearts, lest it extend its malignant influence to our daily walk among men.

Thou shalt not go up and down as a talebearer among
thy people....Thou shalt in any wise rebuke thy neighbour,
and not suffer sin upon him.
—Leviticus 19:16–17

alebearing emits a threefold poison: it injures the teller, the hearer, and the person concerning whom the tale is told. Whether the report is true or false, we are forbidden by this precept of God's Word to spread it. The reputations of the Lord's people should be very precious in our sight, and we should be ashamed to help the devil to dishonor the church and the name of the Lord. Some tongues need a bridle rather than a spur. Many glory in pulling down their brethren, as if thereby they raised themselves. Noah's wise sons cast a mantle over their father, and he who exposed him earned a fearful curse. We may ourselves one of these dark days need forbearance and silence from our brethren, so let us render it cheerfully to those who require it now. Let this be our family rule and our personal bond: Speak no evil of any man.

The Holy Spirit, however, permits us to censure sin and prescribes the way in which we are to do it. It must be done by rebuking our brother to his face, not by railing behind his back. This course is manly, brotherly, Christlike, and under God's blessing will be useful. Does the flesh shrink from it? Then we must lay greater stress on our consciences and keep ourselves to the work, lest by accepting our friend's sin, we ourselves become partakers of it. Hundreds have been saved from gross sins by the timely, wise, affectionate warnings of faithful ministers and friends. Our Lord Jesus has given us a gracious example of how to deal with erring friends in His warning given to Peter, the prayer with which He preceded it, and the gentle way in which He bore with Peter's boastful denial that he needed such a caution.

And Amaziah said to the man of God, But what shall we do
for the hundred talents which I have given to the army of Israel?
And the man of God answered, The LORD is able
to give thee much more than this.
—2 Chronicles 25:9

This seemed to be a very important question to the
king of Judah, and possibly it is of even more weight
with the tried and tempted Christian. To lose money
is at no times pleasant, and when a principle is involved, the
flesh is not always ready to make the sacrifice. "Why lose
that which may be so useful to us? May not the truth itself
be bought at too costly a price? What will we do without
it? Remember the children and our small income!" All these
things and a thousand more would tempt the Christian to
put forth his hand to unrighteous gain or keep him from
carrying out his conscientious convictions, when they involve serious loss. All men cannot view these matters in the
light of faith; and even with the followers of Jesus, the doctrine of "we must live" has quite sufficient weight. "The
Lord is able to give you much more than this" is a very satisfactory answer to the anxious question. Our Father holds
the purse strings, and what we lose for His sake, He can
repay a thousandfold. It is ours to obey His will, and we
may rest assured that He will provide for us. The Lord will
be no man's debtor at the last. Saints know that a grain of
heart's rest is of more value than a ton of gold. He who
wraps a threadbare coat about a good conscience has gained
a spiritual wealth far more desirable than any he has lost.
God's smile and a dungeon are enough for a true heart; His
frown and a palace would be hell to a gracious spirit. Let
the worst come to the worst, let all talents go, and we still
have not lost our treasure, for that is above, where Christ
sits at the right hand of God. Meanwhile, even now, the
Lord makes the meek to *"inherit the earth"* (Matt. 5:5), and
"no good thing will he withhold from them that walk uprightly"
(Ps. 84:11).

Thou hast made summer and winter.
—Psalm 74:17

My soul, begin this wintry month with your God. The cold snows and the piercing winds both remind you that He keeps His covenant with day and night, and they tend to assure you that He will also keep that glorious covenant that He has made with you in the person of Christ Jesus. He who is true to His word in the revolutions of the seasons of this poor, sin-polluted world will not prove unfaithful in His dealings with His own well-beloved Son. Winter in the soul is by no means a comfortable season, and if it is on you just now, it will be very painful to you. But there is this comfort: namely, that the Lord makes it. He sends the sharp blasts of adversity to nip the buds of expectation. He scatters the frost like ashes over the once verdant meadows of our joy. He casts forth His ice like morsels freezing the streams of our delight. He does it all. He is the great King of winter, and He rules in the realms of frost; therefore, you cannot complain. Losses, crosses, heaviness, sickness, poverty, and a thousand other ills are of the Lord's sending, and they come to us with wise design. Frost kills deadly insects and limits raging diseases; it breaks up the clods and sweetens the soul. Oh, that such good results would always follow our winters of affliction! How we prize the fire just now! How pleasant is its cheerful glow! Let us prize our Lord in the same manner, who is the constant source of warmth and comfort in every time of trouble. Let us draw near to Him and find joy and peace in believing. Let us wrap ourselves in the warm garments of His promises and go forth to labors that are appropriate to the season. To be like the sluggard who will not plough because of the cold will result in severe consequences, for he will have to beg even in the summer and will have nothing.

Thou art all fair, my love.
—Song of Solomon 4:7

he Lord's admiration of His church is wonderful, and His description of her beauty is glowing. She is not merely fair, but *"all fair."* He views her in Himself, washed in His sin-atoning blood and clothed in His meritorious righteousness. He considers her to be full of comeliness and beauty. No wonder that such is the case, since it is but His own perfect excellency that He admires. The holiness, glory, and perfection of His church are His own glorious garments on the back of His own well-beloved spouse. She is not simply pure or well-proportioned; she is positively lovely and fair! She has actual merit! Her deformities of sin are removed. In addition, she has, through her Lord, obtained a meritorious righteousness by which an actual beauty is conferred on her. Believers have a positive righteousness given to them when they become *"accepted in the beloved"* (Eph. 1:6). Nor is the church merely lovely; she is superlatively so. Her Lord calls her *"fairest among women"* (Song 1:8). She has real worth and excellence that cannot be rivaled by all the nobility and royalty of the world. If Jesus could exchange His elect bride for all the queens and empresses of earth, or even for the angels in heaven, He would not, for He puts her first and foremost—*"fairest among women."* Like the moon, she far outshines the stars. Nor is this an opinion that He is ashamed of, for He invites all people to hear it. He sets a *"behold"* before it, a special note of exclamation, inviting and arresting attention. *"Behold, thou art fair, my love; behold, thou art fair"* (Song 4:1). He publishes His opinion abroad even now, and one day from the throne of His glory, He will declare the truth of it before the assembled universe. *"Come, ye blessed of my Father"* (Matt. 25:34) will be His solemn affirmation of the loveliness of His elect.

There is no spot in thee.
—Song of Solomon 4:7

Having pronounced His church positively full of beauty, our Lord confirms His praise by a precious negative, *"There is no spot in thee."* It is as if the thought occurred to the Bridegroom that the critical world would insinuate that He had only mentioned her comely parts and had purposely omitted those features that were deformed or defiled. He sums up all by declaring her universally and entirely fair and utterly devoid of stain. A spot may soon be removed; it is the very least thing that can disfigure beauty. But even from this little blemish, the believer is delivered in his Lord's sight. If He had said there is no hideous scar, no horrible deformity, no deadly ulcer, we might have marveled even then; but when He testifies that she is free from the slightest spot, all these other forms of defilement are included, and the depth of wonder is increased. If He had but promised to remove all spots by and by, we would have had eternal reason for joy; but when He speaks of it as already done, who can restrain the most intense emotions of satisfaction and delight? My soul, here is *"marrow and fatness"* (Ps. 63:5) for you; eat your full, and be satisfied with royal delicacies. Christ Jesus has no quarrel with His spouse. She often wanders from Him and grieves His Holy Spirit, but He does not allow her faults to affect His love. He sometimes chides, but it is always in the tenderest manner, with the kindest intentions: it is *"my love"* (Song 4:1), even then. There is no remembrance of our wrongdoing. He does not cherish evil thoughts of us, but He pardons and loves as well after the offense as before it. His forgiveness is beneficial to us, for if Jesus were as mindful of injuries as we are, how could He commune with us? Many times a believer will put himself out of sorts with the Lord for some slight turn in providence, but our precious Husband knows our silly hearts too well to take any offense at our bad manners.

I have much people in this city.
—Acts 18:10

oday's text should be a great encouragement to try to do good, since God has among the vilest of the vile, the most reprobate, the most debauched and drunken, an elect people who must be saved. When you take the Word to them, you do so because God has ordained you to be the messenger of life to their souls, and they must receive it, for so the decree of predestination runs. They are as much redeemed by blood as the saints before the eternal throne. They are Christ's property, and yet, perhaps, they are lovers of the tavern and haters of holiness; but if Jesus Christ purchased them, He will have them. God is not unfaithful to forget the price that His Son has paid. He will not suffer His substitution to be in any case an ineffective, dead thing. Tens of thousands of redeemed ones are not regenerated yet, but regenerated they must be. This is our comfort when we go forth to them with the quickening Word of God. Even more, these ungodly ones are prayed for by Christ before the throne. *"Neither pray I for these alone,"* said the great Intercessor, *"but for them also which shall believe on me through their word"* (John 17:20). Poor, ignorant souls, they know nothing about prayer for themselves, but Jesus prays for them. Their names are on His breastplate, and before long, they must bow their stubborn knee, breathing the penitential sigh before the throne of grace. *"The time of figs [is] not yet"* (Mark 11:13). The predestined moment has not struck; but, when it comes, they will obey, for God will have His own. They must, for the Spirit is not to be resisted when He comes forth with fullness of power. They must become the willing servants of the living God. My people *"shall be willing in the day of [My] power"* (Ps. 110:3). *"He shall see of the travail of his soul, and shall…justify many"* (Isa. 53:11). *"I will divide him a portion with the great, and he shall divide the spoil with the strong"* (v. 12).

Ask, and it shall be given you.
—Matthew 7:7

I know of a place in England where a ration of bread was served to every passerby who chose to ask for it. Whoever the traveler was, he had only to knock at the door of St. Cross Hospital, and there was a portion of bread for him. Jesus Christ so loves sinners that He has built a St. Cross Hospital, so that whenever a sinner is hungry, he has only to knock and have his needs supplied. No, He has done better. He has attached to this Hospital of the Cross a bath; whenever a soul is black and filthy, he has but to go there and be washed. The fountain is always full, always efficacious. No sinner ever went into it and found that it could not wash away his stains. Sins that were scarlet and crimson have all disappeared, and the sinner has been made whiter than snow. As if this were not enough, there is attached to this Hospital of the Cross a wardrobe, and a sinner making application simply as a sinner may be clothed from head to foot. If he wishes to be a soldier, he may not merely have clothes for ordinary wear, but armor, which will cover him from the sole of his foot to the crown of his head. If he asks for a sword, he will have that given to him, and a shield, too. Nothing that is good for him will be denied him. He will have spending money as long as he lives, and he will have an eternal heritage of glorious treasure when he enters into the joy of his Lord. If all these things are to be had by merely knocking at mercy's door, O my soul, knock hard this morning. Ask largely of your generous Lord. Do not leave the throne of grace until all your needs have been spread before the Lord, and until by faith you have a comforting assurance that they will all be supplied. No bashfulness should hold you back when Jesus invites. No unbelief should hinder when Jesus promises. No coldheartedness should restrain when such blessings are to be obtained.

As is the heavenly, such are they also that are heavenly.
—1 Corinthians 15:48

he Head and members of the body of Christ are of one nature, and not like that monstrous image that Nebuchadnezzar saw in his dream. Its head was of fine gold, but the belly and thighs were of brass, the legs of iron, and the feet were part iron and part clay. Christ's mystical body is no absurd combination of opposites. The members were mortal; therefore, Jesus died. The glorified Head is immortal; therefore, the body is immortal, too, for thus the record stands, *"Because I live, ye shall live also"* (John 14:19). As is our loving Head, such is the body, and every member in particular. A chosen Head and chosen members; an accepted Head and accepted members; a living Head and living members. If the Head is pure gold, all the parts of the body are of pure gold also. Thus is there a double union of nature as a basis for the closest communion. Pause here, devout reader, and see if you can, without ecstatic amazement, contemplate the infinite condescension of the Son of God in thus exalting your wretchedness into blessed union with His glory. You are so lowly that in remembrance of your mortality, you may say to corruption, "You are my father," and to the worm, "You are my sister." Yet in Christ, you are so honored that you can say to the Almighty, "Abba, Father," and to the Incarnate God, "You are my brother and my husband." Surely if relationships to ancient and noble families make men think highly of themselves, we have much more reason to glory over them all. Let the poorest and most despised believer lay hold of this privilege. May a senseless laziness not make him negligent to trace his pedigree. Let him allow no foolish attachment to present vanities to occupy his thoughts to the exclusion of this glorious, heavenly honor of union with Christ.

Base things of the world...hath God chosen.
—1 Corinthians 1:28

alk the streets by moonlight, if you dare, and you will see sinners then. Watch when the night is dark, the wind is howling, and the burglar is hiding in the doorway, and you will see sinners then. Go to the jail and walk through the wards; you will observe men with heavy overhanging brows, men whom you would not like to meet at night, and you will find sinners there. Go to the reformatories, and note those who have revealed a rampant juvenile depravity, and you will see sinners there. Go across the seas to the place where a man will gnaw a bone on which is reeking human flesh, and there is a sinner there. Go where you will, for you need not ransack the earth to find sinners, for they are common enough. You may find them in every street of every city, town, village, and hamlet. It is for such that Jesus died. If you will select the grossest specimen of humanity, if he is but born of woman, I would have hope for him yet, because Jesus Christ *"is come to seek and to save that which was lost"* (Luke 19:10). Electing love has selected some of the worst to be made the best. Pebbles from the brook Grace turn into jewels for the royal crown. He transforms worthless dross into pure gold. Redeeming love has set apart many of the worst of mankind to be the reward of the Savior's passion. Effectual grace calls forth many of the vilest of the vile to sit at the table of mercy; therefore, let none despair. Reader, by that love looking out of Jesus' tearful eyes; by that love streaming from those bleeding wounds; by that faithful love, that strong, pure, impartial, and abiding love; by the heart of the Savior's compassion, we charge you not to turn away as though it were nothing to you. Believe on Him, and you will be saved. Trust your soul with Him, and He will bring you to His Father's right hand in glory everlasting.

Thou hast a few names even in Sardis which have not defiled their garments; and they shall walk with me in white: for they are worthy.
—Revelation 3:4

We may understand this to refer to justification. *"They shall walk with me in white"*; that is, they will enjoy a constant sense of their own justification by faith; they will understand that the righteousness of Christ is imputed to them, that they have all been washed and made whiter than the newly fallen snow. Again, it refers to joy and gladness, for white robes were holiday attire among the Jews. They who have not defiled their garments will have their faces always bright. They will understand what Solomon meant when he said *"Go thy way, eat thy bread with joy, and drink thy wine with a merry heart; for God now accepteth thy works. Let thy garments be always white"* (Eccl. 9:7–8). He who is accepted by God will wear white garments of joy and gladness, while he walks in sweet communion with the Lord Jesus. Why are there so many doubts, so much misery, and mourning? It is because so many believers defile their garments with sin and error and, thus, they lose the joy of their salvation and the comfortable fellowship of the Lord Jesus. They do not walk in white here on earth. The promise also refers to walking in white before the throne of God. Those who have not defiled their garments here will most certainly walk in white up yonder, where the white-robed hosts sing perpetual hallelujahs to the Most High. They will possess inconceivable joy, happiness beyond a dream, bliss that imagination cannot know, blessedness that even the stretch of desire has not reached. The *"undefiled in the way"* (Ps. 119:1) will have all this—not by merit or of works, but by grace. They will walk with Christ in white, for He has made them *"worthy."* In His sweet company, they will drink of the living fountains of waters.

Therefore will the LORD wait, that he may be gracious unto you.
—Isaiah 30:18

God often delays in answering prayer. We have several instances of this in sacred Scripture. Jacob did not get the blessing from the angel until near the dawn of day; he had to wrestle all night for it. The poor woman of Syrophenicia was not answered a word for a long while. Paul sought the Lord three times, asking that the *"thorn in the flesh"* (2 Cor. 12:7) might be taken from him. He received no assurance that it would be taken away; instead, he was given a promise that God's grace would be sufficient for him. If you have been knocking at the gate of mercy and have received no answer, shall I tell you why the mighty Maker has not opened the door and let you in? Our Father has reasons known only to Himself for thus keeping us waiting. Sometimes it is to show His power and His sovereignty so that men may know that Jehovah has a right to give or to withhold. More frequently the delay is for our profit. Perhaps you are kept waiting in order that your desires may be more fervent. God knows that delay will quicken and increase desire, and that if He keeps you waiting, you will see your need more clearly and will seek more earnestly. He also knows that you will prize the mercy all the more for its long delay. There may also be something wrong in you that needs to be removed before the joy of the Lord is given. Perhaps your views of the gospel plan are confused, or you may be placing some reliance on yourself, instead of trusting simply and entirely on the Lord Jesus. Or God makes you wait for a while so that He may the more fully display the riches of His grace to you at last. Your prayers are all filed in heaven, and if not immediately answered, they are certainly not forgotten. In a little while, they will be fulfilled to your delight and satisfaction. Do not let despair make you silent, but continue faithfully in earnest supplication.

So shall we ever be with the Lord.
—1 Thessalonians 4:17

ven the sweetest visits from Christ are brief and transitory. One moment our eyes see Him, and we *"rejoice with joy unspeakable and full of glory"* (1 Pet. 1:8), but in a little while, we do not see Him, for our Beloved withdraws Himself from us. Like a roe or a young deer, He leaps over the mountains. He is gone to the land of spices and feeds no more among the lilies.

> If today He deigns to bless us
>   With a sense of pardoned sin,
> He tomorrow may distress us,
>   Make us feel the plague within.

Oh, how sweet the prospect of the time when we will not behold Him at a distance, but see Him face-to-face! When He will not be as a wayfaring man tarrying but for a night, but will eternally enfold us in the heart of His glory! We will not see Him for a little season, but

> Millions of years our wondering eyes,
>   Shall o'er our Savior's beauties rove;
> And myriad ages we'll adore,
>   The wonders of His love.

In heaven there will be no interruptions from care or sin. No weeping will dim our eyes, and no earthly business will distract our happy thoughts. We will have nothing to hinder us from gazing forever with unwearied eyes on the Sun of Righteousness. Oh, if it is so sweet to see Him now and then, how sweet to gaze on that blessed face forever and never have a cloud rolling between or never have to turn one's eyes away to look on a world of weariness and woe! Blessed day, when will you dawn? Rise, unsetting sun! The joys of the tangible world may leave us as soon as they will, for this will make glorious amends. If to die is but to enter into uninterrupted fellowship with Jesus, then death is indeed gain, and the black drop is swallowed up in a sea of victory.

Faithful is he that calleth you, who also will do it.
—1 Thessalonians 5:24

eaven is a place where we will never sin and where we will cease our constant watch against an indefatigable enemy, because there will be no tempter to ensnare our feet. There the wicked cease from troubling, and the weary are at rest. Heaven is the *"inheritance incorruptible, and undefiled"* (1 Pet. 1:4). It is the land of perfect holiness and therefore of complete security. But do not the saints even on earth sometimes taste the joys of blissful security? The doctrine of God's Word is that all who are in union with the Lamb are safe; that all the righteous will hold on their way; and that those who have committed their souls to the keeping of Christ will find Him a faithful and immutable Preserver. Sustained by such a doctrine, we can enjoy security even on earth—not that high and glorious security that renders us free from every slip, but that holy security that arises from the sure promise of Jesus that none who believe in Him will ever perish, but will be with Him where He is. Believer, let us often reflect with joy on the doctrine of the perseverance of the saints and honor the faithfulness of our God by a holy confidence in Him. May our God bring home to you a sense of your safety in Christ Jesus! May He assure you that your name is graven on His hand and whisper in your ear the promise, *"Fear not: for I am with thee"* (Isa. 43:5). Look on Him, the great Surety of the covenant, as faithful and true, and, therefore, bound and engaged to present you, the weakest of the family, with all the chosen race, before the throne of God. In such a sweet contemplation, you will drink the juice of the spiced wine of the Lord's pomegranate and taste the dainty fruits of paradise. You will have a taste of the enjoyments that delight the souls of the perfect saints above, if you can believe with unstaggering faith that *"faithful is he that calleth you, who also will do it."*

His ways are everlasting.
—Habakkuk 3:6

hat God has done at one time, He will do yet again. Man's ways are changeable, but God's ways are everlasting. There are many reasons for this most comforting truth. Among them are the following: the Lord's ways are the result of wise deliberation. He orders all things according to the *"counsel of his own will"* (Eph. 1:11). Human action is frequently the hasty result of passion or fear and is followed by regret and alteration. But nothing can take the Almighty by surprise or happen otherwise than He has foreseen. His ways are the outgrowth of an immutable character, and in them the fixed and settled attributes of God are clearly to be seen. Unless the eternal One Himself can undergo change, His ways, which are Himself in action, must remain forever the same. Is He eternally just, gracious, faithful, wise, and tender? Then His ways must ever be distinguished for the same excellence. Human beings act according to their nature. When those natures change, their conduct varies also; but since God cannot know the *"shadow of turning"* (James 1:17), His ways will abide everlastingly the same. Moreover there is no reason from without that could reverse the divine ways, since they are the embodiment of irresistible might. Habbakuk said that God divided the earth with rivers; that mountains saw Him and trembled; that the deep lifted up its hands; and that the sun and moon stood still when Jehovah marched forth for the salvation of His people (Hab. 3:9–12). Who can stay His hand or say to Him, "What are You doing?" But it is not might alone that gives stability. God's ways are the manifestation of the eternal principles of right and, therefore, can never pass away. Wrong breeds decay and involves ruin, but the true and the good have a vitality that ages cannot diminish. This morning let us go to our heavenly Father with confidence, remembering that Jesus Christ is the *"same yesterday, and to day, and for ever"* (Heb. 13:8), and the Lord is ever gracious to His people.

Salt without prescribing how much.
—Ezra 7:22

alt was used in every offering made by fire to the Lord. From its preserving and purifying properties, it was the grateful symbol of divine grace in the soul. It is worthy of our attention that when Artaxerxes gave salt to Ezra the priest, he set no limit to the quantity (Ezra 6:9); we may be quite certain that when the King of Kings distributes grace among His royal priesthood, the supply is not cut short by Him. Often we are restricted in ourselves, but never in the Lord. He who chooses to gather much manna will find that he may have as much as he desires. There is no famine in Jerusalem such that the citizens must limit the portions of their bread and water. Some things in the economy of grace are measured; for instance, our vinegar and gall are given to us with such exactness that we never have a single drop too much, but of the salt of grace no restriction is made: *"Whatsoever thou wilt ask of God, God will give it thee"* (John 11:22). Parents need to lock up the fruit cupboard and the candy jars, but there is no need to keep the salt shaker under lock and key, for few children will eat too greedily from that. A man may have too much money or too much honor, but he cannot have too much grace. Jeshurun *"waxed fat, and kicked"* (Deut. 32:15) against God, but there is no fear of a man's becoming too full of grace. It is impossible to have too much grace. More wealth brings more care, but more grace brings more joy. Increased wisdom is increased sorrow, but abundance of the Spirit is fullness of joy. Believer, go to the throne for a large supply of heavenly salt. It will season your afflictions, which are unsavory without salt. It will preserve your heart, which corrupts if salt is absent, and it will kill your sins even as salt kills reptiles. You need much. Seek much, and you will have much.

They go from strength to strength.
—Psalm 84:7

hey go from strength to strength." There are various renderings of these words, but all of them contain the idea of progress. Our own good translation of the King James Version is enough for us this morning. *"They go from strength to strength."* That is, they grow stronger and stronger. Usually, if we are walking, we go from strength to weakness. We start fresh and in good order for our journey, but as time passes, the road is rough, and the sun is hot; we sit down by the wayside, and then again painfully pursue our weary way. But the Christian pilgrim, having obtained fresh supplies of grace, is as vigorous after years of toilsome travel and struggle as when he first set out. He may not be quite so elated and buoyant or perhaps quite so hot and hasty in his zeal as he once was, but he is much stronger in all that constitutes real power. He travels, if more slowly, far more surely. Some gray-haired veterans have been as firm and as zealous in their grasp of truth as they were in their younger days; however, it must be confessed that it is often otherwise, *"because iniquity shall abound, the love of many shall wax cold"* (Matt. 24:12). But this is their own sin and not the fault of the promise that still holds good: *"The youths shall faint and be weary, and the young men shall utterly fall: but they that wait upon the LORD shall renew their strength; they shall mount up with wings as eagles; they shall run, and not be weary; and they shall walk, and not faint"* (Isa. 40:30–31). Fretful spirits sit down and trouble themselves about the future. "Alas!" they say, "we go from affliction to affliction." Very true, you of little faith, but then you go *"from strength to strength"* also! You will never find a bundle of affliction that does not have sufficient grace bound up in the midst of it. God will give the strength of mature manhood with the burden allotted to full-grown shoulders.

Orpah kissed her mother in law; but Ruth clave unto her.
—Ruth 1:14

Both Orpah and Ruth had affection for Naomi. That is why they set out with her on her return to the land of Judah. But the hour of testing came. Naomi most unselfishly set before each of them the trials that awaited them. If they cared for ease and comfort, she encouraged them to return to their Moabite friends. At first both of them declared that they would cast in their lot with the Lord's people; but on further consideration, Orpah, with much grief and a respectful kiss, left her mother-in-law and her people and her God. She went back to her idolatrous friends. Ruth, however, with all her heart gave herself up to the God of her mother-in-law. It is one thing to love the ways of the Lord when all is fair, and quite another to cleave to them under all discouragement and difficulties. The kiss of outward profession is very cheap and easy, but the practical cleaving to the Lord, which must show itself in holy decision for truth and holiness, is not so small a matter. How does the case stand with us? Are our hearts fixed on Jesus? Is the sacrifice bound with cords to the horns of the altar? Have we counted the cost, and are we solemnly ready to suffer all worldly loss for the Master's sake? The future gain will be an abundant recompense, for Egypt's treasures are not to be compared with the glory to be revealed. Orpah is heard of no more; in glorious ease and idolatrous pleasure her life melts into the gloom of death. But Ruth lives in history and in heaven, for grace has placed her in the noble line from which came the King of Kings. Blessed among women will those be who for Christ's sake can renounce all; but forgotten and worse than forgotten will those be who in the hour of temptation do violence to conscience and turn back to the world. Oh, that this morning we may not be content with the form of devotion, which may be no better than Orpah's kiss, but may the Holy Spirit work in us a cleaving of our whole hearts to our Lord Jesus.

Come unto me.
—Matthew 11:28

he cry of the Christian religion is the gentle word, *"Come."* The Jewish law harshly said, "Go, take heed to your steps as to the path in which you will walk. Break the commandments, and you will perish; keep them, and you will live." The law was a dispensation of terror, which drove men before it like a scourge. The Gospel draws with bands of love. Jesus is the Good Shepherd going before His sheep, inviting them to follow Him, and always leading them onward with the sweet word, *"Come."* The law repels; the Gospel attracts. The law shows the distance there is between God and man; the Gospel bridges that awful chasm and brings the sinner across it. From the first moment of your spiritual life until you are ushered into glory, the language of Christ to you will be, *"Come unto me."* As a mother puts out her finger and coaxes her little child to walk by saying, "Come," even so does Jesus. He will always be ahead of you, bidding you to follow Him as the soldier follows his captain. He will always go before you to pave your way and clear your path, and you will hear His animating voice calling you after Him all through life. While you face the solemn hour of death, His sweet words with which He will usher you into the heavenly world will be: *"Come, ye blessed of my Father"* (Matt. 25:34). Further, this is not only Christ's cry to you, but, if you are a believer, this is your cry to Christ: "Come! Come!" You will be longing for His second coming. You will be saying, "Come quickly. *'Even so, come, Lord Jesus'* (Rev. 22:20)." You will be panting for nearer and closer communion with Him. As His voice calls to you, "Come," your response to Him will be, "Come, Lord, and abide with me. Come, and occupy alone the throne of my heart. Reign there without a rival, and consecrate me entirely to Your service."

I remember thee.
—Jeremiah 2:2

et us note that Christ delights to think about His church and to look on her beauty. As the bird returns often to its nest and the wayfarer hurries to his home, so does the mind continually pursue the object of its choice. We cannot look too often on the face that we love; we desire always to have our precious things in our sight. It is even so with our Lord Jesus. From all eternity His *"delights were with the sons of men"* (Prov. 8:31). His thoughts rolled onward to the time when His elect would be born into the world. He viewed them in the mirror of His foreknowledge. *"In thy book,"* David wrote, *"all my members were written, which in continuance were fashioned, when as yet there was none of them"* (Ps. 139:16). When the world was set on its pillars, He was there, and He set the bounds of the people according to the number of the children of Israel. Many times before His incarnation, He descended to earth in the likeness of a man: on the plains of Mamre, by the brook of Jabbok, beneath the walls of Jericho, and in the fiery furnace of Babylon, the Son of Man visited His people. Because His soul delighted in them, He could not rest away from them, for His heart longed after them. Never were they absent from His heart, for He had written their names on His hands and engraved them on His side. As the breastplate containing the names of the tribes of Israel was the most brilliant ornament worn by the high priest, so the names of Christ's elect were His most precious jewels, and they glittered on His heart.

We may often forget to meditate on the perfections of our Lord, but He never ceases to remember us. Let us chide ourselves for past forgetfulness, and pray for grace always to bear Him in fondest remembrance. Lord, paint on the eyes of my soul the image of Your Son.

Rend your heart, and not your garments.
—Joel 2:13

earing one's garments and other outward signs of religious emotion are easily manifested and are frequently hypocritical. To feel true repentance is far more difficult; consequently, it is far less common. Men will attend to the most multiplied and minute ceremonial regulations, for such things are pleasing to the flesh. True religion, however, is too humbling, too heart-searching, too thorough for the tastes of carnal men. They prefer something more ostentatious, flimsy, and worldly. Outward observances are temporarily comfortable; eye and ear are pleased, self-conceit is fed, and self-righteousness is puffed up. But they are ultimately misleading, for at the point of death, and on the Judgment Day, the soul needs something more substantial than ceremonies and rituals to lean on. Apart from vital godliness, all religion is utterly vain. Offered without a sincere heart, every form of worship is a solemn sham and an impudent mockery of the majesty of heaven. Heartrending is a divine operation and is solemnly felt. It is a secret grief that is personally experienced, not in mere form, but as a deep, soul-moving work of the Holy Spirit on the inmost heart of each believer. It is not a matter to be merely talked about and believed in, but keenly and sensitively felt in every living child of the living God. It is powerfully humiliating and completely sin-purging; but then, it is sweetly preparative for those gracious consolations that proud spirits are unable to receive. It is distinctly discriminating, for it belongs to the elect of God, and to them alone. The text commands us to rend our hearts, but they are naturally hard as marble. How, then, can this be done? We must take them to Calvary. A dying Savior's voice rent the rocks once, and it is as powerful now. Blessed Spirit, let us hear the death cries of Jesus, and our hearts will be rent even as men tear their clothes in the times of great sorrow.

*The lot is cast into the lap; but the whole
disposing thereof is of the LORD.*
—Proverbs 16:33

If the disposal of the lot is the Lord's, whose is the arrangement of our whole lives? If the simple casting of a lot is guided by Him, how much more the events of our entire lives, especially when we are told by our blessed Savior, *"The very hairs of your head are all numbered"* (Matt. 10:30). Not a sparrow falls to the ground apart from your Father's will (v. 29). It would bring a holy calm over your mind, dear friend, if you were always to remember this. It would relieve your mind from anxiety, so that you would be better able to walk in patience, quiet, and cheerfulness as a Christian should. When a man is anxious, he cannot pray with faith. When he is troubled about the world, he cannot serve his Master; his thoughts are serving himself. If you would *"seek...first the kingdom of God, and his righteousness"* (Matt. 6:33), all things would then be added unto you. You are meddling with Christ's business and neglecting your own when you fret about your lot and circumstances. You have been trying "providing" work and forgetting that it is yours to obey. Be wise and attend to the obeying; let Christ manage the providing. Come and survey your Father's storehouse, and ask whether He will let you starve while He has laid up so great an abundance in His garner. Look at His heart of mercy. See if that can ever prove unkind! Look at His inscrutable wisdom. See if that will ever be at fault. Above all, look to Jesus Christ, your Intercessor, and ask yourself, while He pleads, can your Father deal ungraciously with you? If He remembers even sparrows, will He forget one of the least of His poor children? *"Cast thy burden upon the LORD, and he shall sustain thee: he shall never suffer the righteous to be moved"* (Ps. 55:22).

My soul, rest happy in thy low estate,
    Nor hope nor wish to be esteem'd or great;
To take the impress of the Will Divine,
    Be that thy glory, and those riches thine.

Yea, I have loved thee with an everlasting love.
—Jeremiah 31:3

ometimes the Lord Jesus tells His church His love thoughts. R. Erskine states: "He does not think it enough behind her back to tell it, but in her very presence, He says, *'Thou art all fair, my love'* (Song 4:7). It is true that this is not His ordinary method. He is a wise lover and knows when to keep back the intimation of love and when to let it out, but there are times when He will make no secret of it—times when He will put it beyond all dispute in the souls of His people." The Holy Spirit is often pleased, in a most gracious manner, to witness with our spirits of the love of Jesus. He takes of the things of Christ and reveals them to us. (See John 16:13–15.) No voice is heard from the clouds, and no vision is seen in the night, but we have a testimony more sure than either of these. If an angel should fly from heaven and inform the saint personally of the Savior's love for him, the evidence would not be one bit more satisfactory than that which is borne in the heart by the Holy Spirit. Ask those of the Lord's people who have lived the nearest to the gates of heaven, and they will tell you that they have had seasons when the love of Christ toward them has been a fact so clear and sure that they could no more doubt it than they could question their own existence. Yes, beloved believer, you and I have had times of refreshing from the presence of the Lord, and then, our faith has mounted to the topmost heights of assurance. We have had confidence to lean our heads on the bosom of our Lord. We have no more questioned our Master's affection for us than John did when he was in that same blessed posture. No, we have not even been moved to ask the dark question, "Lord, is it I that will betray You?" That thought has been put far from us. He has kissed us with the kisses of His mouth and killed our doubts by the closeness of His embrace. His love has been sweeter than wine to our souls.

He hath made with me an everlasting covenant.
—2 Samuel 23:5

his covenant is divine in its origin. *"He hath made with me an everlasting covenant."* Oh, that great word *"He"*! Stop, my soul. God, the everlasting Father, has positively made a covenant with you—yes, that God who spoke the world into existence by a word! He, stooping from His majesty, takes hold of your hand and makes a covenant with you. Is not the stupendous condescension of this act enough to ravish our hearts forever if we could really understand it? *"He hath made with me an everlasting covenant."* A king has not made a covenant with me—that would be something; but the Prince of the kings of the earth, Shaddai, the Lord All-sufficient, the Jehovah of ages, the everlasting Elohim, *"He hath made with me an everlasting covenant."* But notice, it is particular in its application. *"He hath made with **me** an everlasting covenant"* (emphasis added). Here lies the sweetness of it to each believer. It is nothing to me that He made peace for the world; I need to know whether He has made peace for me! It is little that He has made a covenant; I want to know whether He has made a covenant with me. Blessed is the assurance that He has made a covenant with me! If God the Holy Spirit gives me assurance, then His salvation is mine, His heart is mine, He Himself is mine—He is my God. This covenant is everlasting in its duration. An everlasting covenant means a covenant that had no beginning and that will never, never end. How sweet, amid all the uncertainties of life, to know that the *"foundation of God standeth sure"* (2 Tim. 2:19), and to have God's own promise, *"My covenant will I not break, nor alter the thing that is gone out of my lips"* (Ps. 89:34). Like dying David, I will sing of this, even though all the affairs and members of my house may not be in the place that my heart desires before God.

I will strengthen thee.
—Isaiah 41:10

God has a strong reserve with which to discharge this engagement, for He is able to do all things. Believer, until you can drain dry the ocean of omnipotence, until you can break into pieces the towering mountains of almighty strength, you never need to fear. Do not think that the strength of man will ever be able to overcome the power of God. While the earth's huge pillars stand, you have enough reason to abide firm in your faith. The same God who directs the earth in its orbit, who feeds the burning furnace of the sun, and trims the lamps of heaven has promised to supply you with daily strength. While He is able to uphold the universe, do not think that He will prove unable to fulfill His own promises. Remember what He did in the days of old, in the former generations. Remember how He spoke, and it was done; how He commanded, and it stood fast. Will He who created the world grow weary? He hangs the world on nothing; will He who does this be unable to support His children? Will He be unfaithful to His word for lack of power? Who is it that restrains the tempest? Does He not ride on the wings of the wind, make the clouds His chariots, and hold the ocean in the hollow of His hand? How can He fail you? When He has put such a faithful promise as this on record, will you for a moment indulge the thought that He has outpromised Himself and gone beyond His power to fulfill? Ah, no! You can doubt no longer. You who are my God and my strength, I can believe that this promise will be fulfilled, for the boundless reservoir of Your grace can never be exhausted, and the overflowing storehouse of Your strength can never be emptied by Your friends or pilfered by Your enemies.

> Now let the feeble all be strong,
> And make Jehovah's arm their song.

Friend, go up higher.
—Luke 14:10

When the life of grace first begins in the soul, we do indeed draw near to God, but it is with great fear and trembling. The soul, conscious of its guilt and humbled thereby, is in awe over the solemnity of its position. It is cast to the earth by a sense of the grandeur of Jehovah, in whose presence it stands. With unfeigned bashfulness, it takes the lowest room. But later, as the Christian grows in grace, although he will never forget the solemnity of his position and will never lose that holy awe that must encompass a gracious man when he is in the presence of the God who can create or can destroy, his fear has all its terror taken out of it. It becomes a holy reverence and no longer an overshadowing dread. He is called up higher to greater access to God in Christ Jesus. Then the man of God, walking amid the splendors of deity and veiling his face like the glorious cherubim with those twin wings—the blood and righteousness of Jesus Christ—will approach the throne reverently and bowed in spirit. Seeing there a God of love, of goodness, and of mercy, he will realize the covenant character of God rather than His absolute deity. He will see in God His goodness rather than His greatness and more of His love than of His majesty. Then, the soul, bowing still as humbly as before, will enjoy a more sacred liberty of intercession. While prostrate before the glory of the Infinite God, it will be sustained by the refreshing consciousness of being in the presence of boundless mercy and infinite love, and by the realization of its acceptance *"in the beloved"* (Eph. 1:6). Thus the believer is invited to come up higher and is enabled to exercise the privilege of rejoicing in God and drawing near to Him in holy confidence, saying, *"Abba, Father"* (Rom. 8:15).

> So may we go from strength to strength,
>   And daily grow in grace,
> Till in Thine image raised at length,
>   We see Thee face to face.

Though he was rich, yet for your sakes he became poor.
—2 Corinthians 8:9

he Lord Jesus Christ was eternally rich, glorious, and exalted, but *"though he was rich, yet for your sakes he became poor."* The rich saint cannot be true in his communion with his poor brethren unless he gives of his substance to meet their needs. Likewise, the same rule applies to the Head and the members of the body of Christ. It is impossible that our divine Lord could have had fellowship with us unless He had imparted to us of His own abundant wealth and had become poor to make us rich. Had He remained on His throne of glory, and had we continued in the ruins of the Fall without receiving His salvation, communion would have been impossible on both sides. Our position by the Fall, apart from the covenant of grace, made it as impossible for fallen man to communicate with God as it is for Belial to be in agreement with Christ. In order, therefore, that communion might be achieved, it was necessary that the rich Kinsman would bestow His estate to His poor relatives, that the righteous Savior would give to His sinning brethren of His own perfection, and that we, the poor and guilty, would receive of His fullness *"grace for grace"* (John 1:16). Thus, in giving and receiving, the One might descend from the heights and the other ascend from the depths, and so be able to embrace each other in true and hearty fellowship. Poverty must be enriched by Him in whom are infinite treasures before it can proceed to commune; guilt must lose itself in imputed and imparted righteousness before the soul can walk in fellowship with purity. Jesus must clothe His people in His own garments, or He cannot admit them into His palace of glory. He must wash them in His own blood, or else they will be too defiled for the embrace of His fellowship. Believer, herein is love! For your sake the Lord Jesus *"became poor"* so that He might lift you up into communion with Himself.

Behold, a virgin shall conceive, and bear a son,
and shall call his name Immanuel.
—Isaiah 7:14

et us go today to Bethlehem, and, in company with wondering shepherds and adoring Magi, let us see Him who was born King of the Jews; for we, by faith, can claim an interest in Him and can sing, *"Unto us a child is born, unto us a son is given"* (Isa. 9:6). Jesus is Jehovah incarnate, our Lord and our God, yet our Brother and Friend. Let us adore and admire Him. Let us notice at the very first glance His miraculous conception. It was a thing unheard of before, and unparalleled since, that a virgin should conceive and bear a son. *"The LORD hath created a new thing in the earth, a woman shall compass a man"* (Jer. 31:22). The first promise involved the seed of the woman—not the offspring of the man. Since adventuresome woman led the way in the sin that brought forth Paradise lost, she, and she alone, ushers in the One who could regain paradise. Our Savior, although truly Man, was, as to His human nature, the Holy One of God. By the power of the Holy Spirit, He was born of the virgin without the taint of original sin, which belongs to all those who are born of the flesh. Let us reverently bow before the holy Child, whose innocence restores to manhood its ancient glory. Let us pray that He may be formed in us, *"the hope of glory"* (Col. 1:27). Do not fail to note His humble parentage. Our morning portion describes His mother as simply *"a virgin,"* not a princess, prophetess, or a matron of a large estate. True, her lineage was not to be despised, for the blood of kings ran in her veins; nor was her mind a weak and untaught one, for she could sing most sweetly a song of praise. Yet how humble her position, how poor the man to whom she stood betrothed, and how miserable the accommodation afforded to the newborn King! Thus has poverty become consecrated, and men of low estate are exalted to honor. Every believer is a portrait of Christ, but a poor saint is the same well-drawn picture hung in the same frame of poverty that surrounds the Master's image.

We esteem every day alike, but still, as the seasons and the general custom suggest thoughts of Jesus, let us joyfully remember our dear Redeemer's glorious birth. To a renewed soul, every day should be the birthday of the Savior. Amid all that is humiliating, there is much that is honorable in the circumstances of the birth of our Immanuel. Whose birth was ever ushered in by a long train of prophecy or longed for by such a multitude of hearts? Who but He can boast of a forerunner who marked Him as the coming Man? When did angels indulge in midnight songs or did God ever hang a new star in the sky before? To whose cradle did rich and poor make so willing a pilgrimage and offer such hearty, unsought acts of worship? Well may earth rejoice; well may all men cease their labors to celebrate the great birthday of Jesus. Bethlehem, house of bread, we see in you our hopes forever gratified. 'Tis He, the Savior, long foretold, who will usher in the age of gold. Let gladness rule the hour. Let holy songs and sweet heart-music accompany our souls in their raptures of delight.

The golden name, Immanuel, is inexpressibly delightful. It is a word fit for the lips of cherubim for its majesty, but, because of its marvelous condescension, none but men can utter it. He is not so with seraphs as He is with us. Immanuel, *"God with us"* (Matt. 1:23)—in our nature, in our sorrow, in our lifework, in our punishment, in our grave, and now with us, or rather, we with Him, in resurrection, ascension, triumph, and Second Advent splendor. The babe of Bethlehem appears to be manifestly with us in weakness and in poverty. Let us not forget that He is equally with us in His glory and honor. Faith clasps the child, and love kisses Him with the kisses of her lips. Oh, for true spiritual fellowship with Immanuel all this day!

The last Adam.
—1 Corinthians 15:45

Jesus is the Head of His elect. In Adam, every heir of flesh and blood has a personal interest because Adam is the covenant head and representative of the race as considered under the law of works. Under the law of grace, every redeemed soul is one with the Lord from heaven, since He is the Second Adam, the Sponsor and Substitute of the elect in the new covenant of love. The apostle Paul declared that Levi was in the loins of Abraham when Melchisedec met him. It is a certain truth that the believer was in the loins of Jesus Christ, the Mediator, when, in old eternity, the covenant settlements of grace were decreed, ratified, and made sure forever. Thus, whatever Christ has done, He has done for the whole body of His church. We were crucified and *"buried with him"* (Col. 2:12), and to make it still more wonderful, we are risen with Him and even ascended with Him to *"sit together in heavenly places"* (Eph. 2:6). It is thus that the church has fulfilled the law and is *"accepted in the beloved"* (Eph. 1:6). It is thus that she is regarded with pleasure by the just Jehovah, for He views her in Jesus and does not look on her as separate from her covenant Head. As the anointed Redeemer of Israel, Christ Jesus has nothing separate from His church, but all that He has, He holds for her. Adam's righteousness was ours as long as he maintained it, and his sin was ours the moment that he committed it. In the same manner, all that the Second Adam is or does is ours as well as His, seeing that He is our Representative. Here is the foundation of the covenant of grace. This gracious system of representation and substitution—that moved Justin Martyr to cry out, "O blessed change, O sweet permutation!"—is the very groundwork of the Gospel of our salvation, and it is to be received with strong faith and rapturous joy.

Can the rush grow up without mire?
—Job 8:11

he rush plant is spongy and hollow, and so is a hypocrite. There is no substance or stability in him. The rush is shaken to and fro in every wind, just as formalists yield to every influence. For this reason the rush is not broken by the tempest; neither are hypocrites troubled with persecution. I would not willingly be a deceiver or be deceived; perhaps the text for this day may help me to examine myself to see whether or not I am a hypocrite. The rush by nature lives in water, and it owes its very existence to the mire and moisture wherein it has taken root. If the marsh becomes dry, the rush withers very quickly. Its greenness is absolutely dependent on circumstances; a present abundance of water makes it flourish, and a drought destroys it right away. Is this my case? Do I serve God only when I am in good company, or when religion is profitable and respectable? Do I love the Lord only when temporal comforts are received from His hands? If so, I am a base hypocrite; and like the withering rush, I will perish when death deprives me of outward joys. But can I honestly assert that when bodily comforts have been few and my surroundings have been rather adverse to grace than at all helpful to it, I have still held fast my integrity? Then I have hope that there is a genuine, vital godliness in me.

The rush cannot grow without moisture, but plants that belong to the Lord can and do flourish, even in the year of drought. A godly man often grows best when his worldly circumstances decay. He who follows Christ for gain is a Judas. Those who follow for loaves and fish are children of the devil, but those who walk with Him out of love for Himself are His own beloved ones. Lord, let me find my life in You, and not in the mire of this world's favor or gain.

The life which I now live in the flesh I live
by the faith of the Son of God.
—Galatians 2:20

When the Lord in mercy passed by and saw us in our blood, He first of all said, "Live." He did this first, because life is one of the absolutely essential things in spiritual matters. Until it is given, we are incapable of partaking in the things of the kingdom. Now the life that grace confers on the saints at the moment of their quickening is none other than the life of Christ. Like the sap from the stem, faith runs into us—the branches—and it establishes a living connection between our souls and Jesus. Faith is the grace that perceives this union, having proceeded from it as its firstfruit. It is the neck that joins the body of the church to its all-glorious Head.

> Oh, Faith, thou bond of union with the Lord,
>   Is not this office thine? And thy fit name,
> In the economy of gospel types,
>   And symbols apposite—the Church's neck;
> Identifying her in will and work
>   With Him ascended?

Faith lays hold of the Lord Jesus with a firm and determined grasp. It knows His excellence and worth, and no temptation can induce it to repose its trust elsewhere. Christ Jesus is so delighted with this heavenly grace that He never ceases to strengthen and sustain it by the loving embrace and all-sufficient support of His eternal arms. Here, then, is established a living, sensible, and delightful union that casts forth streams of love, confidence, sympathy, pleasure, and joy, whereof both the bride and Bridegroom love to drink. When the soul can evidently perceive this oneness between itself and Christ, the pulse may be felt as beating for both, and the one blood as flowing through the veins of each. Then is the heart as near heaven as it can be on earth and is prepared for the enjoyment of the most sublime and spiritual kind of fellowship.

Hitherto hath the LORD helped us.
—1 Samuel 7:12

he word *"hitherto"* seems like a hand pointing in the direction of the past. Whether for twenty years or seventy, *"hitherto hath the LORD helped us"!* Through poverty, through wealth, through sickness, through health, at home, abroad, on the land, on the sea, in honor, in dishonor, in perplexity, in joy, in trial, in triumph, in prayer, in temptation, *"hitherto hath the LORD helped us"!* We delight to look down a long avenue of trees. It is delightful to gaze from end to end of the long vista, a sort of verdant temple, with its branching pillars and its arches of leaves; in the same way, look down the long aisles of your years, at the green boughs of mercy overhead, and the strong pillars of lovingkindness and faithfulness that bear up your joys. Are there no birds in the branches singing? Surely there must be many, and they all sing of mercy received *"hitherto."* But the word also points forward. For when a man gets up to a certain mark and writes "hitherto," he is not yet at the end; there is still a distance to be traversed. More trials, more joys; more temptations, more triumphs; more prayers, more answers; more toils, more strength; more fights, more victories; and then come sickness, old age, disease, and death. Is it over now? No! There is still more awakening in Jesus' likeness, thrones, harps, songs, psalms, white raiment, the face of Jesus, the society of saints, the glory of God, the fullness of eternity, the infinity of bliss. Oh, be of good courage, believer, and with grateful confidence raise your Ebenezer, for He who has helped you *"hitherto"* will help you all your journey through. When read in heaven's light, how glorious and marvelous a prospect will your *"hitherto"* unfold to your grateful eyes!

Better is the end of a thing than the beginning thereof.
—Ecclesiastes 7:8

Look at our Lord and Master, and see His beginning. He was *"despised and rejected of men; a man of sorrows, and acquainted with grief"* (Isa. 53:3). Would you see the end? He sits at His Father's right hand, expectant, waiting until His enemies are made His footstool (Ps. 110:1). *"As he is, so are we in this world"* (1 John 4:17). You must bear the cross, or you will never wear the crown; you must wade through the mire, or you will never walk the golden pavement. Cheer up, then, poor Christian. *"Better is the end of a thing than the beginning thereof."* See that creeping worm; how contemptible is its appearance! It is the beginning of a thing. Notice that insect with gorgeous wings, playing in the sunbeams, sipping at the flower bells, full of happiness and life; that is the end thereof. That caterpillar is you, until you are wrapped up in the chrysalis of death; but when Christ appears, you will *"be like him; for [you] shall see him as he is"* (1 John 3:2). Be content to be like Him, so that like Him you may *"be satisfied, when [you] awake, with [His] likeness"* (Ps. 17:15). That rough-looking diamond is put on the wheel of the lapidary. He cuts it on all sides. It loses much—much that seemed costly to itself. The king is crowned; the diadem is put on the monarch's head with the trumpet's joyful sound. A glittering ray flashes from that coronet, and it beams from that very diamond that was so recently sorely vexed by the lapidary. You may venture to compare yourself to such a diamond, for you are one of God's people; this is the time of the cutting process. Let faith and *"patience have [their] perfect work"* (James 1:4), for in the day when the crown will be set on the head of the *"King eternal, immortal, invisible"* (1 Tim. 1:17), one ray of glory will stream from you. *"They shall be mine, saith the LORD of hosts, in that day when I make up my jewels"* (Mal. 3:17). *"Better is the end of a thing than the beginning thereof."*

In the last day, that great day of the feast, Jesus stood and cried,
saying, If any man thirst, let him come unto me, and drink.
—John 7:37

atience had *"her perfect work"* (James 1:4) in the Lord Jesus, and until the last day of the feast, He pleaded with the Jews. Even as on this last day of the year, He pleads with us and waits to be gracious to us. Admirable indeed is the longsuffering of the Savior in bearing with some of us year after year, notwithstanding our provocations, rebellions, and resistance of His Holy Spirit. Wonder of wonders that we are still in the land of mercy!

Pity expressed herself most plainly, for Jesus *"cried,"* which implies not only the loudness of His voice, but the tenderness of His tones. He entreats us to be reconciled. *"As though God did beseech you by us: we pray you in Christ's stead"* (2 Cor. 5:20), said the apostle Paul. What earnest, pathetic terms are these! How deep must be the love that makes the Lord weep over sinners, and like a mother coax His children to His bosom! Surely at the call of such a cry our willing hearts will come.

Provision is made most plenteously; all is provided that man can need to quench his soul's thirst. The Atonement brings peace to his conscience; the Gospel brings the richest instruction; the person of Jesus is the noblest object of affection to his heart; the truth as it is in Jesus supplies the purest nutriment to the whole man. Thirst is terrible, but Jesus can remove it. Though the soul were utterly famished, Jesus could restore it.

Proclamation is made most freely, so that every thirsty one is welcome. No other distinction is made but that of thirst. Whether it is the thirst of avarice, ambition, pleasure, knowledge, or rest, he who suffers from it is invited. The thirst may be bad in itself, and be no sign of grace, but rather a mark of inordinate sin longing to be gratified with deeper draughts of lust; but it is not goodness in the creature that brings him the invitation. The Lord Jesus sends it freely, and without respect of persons.

Personality is declared most fully. The sinner must come to Jesus, not to works, ordinances, or doctrines, but to a personal Redeemer, who His own self bare our sins in His own body on the tree. The bleeding, dying, rising Savior is the only star of hope to a sinner. Oh, for grace to come now and drink, before the sun sets on the year's last day!

No waiting or preparation is so much as hinted at. Drinking represents a reception for which no suitability is required. A fool, a thief, or a harlot can drink; and so sinfulness of character is no bar to the invitation to believe in Jesus. We want no golden cup, no bejeweled chalice, in which to convey the water to the thirsty; the mouth of poverty is welcome to stoop down and drink deeply of the flowing flood. Blistered, leprous, filthy lips may touch the stream of divine love; they cannot pollute it, but will themselves be purified. Jesus is the fount of hope. Dear reader, hear the dear Redeemer's loving voice as He cries to each of us, *"If any man thirst, let him come unto me, and drink."*

About the Author

harles Haddon Spurgeon was born on June 19, 1834, at Kelvedon, Essex, England, the firstborn of eight surviving children. His parents were committed Christians, and his father was a preacher. Spurgeon was converted in 1850 at the age of fifteen. He began to help the poor and to hand out tracts, and he was known as "The Boy Preacher."

He preached his first sermon at the age of sixteen. At age eighteen, he became the pastor of Waterbeach Baptist Chapel, preaching in a barn. By 1854, he was well-known as a preacher and was asked to become the pastor of New Park Street Chapel in London. In 1856, Spurgeon married Susannah Thompson; they had twin sons, both of whom later entered the ministry.

Spurgeon's compelling sermons and lively preaching style drew multitudes of people, and many came to Christ. Soon the crowds had grown so large that they blocked the narrow streets near the church. Services eventually had to be held in rented halls, and he often preached to congregations of more than ten thousand. The Metropolitan Tabernacle was built in 1861 to accommodate the large numbers of people.

Spurgeon published over thirty-five hundred sermons, which were so popular that they sold by the ton. At one point his sermons sold twenty-five thousand copies every week. An 1870 edition of the English magazine Vanity Fair called him an "original and powerful preacher...honest, resolute, sincere; lively, entertaining." The prime minister of England, members of the royal family, and Florence Nightingale, among others, went to hear him preach. Spurgeon preached to an estimated ten million people throughout his lifetime. Not surprisingly, he is called the "Prince of Preachers."

In addition to his powerful preaching, Spurgeon founded and supported charitable outreaches, including educational institutions. His pastors' college, which is still in existence today, taught nearly nine hundred students in Spurgeon's time. He also founded the famous Stockwell Orphanage.

Charles Spurgeon died in 1892, and his death was mourned by many.

ANOTHER POWERFUL **B**OOK

from Whitaker House

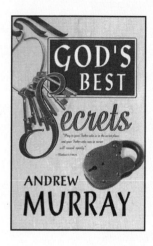

ISBN: 0-88368-559-0
Trade
304 pages

God's Best Secrets
Andrew Murray

In this devotional, Andrew Murray shares the personal revelation that he gained from spending quiet time alone with God. Discover the secrets of fellowship, prayer, faith, and more as you enter into the wonderful privileges that are open to you in *God's Best Secrets*.

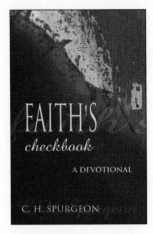